The Macmillan Book of
Business and Economic Quotations

Also by the Author

Crown's Book of Political Quotations

The
Macmillan Book of
BUSINESS
AND
ECONOMIC
QUOTATIONS

Edited by

Michael Jackman

Macmillan Publishing Company

New York

Macmillan Publishing Company
866 Third Avenue, New York, N.Y. 10022
Collier Macmillan Canada, Inc.

Library of Congress Cataloging in Publication Data
Main entry under title:
The Macmillan book of business and economic quotations.
Includes indexes.
1. Business—Quotations, maxims, etc. 2. Economics—
Quotations, maxims, etc. I. Jackman, Michael.
II. Macmillan Publishing Company.
PN6084.B87M33   1984   081   84-14415
ISBN 0-02-558220-8

Macmillan books are available at special discounts
for bulk purchases for sales promotions, premiums,
fund-raising, or educational use. Special editions
or book excerpts can also be created to specification.
For details, contact:

Special Sales Director
Macmillan Publishing Company
866 Third Avenue
New York, New York 10022

10 9 8 7 6 5 4 3 2 1

Printed in the United States of America

CONTENTS

INTRODUCTION

Economics. Business. For many people these words inspire visions of bar graphs, equations and an irrelevant school of thought that translates everything into numbers. The bottom line.

But economics is central to almost every decision you make, from the destination of your next vacation to the merits of getting a master's degree. Like any other discipline—whether it's Renaissance poetry or cellular biology—economics is a study of relationships and behavior.

How do you handle your money? Or someone else's money? What value do you put on your car? A pint of ice cream? Your working conditions? Your free time?

Economics measures and predicts behavior. What would you do if . . . ? And more important, when would you do it? We're never sure, yet economists stake their reputations on their understanding of human behavior. Beyond the laughable forecasts and shaky assumptions, there is a strong body of facts that can usually explain why your stock dropped in a bull market.

How you respond to wealth, rising prices, unemployment, taxes, debt, or self-serve versus full-serve is a more accurate picture of who you are and what you believe in than a lifetime of cocktail party opinions. This is not to minimize the importance of idle speculation. Every day, each of us functions as an economic theorist, hedging our bets, making assessments of true and false bargains, predicting our future employment opportunities and the cost of our child's tuition fifteen years hence.

Governments, grocery stores, and marriages rise and fall on their ability to manage their resources. How each of these economic units survives depends largely on how well they relate to each other.

The Macmillan Book of Business and Economic Quotations is a survival tool for individuals and economics consultants who face the chaos of making ends meet. Tracing the economic thoughts of man throughout history, *The Macmillan Book of Business and Economic Quotations* is a guide to our continuing efforts to explain how society works—or doesn't.

   In short, the utility of using this book increases as your marginal propensity to consume approaches the currency velocity of your money supply, divided by the number of days for your check to clear.

Michael R. Jackman
April 1984
San Francisco

HOW TO USE THIS BOOK

The following quotations are listed under category headings arranged in alphabetical order. Within each category, quotations are arranged chronologically.

To locate a subject area that is *not* a category heading, refer to the key word index in the back of the book.

A biographical index is also provided in the back of the book.

CATEGORY HEADINGS

The Macmillan Book of
Business and Economic Quotations

Advertising

Advertisements are now so numerous that they are very negligently perused, and it is therefore become necessary to gain attention by magnificence of promises, and by eloquences sometimes sublime and sometimes pathetic.
SAMUEL JOHNSON, 1758

Promise, large promise, is the soul of an advertisement.　　SAMUEL JOHNSON, 1761

Yes, sir, puffing is of various sorts; the principal are the puff direct, the puff preliminary, the puff collateral, the puff collusive, and the puff oblique, or puff by implication.
RICHARD B. SHERIDAN, 1779

Advertisements contain the only truths to be relied on in a newspaper.
THOMAS JEFFERSON, 1819

Braggin' saves advertisin'.
THOMAS C. HALIBURTON, 1855

The man who on his trade relies
Must either bust or advertise.
THOMAS LIPTON, 1870

Half the money I spend on advertising is wasted, and the trouble is I don't know which half.
JOHN WANAMAKER, 1885

Consider the soul reflected on the advertising page. . . . Commercial man has set his image therein; let him regard himself when he gets time.　　VOLTAIRE DE CLEYRE, 1887

Publicity, publicity, publicity, is the greatest moral factor and force in our public life.
JOSEPH PULITZER, 1895

Many a small thing has been made large by the right kind of advertising.
MARK TWAIN, 1897

Advertising in the final analysis should be news. If it is not news it is worthless.
ADOLPH S. OCHS, 1898

Advertising may be described as the science of arresting the human intelligence long enough to get money from it.
STEPHEN LEACOCK, 1906

The war [World War I] taught us the power of propaganda. Now when we have anything to sell to the American people, we know how to sell it. We have the school, the pulpit, and the press.　　ROGER BABSON, 1921

Advertising ministers to the spiritual side of trade.　　CALVIN COOLIDGE, 1923

One Ad is worth more to a paper than forty Editorials.　　WILL ROGERS, 1924

Advertising promotes that divine discontent which makes people strive to improve their economic status. RALPH STARR BUTLER, 1925

One-third of the people in the United States promote, while the other two-thirds provide. WILL ROGERS, 1927

The product that will not sell without advertising, will not sell profitably with advertising. ALBERT LASKER, 1927

There is no detail too trivial to influence the public in a favorable or unfavorable sense. EDWARD BERNAYS, 1928

You can tell the ideals of a nation by its advertisements. NORMAN DOUGLAS, 1930

We grew up founding our dreams on the infinite promise of American advertising. ZELDA FITZGERALD, 1932

All economic movements, by their very nature, are motivated by crowd psychology. BERNARD BARUCH, 1932

Advertising is legalized lying. H. G. WELLS, 1934

Advertising is a racket . . . its constructive contribution to humanity is exactly minus zero. F. SCOTT FITZGERALD, 1935

I remember well the time when a cabbage could sell itself just by being a cabbage. JEAN GIRAUDOUX, 1935

Advertising is the rattling of a stick inside a swill bucket. GEORGE ORWELL, 1941

Advertising is a valuable economic factor because it is the cheapest way of selling goods, particularly if the goods are worthless. SINCLAIR LEWIS, 1943

When the producers want to know what the public wants, they graph it as curves. When they want to tell the public what to get, they say it in curves. MARSHALL MCLUHAN, 1951

The modern Little Red Riding Hood, reared on singing commercials, has no objection to being eaten by the wolf. MARSHALL MCLUHAN, 1951

The trouble with us in America isn't that the poetry of life has turned to prose, but that it has turned to advertising copy. LOUIS KRONENBERGER, 1954

Sanely applied advertising could remake the world. STUART CHASE, 1954

The only thing you can tell an advertising man is that he is fortunate that he isn't in some other business. FRED ALLEN, 1954

Advertising is 85% confusion and 15% commission. FRED ALLEN, 1954

Public relations is the attempt, by information, persuasion, and adjustment, to engineer public support for an activity, cause, movement, or institution. EDWARD L. BERNAYS, 1955

Good times, bad times, there will always be advertising. In good times, people want to advertise; in bad times, they have to. BRUCE BARTON, 1955

If advertising encourages people to live beyond their means, so does matrimony. BRUCE BARTON, 1955

Advertising is the principal reason why the business man has come to inherit the earth. JAMES RANDOLPH ADAMS, 1956

Doing business without advertising is like winking at a girl in the dark. You know what you are doing, but nobody else does.
STUART H. BRITT, 1956

The consumer is not a moron. She is your wife.
DAVID OGILVY, 1956

Advertising is the foot on the accelerator, the hand on the throttle, the spur on the flank that keeps our economy surging forward.
ROBERT W. SARNOFF, 1956

On some not distant day, the voice of each individual seller may well be lost in the collective roar of all together. Like injunctions to virtue and warnings of socialism, advertising will beat helplessly on ears that have been conditioned by previous assault to utter immunity.
JOHN KENNETH GALBRAITH, 1958

Few people at the beginning of the nineteenth century needed an adman to tell them what they wanted. JOHN KENNETH GALBRAITH, 1958

Public relations specialists make flower arrangements of the facts, placing them so that the wilted and less attractive petals are hidden by sturdy blooms.
ALAN HARRINGTON, 1959

Advertising is found in societies which have passed the point of satisfying the basic animal needs. MARION HARPER, JR., 1960

We have got to understand women the way they do each other. We must learn to use a woman's inconsistency as the key to approaching her.
CHARLES REVSON, 1961

You know why Madison Avenue advertising has never done well in Harlem? We're not the only ones who know what it means to be Brand X.
DICK GREGORY, 1962

What self-respecting woman wants anything common around if she can buy something preferred? . . . Women like quality-brand.
ALBERT SCHWABACHER, JR., 1963

Publicity is stronger than sanity: given the right PR, armpit hair on female singers could become a national fetish. LENNY BRUCE, 1963

Commercials on television are similar to sex and taxes; the more talk there is about them, the less likely they are to be curbed.
JACK GOULD, 1963

The motion picture industry has provided a window on the world, and the colonized nations have looked through that window and have seen the things of which they have been deprived. It is perhaps not generally realized that a refrigerator can be a revolutionary symbol—to a people who have no refrigerators.
ACHMED SUKARNO, 1967

Advertising has done more to cause the social unrest of the twentieth century than any other single factor. CLIVE BARNES, JR., 1969

The advertising media in this country continuously inform the American male of his need for indispensable signs of his virility.
FRANCES M. BEAL, 1970

If we define pornography as any message from any commercial medium that is intended to arouse sexual excitement, then it is clear that most advertisements are covertly pornographic.
PHILIP SLATER, 1970

Great parts of our economy are directly dependent upon women having a weak self-concept. A multi-billion dollar fashion-cosmetic industry testifies to the validity of this approach. A woman who does not know who she is can be sold anything. GABRIELLE BURTON, 1972

The conscious and intelligent manipulation of the organized habits and opinions of the masses is an important element in a democratic society. Those who manipulate this unseen mechanism of society constitute an invisible government which is the true ruling power of our country.

EDWARD L. BERNAYS, 1978

Commercials are the last thing in life you can count on for a happy ending.

ROBERT MORLEY, 1978

A businessman can make no worse mistake than to try to use the muscle of his advertising dollar to influence the news.

STANLEY MARCUS, 1978

Advertising undermines the horror of indebtedness, exhorting the consumer to buy now and pay later. As the future becomes menacing and uncertain, only fools put off until tomorrow the fun they can have today.

CHRISTOPHER LASCH, 1979

Hype makes no critical judgements. The thing or person to be sold may be good quality or trash. Hype works on the theory that Americans will put their money where the noise is.

RUSSELL BAKER, 1979

If I were asked to name the deadliest subversive force within capitalism—the single greatest source of its waning morality—I would without hesitation name advertising.

ROBERT L. HEILBRONER, 1981

Quite clearly, it makes no sense to build a better mousetrap and then keep it a secret. Advertising has emerged and evolved as the most efficient way to tell or to find out about products and services.   EDWARD N. NEY, 1982

Agriculture

A farmer is always going to be rich next year.

PHILEMON, 300 B.C.

Husbandry is not governed by judgement and labor, but by the most uncertain of things, winds and tempests.   CICERO, c. 70 B.C.

When by the improvement and cultivation of land the labor of one family can provide food for two, the labor of half the society becomes sufficient to provide food for the whole. The other half, therefore, or at least the greater part of them, can be employed in providing other things, or in satisfying the other wants and fancies of mankind.   EDWARD GIBBON, 1776

Population, when unchecked, increases in a geometrical ratio. Subsistence only increases in an arithmetical ratio.

THOMAS MALTHUS, 1798

He [the farmer], more than any other class of the community, is benefited by the depreciation of money, and injured by the increase of its value.   DAVID RICARDO, 1811

I believe the first receipt to farm well is to be rich.   SYDNEY SMITH, 1818

In agriculture, the state of the art being given, doubling the labor does not double the produce.   JOHN STUART MILL, 1848

The farmer is covetous of his dollar, and with reason. . . . He knows how many strokes of labor it represents. His bones ache with the day's work that earned it.
                RALPH WALDO EMERSON, 1862

The foundation of every division of labor that is well developed and brought about by the exchange of commodities is the separation between town and country. It may be said, that the whole economical history of society is summed up in the movement of this antithesis.
                KARL MARX, 1873

He was a very inferior farmer when he first began, . . . and he is now fast rising from affluence to poverty.   MARK TWAIN, 1894

Bowed by the weight of centuries he leans
Upon his hoe and gazes on the ground,
The emptiness of ages in his face,
And on his back the burden of the world.
                EDWIN MARKHAM, 1899

Just as the price which the farmer received for the commodities he sold seemed to him to be fixed by those to whom he sold, so also, he felt that the price of his supplies was fixed by those from whom he bought.
                SOLON J. BUCK, 1913

Farming is one of the finest occupations in the world if taken in moderation.
                PETER MCARTHUR, 1915

Whatever the future may contain, the past has shown no more excellent social order than that in which the mass of the people were the masters of the holdings which they ploughed and of the tools with which they worked.
                RICHARD H. TAWNEY, 1920

The country town of the Great American farming region is the perfect flower of self-help and cupidity standardized on the American plan.
                THORSTEIN VEBLEN, 1923

Farming is not really a business; it is an occupation.   WILLIAM E. WOODWARD, 1932

Agriculture appears to have its own cycles, whose timing has no clear or regular relation to the cycles of general business. This is true whether we consider physical production, prices at the farm, or the product of the two, which may be taken to measure the total purchasing power which agriculture generates and has to offer in the general market.
                JOHN MAURICE CLARK, 1934

Some people tell us that there ain't no Hell,
But they never farmed, so how can they tell?
                Down on the Farm, 1940

A good farmer is nothing more nor less than a handyman with a sense of humor.
                E. B. WHITE, 1944

A study of depression since the Civil War brings out the conclusion that if a decline in the agricultural purchasing power did not actually start the general economic collapse it added almost immediately its immense weight to the general collapse with a vast and devastating impetus.
                LOUIS BROMFIELD, 1949

The farmer is the only man in our economy who buys everything he buys at retail, sells everything he sells at wholesale, and pays the freight both ways.   JOHN F. KENNEDY, 1960

American agricultural abundance can be forged into both a significant instrument of foreign policy and a weapon against domestic hardship and hunger.   JOHN F. KENNEDY, 1961

Italians come to ruin most generally in three ways—women, gambling and farming. My family chose the slowest one.
                    POPE JOHN XXIII, 1961

The state pays the owners of farm property not to produce, but pays virtually nothing to farm workers who become unemployed as a result of this dole to property owners.
                    HOWARD WACHTEL, 1971

Food is a weapon . . . one of the principal tools in our negotiating kit.   EARL BUTZ, 1975

My life on the farm during the Great Depression more nearly resembled farm life of fully 2,000 years ago than farm life today.
                    JIMMY CARTER, 1975

Without socialization of agriculture, there can be no complete, consolidated socialism.
                    MAO ZEDONG, 1976

For the last 20 years, America's influence on Europe has had more to do with food and animal feed than with high politics or low diplomacy.   EMMA ROTHSCHILD, 1978

American farmers have become welfare addicts, protected and assisted at every turn by a network of programs paid for by their fellow citizens. If Americans still believe in the virtue of self-reliance, they should tell Washington to get out of the way and let farmers practice it.
                    STEPHEN CHAPMAN, 1982

America

So one finds that love of money is either the chief or a secondary motive at the bottom of everything the Americans do.
                    ALEXIS DE TOCQUEVILLE, 1836

In no other country in the world is the love of property more active and more anxious than in the United States; nowhere does the majority

display less inclination for those principles which threaten to alter, in whatever manner, the laws of property.   ALEXIS DE TOCQUEVILLE, 1836

Business is the very soul of an American: he pursues it, not as a means of procuring for himself and his family the necessary comforts of life, but as the foundation of all human felicity; and shows as much enthusiastic ardor in his application to it as any crusader has ever evinced for the conquest of the Holy Land, or the followers of Mohammed for the spreading of the Koran.

FRANCIS J. GRUND, 1837

There is, probably, no people on earth with whom business constitutes pleasure, and industry amusement, in an equal degree with the inhabitants of America. Active occupation is not only the principal source of their happiness, and the foundation of their national greatness, but they are absolutely wretched without it.

FRANCIS J. GRUND, 1843

There is no doubt but that the natural circumstances of North America point especially to the profitable cultivation of the extremely cheap land, and that it will continue to be an agricultural country . . . for a long time to come.

FREDERICK VON RAUMER, 1846

Everyone is running to and fro, pressed by the stomach ache of business.

FRÉDÉRIC AUGUSTE BARTHOLDI, 1871

To me, the wonder is that a poor man ever consents to live out of America, or a rich man to live in it.   RICHARD F. BURTON, 1888

The chief business of America is business.

CALVIN COOLIDGE, 1925

The American system of ours, call it Americanism, call it Capitalism, call it what you like, gives each and every one of us a great opportunity if we only seize it with both hands and make the most of it.   AL CAPONE, 1929

There is something about prosperity, the hunger for it, the pretense in all these middle-class Americans, that makes the soul sick.

SHERWOOD ANDERSON, 1931

The typical successful American businessman was born in the country where he worked like hell so he could live in the city where he worked like hell so he could live in the country.

DON MARQUIS, 1935

The reason American cities are prosperous is that there is no place to sit down.

ALFRED J. TALLEY, 1935

America is not a land of money, but of wealth— not a land of rich people, but successful workers.   HENRY FORD, 1935

The glory of the United States is business.

WENDELL L. WILLKIE, 1936

The economic vice of Europeans is avarice, while that of Americans is waste.

W. H. AUDEN, 1940

When most Americans read about the corruption and ruthlessness of the rich, they are inclined to grin. These malefactors are their dreamselves. The American does not aspire to overthrow the thieves and oppressors half as much as he does to become one of them.

BEN HECHT, 1954

The worst country to be poor in is America.

ARNOLD TOYNBEE, 1954

It is a gross perversion not only of the concept of loyalty but of the concept of Americanism to identify it with a particular economic system.

HENRY STEELE COMMAGER, 1954

An American who can make money, invoke God, and be no better than his neighbor, has nothing to fear but truth itself.

MARYA MANNES, 1958

We boast the highest standard of living when it's only the biggest.

FRANK LLOYD WRIGHT, 1959

Business occupies in the American scheme of things a place it occupies nowhere else in the world. The position of business in the American institutional framework is one of major significance.   JAMES C. WORTHY, 1959

In the old days we used to say that when the U.S. economy sneezed the rest of the world went to bed with pneumonia. Now when the U.S. economy sneezes the other countries say "Gesundheit."   WALTER HELLER, 1961

America has the best-dressed poverty the world has ever known.
          MICHAEL HARRINGTON, 1962

The organization of American society is an interlocking system of semi-monopolies notoriously venal, an electorate notoriously unenlightened, misled by mass media notoriously phony.   PAUL GOODMAN, 1962

Science and time and necessity have propelled us, the United States, to be the general store for the world, dealers in everything. Most of all, merchants for a better way of life.
          LADY BIRD JOHNSON, 1963

The strongest argument for the unmaterialistic character of American life is that we tolerate conditions that are, from a materialistic point of view, intolerable.
          MARY MCCARTHY, 1964

Americans: People who laugh at . . . African witch doctors and spend 100 million dollars on fake reducing systems.
          LEONARD LOUIS LEVINSON, 1967

The entire essence of America is the hope to first make money—then make money with money—then make lots of money with lots of money.
          PAUL ERDMAN, 1967

Only Americans have mastered the art of being prosperous though broke.
          KELLY FORDYCE, 1969

I think that New York is not the cultural center of America, but the business and administrative center of American culture.
          SAUL BELLOW, 1969

The American economy has been a junkie since World War I.   DOUGLAS DOWD, 1974

An economic system prouder of the distribution of its products than of the products themselves.
          MURRAY KEMPTON, 1977

The U.S. is the fastest "undeveloping" country in the world.   ARTHUR LAFFER, 1979

Banking

Jesus went into the temple, . . . overthrew the tables of the moneychangers, and the seats of them that sold doves.

MARK 11:15, C. A.D. 70

A money lender. He serves you in the present tense; he lends you in the conditional mood; keeps you in the subjunctive; and ruins you in the future.   JOSEPH ADDISON, 1712

This free competition, too, obliges all bankers to be more liberal in their dealings with their customers, lest their rivals should carry them away.   ADAM SMITH, 1776

It is not by augmenting the capital of the country, but by rendering a greater part of that capital active and productive than would otherwise be so, that the most judicious operations of banking can increase the industry of the country.   ADAM SMITH, 1776

Banks have done more injury to the religion, morality, tranquility, prosperity, and even wealth of the nation than they can have done or ever will do good.   JOHN ADAMS, 1799

The whole community derives benefit from the operation of the bank. It facilitates the commerce of the country. It quickens the means of purchasing and paying for country produce and hastens on the exportation of it. The emolument, therefore, being to the community, it is the office and duty of government to give protection to the bank.   THOMAS PAINE, 1804

I sincerely believe that banking establishments are more dangerous than standing armies.

THOMAS JEFFERSON, 1816

All money corporations are detrimental to national wealth. They are always created for the benefit of the rich, and never for the poor. The poor have no money to vest in them and can therefore derive no advantage from such corporations.   DANIEL RAYMOND, 1820

The bank, Mr. Van Buren, is trying to kill me, but I will kill it.   ANDREW JACKSON, 1832

A power has risen up in the government greater than the people themselves, consisting of many and various and powerful interests . . . held together by the cohesive power of the vast surplus in the banks.   JOHN C. CALHOUN, 1836

It has come to be a proverb that banks never originate with those who have money to lend, but with those who wish to borrow.

AMASA WALKER, 1857

Rich men die but banks are immortal.

WENDELL PHILLIPS, 1863

Adventure is the life of commerce, but caution, I had almost said timidity, is the life of banking.

WALTER BAGEHOT, 1873

The Dealers in money have always, since the day of Moses, been the dangerous class.

PETER COOPER, 1876

These heroes of finance are like beads on a string—when one slips off, all the rest follow.

HENRIK IBSEN, 1879

Banking is a watchful, but not a laborious trade. A banker, even in large business, can feel pretty sure that all his transactions are sound, and yet have much spare mind.

WALTER BAGEHOT, 1888

A banker is a fellow who lends his umbrella when the sun is shining and wants it back the minute it begins to rain.   MARK TWAIN, 1893

If a man needs beef, he goes to a butcher; if he needs gold, he goes to a banker; if he needs a great deal of beef, he goes to a big butcher; if he requires a great deal of gold, he must go to a big banker and pay his price for it.

GROVER CLEVELAND, 1895

What the establishment of [bank] branches would actually do would be to destroy the local money power which now practically stifles many forms of legitimate industry by the pressure of excessive interest rates.

H. PARKER WILLIS, 1902

There have been three great inventions since the beginning of time: fire, the wheel, and central banking.   WILL ROGERS, 1920

Will you please tell me what you do with all the Vice Presidents a bank has? I guess that's to get you discouraged before you can see the President. Why, the United States is the biggest institution in the world and they only have one Vice President and nobody has ever found anything for him to do.   WILL ROGERS, 1922

Financial sense is knowing that certain men will promise to do certain things, and fail.

E. W. HOWE, 1926

In the course of my life I have met a certain sprinkling of bankers, and I do not think there is any sort of human being more marvelous and incredible. They take money for granted as a terrier takes rats; when they see it, they go for it; but they are absolutely immune to any philosophic curiosity about it.

H. G. WELLS, 1926

What is robbing a bank compared with founding a bank?   BERTOLT BRECHT, 1928

Competition for deposits is often so great as to cause banks to pay such high rates of interest on their balances left with them as to make a large part of the deposit business of banks unprofitable.   JAMES TRANT, 1931

Verily what bishops are to the English, bankers are to Americans.   MABEL ULRICH, 1932

It is safer to keep your money in a reopened bank than under your mattress.

FRANKLIN D. ROOSEVELT, 1933

Finance is a means for assuring the flow of capital. Historically it has also been a means for guiding that flow. In the first use, it is a mechanism in aid of the industrial system as we know it. In the second, it is a power controlling it.

ADOLF A. BERLE, JR., 1933

In any business extending credit success depends on knowing what not to believe in accounting.   ROBERT H. JACKSON, 1934

It is better that a man should tyrannize over his bank balance than over his fellow citizens.

JOHN MAYNARD KEYNES, 1936

Our greatest single asset is our loaning policy. Businessmen get to know about that from friends, customers and competitors—not from our advertising.　　GAYLORD FREEMAN, 1950

Every Republican candidate for President since 1936 has been nominated by the Chase National Bank.　　ROBERT A. TAFT, 1952

Bankers are just like anyone else except richer.
　　OGDEN NASH, 1953

Banking, too, still has its well-read men, though most of them seem to belong to that generation that is passing. The way things are going, we shall not have many well-read bankers around for long. For in banking as well as manufacturing or selling, the executive now is the least-leisured man in the world.
　　RUSSELL KIRK, 1957

Ours is essentially a decentralized system of community banks.
　　WILLIAM BRENNAN, 1963

Foundations of a new religion can be laid only with the blessing of bankers.
　　SALVADOR DALI, 1965

A bank is a place that will lend you money if you can prove that you don't need it.
　　BOB HOPE, 1967

Banking may well be a career from which no man really recovers.
　　JOHN KENNETH GALBRAITH, 1968

The process by which banks create money is so simple that the mind is repelled.
　　JOHN KENNETH GALBRAITH, 1968

The largest single cause of bank failures is misuse of banking assets by directors and officers.
　　JACK T. CONN, 1973

Banking is perhaps the most personal of the big businesses.　　MARTIN MAYER, 1974

Just remember this: if bankers were as smart as you [lawyers] are, you would starve to death.
　　HENRY HARFIELD, 1974

Our banking system grew up by accident; and whenever something happens by accident, it becomes a religion.　　WALTER WRISTON, 1975

Next to the church, credit unions do more good for the people than any other institution.
　　WRIGHT PATMAN, 1976

What else do the bankers do—walk in and turn off the lights in the country.
　　WILLIAM SLEE, 1978

If I owe a million dollars, then I am lost. But if I owe fifty billions, the bankers are lost.
　　CELSO MING, 1980

But what is left us after the banks are nationalized? One can become a hairdresser, a butcher, one can buy a few stores. But that is not our métier. We have a calling; our name is in the dictionary.
　　BARON GUY DE ROTHSCHILD, 1981

Business

He that hath little business shall become wise.
ECCLESIASTICUS 38, c. 210 B.C.

Many shall run to and fro, and knowledge shall be increased. DANIEL 12:4, c. 165 B.C.

Do you fear to trust the word of a man, whose honesty you have seen in business?
TERENCE, c. 160 B.C.

You have a mind careful in business, and unmoved either in times of prosperity or of doubt.
HORACE, c. 19 B.C.

It is easy to escape from business, if you will only despise the rewards of business.
SENECA, c. A.D. 35

The playthings of our elders are called business.
ST. AUGUSTINE, 399

Business men boast of their skill and cunning,
But in philosophy they are like little children.
Bragging to each other of successful depredations,
They neglect to consider the ultimate fate of the body.
CH'EN TZU-AGIG, seventh century

This estimable merchant so had set
His wits to work, none knew he was in debt,

He was so stately in negotiation,
Loan, bargain, and commercial obligation.
GEOFFREY CHAUCER, 1482

What takes place after dinner must never be taken as counsel.
PHILIPPE DE COMMYNES, 1524

The greatest part of the business of the world is the effect of not thinking.
GEORGE SAVILE, 1693

A true-bred merchant is the best gentleman in the nation. DANIEL DEFOE, 1719

Men of business must not break their word twice. THOMAS FULLER, 1732

Commerce is the school of cheating.
MARQUIS DE VAUVENARGUES, 1746

A man who cannot command his temper should not think of being a man of business.
LORD CHESTERFIELD, 1760

A merchant may, perhaps, be a man of an enlarged mind, but there is nothing in trade connected with an enlarged mind.
SAMUEL JOHNSON, 1761

To cultivate kindness is a valuable part of the business life. SAMUEL JOHNSON, 1761

14

I am a bad Englishman, because I think the advantages of commerce are dearly bought for some by the lives of many more.

HORACE WALPOLE, 1762

It is the interest of the commercial world that wealth should be found everywhere.

EDMUND BURKE, 1775

The propensity to truck, barter, and exchange . . . is common to all men, and to be found in no other race of animals.

ADAM SMITH, 1776

A dinner lubricates business.

WILLIAM SCOTT, 1781

Commerce gives rise to a large class disposed to external peace, internal tranquility, and attached to the established government.

JOSEPH BARNAVE, 1791

Let your discourse with men of business always be short and comprehensive.

GEORGE WASHINGTON, 1798

Business, you know, may bring money, but friendship hardly ever does.

JANE AUSTEN, 1804

The selfish spirit of commerce knows no country, and feels no passion or principle but that of gain.

THOMAS JEFFERSON, 1809

Merchants have no country. The mere spot they stand on does not constitute so strong an attachment as that from which they draw their gains.

THOMAS JEFFERSON, 1814

I know of nothing more opposite to revolutionary attitudes than commercial ones. Commerce is naturally adverse to all the violent passions; it loves to temporize, takes delight in compromise, and studiously avoids irritation. It is patient, insinuating, flexible, and never has recourse to extreme measures until obliged by the most absolute necessity. Commerce renders men independent of one another, . . . it therefore prepares men for freedom, but preserves them from revolutions.

ALEXIS DE TOCQUEVILLE, 1839

Everybody's business is nobody's business.

THOMAS MACAULEY, 1843

Most are engaged in business the greater part of their lives, because the soul abhors a vacuum and they have not discovered any continuous employment for man's nobler faculties.

HENRY DAVID THOREAU, 1854

Commerce is, in its very essence, satanic. Commerce is return of the loan, a loan in which there is the understanding: give me more than I give you.

CHARLES BAUDELAIRE, 1856

Business? That's very simple: it's other people's money.

ALEXANDRE DUMAS, *fils*, 1857

The first of all the English games is making money. This is an all-absorbing game; and we knock each other down oftener in playing at that, than at football, or any other roughest sport; and it is absolutely without purpose; no one who engages heartily in that game ever knows why. He doesn't make it to do anything with it. He gets it only that he may get it.

JOHN RUSKIN, 1866

The summits of the various kinds of business are, like the tops of mountains, much more alike than the parts below—the bare principles are much the same; it is only the rich variegated details of the lower strata that so contrast with one another. But it needs travelling to know that the summits *are* the same. Those who live on one mountain believe that *their* mountain is wholly unlike all others.

WALTER BAGEHOT, 1867

Men of business have a solid judgement, a wonderful guessing power of what is going to happen, each in his own trade, but they have never practiced themselves in reasoning out their judgements and in supporting their guesses by argument; probably if they did so, some of the finer and correcter parts of their anticipations would vanish. They are like the sensible lady to whom Coleridge said, "Madam, I accept your conclusion, but you must let me find the logic for it."   WALTER BAGEHOT, 1873

Business should be like religion or science; it should know neither love nor hate.

SAMUEL BUTLER, 1873

The happiest time in any man's life is when he is in red-hot pursuit of a dollar with a reasonable prospect of overtaking it.

JOSH BILLINGS, 1876

Commerce links all mankind in one common brotherhood of mutual dependence and interests.   JAMES A. GARFIELD, 1881

It is not by any means certain that a man's business is the most important thing he has to do.

ROBERT LOUIS STEVENSON, 1882

Merchant and pirate were for a long period one and the same person. Even today mercantile morality is really nothing but a refinement of piratical morality.

FRIEDRICH NIETZSCHE, 1885

There is no better ballast for keeping the mind steady on its keel, and saving it from all risk of crankiness, than business.

JAMES RUSSELL LOWELL, 1887

Have not great merchants, great manufacturers, great inventors, done more for the world than preachers and philanthropists? . . . Can there be any doubt that cheapening the cost of necessaries and conveniences of life is the most powerful agent of civilization and progress?

CHARLES ELLIOTT PERKINS, 1888

A financier is a pawnbroker with imagination.

A. W. PINERO, 1893

When two men in business always agree, one of them is unnecessary.

WILLIAM WRIGLEY, JR., 1896

There is no way of making a business successful that can vie with the policy of promoting those who render exceptional service.

ANDREW CARNEGIE, 1902

The supreme vice of commercialism is that it is without an ideal.   HENRY POTTER, 1902

A man is known by the company he organizes.

AMBROSE BIERCE, 1906

Commerce, n. A kind of transaction in which A plunders from B the goods of C, and for compensation B picks the pocket of D of money belonging to E.   AMBROSE BIERCE, 1906

A committee is a thing which takes a week to do what one good man can do in an hour.

ELBERT HUBBARD, 1910

Somehow the man who attends strictly to his own business never acquires a reputation as an entertaining conversationalist.

BOB EDWARDS, 1913

How unreasonable to expect that the pursuit of business should be itself a culture of the imagination, in breadth and refinement; that it should directly, and not through the money which it supplies, have social services for its animating principle and be conducted as an enterprise in behalf of social organization.

JOHN DEWEY, 1916

If you can forgive the magnificence and vanity of a successful politician, why are you unable to forgive a successful business man? Every time I strike a match, or turn an electric button, or use the telephone, I am indebted to a business man, but if in debt to any politician, I do not know it. EDGAR W. HOWE, 1918

It takes no more actual sagacity to carry on the everyday hawking and haggling of the world, or to ladle out its normal doses of bad medicine and worse law, than it takes to operate a taxicab or fry a pan of fish.

H. L. MENCKEN, 1922

Mr. [Henry] Ford was for Mr. Wilson when Mr. Wilson was president. Mr. Ford was for Mr. Harding when Mr. Harding was president. Mr. Ford is for Mr. Coolidge while Mr. Coolidge is president. Mr. Ford is a marvelous businessman. HIRAM JOHNSON, 1923

One of the chief sources of success in manufacturing is the introduction and strict maintenance of a perfect system of accounting so that responsibility for money or materials can be brought home to every man.

ANDREW CARNEGIE, 1924

If you build up a business big enough, it's respectable. WILL ROGERS, 1924

A businessman is a hybrid of a dancer and a calculator. PAUL VALÉRY, 1924

Financial sense is knowing that certain men will promise to do certain things and fail.

EDGAR W. HOWE, 1926

A "tired businessman" is one whose business is usually not a successful one.

JOSEPH R. GRUNDY, 1928

Business is a combination of war and sport.

ANDRÉ MAUROIS, 1930

A great society is a society in which its men of business think greatly of their functions.

ALFRED NORTH WHITEHEAD, 1933

Regarded as a means, the businessman is tolerable; regarded as an end he is not so satisfactory. JOHN MAYNARD KEYNES, 1933

If I had my life to live over again, I would elect to be a trader of goods rather than a student of science. I think barter is a noble thing.

ALBERT EINSTEIN, 1934

Commerce is the most important activity on the face of the earth. It is the foundation on which civilization is built. Religion, society, education—all have their roots in business, and would have to be reorganized in their material aspects should business fail. JAMES R. ADAMS, 1937

Things that are bad for business are bad for the people who work for business.

THOMAS E. DEWEY, 1940

Nothing is ever accomplished by a committee unless it consists of three members, one of whom happens to be sick and the other absent.

HENDRIK VAN LOON, 1942

No grand idea was ever born in a conference, but a lot of foolish ideas have died there.

F. SCOTT FITZGERALD, 1945

The Swiss are not a people so much as a neat clean quite solvent business.

WILLIAM FAULKNER, 1948

He [the business person] is the only man who is forever apologizing for his occupation.

H. L. MENCKEN, 1949

Romance without finance ain't got no chance.

CHARLIE PARKER, 1951

The farmer spends his time in the fields, the laborer at his machine, and the businessman at meetings. . . . The object of a meeting is not, as the very young believe, to solve the problem at hand, but to impress the people there.

SHEPHERD MEAD, 1952

A committee is a group that keeps minutes and loses hours.　　MILTON BERLE, 1954

A conference is a gathering of important people who singly can do nothing, but together can decide that nothing can be done.

FRED ALLEN, 1954

Whenever you're sitting across from some important person, always picture him sitting there in a suit of long red underwear. That's the way I always operated in business.

JOSEPH P. KENNEDY, 1956

My father always told me that all businessmen were sons-of-bitches, but I never believed it till now.　　JOHN F. KENNEDY, 1962

Finance is the art of passing currency from hand to hand until it finally disappears.

ROBERT W. SARNOFF, 1964

I believe that the able industrial leader who creates wealth and employment is more worthy of historical notice than politicians or soldiers.

J. PAUL GETTY, 1968

Business activity rewards the individual who can operate in a rational, foresighted, utilitarian manner, who pursues discreet goals and husbands his resources in a mode of disciplined efficiency.　　ROBERT N. WILSON, 1968

The length of a meeting rises with the square of the number of people present.

EILEEN SHANAHAN, 1968

The secret of business is to know something that nobody else knows.

ARISTOTLE ONASSIS, 1969

It was business, and none of them had allegiances or attachments or involvements with any nations, not even their own.

TAYLOR CALDWELL, 1972

I feel very sorry commercialism has gone so far.

EILEEN O'CASEY, 1974

I don't know of anyone today that has less influence in this country than business.

RONALD REAGAN, 1975

Nobody is a gentleman when big money is involved.　　JOHN LEONARD, 1976

I don't care how many martinis anyone has with lunch. But I do care who picks up the check.

JIMMY CARTER, 1978

Entertaining is to the selling business the same thing as fertilizer is to the farming business—it increases the yield.　　RUSSELL LONG, 1978

Business Cycles

Remember that there is nothing stable in human affairs; therefore avoid undue elation in prosperity, or undue depression in adversity.

SOCRATES, C. 399 B.C.

In all things there is a kind of law of cycles.

TACITUS, C. A.D. 105

Panics, in some cases, have their uses; they produce as much good as hurt.

THOMAS PAINE, 1787

And since business will have its floods and ebbs, and the spirit of enterprise and production must be checked, for a time, the more promptly and approaching crisis can be seen and provided against, as far as practicable, the less the community will suffer.   WILLIAM PHILLIPS, 1828

Millions of men will depend for subsistence on the demand for a particular manufacture, and yet this demand will of necessity be liable to perpetual fluctuation. When the pendulum vibrates in one direction, there will be an influx of wealth and prosperity; when it vibrates in the other, misery, discontent, and turbulence will spread through the land.

THOMAS HAMILTON, 1833

The history of what we are in the habit of calling "the state of trade" is an instructive lesson.

We find it subject to various conditions which are periodically returning; it revolves apparently in an established cycle. First we find it in a state of quiescence—next, improvement—growing confidence—prosperity—excitement—overtrading — convulsion — pressure — stagnation—distress—ending again in quiescence.

SAMUEL JONES LLOYD, 1837

All active, enterprising, commercial countries are necessarily subject to commercial crises. A series of prosperous years almost necessarily produces overtrading. These revolutions will be more frequent and greater in proportion to the spirit of enterprise and to the extension or abuse of credit.   ALBERT GALLATIN, 1841

The demand for loans varies much more largely than the supply, and embraces longer cycles of years in its aberrations.

JOHN STUART MILL, 1848

The disturbances are the accompaniment of another wave which appears to have a decennial period, and in the generation of which moral [psychological] causes have no doubt an important part. The prompting cause of these convulsive movements appears to lie in the inordinate use of credit.   WILLIAM LANGTON, 1857

Bad times have a scientific value. These are occasions a good learner would not miss.

RALPH WALDO EMERSON, 1860

The malady of commercial crises is not, in essence, a matter of the purse but of the mind.

JOHN STUART MILL, 1867

The ultimate reason for all real crises always remains the poverty and restricted consumption of the masses as opposed to the drive of capitalist production to develop the productive forces as though only the absolute consuming power of society constituted their limit.

KARL MARX, 1867

A panic, in a word, is a species of neuralgia, and according to the rules of science you must not starve it. . . . In wild periods of alarm, one failure makes many, and the best way to prevent the derivative failures is to arrest the primary failure that causes them.

WALTER BAGEHOT, 1873

If the planets govern the sun, and the sun governs the vintages and harvests, and thus the prices of foods and raw materials and the state of the money market, it follows that the configurations of the planets may prove to be the remote causes of the greatest commercial disasters.

W. STANLEY JEVONS, 1875

The chief cause of the evil [depressions] is a want of confidence. The greater part of it could be removed almost in an instant if confidence could return, touch all industries with her magic wand, and make them continue their production, and their demand for the wares of others.

ALFRED MARSHALL, 1879

As credit by growing makes itself grow, so when distrust has taken the place of confidence. failure and panic breed panic and failure. The commercial storm leaves its path strewn with ruin. When it is over, there is a calm, but a dull heavy calm. Those who have saved themselves are in no mood to venture again.

ALFRED MARSHALL, 1879

It seems probable that commercial crises are connected with a periodic variation of weather affecting all parts of the earth, and probably arising from increased waves of heat received from the sun at average intervals of ten years and a fraction.   W. STANLEY JEVONS, 1884

Your system was liable to periodical convulsions, overwhelming alike the wise and the unwise, the successful cutthroat as well as its victim. I refer to the business crises at intervals of five to ten years, which wrecked the industries of the nation.   EDWARD BELLAMY, 1887

There is no question but that crises promote rather than diminish inequalities in the distribution of wealth, for in the extremity of the man of ordinary means lies the opportunity of men of very large wealth.

EDWARD D. JONES, 1900

A crisis is certainly a disturbance of the equilibrium between demand and supply.

EDWARD D. JONES, 1900

The real difference between prosperity and depression consists in the increasing or decreasing production of fixed capital and in the decreasing or increasing store of investment-seeking capital.   ARTHUR SPIETHOFF, 1902

The very word "panic" denotes a fear so great as to make those who experience it to become for the time being crazy; and when crazy with fear men both say and do foolish things, and moreover, always seek for someone to hold responsible for their sufferings.

THEODORE ROOSEVELT, 1907

The right proportion of saving to spending at any given time depends upon the present condition of the arts of production and consumption, and the probabilities of such changes in modes of work or living as shall provide social utility for new forms of capital within the near or calculable future.

JOHN A. HOBSON, 1910

Under perfectly steady prices there would still be great booms and depressions in the capital-making industries, and resulting booms and depressions in industry at large.

JOHN MAURICE CLARK, 1917

A period of boom is one of special increase in the production of fixed capital; a period of decline or a depression is one in which this production falls below the point it had previously reached. GUSTAV CASSEL, 1918

The typical trade boom does not mean over-production or an over-estimate of the demands of the consumers or the needs of the community for the services of fixed capital, but an over-estimate of the supply of capital or of the amount of savings available for taking over the real capital produced. GUSTAV CASSEL, 1918

At present, it is less likely that the existence of business cycles will be denied than that their regularity will be exaggerated.

WESLEY CLAIR MITCHELL, 1923

I do not think it is even nearly true that if all business men always made, and acted upon, true judgements about their own self-interest, industrial fluctuations of a fairly rhythmical character would disappear.

DENNIS H. ROBERTSON, 1926

My principal thesis is that the chief responsibility for cyclical fluctuations should be assigned to one of the characteristics of modern industrial techniques, namely, the long period required for the production of fixed capital.

ALBERT AFTALION, 1927

Business will be better or worse.

CALVIN COOLIDGE, 1928

With the assistance of the Federal Reserve System, we may expect freedom from the unwarranted and annoying financial panics of the past. PAUL M. MAZUR, 1928

Only by studying the changes of the capitalistic structure of production will we learn to understand the factors which govern it, and it seems that the trade cycle is the most important manifestation of these changes.

FRIEDRICH A. HAYEK, 1929

Let the slump liquidate itself. Liquidate labor, liquidate stocks, liquidate the farmers, liquidate real estate. . . . It will scourge the rottenness out of the system. High costs of living will come down. People will work harder, live a more moral life. Values will be adjusted, and enterprising people will pick up the wrecks from less competent people. ANDREW MELLON, 1930

Economic depression cannot be cured by legislative action or executive pronouncement. Economic wounds must be healed by the action of the cells of the economic body, the producers and consumers themselves.

HERBERT HOOVER, 1931

But with the slow menace of a glacier, depression came on. No one had any measure of its progress; no one had any plan for stopping it. Everyone tried to get out of its way.

FRANCES PERKINS, 1934

The trouble seems to be not so much that business men mistake their interests—though that does happen, and aggravates some of the difficulties—as that their actual interests lie in doing the things which bring on the cycle, so long as they are acting as individual business men or representatives of individual business interests.

JOHN MAURICE CLARK, 1934

[The] volume of credits seems to respond in the main to the demands of the volume of trade. It is an important enabling cause or condition, but hardly an initiating one in the typical case [of business cycles].   JOHN MAURICE CLARK, 1934

The responses of the business system seem to form a closely knit sequence of cause and effect, in which a state of over-contraction appears to set in motion forces leading to over-expansion, and this in turn to over-contraction once more.   JOHN MAURICE CLARK, 1934

Excessive debts sooner or later precipitate excessive liquidation. Thus are booms the cause of depressions.   IRVING FISHER, 1934

Even apart from the instability due to speculation, there is the instability due to the characteristic of human nature that a large proportion of our positive activities depend on spontaneous optimism rather than on a mathematical expectation, whether moral or hedonistic or economic.   JOHN MAYNARD KEYNES, 1936

A boom is a situation in which over-optimism triumphs over a rate of interest which, in a cooler light, would be seen to be excessive.   JOHN MAYNARD KEYNES, 1936

The frequent recurrence of economic crises and depressions is evidence that the automatic functioning of our business system is defective.   WESLEY CLAIR MITCHELL, 1937

Cycles are not, like tonsils, separable things that might be treated by themselves, but are, like the beat of its heart, at the essence of the organism that displays them.   JOSEPH A. SCHUMPETER, 1939

[The] trade cycle is properly envisaged not as a passing rash on the fair face of a static equilib-rium but as a deep-seated rate of organic growth.   DENNIS H. ROBERTSON, 1940

Economic progress, in capitalist society, means turmoil.   JOSEPH A. SCHUMPETER, 1942

We may expect that expansion of specific cycles in individual economic activities will tend to be longer and more boisterous, and contractions are shorter and milder, when the "trend" of prices is upward than when it is downward.   ARTHUR F. BURNS AND   WESLEY CLAIR MITCHELL, 1946

A society in which there is widespread economic insecurity can turn freedom into a barren and vapid right for millions of people.   ELEANOR ROOSEVELT, 1948

Keynesian economics, in spite of all that is has done for our understanding of business fluctuations, has beyond doubt left at least one major thing unexplained; and that thing is nothing less than the business cycle itself.   J. R. HICKS, 1950

An economy may be in equilibrium from a short-period point of view and yet contain within itself incompatibilities that are soon going to knock it out of equilibrium.   JOAN ROBINSON, 1962

No longer do we view our economic life as a relentless tide of ups and downs. No longer do we fear that automation and technical progress will rob workers of jobs rather than help us to achieve greater abundance. No longer do we consider poverty and unemployment landmarks on our economic scene.   LYNDON B. JOHNSON, 1969

There's a lot of nostalgia for the Depression, though obviously by people who didn't live through it.   HILTON KRAMER, 1972

Normality is a fiction of economic textbooks.
JOAN ROBINSON, 1972

As the economy gets better, everything else gets worse.   ART BUCHWALD, 1972

An economist's "lag" may be a politician's catastrophe.   GEORGE P. SCHULTZ, 1974

There are two ways to fight threatening recession: by fiscal tax cuts and expenditure increases; or by Federal Reserve expansion of the money and credit supplies sufficient to bring down mortgage rates on housing, interest rates on funds needed for investment and durable consumer goods, and the cost of equity capital to corporate employers.
PAUL A. SAMUELSON, 1974

What really scares me is signs of a worldwide slowdown at a time when the economies of the West have become increasingly synchronized.
LAWRENCE KLEIN, 1976

Listening to the economics wizards talk about the recession, you get the feeling that things are going to get better as soon as they get worse.
RUSSELL BAKER, 1980

We have learned that our economy is like a big, soft balloon. You put in your finger in one place and it pops out in another wholly unexpected spot.   LEO ROSTEN, 1981

A depression is when an economy, through a sequence of degenerative events, finds itself literally on the wrong end of the Laffer Curve.
ARTHUR LAFFER, 1982

A depression is either a 12 percent unemployment rate for nine months or more, or a 15 percent unemployment rate for three to nine months.   ALAN GREENSPAN, 1982

Capital

As capitalists increase in any country, the profits which can be made by employing them necessarily diminish. It becomes gradually more and more difficult to find within the country a profitable method of employing any new capital.
ADAM SMITH, 1776

For no nation, without injury to the progress of its wealth, can thus rapidly increase its capital,

at the expense of abstracting annually so large a sum from expenditures in consumable commodities.   LORD LAUDERDALE, 1804

Rent is always the difference between the produce obtained by the employment of two equal quantities of capital and labor.
DAVID RICARDO, 1817

With a population pressing against the means of subsistence, the only remedies are either a reduction of people, or a more rapid accumulation of capital. DAVID RICARDO, 1817

Capital is commodities. JAMES MILL, 1821

If you divorce capital from labor, capital is hoarded, and labor starves. DANIEL WEBSTER, 1831

Failure is more frequently from want of energy than from want of capital. DANIEL WEBSTER, 1838

The great original capital of head, heart and hand. JOHN RUSKIN, 1846

Even in a progressive state of capital, in old countries, a conscientious or prudential restraint on population is indispensable, to prevent the increase of numbers from outstripping the increase of capital, and the condition of the classes who are at the bottom of society from being deteriorated. JOHN STUART MILL, 1848

That part of capital which is represented by the means of production, by the raw materials and the instruments of labor, does not in the process of production undergo any quantitative alteration of value. I therefore call it the constant part of capital. . . . On the other hand, that part of capital represented by labor power does, in the process of production, undergo an alteration in value. I therefore call it the variable part of capital. KARL MARX, 1867

Abstinence from enjoyment is the only source of capital. THOMAS BRASSEY, 1885

While the part which nature plays in production shows a tendency to diminishing return, the part which man plays shows a tendency to increasing return. ALFRED MARSHALL, 1890

Capital consists in a great part of knowledge and organization: and of this some part is private property and the other part is not. ALFRED MARSHALL, 1890

Capital is that part of wealth which is devoted to obtaining further wealth. ALFRED MARSHALL, 1890

The employer put his money into . . . business and the workman his life. The one has as much right as the other to regulate that business. CLARENCE DARROW, 1909

Financiers live in a world of illusion. They count on something which they call the capital of the country, which has no existence. GEORGE BERNARD SHAW, 1911

Capital has a right to a just share of the profits, but only to a just share. WILLIAM H. O'CONNELL, 1912

When we oppose labor and capital, labor means the group that is selling its products, and capital all the other groups that are buying it. OLIVER WENDELL HOLMES, JR., 1913

The movements of the trade cycle are merely expressions of the fluctuations in the production of fixed capital. GUSTAV CASSEL, 1918

Thought, not money, is the real business capital, and if you know absolutely that what you are doing is right, then you are bound to accomplish it in due season. HARVEY S. FIRESTONE, 1922

The highest use of capital is not to make more money, but to make money do more for the betterment of life. HENRY FORD, 1931

The schedule of the marginal efficiency of capital is of fundamental importance because it is mainly through this factor (more than through the rate of interest) that the expectations of the future influence the past.

JOHN MAYNARD KEYNES, 1936

Capital as such is not evil; it is its wrong use that is evil. MOHANDAS GANDHI, 1937

There is always plenty of capital for those who can create practical plans for using it.

NAPOLEON HILL, 1937

Owning capital is not a productive activity.

JOAN ROBINSON, 1947

Capital is the sum of money equivalent of all assets minus the sum of the money equivalent of all liabilities as dedicated at a definite date to the conduct of the operations of a definite business unit. LUDWIG VON MISES, 1949

It is highly doubtful whether the achievements of the Industrial Revolution would have been permitted if the franchise [voting] had been universal. It is very doubtful because a great deal of the capital aggregations that we are at present enjoying are the results of the wages that our fathers went without.

ANEURIN BEVAN, 1950

The essential measure of the success of the economy is not production and consumption at all, but the nature, extent, quality, and complexity of the total capital stock, including in this the state of the human bodies and minds included in the system.

KENNETH E. BOULDING, 1973

Capitalism

The whole annual produce of the land and labor of every country naturally divides itself . . . into three parts; the rent of the land, the wages of labor, and the profits of stock; and constitutes a revenue to three different orders of people; to those who live by rent, to those who live by wages, and to those who live by profit.

ADAM SMITH, 1776

Nobody ever saw a dog make a fair and deliberate exchange of one bone for another with another dog. ADAM SMITH, 1776

These capitalists generally act harmoniously and in concert, to fleece the people.

ABRAHAM LINCOLN, 1837

Capitalists are almost as much interested as laborers, in placing the operations of industry on such a footing that those who labor for them may feel the same interest in the work which is felt by those who labor on their own account.

JOHN STUART MILL, 1848

Nothing is implied in property but the right of each to his (or her) own faculties, to what he can produce by them, and to whatever he can get for them in a fair market; together with his right to give this to any other person if he chooses, and the right of that other to receive and enjoy it.   JOHN STUART MILL, 1848

He is called upon to estimate, with tolerable accuracy, the importance of the specific product, the probable amount of the demand, and the means of production; sometimes to employ a great number of hands; again to buy or order raw materials, to combine the workers, find customers, to exercise a spirit of order and economy, in short, the ability of the administrator.   JEAN-BAPTISTE SAY, 1861

On one side employers are interested, because of profit, to keep down the price of labor; while on the other side, the employees are justified, on account of self-interest, to keep up wages. Thus labor and capital are antagonistic.

WILLIAM SYLVIS, 1864

What a fine arrangement that permits a factory girl to sweat for twelve hours so that the employer can use a portion of her unpaid labor to hire her sister as a maid, her brother as a groom, and her cousin as a soldier or a policeman.

KARL MARX, 1867

Capital is good; the capitalist is a helper, if he is not also a monopolist. We can safely let any one get as rich as he can if he will not despoil others in doing so.   HENRY GEORGE, 1879

This new psychological state woven together of the bourgeois spirit and the entrepreneurial spirit, I call the capitalist spirit. It has created capitalism.   WERNER SOMBART, 1899

Man does not by nature wish to earn more and more money.   MAX WEBER, 1904

The basic law of capitalism is you or I, not both you and I.   KARL LIEBKNECHT, 1907

It's too bad the golden days have passed. Capital still pats labor on th' back, but on'y with an axe. Labor rayfuses to be treated as a friend. It wants to be treated as an inimy. It thinks it gets more that way. They ar-re still a happy fam'ly, but it's none like an English fam'ly. They don't speak.   FINLEY PETER DUNNE, 1910

The general result of the struggle between capitalism and simple commodity production is this: after substituting commodity economy [peasant economy] for natural economy [primitive systems], capital takes the place of simple commodity economy. Non-capitalist organizations provide a fertile soil for capitalism; more strictly: capital feeds on the ruins of such organizations, and although this non-capitalist milieu is indispensable for accumulation, the latter proceeds at the cost of this medium nevertheless, by eating it up.   ROSA LUXEMBURG, 1913

Capitalists are no more capable of self-sacrifice than a man is capable of lifting himself by his own bootstraps.   NIKOLAI LENIN, 1917

Under the old type of capitalism, when free competition prevailed, the export of commodities was the most typical feature. Under modern capitalism, when monopolies prevail, the export of capital has become the typical feature.

NIKOLAI LENIN, 1917

Capitalism is hell compared to Socialism, but heaven compared to Feudalism.

NIKOLAI LENIN, 1917

Capitalism is itself a crisis.

GILBERT K. CHESTERTON, 1917

I believe the most useful man who has ever lived is John D. Rockefeller.

EDGAR W. HOWE, 1918

Very few of us realize with conviction the intensely unusual, unstable, complicated, unreliable temporary nature of the economic organization by which Western Europe has lived for the last half century.

JOHN MAYNARD KEYNES, 1919

I am going to fight capitalism even if it kills me. It is wrong that people like you should be comfortable and well fed while all around you people are starving. SYLVIA PANKHURST, 1921

Competition as it runs under the rule of this decayed competitive system is chiefly the competition between the business concerns that control production, on one side, and the consuming public on the other side.

THORSTEIN VEBLEN, 1923

There is no more demoralizing theory than that which imputes all human evils to Capitalism or any other single agency.

SAMUEL GOMPERS, 1925

The capitalistic system has grown up and it is in use because, and only because, the experience of mankind has proven it to be the best way of doing what has to be done.

CLIFFORD SIFTON, 1925

We are coming to see that there should be no stifling of Labor by Capital, or of Capital by Labor; and also that there should be no stifling of Labor by Labor, or of Capital by Capital.

JOHN D. ROCKEFELLER, JR., 1926

The word Capitalism is misleading. The proper name for our system is Proletarianism.

GEORGE BERNARD SHAW, 1928

The modern capitalist is a fair-weather sailor. As soon as a storm arises he abandons the duties of navigation and even sinks the boats which might carry him to safety by his haste to push his neighbors off and himself in.

JOHN MAYNARD KEYNES, 1931

The idea that everyone can be a capitalist is an American concept of capitalism. It is a socialist concept of capitalism.

LEON SAMPSON, 1933

The defects of the capitalist system have been increasingly robbing us of its benefits. They are now threatening its existence.

ARTHUR SALTER, 1934

The outstanding faults of the economic society in which we live are its failure to provide for full employment and its arbitrary and inequitable distribution of wealth and incomes.

JOHN MAYNARD KEYNES, 1936

The movement from feudalism to capitalism is a movement from a world in which individual well-being is regarded as the outcome of action socially controlled to one in which social well-being is regarded as the outcome of action individually controlled. HAROLD LASKI, 1936

The forces of a capitalist society, if left unchecked, tend to make the rich richer and the poor poorer. JAWAHARLAL NEHRU, 1936

Capitalism is that form of private property economy in which innovations are carried out by means of borrowed money, which in general, though not by logical necessity, implies credit creation.

JOSEPH A. SCHUMPETER, 1939

Not only the modern mechanized plant and the volume of the output that pours forth from it, not only modern technology and economic organization, but all the features and achievements of modern civilization are, directly or indirectly, the products of the capitalist process.

JOSEPH A. SCHUMPETER, 1942

Capitalist economic power constitutes a direct, continuous, and fundamental threat to the whole

structure of democratic authority everywhere and
always.   ROBERT LYND, 1943

The market is not something invented by businessmen and speculators for their profit, or by
the classical economists for their intellectual
pleasure. The market is the only possible method
by which labor that has been analyzed into separate specialties can be synthesized into useful
work.   WALTER LIPPMANN, 1943

The revolt against capitalism has its source, not
merely in material miseries, but in resentment
against an economic system which dehumanizes
existence by treating the mass of mankind, not
as responsible partners in the co-operative enterprise of subduing nature to the service of man,
but as instruments to be manipulated for the pecuniary advantage of a minority of property
owners, who themselves, in proportion as their
aims are achieved, are too often degraded by
the attainment of them.
                  RICHARD H. TAWNEY, 1949

There is a good deal of solemn cant about the
common interests of capital and labor. As matters stand, their only common interest is that of
cutting each other's throat.
                  BROOKS ATKINSON, 1951

We can no longer ask the invisible hand to do
our dirty work for us.   E. H. CARR, 1951

The classical justification for a profits system is
that, on the whole, profits are made by being
serviceable. Businesses can only thrive by selling
people things that they want at prices which they
can afford and which will enable the business
to attract the resources necessary. This is less
romantic than selling people what you think is
good for them, like glory, death, progress and
salvation, but it at least exhibits a decent
humility.   KENNETH E. BOULDING, 1957

American capitalism has been both overpraised
and overindicted . . . it is neither the Plumed
Knight nor the monstrous Robber Baron.
                  MAX LERNER, 1958

We fear that the word capitalism is unpopular.
So we talk about the "free enterprise system"
and run to cover in the folds of the flag and talk
about the American way of life.
                  ERIC A. JOHNSTON, 1958

I am fearful of stumbling capitalism as well as
of creeping socialism.
                  G. BROMLEY OXNAM, 1958

The growth of nineteenth-century capitalism
depended largely on the general acceptance of a
reasoned justification of the system on moral as
well as on political and economic grounds.
                  E. S. MASON, 1958

A conception of an efficient allocation of resources ultimately rests upon a value judgement
as to what the optimum composition of output
ought to be. As a result, there is obviously no
scientific way of proving (or, by the same token,
of disproving) that social imbalance actually
exists.   C. R. MCCONNELL, 1961

Capitalism and altruism are incompatible; they
are philosophical opposites; they cannot co-
exist in the same man or in the same society.
                  AYN RAND, 1961

History suggests that capitalism is a necessary
condition for political freedom. Clearly it is not
a sufficient condition.
                  MILTON FRIEDMAN, 1962

Viewed as a means to the end of political freedom, economic arrangements are important because of their effect on the concentration or
dispersal of power. The kind of economic organization that provides economic freedom directly, namely, competitive capitalism, also pro-

motes political freedom because it separates economic power from political power and in this way enables the one to offset the other.

MILTON FRIEDMAN, 1962

Few trends could so thoroughly undermine the very foundation of our free society as the acceptance by corporate officials of a social responsibility other than to make as much money for their stockholders as possible.

MILTON FRIEDMAN, 1962

Why should there be a perverse empirical relationship between the degree to which public opinion is, in fact, tolerant and the degree to which it relies on free markets? In our history, the days of most rugged individualism—the Gilded Age and the 1920s—seem to have been the ages least tolerant of dissenting opinion.

PAUL A. SAMUELSON, 1964

You show me a capitalist, I'll show you a bloodsucker. MALCOLM X, 1965

The dynamics of capitalism is postponement of enjoyment to the constantly postponed future.

NORMAN O. BROWN, 1966

Power goes to two poles—to those who've got money and those who've got people.

SAUL ALINSKY, 1966

Now it is a simple fact that most of Marx's "laws of motion of capitalism" have *not* revealed themselves on the surface of economic reality, at any rate during the last quarter century and at any rate in the advanced capitalist countries.

RONALD MEEK, 1967

Capitalism with near-full employment was an impressive spectacle.

JOAN ROBINSON, 1972

Nothing could discredit capitalism more than a decision by the Russians to try it.

JACK TANNER, 1976

Capitalism is a hotel. Its penthouse suites are always filled, but not necessarily with the same people this decade as last. And its basement dungeons are also jam-packed, but not with the same faces and bodies.

PAUL A. SAMUELSON, 1977

Not every problem someone has with his girlfriend is necessarily due to the capitalist mode of production. HERBERT MARCUSE, 1978

I'd say capitalism's worst excess is in the large number of crooks and tinhorns who get too much of the action.

MALCOLM FORBES, 1979

I sometimes suspect that many American capitalists actually distrust the market as much as capitalism's enemies do. . . . There are whole industries today that prefer to escape the market's discipline. HENRY FORD II, 1979

No better weapon against poverty, disease, illiteracy, and tyranny has yet been found than capitalism. The techniques, human skills, and changes of cultural habit necessary to expand the productive capacity of the earth has been pioneered by democratic capitalism.

MICHAEL NOVAK, 1979

Careers

Let a man practice the profession which he best knows.   CICERO C. 76 B.C.

Always believe the expert.   VIRGIL, 19 B.C.

Why, Hal, 'tis my vocation, Hal; 'tis no sin for a man to labour in his vocation.
WILLIAM SHAKESPEARE
Henry IV, Part I (I, ii), 1598

The most important thing in life is the choice of a calling, but that is left to chance.
BLAISE PASCAL, 1656

Be the business never so painful, you may have it done for money.   THOMAS FULLER, 1732

In every age and clime we see
Two of a trade can never agree.
JOHN GAY, 1738

It is an infallible consequence of all industrious professions, to . . . make the love of gain prevail over the love of pleasure.
DAVID HUME, 1754

He that hath a trade hath an estate and he that hath a calling hath an office of profit and honor.
BENJAMIN FRANKLIN, 1757

The contempt of risk and the presumptuous hope of success, are in no period of life more active than at the age at which young people choose their professions.   ADAM SMITH, 1776

Jack of all trades and master of none.
MARIA EDGEWORTH, 1800

Of the professions, it may be said that soldiers are becoming too popular, parsons too lazy, physicians too mercenary, and lawyers too powerful.   CHARLES C. COLTON, 1820

Never fear the want of business. A man who qualifies himself well for his calling, never fails of employment.   THOMAS JEFFERSON, 1826

Serious occupation is labor that has reference to some want.   GEORG HEGEL, 1832

Vocations which we wanted to pursue, but didn't, bleed, like colors, on the whole of our existence.   HONORÉ DE BALZAC, 1838

The ugliest of trades have their moments of pleasure. Now, if I were a gravedigger, or even a hangman, there are some people I could work for with a great deal of enjoyment.
DOUGLAS JERROLD, 1839

To do nothing and get something, formed a boy's ideal of a manly career.
BENJAMIN DISRAELI, 1845

The best business you can go into you will find on your father's farm or in his workshop. If you have no family or friends to aid you, and no prospect open to you there, turn your face to the great West and there build up your home and fortune.   HORACE GREELEY, 1846

Beware of Enterprises that require new clothes.
HENRY DAVID THOREAU, 1854

A man who goes driving about from one trade to another is sure to drive himself into ruin eventually.   BERTHOLD AUERBACH, 1856

Who does not teach his child a trade or profession brings him up to steal, say the Persians.
RALPH WALDO EMERSON, 1863

If a man loves the labor of his trade, apart from any question of success or fame, the gods have called him.
ROBERT LOUIS STEVENSON, 1882

The very first step towards success in any occupation is to become interested in it.
WILLIAM OSLER, 1892

Employments fall into a hierarchical gradation of reputability. Those which have to do immediately with ownership on a large scale are the most reputable. . . . Next to these in good repute come those employments that are immediately subservient to ownership and financing such as banking and law.
THORSTEIN VEBLEN, 1899

A man with a career can have not time to waste upon his wife and friends; he has to devote it wholly to his enemies.
JOHN OLIVER HOBBES, 1902

All professions are conspiracies against the laity.   GEORGE BERNARD SHAW, 1906

Of all the damnable waste of human life that ever was invented, clerking is the very worst.
GEORGE BERNARD SHAW, 1910

Always take a job that is too big for you.
HARRY EMERSON FOSDICK, 1928

People don't choose their careers: They are engulfed by them.   JOHN DOS PASSOS, 1936

A human being must have occupation if he or she is not to become a nuisance to the world.
DOROTHY L. SAYERS, 1947

An expert is a man who has made all the mistakes which can be made in a very narrow field.
NIELS BOHR, 1953

When white-collar people get jobs, they sell not only their time and energy, but their personalities as well. They sell by the week, or month, their smiles and their kindly gestures, and they must practice that prompt repression of resentment and aggression.
C. WRIGHT MILLS, 1956

The price one pays for pursuing any profession, or calling, is an intimate knowledge of its ugly side.   JAMES BALDWIN, 1961

Every profession considers itself the proper body to set the terms in which some aspect of society, life or nature is to be thought of, and to define the general lines, or even the details of public policy concerning it.
EVERETT C. HUGHES, 1963

I cannot honestly claim that I possessed any innate talent nor even any particular desire for a business career.   J. PAUL GETTY, 1964

Money demands that you sell, not your weakness to men's stupidity, but your talent to their reason.   AYN RAND, 1966

Did you ever hear of a kid playing accountant—
even if he wanted to be one?
                          JACKIE MASON, 1969

It is so difficult to become a specialist that the
mediocre man has been very eager to cry wolf
to the specialist, often before it was actually
necessary.   REBECCA WEST, 1969

We find the emergence of a new kind of organization man—a man who, despite his many af-
filiations, remains basically uncommitted to any
organization. He is willing to employ his skills
and creative energies to solve problems with
equipment provided by the organization, and
within temporary groups established by it. But
he does so only so long as the problems interest
him. He is committed to his own career, his own
self-fulfillment.   ALVIN TOFFLER, 1970

Consultants are people who borrow your watch
and tell you what time it is, and then walk off
with the watch.   ROBERT TOWNSEND, 1970

The trouble with specialists is that they tend to
think in grooves.   ELAINE MORGAN, 1972

Is a certified public accountant upper lower
middle class or lower upper middle class?
                   CHARLES MERRILL SMITH, 1972

Consultant: any ordinary guy more than fifty
miles from home.   ERIC SEVAREID, 1974

I have always been overpaid to do that which I
would pay to do.
                   PAUL A. SAMUELSON, 1974

Professions, like nations, are civilized to the degree to which they can satirize themselves.
                   PETER DE VRIES, 1974

I believe that the true road to preeminent success in any line is to make yourself master of
that line.   DAVID FROST, 1975

The best careers advice given to the young is
"Find out what you like doing best and get
someone to pay you for doing it."
                   KATHARINE WHITEHORN, 1975

Nothing is more boring than a man with a
career.   ALEKSANDR SOLZHENITSYN, 1976

Professionalism is a cheap and easy way of dis-
ciplining labor.
                   NICHOLAS VON HOFFMAN, 1978

Civil Rights

Whatever day
Makes man a slave, takes half his worth away.
                   HOMER, C. 1000 B.C.

The work done by freemen comes cheaper in
the end than that performed by slaves.
                   ADAM SMITH, 1759

The flour-merchant, the house-builder, and the postman charge us no less on account of our sex; but when we endeavor to earn money to pay all these, then, indeed we find the difference. LUCY STONE, 1855

Cotton is king; or slavery in the Light of Political Economy. DAVID CHRISTY, 1855

It was not by any change in the distribution of material interests, but by the spread of moral conditions that negro slavery has been put an end to in the British Empire and elsewhere. JOHN STUART MILL, 1861

I recognize for myself no narrow sphere. Where you may work, my brother, I may work. LUCY N. COLEMAN, 1863

We all get about the same amount of ice. The rich get it in Summer and the poor in Winter. BAT MASTERSON, c. 1900

An occupation that has no basis in sex-determined gifts can now recruit its ranks from twice as many potential artists. MARGARET MEAD, 1935

The American economy, the American society, the American unconscious are all racist. MICHAEL HARRINGTON, 1962

I wouldn't mind paying my income tax if I knew it was going to a friendly country. DICK GREGORY, 1962

This book is dedicated to Abraham Lincoln. If it wasn't for Abe, I'd still be on the open market. DICK GREGORY, 1962

The Negro may wind up with a mouthful of civil rights, but an empty stomach and living in a hovel. WHITNEY M. YOUNG, JR., 1963

Money is the most egalitarian force in society. It confers power on whoever holds it. ROGER STARR, 1968

We think that anybody who talks about black capitalism or black control of black communities in a system of international imperialism is insane. PHIL HUTCHINGS, 1968

We've never been in a democracy; we've always been in a pallocracy. FRANÇOIS PARTURIER, 1968

Most hierarchies were established by men who now monopolize the upper levels, thus depriving women of their rightful share of opportunities for incompetence. LAURENCE PETER, 1969

Unless a person is prepared to accept the "might makes right" philosophy, he must respect another's right to live, to produce, and to consume, keep, exchange, sell, or give away that which he has produced. WILLIAM W. BAYES, 1970

The only jobs for which no man is qualified are human incubator and wet nurse. Likewise, the only job for which no woman is or can be qualified is sperm donor. WILMA SCOTT HEIDE, 1971

I fired my female employees because they weren't beautiful anymore. TAIJI KAWATE, 1972

We [black Americans] buy more Cadillacs than anybody else. If we stopped buying them, they would have to stop making them. LEON H. SULLIVAN, 1972

Male chauvinism is . . . a shrewd method of extracting the maximum of work for the minimum of compensation. MICHAEL KORDA, 1973

There are very few jobs that actually require a penis or vagina. All other jobs should be open to everybody.   FLORYNCE R. KENNEDY, 1974

Government cannot devise an efficient benefit scheme of taxation. In the multiracial society, taxes are collected from members of all communities, but political minorities can be excluded from consuming all the public goods their funds pay for.   ALVIN RABUSHKA, 1974

Just because a child's parents are poor or uneducated is no reason to deprive the child of basic human rights to health care, education, proper nutrition.   MARIAN WRIGHT EDELMAN, 1975

Class

There are three classes of citizens. The first are the rich, who are indolent and yet always crave more. The second are the poor, who have nothing, are full of envy, hate the rich, and are easily led by demagogues. Between the two extremes lie those who make the state secure and uphold the laws.   EURIPIDES, 421 B.C.

When quarrels and complaints arise, it is when people who are equal have not got equal shares or vice versa.   ARISTOTLE, C. 330 B.C.

Money doesn't change your birth.   HORACE, 30 B.C.

High descent and meritorious deeds, unless united to wealth, are as useless as seaweed.   HORACE, C. 30 B.C.

What difference does it make how much you have? What you do not have amounts to much more.   SENECA, C. A.D. 62

If you are poor today, you will always be poor. Only the rich now have riches.   MARTIAL, C. A.D. 95

They have wine and spices and fair bread; and we have oat-cake and straw, and water to drink. They have leisure and fine houses; we have pain and labor, the rain and the wind in the fields. And yet it is of us and our toil that these men hold their state.   JOHN BALL, 1381

A beggar wisheth he might be a monarch while he lives, and the great potentate wisheth he had lived a beggar when he comes to die.   JOSEPH HALL, 1606

After man has satisfied the desires which he has in common with the animals and which relate to the preservation of the individual and of the species, there is no stronger and more violent passion than that for distinction and superiority over others. . . . Goods which satisfy it have a very high value.

FERDINANDO GALIANI, 1764

A landed interest, a manufacturing interest, a mercantile interest, with many lesser interests grow up of necessity in civilized nations and divide them into different classes actuated by different sentiments and views. The regulation of these various and interfering interests forms the principal task of modern legislation.

JAMES MADISON, 1787

There never has yet existed a wealthy and civilized society in which one portion of the community did not, in point of fact, live on the labor of the other.   JOHN C. CALHOUN, 1837

Among aristocratic nations money reaches only to a few points on that vast circle of man's desires; in democracies it seems to lead to all.

ALEXIS DE TOCQUEVILLE, 1839

The whole composition of our society is arithmetical; each gentleman ranking according to the numerical index of his property.

FRANCIS J. GRUND, 1839

In all civilized countries, as they are called, society is divided into idlers and producers—into those who obtain double allowance for doing nothing; and those who obtain only half-allowance for doing double work.

JOHN FRANCIS BRAY, 1839

The English laborer does not find his worst enemy in the nobility, but in the middling class.

ORESTES A. BROWNSON, 1840

There is no society, however free and democratic, where wealth will not create an aristocracy.

EDWARD G. BULWER-LYTTON, 1843

Competition is the most extreme expression of that war of all against all which dominates modern middle-class society.

FRIEDRICH ENGELS, 1844

I was told that the Privileged and the People formed Two Nations.

BENJAMIN DISRAELI, 1845

The history of all hitherto existing society is the history of class struggles.

KARL MARX AND
FRIEDRICH ENGELS, 1848

You who have read the history of nations, from Moses down to our last election, where have you ever seen one class looking after the interests of another?

ELIZABETH CADY STANTON, 1854

Middle-class people are apt to live up to their incomes, if not beyond them; affecting a degree of "style" which is most unhealthy in its effects upon society at large.

SAMUEL SMILES, 1858

There is always more misery among the lower classes than there is humanity in the higher.

VICTOR HUGO, 1862

Which of us, in brief word, is to do the hard and dirty work for the rest, and for what pay? Who is to do the pleasant and clean work, and for what pay? Who is to do no work, and for what pay?   JOHN RUSKIN, 1865

There is really very little in the present industrial régime to stimulate the intelligence, excite the ambition, and sweeten the toil of ordinary mortals. The work is, after all, another man's work; the gain is to be his, and the honor of success is to be his too.   E. L. GODKIN, 1867

Thus, it has been said, does society divide itself into four classes—noblemen, gentlemen, gigmen, and men.   THOMAS CARLYLE, 1871

Our dangerous class is not at the bottom, it is near the top of society. Riches without law are more dangerous than is poverty without law.
                                 HENRY WARD BEECHER, 1873

Be neither rich nor a beggar.
                                 FRIEDRICH NIETZSCHE, 1876

[Aristocrat] — A demokrat with hiz pockets filled.   JOSH BILLINGS, 1877

I can hire one-half of the working class to kill the other half.   JAY GOULD, 1886

It is the tendency of all social burdens to crush out the middle class, and to force society into an organization of only two classes, one at each social extreme.   WILLIAM G. SUMNER, 1887

The state, it cannot too often be repeated, has nothing, and can give nothing, which it does not take from somebody. Its victims must be those who have earned and saved, and they must be the broad, strong, middle classes, from whom alone any important contributions can be drawn.   WILLIAM G. SUMNER, 1887

There is only one class in the community that thinks more about money than the rich, and that is the poor. The poor can think of nothing else. That is the misery of being poor.
                                 OSCAR WILDE, 1891

What a social class gets is, under natural law, what it contributes to the general output of industry.   JOHN BATES CLARK, 1891

In Boston they ask, How much does he know? In New York, How much is he worth? In Philadelphia, Who were his parents?
                                 MARK TWAIN, 1895

Keeping up appearances is the most expensive thing in the world.
                        ARTHUR CHRISTOPHER BENSON, 1896

Make money; and the whole nation will conspire to call you a gentleman.
                                 GEORGE BERNARD SHAW, 1904

There is no man who has an ounce of honesty in his make-up but recognizes the fact that there is a continuous struggle between the two classes.   BILL HAYWOOD, 1905

I did not know the working classes were so united. . . . Perhaps this is because the working people feel that there is a class struggle, and the leisure class does not know it yet.
                                 MAUD YOUNGER, 1907

The question is not now asked, "Is So-and-so clever?" but, "Is So-and-so rich?"
                                 DOROTHY NEVILL, 1907

To regard self-culture . . . as a means of getting past others in the world . . . rather than as a power to elevate the character and expand the spiritual nature, is to place it on a very low level.   SAMUEL SMILES, 1907

Aristocracy is not a government, it is a riot; the most effective kind of riot, a riot of the rich.
                                 GILBERT K. CHESTERTON, 1910

It is not good for trade unions that they should be brought into contact with the courts. Where class issues are involved, it is impossible to pretend that the courts command the same degree of general confidence.
                                 WINSTON CHURCHILL, 1911

There is coming to be visible a lack of respect and affection for the vested interests, whether of business or of privilege; and it rises to the pitch of distrust and plain disallowance among those peoples on whom the preconceptions of the 18th century sit more lightly and loosely.

THORSTEIN VEBLEN, 1920

Why! Why! Why is the middle-class so stodgy—so utterly without a sense of humor?

KATHERINE MANSFIELD, 1920

Economic privileges must be abolished not, primarily, because they hinder the production of wealth, but because they produce sickness.

RICHARD H. TAWNEY, 1926

It is no longer a distinction to be rich. . . . What we accumulate by way of useless surplus does us no honor.

HENRY FORD, 1926

Do not mistake a crowd of big wage-earners for a leisure class.

CLIVE BELL, 1928

What is repulsive is not that one man should earn more than others, for where community of environment, and common education and a habit of life have bred a common tradition of respect and consideration, these details of the counting-house are forgotten or ignored. It is that some classes should be excluded from the heritage of civilization which others enjoy, and that the fact of human fellowship, which is ultimate and profound, should be obscured by economic contrasts, which are trivial and superficial.

RICHARD H. TAWNEY, 1929

The forgotten man at the bottom of the economic pyramid.

FRANKLIN D. ROOSEVELT, 1932

Half of the working class is slaving away to pile up riches of which they will be plundered by the upper class. The other half is plundering the plunderers.

GEORGE BERNARD SHAW, 1933

The middle class, that prisoner of the barbarian 20th century.

SINCLAIR LEWIS, 1935

We of the sinking middle class . . . may sink without further struggles into the working class where we belong, and probably when we get there it will not be so dreadful as we feared, for, after all, we have nothing to lose but our aitches.

GEORGE ORWELL, 1937

This is a middle-class country, and the middle class will have its will and say. For the middle class is the real owner of American industry.

WILLIAM A. WHITE, 1937

There is no prettier sight in this pretty world than the sight of the privileged class enjoying their privileges.

PHILIP BARRY, 1939

How right the working classes are in their "materialism." How right they are to realize that the belly comes before the soul, not in the scale of values but in point of time.

GEORGE ORWELL, 1941

The force of the drive toward higher living standards—that is, toward the purchase of superior goods—is greatly strengthened in our society by the characteristics of our social structure. Ours is a society, which is formally classless, but which is nevertheless characterized by a system of differentiated social status.

JAMES S. DUESENBERRY, 1949

It is no longer clear which way is up even if one wants to rise.

DAVID RIESMAN, 1950

Madame loves the unusual! It's a middle-class failing—she says—to run away from the unusual.

ENID BAGNOLD, 1953

The wealthy and the poverty-stricken are in like case: both are too preoccupied with finance to use time to better purpose. Perhaps that is a sound argument for sweeping both classes away.

EDEN PHILLPOTTS, 1954

The man at the top of the intellectual pyramid contributes the most to all those below him, but he gets nothing except his materials payment, receiving no intellectual bonus from others to add to the value of his time. The man at the bottom who, left to himself, would starve in his hopeless ineptitude contributes nothing to those above him, but receives the bonus of all of their brains. Such is the nature of the "competition" between the strong and the weak of the intellect.   AYN RAND, 1957

"The difference between the rich and poor," said Francie, "is that the poor do everything with their own hands and the rich hire hands to do things."   BETTY SMITH, 1958

The class war is obsolete.
                        HAROLD MACMILLAN, 1959

To have the license number of one's automobile as low as possible is a social advantage in America.   ANDRÉ MAUROIS, 1959

The Communist pie is nothing but crust. In America we have an upper crust and a lower crust, but it's what's between—the middle class— that gives the real flavor.
                    VIRGINIA L. MCCLEARY, 1960

Nowadays people can be divided into three classes—the Haves, the Have-Nots, and the Have-Not-Paid-For-What-They-Haves.
                           EARL WILSON, 1964

In class society everyone lives as a member of a particular class, and every kind of thinking, without exception, is stamped with the brand of class.   MAO ZEDONG, 1966

To put it quite crudely . . . the poor don't really know how the rich live, and the rich don't know how the poor live, and to find out is really enchanting to both of them.
                        AGATHA CHRISTIE, 1967

I'd like to live like a poor man with lots of money.   PABLO PICASSO, 1967

The best way to attract money, she had discovered, was to give the appearance of having it.
                          GAIL SHEEHY, 1970

The advantage of a working class background is that I do not make the mistake of thinking every worker is a revolutionary.
                          JANOS KADAR, 1974

The ship follows Soviet custom: it is riddled with class distinctions so subtle, it takes a trained Marxist to appreciate them.
                          PAUL THEROUX, 1975

One thing I've learned is that money never buys you out of being working class. The middle classes never let you forget where you've come from.   ROGER DALTRY, 1976

When class authority declines, money talks.
                     EDWARD D. BALTZELL, JR., 1978

Our problem is a ruling class of people who have no vision of this country existing beyond their next dividend check.
                     HUNTER S. THOMPSON, 1984

Consumption

As a nail sticketh fast between the joinings of the stones: so doth sin stick close between buying and selling.

ECCLESIASTICUS 27, c. 210 B.C.

Good merchandise, even when hidden, soon finds buyers. PLAUTUS, c. 190 B.C.

Nothing stings more sharply than the loss of money. TITUS LIVIUS, C. A.D. 5

It is the superfluous things for which men sweat. SENECA, C. A.D. 63

For a dear bargain is always annoying particularly on this account, that it is a reflection on the judgement of the buyer.

PLINY THE YOUNGER, c. 100

He who spends too much is a robber.

ST. AMBROSE, c. 375

Bargains made in speed are commonly repented at leisure. GEORGE PETTIE, 1576

No man divulges his revenue, or at least which way it comes in; but everyone publishes his acquisitions. MICHEL DE MONTAIGNE, 1580

But in the way of bargain, mark ye me,
I'll cavil in the ninth part of a hair.

WILLIAM SHAKESPEARE,
Henry IV, Part I (III, i), 1598

I can get no remedy against this consumption of the purse: borrowing only longers and lingers it out, but the disease is incurable.

WILLIAM SHAKESPEARE,
Henry IV, Part II (I, ii), 1600

All kind of bounty and pomp is not to be avoided, for if we become so frugal that we would use few or no foreign wares, how shall we then vent our own commodities?

THOMAS MUN, 1621

He is my friend that grindeth at my mill.

JOHN CLARKE, 1639

On a good bargain think twice.

GEORGE HERBERT, 1640

The buyer needs a hundred eyes, the seller not one. GEORGE HERBERT, 1640

As in other things, so in men, not the seller, but the buyer determines the price. For let a man, as most men do, rate themselves at the highest value they can; yet their true value is no more than it is esteemed by others.

THOMAS HOBBES, 1651

Truly it is a reproach to a man that he knows not when he hath enough; when to leave off; when to be satisfied. WILLIAM PENN, 1668

Make every bargain clear and plain,
That none may afterward complain.

JOHN RAY, 1670

He who pays the piper can call the tune.

JOHN RAY, 1670

The exhorbitant appetites of men are the main spur to trade, or rather to industry and ingenuity.   DUDLEY NORTH, 1691

On the soft beds of luxury most kingdoms have expired.   EDWARD YOUNG, 1725

Can wealth give happiness? look round and see
What gay distress! what splendid misery!
Whatever fortune lavishly can pour,
The mood annihilates, and calls for more!

EDWARD YOUNG, 1728

He that payeth beforehand shall have his work ill done.   THOMAS FULLER, 1732

If you buy the cow take the tail into the bargain.

THOMAS FULLER, 1732

Republics end through luxury; monarchies through poverty.   C. S. MONTESQUIEU, 1748

Luxury may possibly contribute to give bread to the poor; but if there were no luxury, there would be no poor.   HENRY HOME, 1751

Necessity never made a good bargain.

BENJAMIN FRANKLIN, 1758

Beware of little expenses. A small leak will sink a great ship.   BENJAMIN FRANKLIN, 1758

He that speaks ill of the mare will buy her.

BENJAMIN FRANKLIN, 1767

Thrift is care and scruple in the spending of one's means. It is not a virtue, and it requires neither skill nor talent.   IMMANUEL KANT, 1775

With the great part of rich people, the chief employment of riches consists in the parade of riches.   ADAM SMITH, 1776

In general, there is not, perhaps, any one article of expense or consumption by which the liberality or narrowness of a man's whole expense can be better judged of, than by his house-rent.

ADAM SMITH, 1776

A person who can acquire no property, can have no other interest but to eat as much, and labor as little as possible. Whatever work he does beyond what is sufficient to purchase his own maintenance, can be squeezed out of him by violence only, and not by any interest of his own.   ADAM SMITH, 1776

It is absolutely necessary that a country with great powers of production should possess a body of unproductive consumers.

THOMAS MALTHUS, 1798

Never spend your money before you have it.

THOMAS JEFFERSON, 1813

If men ceased to consume, they would cease to produce.   DAVID RICARDO, 1817

Extravagant habits are a more frequent cause of a scarcity of capital and high profits, than high profits are a cause of extravagant habits.

THOMAS MALTHUS, 1820

Most men place some limits, however variable, to the quantity of conveniences and luxuries which they will labor for.

THOMAS MALTHUS, 1820

Consumption, in the sense in which the word is used in this science, is synonymous with use; and is, in fact, the great end and object of industry.   JOHN R. MCCULLOCH, 1825

To increase the sale of the produce of the industry and labor of man, it is not the income of the rich but the income of the poor which must be increased. It is their wage that must be increased, for the poor are the only purchasers who can add greatly to the extent of the market.

JEAN C. L. SISMONDI, 1834

The taste for well-being is the prominent and indelible feature of democratic times.

ALEXIS DE TOCQUEVILLE, 1835

We can do without any article of luxury we have never had; but when once obtained, it is not human nature to surrender it voluntarily.

THOMAS C. HALIBURTON, 1836

Each successive addition to the population brings a consumer and a producer.

HENRY CHARLES CAREY, 1840

My old father used to have a saying: If you make a bad bargain, hug it all the tighter.

ABRAHAM LINCOLN, 1842

Although he who sells, really sells only to buy, he need not buy at the same moment when he sells.   JOHN STUART MILL, 1844

I know not why it should be matter of congratulation that persons who are already richer than anyone needs to be, should have doubled their means of consuming things which give little or no pleasure except as representatives of wealth.

JOHN STUART MILL, 1848

Almost any man knows how to earn money, but not one in a million knows how to spend it.

HENRY DAVID THOREAU, 1854

Give us the luxuries of life, and we will dispense with its necessaries.

OLIVER WENDELL HOLMES, SR., 1858

Consumption is the crown of production and the wealth of a nation is only to be estimated by what it consumes.   JOHN RUSKIN, 1862

The theory of economics must begin with a correct theory of consumption.

W. STANLEY JEVONS, 1871

We may safely call that man happy who, however lowly his position and limited his possessions, can always hope for more than he has, and can feel that every moment of exertion tends to realize his aspirations. He, on the contrary, who seizes the enjoyment of the passing moment without regard to coming times, must discover sooner or later that his stock of pleasure is on the wane, and that even hope begins to fail.   W. STANLEY JEVONS, 1871

The best form of charity is extravagance. . . . The prodigality of the rich is the providence of the poor.   ROBERT G. INGERSOLL, 1883

For every man who consumes more than he creates, there must of necessity be another man who has to consume less than he creates.

EDWARD CARPENTER, 1887

Before buying anything, it is well to ask if one could do without it.   JOHN LUBBOCK, 1889

It is true that in times of depression the disorganization of consumption is a contributory cause to the continuance of the disorganization of credit and of production. But the remedy is not to be got by a study of consumption as has been alleged by some hasty writers.

ALFRED MARSHALL, 1890

The higher study of consumption must come after, and not before, the main body of economic analysis; and though it may have its beginning within the proper domain of economics, it cannot find its conclusion there, but must extend far beyond.

ALFRED MARSHALL, 1890

The man who possesses a fortune is nolens volens a benefactor to the community. He may be a misanthrope and atheist. But if such a man moves into a western city and begins to spend his money in the most selfish and ostentatious luxury, he is an involuntary benefactor of that city.   WILLIAM P. FAUNCE, 1893

As the priestess of the temple of consumption, as the limitless demander of things to use up, her economic influence is reactionary and injurious.

CHARLOTTE PERKINS GILMAN, 1898

Conspicuous consumption of valuable goods is a means of reputability to the gentleman of leisure.   THORSTEIN VEBLEN, 1899

In order to gain and to hold the esteem of men it is not sufficient merely to possess wealth or power. The wealth or power must be put in evidence, for esteem is awarded only on evidence.

THORSTEIN VEBLEN, 1899

He practiced the utmost economy in order to keep the most expensive habits.

GEORGE BERNARD SHAW, 1904

Business success means "getting the best of the bargain."   THORSTEIN VEBLEN, 1904

There are two halves to ivry dollar. Wan is knowing how to make it an' th' other is not knowin' how to spend it confortably.

FINLEY PETER DUNNE, 1910

The right proportion of saving to spending at any given time depends upon the present condition of the arts of production and consumption, and the probabilities of such changes in modes of work or living as shall provide social utility for new forms of capital within the near or calculable future.

JOHN A. HOBSON, 1910

Where the production of an economic society has grown so far as to yield a considerable and a growing surplus beyond that required for survival purposes, this surplus is liable to several abuses. Instead of being applied as food and stimulus to the physical and spiritual growth of individual and social life, it may be squandered, either upon excessive satisfaction of existing routine wants in any class or classes, or in the stimulation and satisfaction of more routine wants and the evolution of a complex conventional standard of consumption, containing in its new factors a diminishing amount of human utility or even an increasing amount of human costs.   JOHN A. HOBSON, 1914

We owe something to extravagance, for thrift and adventure seldom go hand in hand.

EMILIE POULSSON, 1915

Impoverished them to such an extent that for three consecutive months they could barely afford the most unnecessary luxuries of life.

NORMAN DOUGLAS, 1917

It is the preoccupation with possession, more than anything else, that prevents men from living freely and nobly.

BERTRAND RUSSELL, 1923

Bargain: something you can't use at a price you can't resist.   FRANKLIN P. JONES, 1924

Extravagance. The price of indulging yourself in your youth in the things you cannot afford is poverty and dependence in your old age.

DOROTHY DIX, 1926

So it has been my policy to force the price of the care down as fast as production would permit and give the benefits to the users and laborers with resulting surprisingly enormous benefits to ourselves.   HENRY FORD, 1926

When we come to the practices which today prevail in buying for ultimate consumption, we find that less than one hundred years of divorce between production and consumption has almost entirely destroyed the consumer's capacity for measuring quality.

RALPH BORSODI, 1927

The instinct of acquisitiveness has more perverts, I believe, than the instinct of sex. At any rate, people seem to me odder about money than about even their amours.

ALDOUS HUXLEY, 1928

We'll hold the distinction of being the only nation in the history of the world that ever went to the poorhouse in an automobile.

WILL ROGERS, 1932

The theory of hard work and thrift as a means of pulling us out of the depression is unsound economically. True, hard work means more production, but thrift and economy mean less consumption. Now reconcile those two forces, will you?   MARRINER ECCLES, 1932

Not only is the marginal propensity to consume weaker in a wealthy community, but, owing to its accumulation of capital being already larger, the opportunities for further investment are less attractive.   JOHN MAYNARD KEYNES, 1936

The workers spend what they get and the capitalists get what they spend.

M. KALECKI, 1939

Never economize on luxuries.

ANGELA THIRKELL, 1940

Investment dollars are high-powered dollars. Consumption dollars are too.

PAUL A. SAMUELSON, 1947

The desire to get superior goods takes on a life of its own. It provides a drive to higher expenditures which may even be stronger than that arising out of the needs which are supposed to be satisfied by that expenditure.

JAMES S. DUESENBERRY, 1949

Today the future occupation of all moppets is to be skilled consumers.

DAVID RIESMAN, 1950

When people come into contact with superior goods or superior patterns of consumption, with new articles or new ways of meeting old wants, they are apt to feel after a while a certain restlessness and dissatisfaction. Their knowledge is extended, their imagination stimulated; new desires are aroused, the propensity to consume is shifted upward.   RAGNAR NURKSE, 1953

Consumption is determined by lifetime consuming power anticipations, and these are best expressed in terms of wealth and the wage rate and *not* by disposable income.

W. HAMBURGER, 1955

An industrial economy faces . . . the problem of maintaining a level of consumption adequate to ever-increasing levels of productiveness. If it fails to solve this problem, an industrial economy is prone to cycles of bust-and-boom.

LOUIS O. KELSO AND
MORTIMER ADLER, 1958

The development of the consumer cooperatives follows the straight line of numerical progression; a considerable portion of civilized mankind is organized today, from the consumption side, on cooperative lines.

MARTIN BUBER, 1958

Wealth has never been a sufficient source of honor in itself. It must be advertised, and the normal medium is obtrusively expensive goods.

JOHN KENNETH GALBRAITH, 1958

The consumer today is the victim of the manufacturer who launches on him a regiment of products for which he must make room in his soul.   MARY MCCARTHY, 1961

When the conception of the rate of profit determined by the rate of accumulation of capital and thriftiness conditions are combined with the conception of a choice of technique from a given spectrum of possibilities, it can be seen that the highest rate of output of consumption goods is achieved when the rate of profit on capital is equal to the rate of accumulation.

JOAN ROBINSON, 1962

The people recognize themselves in their commodities; they find their soul in their automobile, hi-fi set, split-level home, kitchen equipment. The very mechanism which ties the individual to his society has changed, and social control is anchored in the new needs which it has produced.   HERBERT MARCUSE, 1964

Man today is fascinated by the possibility of buying more, better, and especially new things. He is consumption-hungry. The act of buying and consuming has become a compulsive, irrational aim, because it is an end in itself, with little relation to the use or pleasure in the things bought and consumed.

ERICH FROMM, 1965

The economy may suffer if auto sales drop— but that's the American way; we have to buy more cars than we need or we'll never be able to afford them.   JACK WILSON, 1965

There was a time when a fool and his money were soon parted, but now it happens to everybody.   ADLAI STEVENSON, 1966

The American consumer is not notable for his imagination and does not know what he "wants."   ANDREW HACKER, 1966

An honest man is one who knows that he can't consume more than he has produced.

AYN RAND, 1966

The dynamic consumer does not live from day to day. He purchases goods that will serve him in the future. He borrows to acquire housing and durable goods suitable to the status he expects to have and geared to his expected income. By . . . committing future income in advance, his needs and wants exert great pressure toward obtaining a higher income.

GEORGE KATONA, 1971

In a consumer society there are inevitably two kinds of slaves: the prisoners of addiction and the prisoners of envy.   IVAN ILLICH, 1973

Other people's patterns of expenditure and consumption are highly irrational and slightly immoral.   CHARLES P. ISSAWI, 1973

A consumer is born every ten seconds.

EDWIN NEWMAN, 1976

The more the citizen is trained in the consumption of packaged goods and services, the less effective he seems to become in shaping his environment.   IVAN ILLICH, 1978

If you don't appreciate the amount of luxuries your budget can afford, you are getting paid far too much.   DAVID A. OGDEN, 1979

The gap in our economy is between what we have and what we think we ought to have—and that is a moral problem, not an economic one.

PAUL HEYNE, 1983

Corporation

Great businesses turn on a little pin.

GEORGE HERBERT, 1640

The trade of a joint stock company is always managed by a court of directors. This court indeed, is frequently subject, in many respects, to the control of a general court of proprietors. But the greater part of those proprietors seldom pretend to understand anything of the business of the company, and when the spirit of faction happens not to prevail among them, give themselves no trouble about it, but receive contentedly such half yearly or yearly dividend as the directors think proper to make to them.

ADAM SMITH, 1776

Corporate bodies are more corrupt and profligate than individuals, because they have more power to do mischief, and are less amenable to disgrace and punishment.

WILLIAM HAZLITT, 1805

A corporation is an artificial being, invisible, intangible, and existing only in contemplation of law.

JOHN MARSHALL, 1819

It is truly enough said that a corporation has no conscience; but a corporation of conscientious men is a corporation with a conscience.

HENRY DAVID THOREAU, 1854

Corporations, which should be the carefully restrained creatures of the law and the servants of the people, are fast becoming the people's masters.

GROVER CLEVELAND, 1888

The committee sat and sat and sat, till every sensible plan was crushed as flat as a pancake.

CHARLES H. SPURGEON, 1892

We demand that big business give people a square deal.

THEODORE ROOSEVELT, 1904

The biggest corporation, like the humblest private citizen, must be held to strict compliance with the will of the people.

THEODORE ROOSEVELT, 1904

Corporation, n. An ingenious device for obtaining individual profit without individual responsibility.

AMBROSE BIERCE, 1911

Large organization is loose organization. Nay, it would be almost as true to say that organization is always disorganization.

GILBERT K. CHESTERTON, 1926

A holding company is a thing where you hand an accomplice the goods while the policeman searches you.

WILL ROGERS, 1927

45

The notion that a business is clothed with a public interest and has been devoted to the public use is little more than a fiction intended to beautify what is disagreeable to the sufferers.

OLIVER WENDELL HOLMES, JR., 1927

This dissolution of the atom of property (the separation of formal ownership and effective control) destroys the very foundation on which the economic order of the past three centuries has rested.   ADOLF A. BERLE, JR., 1932

We are raising a lot of thoroughly drilled yes Ma'ams in the big corporations, who have no minds of their own; no opinions.

CARL THOMPSON, 1932

What is the use of thinking if after all there is to be organization?   GERTRUDE STEIN, 1937

A big corporation is more or less blamed for being big. It is only because it gives service. If it doesn't give service, it gets small faster than it grew.   WILLIAM S. KNUDSEN, 1946

What is good for the country is good for General Motors, and vice versa.

CHARLES E. WILSON, 1953

Big business breeds bureaucracy and bureaucrats exactly as big government does.

T. K. QUINN, 1953

A corporation . . . may be defined in the light of history as a body created by law for the purpose of attaining public ends through an appeal to private interests.

HENRY CARTER ADAMS, 1954

For the employees, freedom and security, both political and economic, can no longer rest upon individual independence in the old sense. To be free and to be secure is to have an effective control over that upon which one is dependent: the job within the centralized enterprise.

C. WRIGHT MILLS, 1956

The modern corporation has undermined the preconceptions of classical economic theory as effectively as the quantum undermined classical physics at the beginning of the 20th century.

GARDINER MEANS, 1957

I yield to no one in my admiration for the office as a social center, but it's no place actually to get any work done.

KATHARINE WHITEHORN, 1962

Bigness taxes the ability to manage intelligently. . . . The growth of bigness has resulted in ruthless sacrifice of human values. The disappearance of free enterprise has submerged the individual in the impersonal corporation.

WILLIAM O. DOUGLAS, 1963

We presumed that the first purpose in making a capital investment is the establishment of a business that will pay satisfactory dividends and preserve and increase its capital value. The primary object of the corporation, therefore, we declared, was to make money, not just motor cars.   ALFRED P. SLOAN, JR., 1964

The history of General Motors over the past 50 years is far more important than the history of Switzerland or Holland.   ANTONY JAY, 1968

The only things that evolve by themselves in an organization are disorder, friction, and malperformance.   PETER DRUCKER, 1969

Humans must breathe, but corporations must make money.   ALICE EMBREE, 1970

All organizations are at least 50 percent waste—waste people, waste effort, waste space, and waste time.   ROBERT TOWNSEND, 1970

The modern corporation is a political institution; its purpose is the creation of legitimate power in the industrial sphere.

PETER DRUCKER, 1970

At some point in the life cycle of virtually every organization, its ability to succeed in spite of itself runs out.   RICHARD BRIEN, 1970

Reorganization is the permanent condition of a vigorous organization.   ROY L. ASH, 1971

Going to work for a large company is like getting on a train. Are you going sixty miles an hour or is the train going sixty miles an hour and you're just sitting still?
          J. PAUL GETTY, 1971

About the nature of the corporation, there are important differences. I once said half in jest and half in truth that U. S. Steel is the prototype of the corporation of the first third of this century, General Motors is the prototype of the corporation of the second third of the century, and IBM is the prototype of the corporation of the last third of the century.   DANIEL BELL, 1971

General Motors could buy Delaware if DuPont were willing to sell it.   RALPH NADER, 1973

A committee is a cul de sac down which ideas are lured and then quietly strangled.
          BARNETT COCKS, 1973

The large corporation, though still primarily a private economic entity, has such vast social impact that it has become a public trust with a communal constituency.
          STEPHEN B. SHEPARD, 1974

The global corporation is an instrument for accelerating concentration of wealth. As a global distributor it diverts resources from where they are most needed (poor countries and poor regions of rich countries) to where they are least needed (rich countries and rich regions of poor countries).
          RICHARD BARNET AND
          RONALD MULLER, 1974

The multinational corporation is the only organization which has the resources and scope to think, to plan, and to act with worldwide planning of markets and sources. Many international opportunities require capital and technology on a scale only large multinational corporations can supply.
          NASROLLAH FATEM, 1975

They [corporations] usually do not much care what society's rules are so long as the rules are clear.   GEORGE WILL, 1979

The key to the problem of employee theft is to make the employing organization a place that people identify with and "feel good about," and not one that is suspicious and threatening.
          LEONARD SMITH, 1981

Nothing is so important in the defense of the modern corporation as the argument that its power does not exist—that all power is surrendered to the impersonal play of the market, all decision is in response to the instruction of the market.   JOHN KENNETH GALBRAITH, 1983

Credit

Be not a beggar by banqueting upon borrowing.
ECCLESIASTICUS 18:33, c. 210 B.C.

If a man ever pays you what he owes you,
You're greatly beholden to him.
TERENCE, c. 162 B.C.

Nothing so cements and holds together all the parts of society as faith or credit, which can never be kept up unless men are under some force or necessity of honestly paying what they owe to each other. CICERO, c. 65 B.C.

He who loses credit can lose nothing further.
PUBLILIUS SYRUS, c. 43 B.C.

Lend freely, hoping nothing thereby.
LUKE 6:35, c. A.D. 82

'Tis a godlike thing to lend; to owe is a heroic virtue. FRANÇOIS RABELAIS, 1553

Who quick be to borrow, and slow be to pay,
Their credit is naught, go they never so gay.
THOMAS TUSSER, 1573

Neither a borrower nor a lender be:
For loan oft loses both itself and friend,
And borrowing dulls the edge of husbandry.
WILLIAM SHAKESPEARE,
Hamlet (I, iii), 1604

I come to borrow what I'll never lend
And buy what I'll never pay for.
WILLIAM DAVENANT, 1634

Of all beings that have existence only in the minds of men, nothing is more fantastical and nice than Credit; it is never to be forced; it hangs upon opinion; it depends upon our passions of hope and fear; it comes many times unsought for, and often goes away without reason, and when once lost, is hardly to be quite recovered.
CHARLES DAVENANT, 1638

He that hath lost his credit is dead to the world.
GEORGE HERBERT, 1639

Who tells a lie to save his credit wipes his nose on his sleeve to save his napkin.
JAMES HOWELL, 1659

Creditors have better memories than debtors.
JAMES HOWELL, 1659

Some give Men no Rest till they are in their Debt, and then give them no Rest till they are out again; some will credit no body, and some again are for crediting every body; some get Credit till they can pay nothing, and some break tho' they could pay all. DANIEL DEFOE, 1706

He that has but one Coat, cannot lend it.
THOMAS FULLER, 1732

Blest paper-credit! last and best supply!
That lends corruption lighter wings to fly.
ALEXANDER POPE, 1737

If you'd lose a troublesome visitor lend him money.   BENJAMIN FRANKLIN, 1740

If you would know the value of money, go and try to borrow some.
BENJAMIN FRANKLIN, 1757

Take care you don't hurt your credit by offering too much security.
RICHARD SHERIDAN, 1775

I owe you one.   GEORGE COLMAN, JR., 1797

That canker at the heart of national prosperity, the imaginary riches of paper credit.
T. L. PEACOCK, 1817

The human species, according to the best theory I can form of it is composed of two distinct races, the men who borrow, and the men who lend.
CHARLES LAMB, 1818

The best way to keep your friends is to never owe them anything and never lend them anything.   PAUL DE KOCK, 1820

Cash is virtue.   LORD BYRON, 1822

Credit is like a looking glass, which, when once sullied by a breath, may be wiped clear again, but if once cracked can never be repaired.
WALTER SCOTT, 1826

Cash Payment is the only nexus between man and man.   THOMAS CARLYLE, 1843

Credit is . . . the economic judgement on the morality of a man. In credit, man himself, in-stead of metal or paper, has become the media-tor of exchange, but not as man, but as the existence of capital and interest.
KARL MARX, 1844

It is difficult to begin without borrowing, but perhaps it is the most generous course thus to permit your fellowmen to have an interest in your enterprise.   HENRY DAVID THOREAU, 1854

A creditor is worse than a master; for a master owns only your person, a creditor owns your dignity, and can belabor that.
VICTOR HUGO, 1865

Borrowers are nearly always ill-spenders, and it is with lent money that all evil is mainly done and all unjust war protracted.
JOHN RUSKIN, 1865

Credit is like chastity; they can both stand temptation better than suspicion.
JOSH BILLINGS, 1868

Very often he that his money lends
Loses both his gold and his friends.
CHARLES H. SPURGEON, 1869

I hate this shallow Americanism which hopes to get rich by credit.
RALPH WALDO EMERSON, 1870

Credit is a power which may grow, but cannot be constructed. Those who live under a great and firm system of credit must consider that if they break up that one, they will never see an-other, for it will take years upon years to make a successor to it.   WALTER BAGEHOT, 1873

The amount of that cash is so exceedingly small that a bystander almost trembles when he com-pares its minuteness with the immensity of the credit which rests upon it.
WALTER BAGEHOT, 1873

Every innocent man has in his countenance a promise to pay, and hence credit.

RALPH WALDO EMERSON, 1876

The holy passion of Friendship is of so sweet and steady and loyal and enduring a nature that it will last through a whole lifetime, if not asked to lend money.   MARK TWAIN, 1878

Home life ceases to be free and beautiful as soon as it is founded on borrowing and debt.

HENRIK IBSEN, 1879

It is stupid to borrow $30 million, and have to pay moneylenders $66 million for the use of the money.   THOMAS A. EDISON, 1893

It is only by not paying our bills that we can hope to live in the memory of the commercial classes.   OSCAR WILDE, 1895

Creditor, n. One of a tribe of savages dwelling beyond the Financial Straits and dreaded for their desolating incursions.

AMBROSE BIERCE, 1906

The man who won't loan money isn't going to have many friends—or need them.

WILSON MIZNER, 1909

He was an incorrigible borrower of money; he borrowed from all his friends; if he ever repaid a loan the incident failed to pass into history.

MARK TWAIN, 1910

The biggest businessmen in the world today are borrowers.   ELBERT HUBBARD, 1923

No man's credit is as good as his money.

E. W. HOWE, 1926

It's not politics that is worrying this Country; it's the Second Payment.

WILL ROGERS, 1927

Every one, even the richest and most munificent of men, pays much by check more light-heartedly than he pays little in specie.

MAX BEERBOHM, 1928

Freely we lend, for friends are best, we hold,
When "grappled to our soul" with hoops of gold.   MACFLECKNOE, 1932

My dear, I'll be economically independent if I have to borrow every cent!

MAX EASTMAN, 1936

It saves a lot of trouble if, instead of having to earn money and save it, you can just go and borrow it.   WINSTON CHURCHILL, 1939

There can be no doubt that it is a rule of borrowing and lending that "to him that hath shall be lent."   JOHN R. HICKS, 1942

The lender is often a monopolist—a "money master," a malster or corn monger, "a rich priest," who is the solitary capitalist in a community of peasants and artisans. Naturally, he is apt to become their master.

RICHARD H. TAWNEY, 1947

Our whole intricate system of credit depends on the belief that most people are honest most of the time.   REINHOLD NIEBUHR, 1953

Someone has suggested that America's greatest gifts to civilization are three: cornflakes, Kleenex, and credit.   LOUIS P. BENEZET, 1954

Credit . . . is the only enduring testimonial to man's confidence in man.

JAMES BLISH, 1958

Remember when people worried about how much it took to buy something, instead of how long?   EARL WILSON, 1962

A good loan is better than a bad tax.
ROBERT F. WAGNER, 1964

If you think nobody cares if you're alive, try missing a couple of car payments.
EARL WILSON, 1964

Credit buying is much like being drunk. The buzz happens immediately, and it gives you a lift. . . . The hangover comes the day after.
JOYCE BROTHERS, 1971

Children are rarely in the position to lend one a truly interesting sum of money. There are, however, exceptions, and such children are an excellent addition to any party.
FRAN LEBOWITZ, 1974

The rich are different from you and me because they have more credit.
JOHN LEONARD, 1974

It is easier not to pay one's mother than not to pay a creditor.
NORMAN MAILER, 1979

Currency

A substance was selected whose public evaluation exempted it from the fluctuations of the other commodities, thus giving it an always stable external [nominal] value. . . . Hence its exchange value is based, not upon the substance itself, but upon its nominal value.
PAULUS, second century

Money usually depreciates when it becomes too abundant.
NICHOLAS COPERNICUS, 1522

Bad money drives out good money.
THOMAS GRESHAM, 1590

And it is much better for the kingdom to have things dear with plenty of money, whereby men may live in their several callings: than to have things cheap with want of money, which now makes every man complain.
EDWARD MISSELDEN, 1622

Money is but the Fat of the Body-politic, whereof too much doth as often hinder its Agility as too little makes it sick.
WILLIAM PETTY, 1665

What remedy is there if we have too little Money? Answer: We must erect a Bank, which well computed, doth almost double the Effect of our coined money.
WILLIAM PETTY, 1682

It were better for trade, and consequently for everybody (for money would be stirring, and less would do the business), if rents were paid by shorter intervals. . . . A great deal less money would serve for the trade of a country.

JOHN LOCKE, 1691

That, which constantly raises the natural interest of money, is, when money is little, in proportion to the trade of a country.

JOHN LOCKE, 1692

A state must have a certain quantity of money proportioned to the number of its people.

JOHN LAW, 1700

Money is not the value for which goods are exchanged but the value by which they are exchanged: the use of money is to buy goods, and silver while money is of no other use.

JOHN LAW, 1705

If this Colony [Rhode Island] be in any respect happy and flourishing, it is paper money and a right application of it that hath rendered us so. And that we are in a flourishing condition is evident from our trade.

RICHARD WARD, 1740

And any man who travels over Europe at this day, may see, by the prices of commodities, that money, in spite of the absurd jealousy of princes and states, has brought itself nearly to a level; and that the difference between one kingdom and another is not greater in this respect, than it is often between different provinces of the same kingdom.   DAVID HUME, 1752

When the people of any particular country have such confidence in the fortune, probity, and prudence of a particular banker, as to believe that he is always ready to pay upon demand such of his promissory notes as are likely to be at any time presented to him; those notes come to have the same currency as gold and silver, from the confidence that such money can at any time be had for them.   ADAM SMITH, 1776

It is a common saying that plenty or scarcity of money makes all things dear or good or cheap.

ADAM SMITH, 1776

The quantity of money, on the contrary, must in every country naturally increase as the value of the annual produce increases.

ADAM SMITH, 1776

This Currency, as we manage it, is a wonderful machine. It performs its Office when we issue it; it pays and clothes Troops, and provides Victuals and Ammunition; and when we are obliged to issue a Quantity excessive, it pays itself off by Depreciation.

BENJAMIN FRANKLIN, 1779

Most commercial nations have found it necessary to institute banks; and they have proved to be the happiest engines that ever were invented for advancing trade.

ALEXANDER HAMILTON, 1781

We would gladly have borne the tax on tea if we could have been granted the power to create our own money.

BENJAMIN FRANKLIN, 1783

A great deal of small change is useful in a state, and tends to reduce the price of small articles.

THOMAS JEFFERSON, 1784

Too great a quantity of cash in circulation is a much greater evil than too small a quantity.

NOAH WEBSTER, 1785

To suffer either the solicitation of merchants, or the wishes of government, to determine the measure of bank issues is unquestionably to adopt a very false principle of conduct.

HENRY THORNTON, 1802

If we consent to give coin in exchange for goods, it must be from choice, not from necessity. We should not import more goods than we export, unless we had a redundancy of currency, which it therefore suits us to make a part of our exports. DAVID RICARDO, 1810

We must, in a word, use a bank to unbank the banks, to the extent that may be necessary to restore a safe and stable currency—just as we apply snow to a frozen limb in order to restore vitality and circulation.
JOHN C. CALHOUN, 1816

In all states . . . the issue of money ought to be under some check and control; and none seems so proper for that purpose, as that of subjecting the issue of paper money to the obligation of paying their notes in either gold coin or bullion.
DAVID RICARDO, 1817

There is no point more important in issuing paper money than to be fully impressed with the effects that follow from the principle of limitation of quantity. It is not necessary that paper should be payable in specie to secure its value; it is only necessary that its quantity should be regulated. . . DAVID RICARDO, 1817

A circulation can never be so abundant as to overflow; for by diminishing its value, in the same proportion you will increase its quantity, and by increasing its value diminish its quantity.
DAVID RICARDO, 1817

A disordered currency is one of the greatest political evils. DANIEL WEBSTER, 1827

All the perplexities, confusion, and distress in America arise, not from the defects in their constitution or confederation, not from want of honor or virtue, so much as from downright ignorance of the nature of coin, credit, and circulation. JOHN QUINCY ADAMS, 1829

The prices vary much on the road and the eternal confusion with the good and bad money and its different value is enough to weary a bank clerk.
TRAVELER FROM LONDON TO VIENNA, 1829

The Almighty Dollar, that great object of universal devotion throughout our land.
WASHINGTON IRVING, 1835

It is the quantity of money, constituting the revenues of the different orders of the State, under the head of rents, profits, salaries, and wages, destined for current expenditures, that alone forms the limiting principle of the aggregate of money prices, the only prices that can properly come under the designation of general prices. As the cost of production is the limiting principle of supply, so the aggregate of money incomes devoted to expenditure for consumption is the determining and limiting principle of demand. THOMAS TOOKE, 1844

The value of money, other things being the same, varies inversely as its quantity; every increase of quantity lowering the value, and every diminution raising it, in a ratio exactly equivalent. This, it must be observed, is a property peculiar to money. JOHN STUART MILL, 1848

To be able to pay off the national debt, defray the expenses of government without taxation, and in fine, to make the fortunes of the whole community is a brilliant prospect, when once a man is capable of believing that printing a few characters on bits of paper will do it.
JOHN STUART MILL, 1848

Money is the creature of law, and the creation of the original issue of money should be maintained as an exclusive monopoly of the National Government.
ABRAHAM LINCOLN, 1860

No human intelligence can fix the amount of currency that is really needed. . . . So long as the volume of currency depends upon legislative enactment, uncertainty and instability will pervade all financial operations.

HILAND R. HULBURD, 1869

Now that London is the clearinghouse to foreign countries, London has a new liability to foreign countries. At whatever place many people have to make payments, at that place those people must keep money. A large deposit of foreign money in London is now necessary for the business of the world.

WALTER BAGEHOT, 1873

I maintain that the Money Market is as concrete and real as anything else; that it can be described in plain words; that it is the writer's fault if what he says is not clear.

WALTER BAGEHOT, 1873

I am not a believer in any artificial method of making paper money equal to coin, when the coin is not owned or held ready to redeem the promises to pay.   ULYSSES S. GRANT, 1874

I am thankful I have lived to see the day when the greenback can raise its right hand and declare, "I know that my Redeemer liveth."

ROBERT G. INGERSOLL, 1879

No government can afford to be a clipper of coin.   ROBERT G. INGERSOLL, 1880

If a nation legislates a lie and forces its promise of a dollar under a legal-tender act into use in place of the coined metal that carries its own value in its own substance, the people will follow the example; fraud will prevail more and yet more among them until bankruptcy or anarchy forces a return to right methods of legislation.   EDWARD ATKINSON, 1880

Money has little value to its possessor unless it also has value to others.

LELAND STANFORD, 1881

Whoever controls the volume of money in any country is the master of all its legislation and commerce.   JAMES A. GARFIELD, 1881

The principles governing the circulation of money were a perplexing mystery to most of our revolutionary fathers; and even now the haze has not entirely cleared away before every eye.

ALFRED S. BOLLES, 1884

A credit corresponding to his share of the annual produce of the nation is given to every citizen on the public books at the beginning of each year, and a credit card issued him with which he procures at the public storehouses, found in every community, whatever he desires whenever he desires it.   EDWARD BELLAMY, 1887

Patriotism is no substitute for a sound currency.

GROVER CLEVELAND, 1892

Dollars not only count but they rule.

CHARLES THOMAS WALKER, 1900

There is the same distinction in economics between money and commodities that there is in physics between energy and work. It is to increase their potential energy, that is, their reserve of purchasing power, that the aspirations, both of men and nations are directed.

WILLIAM CARLILE, 1901

No great increase of money in any one country or locality can occur without spreading to other countries or localities. As soon as local prices have risen enough to make it profitable to sell at the high prices in that place and buy at the low prices elsewhere, money will be exported.

IRVING FISHER, 1911

In short, the quantity theory asserts that (provided velocity of circulation and volume of trade are unchanged) if we increase the number of dollars, whether by renaming coins, or be debasing coins, or by increasing coinage, or by any other means, prices will be increased in the same proportion.   IRVING FISHER, 1920

The size of a dollar depends entirely upon how many more you have.

ROBERT C. EDWARDS, 1920

The only quality demanded of a monetary system which is of any importance for promoting the trade and general welfare of the world, is stability.   GUSTAV CASSEL, 1922

The actual rate of exchange is largely governed by the expected behavior of the country's monetary authority.

DENNIS H. ROBERTSON, 1922

The youth who can solve the money question will do more for the world than all the professional soldiers of history.

HENRY FORD, 1922

Whatever the state of society, there is a certain volume of their resources which people of different classes taken one with another, care to keep in the form of currency; and, if everything else remains the same, then there is this direct relation between the volume of currency, and the level of prices, that, if one is increased by ten percent, the other also will be increased by ten percent.   ALFRED MARSHALL, 1923

If we are dealing with a closed system, so that there is only one condition of internal equilibrium to fulfill, an appropriate banking policy is always capable of preventing any serious disturbance of the status quo from developing at all. . . . But when the condition of external equilibrium must also be fulfilled, then there will be no banking policy capable of avoiding disturbance of the internal system.

JOHN MAYNARD KEYNES, 1925

There are three main causes that dispose men to madness: love, ambition, and the study of currency problems.   WALTER LEAF, 1926

The aim of monetary policy should surely be not to prevent all fluctuations in the general price-level, but to permit those which are necessary to the establishment of appropriate alterations in output and to repress those which tend to carry the alterations in output beyond the appropriate point.

DENNIS H. ROBERTSON, 1926

The power of taxation by currency depreciation is one which has been inherent in the State since Rome discovered it.

JOHN MAYNARD KEYNES, 1933

We need a quantum of international currency, which is neither determined in an unpredictable and irrelevant manner as, for example, by the technical progress of the gold industry, nor subject to large variations depending on the gold reserve policies of individual countries.

JOHN MAYNARD KEYNES, 1943

An organized money market has many advantages. But it is not a school of social ethics or of political responsibility.

RICHARD H. TAWNEY, 1947

One of the uses of sound money is to produce that pain in the economic body; the ache tells it that by excess and wrong living it is doing its health a damage.   GARET GARRET, 1948

Now if a country is rapidly increasing its supply of money, the same lack of confidence in the future of money which ultimately worms its way into the skull of the thickest-headed citizen, strikes like a flash upon the consciousness of the well-informed and impressionable gentlemen whose business it is to carry on dealings in foreign money. They become highly willing to buy foreign money and to sell the money of their own country.   DENNIS H. ROBERTSON, 1948

The obvious weakness of fixed quantity, as a sole rule of monetary policy, lies in the danger of sharp changes on the velocity side, for no monetary system can function effectively or survive politically in the face of extreme alternations of hoarding and dishoarding.

HENRY SIMONS, 1948

The public's distrust of paper money is too strong, and its increase in every country would only amplify the confusion of the exchange rates and the disorder in international commerce, at the same time as the social crisis . . . the only instrument of international payment which has the confidence of the public is gold.

CHARLES RIST, 1949

A fall in the exchange rate, or in money wages, causes a primary increase in employment in export industries, and in industries producing goods rival to imports.   JOAN ROBINSON, 1949

A good new chairman of the Federal Reserve Bank is worth a $10 billion tax cut.

PAUL H. DOUGLAS, 1955

The worst episodes in recent monetary history—the great inflations—have been marked by the subjection of central bankers to overriding political pressures.   R. S. SAYERS, 1956

A foreign exchange dealers' office during a busy spell is the nearest thing to Bedlam I have struck.   HAROLD WINCOTT, 1958

In today's world of inflation, depreciation is likely to raise prices in the depreciating country, leaving them unchanged in the appreciating country. . . . Depreciation and appreciation . . . will thus raise world prices on balance in ratchet style, and generate dynamic inflationary forces inside separate countries.

CHARLES KINDLEBERGER, 1960

The Great Depression in the United States, far from being a sign of the inherent instability of the private enterprise system, is a testament to

how much harm can be done by mistakes on the part of a few men when they wield vast power over the monetary system of a country.

MILTON FRIEDMAN, 1962

To alter the terms on which the community will accumulate real capital—that is what monetary policy is all about.   JAMES TOBIN, 1963

Monetary changes have often had an independent origin; they have not been simply a reflection of changes in economic activity.

MILTON FRIEDMAN AND
ANNA J. SCHWARTZ, 1963

Some may regret the loss of sovereignty in the monetary and foreign exchange field. But sovereignty is being lost in various spheres—trade, defense, monetary policy, etc.—and it is as useless to weep over it as over the loss of U. S. foreign policy innocence. The household has lost the capacity to feed, clothe, protect itself, and so have the village, town, region, and state. It is sensible to expect growing interdependence of countries and in economic and political fields. It is difficult to see how independence of monetary, fiscal payments, and other economic policy can be preserved.

CHARLES KINDLEBERGER, 1963

To restore the dollar will be a very painful process, but the alternatives are political repression, socialism, and worldwide inflation.

JACQUES RUEFF, 1964

Under the Constitution, it is the right and duty of Congress to create money. It is left entirely to Congress. Congress has farmed out this power—has let it out to the banking system.

WRIGHT PATMAN, 1964

Like England in its heyday, when it was the major center of world trade and finance and sterling was the key currency, the United States in turn emerged from the Second World War as the world's financial center and its currency as the most important medium of exchange.

HENRY G. AUBREY, 1964

We therefore consider it necessary that international exchanges should rest, as was the case before the great world misfortunes, on an indisputable monetary basis bearing the mark of no particular country.

CHARLES DE GAULLE, 1965

All currency is neurotic currency.

NORMAN O. BROWN, 1966

The dollar became an international currency neither by Act of Congress nor by Act of God, but rather because it met various needs of foreign official institutions and foreign private parties more effectively than other financial assets could.

ROBERT ALIBER, 1966

We are in danger of assigning to monetary policy a larger role than it can perform, in danger of asking it to accomplish tasks that it cannot achieve and, as a result, in danger of preventing it from making the contribution that it is capable of making.

MILTON FRIEDMAN, 1967

Monetary theory is less abstract than most economic theory; it cannot avoid a relation to reality, which in other economic theory is sometimes missing. It belongs to monetary history, in a way that economic theory does not always belong to economic history.

JOHN R. HICKS, 1967

A system of floating exchange rates completely eliminates the balance of payment problem—just as in a free market there cannot be a surplus or a shortage in the sense of eager sellers unable to find buyers or eager buyers unable to find sellers. The price may fluctuate but there cannot be a deficit or a surplus threatening an exchange crisis.

MILTON FRIEDMAN, 1967

In the nation, no recipient, holder, or spender of money ever thinks of the existence of a legal debtor who issued the money and continues to "owe" something to the holder. The only thing in the mind of the recipient and holder of money is its transferability to and acceptability by others. The holder of money does not expect to "collect" from the issuing agency, but only to pass on the money to those who have something to sell.

FRITZ MACHLUP, 1968

We may ask why, after a hundred years of international monetary conferences, men still have not resolved their differences. The answer lies in one word—power. That is what one hundred years of international monetary conferences have been about.

EUGENE A. BIRNBAUM, 1968

Monetary policy had not been tried and found wanting. It had not been tried [during the Depression].

MILTON FRIEDMAN, 1970

I don't give a shit about the lira.

RICHARD M. NIXON, 1972

International corporations may at any given moment have an overall balance sheet in a dozen or more currencies. This gives them both the commercial need and the commercial means to protect their interests by "speculating," or (more politely) "taking positions" in the foreign exchange markets.

HUGH STEVENSON, 1972

Even if monetary policy could be depended upon to ultimately restore the economy to full employment, there would still remain the crucial question of the length of time it would need. There would still remain the very real possibility that it would necessitate subjecting the economy to an intolerably long period of dynamic adjustment: a period during which wages, prices, and interest would continue to fall, and—what is most important—a period during which varying numbers of workers would continue to suffer from involuntary unemployment.

DON PATINKIN, 1972

The more we use monetary policy, the less satisfactory it seems.

JAMES S. DUESENBERRY, 1974

Paper money is beginning to act more like paper and less like money.   JEROME SMITH, 1974

The study of money, above all fields in economics, is the one in which complexity is used to disguise truth or to evade truth, not to reveal it.

JOHN KENNETH GALBRAITH, 1975

The value of a pound is what the market says it is.   MILTON FRIEDMAN, 1976

The dollar has become like a hydrant at an international convention of dogs.

ELIOT JANEWAY, 1978

If the price system is not determined by genuine demand but rather by pushing additional money into the market, you direct productive efforts to uses which can continue only so long as this inflation continues, and not so long as it continues, but only so long as it continues to accelerate.   FRIEDRICH A. HAYEK, 1979

Mrs. Thatcher is doing for monetarism what the Boston Strangler did for door-to-door salesmen.   DENIS HEALEY, 1979

The Eurobond market has become one of the world's most exclusive clubs, conferring prestige on banks and borrowers alike.

M. STEFAN MENDELSOHN, 1980

Abstraction is the Achilles' heel of advanced monetary systems. It causes money to be regarded as exercising powers of its own—powers that individuals possessing it can allegedly wield, irrespective of political, social, and economic circumstances.

S. HERBERT FRANKEL, 1980

Debt

It is better to pay a creditor than to give to a friend.   ARISTOTLE, C. 340 B.C.

Debt is the slavery of the free.

PUBLILIUS SYRUS, first century B.C.

I attend to the business of other people, having lost my own.   HORACE, C. 35 B.C.

Economy is too late at the bottom of the purse.

SENECA, C. A.D. 35

A small debt makes a man your debtor, a large one makes him your enemy.

SENECA, C. A.D. 35

Live within your harvest.   PERSIUS, A.D. 62

Forgive us our debts as we forgive our debtors.
MATTHEW 4:12, c. A.D. 62

We should pay our debt first, and that only then we should, if we so decide, make a gift to our creditor in addition.   ST. AUGUSTINE, 397

This estimable merchant so had set
His wits to work, none knew he was in debt,
He was so stately in negotiation,
Loan, bargain, and commercial obligation.
GEOFFREY CHAUCER, 1382

The Lord forbid that I should be out of debt, as if indeed I could not be trusted.
FRANÇOIS RABELAIS, 1532

He that dies, pays all debts.
WILLIAM SHAKESPEARE,
The Tempest (III, ii), 1612

A pound of worry won't pay an ounce of debt.
JOHN RAY, 1670

The man who will live above his present circumstances is in great danger of living, in a little time, much beneath them.
JOSEPH ADDISON, 1712

Rather go to bed supperless than rise in debt.
BENJAMIN FRANKLIN, 1758

Do not accustom yourself to consider debt only as an inconvenience. You will find it a calamity.
SAMUEL JOHNSON, 1758

A man who owes a little can clear it off in a little time, and, if he is prudent, he will: whereas a man, who, by long negligence, owes a great deal, despairs of ever being able to pay, and therefore never looks into his accounts at all.
PHILIP D. STANHOPE, 1774

The principle of spending money to be paid by posterity, under the name of funding, is but swindling futurity on a large scale.
THOMAS JEFFERSON, 1789

It is a sure sign of an improved character, if you like paying debts as much as getting money.
G. C. LICHTENBERG, 1794

I have discovered the philosopher's stone, that turns everything into gold: It is, "Pay as you go."   JOHN RANDOLPH, 1802

Debts shorten life.   JOSEPH JOUBERT, 1824

Dreading that climax of all human ills,
The inflammation of his weekly bills.
LORD BYRON, 1824

It has been long my deliberate judgement that all bankrupts, of whatsoever denomination, civil or religious, ought to be hanged.
CHARLES LAMB, 1829

The beautiful shopkeeper's virtue, which sacrifices everything to meet a note on the day it is due!   HEINRICH HEINE, 1831

Debt is a prolific mother of folly and of crime.
BENJAMIN DISRAELI, 1834

The two greatest stimulants in the world are youth and debt.   BENJAMIN DISRAELI, 1837

When once a people have tasted the luxury of not paying their debts, it is impossible to bring them back to the black broth of honesty.
SYDNEY SMITH, 1843

Youth is in danger until it learns to look upon debts as furies.
EDWARD G. BULWER-LYTTON, 1843

Debt is to a man what the serpent is to the bird; its eye fascinates, its breath poisons, its coil

crushes both sinew and bone, its jaw is the pitiless grave.
                    EDWARD G. BULWER-LYTTON, 1849

Always pay; for first or last you must pay your
entire debt.   RALPH WALDO EMERSON, 1849

Some people use one half their ingenuity to get
into debt, and the other half to avoid paying it.
                        GEORGE D. PRENTICE, 1860

Let us be happy and live within our means, even
if we have to borrow the money to do it.
                            ARTEMUS WARD, 1865

Whenever you receive a letter from a creditor
write fifty lines upon some extraterrestrial subject, and you will be saved.
                        CHARLES BAUDELAIRE, 1867

A man in debt is so far a slave.
                    RALPH WALDO EMERSON, 1870

Wilt thou seal up the avenues of ill?
Pay every debt as if God wrote the bill!
                    RALPH WALDO EMERSON, 1870

Debt is an inexhaustible fountain of dishonesty.
                    HENRY WARD BEECHER, 1873

How far high failure overleaps the bounds of
low success.   LEWIS MORRIS, 1877

The so-called debtor class . . . are not dishonest because they are in debt.
                        GROVER CLEVELAND, 1878

If I owe Smith ten dollars, and God forgives me,
that doesn't pay Smith.
                        ROBERT G. INGERSOLL, 1879

All progress is based on a universal, innate desire of every organism to live beyond its means.
                            SAMUEL BUTLER, 1902

All decent people live beyond their incomes
nowadays, and those who aren't respectable live
beyond other people's. A few gifted individuals
manage to do both.
                        HECTOR HUGH MUNRO, 1905

Debt, n. An ingenious substitute for the chain
and whip of the slave-driver.
                        AMBROSE BIERCE, 1906

As you say, business is business. There are people in this town who say that bankruptcy is good
business.   ARNOLD BENNETT, 1908

Bankruptcy is when you put your money in your
hip pocket and let your creditors take your
coat.   BOB EDWARDS, 1921

Good times are when people make debts to pay
in bad times.   ROBERT QUILLEN, 1923

I am not sure just what the unpardonable sin is,
but I believe it is a disposition to evade the payment of small bills.   ELBERT HUBBARD, 1923

We pay for the mistakes of our ancestors, and
it seems only fair that they should leave us the
money to pay with.   DON MARQUIS, 1924

Money is what the state says it is. The state claims
the right not only to enforce the dictionary, but
also to write the dictionary. The right is claimed
by all modern states and has been so claimed
for some 4,000 years at least.
                    JOHN MAYNARD KEYNES, 1925

In the midst of life we are in debt.
                    ETHEL WATTS MUMFORD, 1928

Debts are not the kind of bond that can unite
the world.   HERBERT FEIS, 1930

Solvency is entirely a matter of temperament and
not of income.
                    LOGAN PEARSALL SMITH, 1931

I've often known people more shocked because you are not bankrupt than because you are.

MARGARET B. SAUNDERS, 1934

The payment of debts is necessary for social order. The non-payment is quite equally necessary for social order. For centuries humanity has oscillated serenely unaware, between these two contradictory necessities.

SIMONE WEIL, 1937

If it isn't the sheriff, it's the finance company. I've got more attachments on me than a vacuum cleaner. JOHN BARRYMORE, 1938

No country has ever been ruined on account of its debts. ADOLF HITLER, 1940

My problem lies in reconciling my gross habits with my net income. ERROL FLYNN, 1946

I'm sure the way to be happy is to live well beyond your means! RUTH GORDON, 1948

People who go broke in a big way never miss any meals. It is the poor jerk who is shy a half slug who must tighten his belt.

ROBERT HEINLEIN, 1950

Do you wish to be remembered? Leave a lot of debts. JOHN W. RAPER, 1954

I've never been poor, only broke. Being poor is a frame of mind. Being broke is only a temporary situation. MICHAEL TODD, 1958

Expenditure rises to meet income. Individual expenditure not only rises to meet income but tends to surpass it.

C. NORTHCOTE PARKINSON, 1958

Owing money has never concerned me so long as I know where it could be repaid.

HENRY CROWN, 1960

What can you say about bills? Curse them if you will, but pay them you must.

GEORGE SANDERS, 1966

Anyone who lives within his means suffers from a lack of imagination.

LIONEL STANDER, 1967

Don't let your mouth write no cheque your tail can't cash. BO DIDDLEY, 1974

If you are going bankrupt, be sure you go bankrupt on a big scale.

PAUL A. SAMUELSON, 1979

Never in the history of human credit has so much been owed. MARGARET THATCHER, 1980

Economics

The business of household management is concerned more with human beings than it is with inanimate property; it is concerned more with the good condition of human beings than with a good condition of property.

ARISTOTLE, C. 336 B.C.

Within a moderate period of time, the fundamentals of political economy will, to a very useful extent, be known to the higher, middle, and a most important portion of the working classes of society in England.

THOMAS MALTHUS, 1798

No law can be laid down respecting quantity, but a tolerably correct one can be laid down respecting proportions. Every day I am more satisfied that the former enquiry is vain and delusive, and the latter only the true objects of the science [of economics].

DAVID RICARDO, 1821

It has been said that figures rule the world; maybe. I am quite sure that it is figures which show us whether it is being ruled well or badly.

JOHANN WOLFGANG GOETHE, 1830

My principles, sir, in these things are, to take as much as I can get, and to pay no more than I can help. These are everyman's principles, whether they be the right principles or not. There, sir, is political economy in a nutshell.

THOMAS LOVE PEACOCK, 1831

A judicious man looks at Statistics not to get knowledge but to save himself from having ignorance foisted on him.

THOMAS CARLYLE, 1840

Except on matters of mere detail, there are perhaps no practical questions, even among those which approach nearest to the character of purely economical questions, which admit of being decided on economic premises alone.

JOHN STUART MILL, 1848

Our aim is simply to describe man's economic nature and economic wants, to investigate the laws and the character of the institutions which are adapted to the satisfaction of these wants, and the greater or less amount of success by which they have been attended. Our task is, therefore, so to speak, the anatomy and physiology of social or national economy.

WILLIAM ROSCHER, 1854

I neither impugn nor doubt the conclusion of the science [economics], if its terms are accepted. I am simply uninterested in them, as I should be of a science of gymnastics which assumed that men had no skeleton.

JOHN RUSKIN, 1862

Most persons appear to hold that the physical sciences form the proper sphere of mathematical method, and that the moral sciences demand some other method, I know not what. My theory of Economics, however, is purely mathematical in character.

W. STANLEY JEVONS, 1871

While the economic condition of countries is bad, men care for Political Economy, which may tell us how it is to be improved; when that condition is improved, Political Economy ceases to have the same popular interest.

WALTER BAGEHOT, 1873

Political economy, in truth, has never pretended to give advice to mankind with no lights but its own; though people who knew nothing but political economy have taken upon themselves to advise, and could only do so by such lights as they had.

JOHN STUART MILL, 1873

Decrees which are ordinarily given to the world in the name of Political Economy, in the main, amount to a handsome ratification of the existing form of society as approximately perfect.

J. E. CAIRNES, 1873

In my vacations, I visited the poorest quarters of several cities and walked through one street after another, looking at the faces of the poorest people. Next, I resolved to make as thorough a study as I could of Political Economy.

ALFRED MARSHALL, 1890

Economics is, on the one side, a Science of Wealth; and, on the other, that part of the Social Science of man's action in society, that deals with his efforts to satisfy his wants, in so far as the efforts and wants are capable of being measured in terms of wealth, or its general representative, i.e., money.

ALFRED MARSHALL, 1890

The Mecca of the economist lies in economic biology rather than in economic dynamics.

ALFRED MARSHALL, 1890

The laws of economics are statements of tendencies expressed in the indicative mood, and not ethical precepts in the imperative.

ALFRED MARSHALL, 1890

When I am Premier, you will not have to look up figures to find out whether you are prosperous: you will know by feeling in your pockets.

WILFRED LAURIER, 1892

Economic facts are the ever recurring decisive forces, the chief points in the process of history.

EDUARD BERNSTEIN, 1899

You cannot feed the hungry on statistics.

DAVID LLOYD GEORGE, 1904

A good mathematical theorem dealing with economic hypotheses was very unlikely to be good economics: and I went more and more on the rules— (1) Use mathematics as a shorthand language, rather than as an engine of inquiry. (2) Keep them till you have done. (3) Translate into English. (4) Then illustrate by examples that are important in real life. (5) Burn the mathematics. (6) If you can't succeed in 4, burn 3.

ALFRED MARSHALL, 1906

Pure economics gives us no truly decisive criterion to choose between a society based upon private property and a socialist form of organization.

VILFREDO PARETO, 1906

There is no such thing as a science of economics, nor ever will be. It is just cant.

RICHARD H. TAWNEY, 1914

GUSTAV VON SCHMOLLER: Sir, there are no natural laws of economics.

VILFREDO PARETO: Do you know of any restau-

rant here where one does not have to pay for
one's meal?

SCHMOLLER: No, certainly not, but there are
cheap ones.

PARETO: Aha, here you have the natural laws of
economics.   c. 1916

There are certain saving clauses in common use.
. . . Among them are these: "Given the state of
the industrial arts"; "Other things remaining the
same"; "In the long run"; "In the absence of
disturbing causes." Now the state of the industrial arts has at no time continued unchanged
during the modern era; consequently other things
have never remained the same; and in the long
run the outcome has always been shaped by the
disturbing causes.

THORSTEIN VEBLEN, 1919

Economic laws are schemes of rational action,
deduced not from the psychological analysis of
the individual but from a theoretical construction of an objective situation, a reconstruction,
by means of ideal types, of the price struggle in
the market.   MAX WEBER, 1920

The theory of economics does not furnish a body
of settled conclusions immediately applicable to
policy. It is a method rather than a doctrine, an
apparatus of the mind, a technique of thinking
which helps its possessor to draw correct
conclusions.   JOHN MAYNARD KEYNES, 1923

There are no economic ends.

LIONEL ROBBINS, 1931

The science which studies human behavior as a
relationship between ends and scarce means
which have alternative uses.

LIONEL ROBBINS, 1932

Experience has shown that each of these three
view-points, that of statistics, economic theory,
and mathematics, is a necessary, but not by itself a sufficient, condition for a real understand-

ing of the quantitative relations in modern economic life. It is the unification of all three that
is powerful. And it is this unification that constitutes econometrics.

RAGNAR FRISCH, 1933

The only way to a position in which our science
[economics] might give positive advice on a larger
scale to politicians and businessmen, leads
through quantitative work. For as long as we
are unable to put our arguments into figures,
the voice of our science, although occasionally
it may help to dispel errors, will never be heard
by practical men. They are, by instinct, econo-
metricians all of them, in their distrust of anything not amenable to exact proof.

JOSEPH A. SCHUMPETER, 1933

The critical reader of general economic literature must be struck by the absence of any attempt accurately to define that competition which
is the principal subject under discussion.

FRANK KNIGHT, 1935

Human decisions affecting the future, whether
personal or political or economic, cannot depend on strict mathematical expectation, since
the basis for making such calculations does not
exist; and that it is our innate urge to activity
which makes the wheels go round, our rational
selves choosing between the alternatives as best
we are able, calculating where we can, but often
falling back for our motive on whim or sentiment or chance.

JOHN MAYNARD KEYNES, 1936

No less than war or statecraft, the history of
economics has its heroic ages.

ALDOUS HUXLEY, 1936

Let us look at these awkward questions squarely
in the face and pass rapidly on.

DENNIS ROBERTSON, 1937

Economics is the study of the price and value aspects of human activities and institutions.
F. B. GARVER AND ALVIN HANSEN, 1937

The society of money and exploitation has never been charged . . . with assuring the triumph of freedom and justice. ALBERT CAMUS, 1943

Statistics are the heart of democracy.
SIMEON STRUNSKY, 1944

Economic problems have no sharp edges; they shade off imperceptively into politics, sociology, and ethics. Indeed, it is hardly an exaggeration to say that the ultimate answer to every economic problem lies in some other field.
KENNETH E. BOULDING, 1945

Religion and art spring from the same root and are close kin. Economics and art are strangers.
WILLA CATHER, 1947

The mathematical economists . . . formulate equations and draw curves which are supposed to describe reality. In fact they describe only a hypothetical and unrealizable state of affairs, in no way similar to the catallactic problems in question. LUDWIG VON MISES, 1949

I don't see that anyone save a sap-head can now think he knows any history until he understands economics. EZRA POUND, 1960

Like theology, and unlike mathematics, economics deals with matters which men consider very close to their lives.
JOHN KENNETH GALBRAITH, 1962

Difficult problems arise when economics leaves the serene field of pure science and enters economic policy where deliberately or otherwise it comes under the influence of non-scientific forces, ideologies, interests and emotions, amidst which it has to hold its own and define its own specific responsibilities. P. HENNIPMAN, 1962

Any economic system requires a set of rules, an ideology to justify them, and a conscience in the individual which makes him strive to carry them out. JOAN ROBINSON, 1962

If ignorance paid dividends most Americans could make a fortune out of what they don't know about economics.
LUTHER HODGES, 1962

Ever since the beginning of economics, macro and micro theory have existed side by side; they will continue to do so in the future. Each is needed, neither is expendable.
FRITZ MACHLUP, 1963

The economic game is a game where the rules are subject to important revisions, say, every ten years, and bears an uncomfortable resemblance to the Queen's croquet game in *Alice in Wonderland*. NORBERT WEINER, 1964

Economics is a subject that does not greatly respect one's wishes.
NIKITA KHRUSHCHEV, 1965

In principle there are no value judgements in economics. MILTON FRIEDMAN, 1967

I learned that economics was not an exact science and that the most erudite men would analyze the economic ills of the world and derive a totally different conclusion.
EDITH SUMMERSKILL, 1967

Economics—which to be sure has always had an uneasy time of it asserting its autonomy as a social science—has become the pliant servant of ideology. WILLIAM F. BUCKLEY, JR., 1968

Economic Theory: A systematic application and critical evaluation of the basic analytic concepts of economic theory, with an emphasis on money and why it's good. WOODY ALLEN, 1970

By divorcing itself from the need to struggle with the elements of the political and social world, however recalcitrant they may be, conventional economics has ensured its technical virtuosity and its internal consistency, but at the cost of its social relevance.

ROBERT L. HEILBRONER, 1970

The weak and all too slowly growing empirical foundation clearly cannot support the proliferating superstructure of pure, or should I say, speculative economic theory.

WASSILY LEONTIEF, 1971

A study of economics usually reveals that the best time to buy anything is last year.

MARTY ALLEN, 1972

Once demystified, the dismal science is nothing less than the study of power.

RICHARD J. BARNET, 1973

I have been gradually coming under the conviction, disturbing for a professional theorist, that there is no such thing as economics.

KENNETH E. BOULDING, 1976

Like other sciences, economics has two sides: the theories and the facts.

WILFRED BECKERMAN, 1976

As a good friend says, most of the modern economics as taught is a form of brain damage.

E. F. SCHUMACHER, 1977

Economics is all about how people make decisions. Sociology is all about why they don't have any decisions to make.

JAMES S. DUESENBERRY, 1978

Economics is only partly an economic problem. It also is a question of fair treatment, power and values. Who suffers, who gains? Who pays, who benefits?

ARTHUR DOBRIN, 1979

Part of the economy dies every day and is replaced by something new.

PAUL HAWKEN, 1983

There are two areas where new ideas are terribly dangerous—economics and sex.

FELIX ROHATYN, 1984

Economists

The age of chivalry is gone. That of sophisters, economists and calculators has succeeded: and the glory of Europe is extinguished for ever.

EDMUND BURKE, 1790

To decide in each case how far these conclusions are to be acted upon, belongs to the act of

government, an act to which Political Economy is only one of many subservient Sciences.

NASSAU SENIOR, 1836

Malthus finds no cover laid at Nature's table for the laborer's son.

RALPH WALDO EMERSON, 1856

Of all the quacks that ever quacked, political economists are the loudest. Instead of telling us what is meant by one's country, by what causes men are happy, moral, religious, or the contrary, they tell us how flannel jackets are exchanged for pork hams, and speak much of the land last taken into cultivation.

THOMAS CARLYLE, 1881

The economist, like everyone else, must concern himself with the ultimate aims of man.

ALFRED MARSHALL, 1890

If all the economists were laid end to end, they would not reach a conclusion.

GEORGE BERNARD SHAW, 1910

In the long run we are all dead. Economists set themselves too easy, too useless a task if in tempestuous seasons they can only tell us that when the storm is long past the ocean is flat again.

JOHN MAYNARD KEYNES, 1923

The economist can, of course, give us the facts. That is his job. He is a good cartographer, but a bad pilot.

VINCENT MASSEY, 1924

The note of gloom and pessimism which distinguished so much of the economic doctrine of the nineteenth century is in no small measure the legacy of Malthus.

ALEXANDER GRAY, 1931

If economists could manage to get themselves thought of as humble, competent people on a level with dentists, that would be splendid!

JOHN MAYNARD KEYNES, 1931

I believe myself to be writing a book [*General Theory*] on economic theory which will largely revolutionize—not, I suppose, at once but in the course of the next ten years—the way the world thinks about economic problems.

JOHN MAYNARD KEYNES, 1935

Practical men . . . are usually the slaves of some defunct economist.

JOHN MAYNARD KEYNES, 1936

As with Marx, it is possible to admire Keynes even though one may consider his social vision to be wrong and every one of his propositions to be misleading.

JOSEPH A. SCHUMPETER, 1936

If an economist becomes certain of the solution of any problem, he can be equally certain that his solution is wrong.

H. A. INNIS, 1936

Marx had a master then? Yes. Real understanding of his economics begins with recognizing that, as a theorist, he was a pupil of Ricardo.

JOSEPH A. SCHUMPETER, 1937

Karl Marx was a philosophical Oscar Wilde, more scandalous because more sober.

ALBERT J. MULLER, 1943

My only regret in life is that I did not drink more champagne.

JOHN MAYNARD KEYNES, 1946

Marx's great achievement was to place the system of capitalism on the defensive.

CHARLES A. MADISON, 1947

The orthodox economists have been much occupied with elegant elaborations of minor problems, which distract the attention of their pupils from the uncongenial realities of the modern world and the development of abstract argument has run far ahead of any possibility of empirical verification.

JOAN ROBINSON, 1947

Keynes wanted to apologize and conserve, while Marx wanted to criticize and destroy.

LAWRENCE KLEIN, 1948

No one in our age was cleverer than Keynes nor made less attempt to conceal it.

R. F. HARROD, 1951

If all the nation's economists were laid end to end, they would still point in all directions.

ARTHUR H. MOTLEY, 1954

I was in search of a one-armed economist so that the guy could never make a statement and then say: "on the other hand."

HARRY S TRUMAN, 1955

The instability of the economy is equaled only by the instability of economists.

JOHN H. WILLIAMS, 1956

His [Keynes's] disciples, as disciples will, went much farther than the master. The view became widespread that "money does not matter."

MILTON FRIEDMAN, 1958

Professor Galbraith is horrified by the number of Americans who have bought cars with tail fins on them, and I am horrified by the number of Americans who take seriously the proposals of Mr. Galbraith.

WILLIAM F. BUCKLEY, JR., 1959

As a year, 1929 has always been peculiarly the property of economists.

JOHN KENNETH GALBRAITH, 1961

Marx's philosophy was, in secular, nontheistic language, a new and radical step forward in the tradition of prophetic Messianism; it was aimed at the full realization of individualism, the very aim that has guided Western thinking from the Renaissance and the Reformation far into the 19th century.   ERICH FROMM, 1961

His [Marx's] most explosive and indeed most original contribution to the cause of revolution was that he interpreted the compelling needs of mass poverty in political terms as an uprising, not for the sake of bread or wealth, but for the sake of freedom as well.

HANNAH ARENDT, 1963

We are all Keynesians now.

MILTON FRIEDMAN, 1965

It is always depressing to go back to Adam Smith, especially on economic development, as one realizes how little we have learned in nearly two hundred years.

KENNETH E. BOULDING, 1966

Another difference between Milton [Friedman] and myself is that everything reminds Milton of the money supply. Well, everything reminds me of sex, but I keep it out of the paper.

ROBERT SOLOW, 1966

Economists are not solely that but also human beings, and their own values undoubtedly affect their economics.   MILTON FRIEDMAN, 1966

When the definitive history of economic analysis during the 1930s comes to be written, a leading character in the drama will be Professor Hayek . . . there was a time when the new theories of Hayek were the principal rival of the new theories of Keynes.

JOHN R. HICKS, 1967

Karl Marx . . . preparing the time bomb which was to go off with shattering effect long after his death.   DEAN ACHESON, 1971

It seems to me that this failure of economists to guide policy more successfully is closely connected with their propensity to imitate as closely as possible the procedures of the brilliantly successful physical sciences—an attempt which in our subject may lead to outright error.

FRIEDRICH A. HAYEK, 1974

[Economists' advice] is something like patent medicine—people know it is largely manufactured by quacks and that a good percentage of the time it won't work, but they continue to buy the brand whose flavor they like.

BARBARA BERGMANN, 1974

Economists are economical, among other things, of ideas; most make those of their graduate days do for a lifetime.

JOHN KENNETH GALBRAITH, 1976

Despite the fact that he [Labor Secretary John Dunlop] is an economist, basically, I have great confidence in him.   GEORGE MEANY, 1976

If Karl Marx were alive today, his problem would be to find parking spaces for the American proletariat rather than break their chains of economic slavery.   G. K. REDDY, 1976

In all recorded history there has not been one economist who has had to worry about where the next meal would come from.

PETER DRUCKER, 1977

All races have produced notable economists, with the exception of the Irish who doubtless can protest their devotion to higher arts.

JOHN KENNETH GALBRAITH, 1977

Much of the world's work, it has been said, is done by men who do not feel quite well. Marx is a case in point.

JOHN KENNETH GALBRAITH, 1977

I am a great friend of Israel. Any country that can stand Milton Friedman as an adviser has nothing to fear from a few million Arabs.

JOHN KENNETH GALBRAITH, 1979

Economists are like police officers and armies. They are most successful when their services are needed least. By that criterion economics has not been doing too well lately.

SHLOMO MAITAL, 1982

Economists are the failed priests of our generation.   LOUIS RUKEYSER, 1983

When economists are wrong, they are likely to be wrong at just the critical time when we most desperately need them to be right.

IRVING KRISTOL, 1983

The intensity with which economists work out their Gini coefficients, and the subtlety with which they measure income trends in the quintules or deciles of the population, is matched— so far as I can see—by the utter lack of interest of the average American in their findings.

IRVING KRISTOL, 1984

Education

The love of money and the love of learning rarely meet.   GEORGE HERBERT, c. 1630

It is important to remember how much income can be earned by professional skill. Capital pro-

vides its owner with an annual income amounting to a twentieth of its value, but with a pound's worth of paints an artist can produce a picture which will earn him fifty.

C. S. MONTESQUIEU, 1717

A man of wit is not incapable of business, but above it. A sprightly, generous horse is able to carry a pack saddle as well as an ass, but he is too good to be put to the drudgery.

ALEXANDER POPE, 1736

It is allowed that vocations and employments of least dignity are of the most apparent use, that the meanest artisan or manufacturer contributes more to the accommodation of life than the profound scholar and argumentative theorist, and that the public would suffer less present inconvenience from the banishment of philosophers than from the extinction of any common trade.　　SAMUEL JOHNSON, 1751

The rich are too indolent, the poor too weak, to bear the insupportable fatigue of thinking.

WILLIAM COWPER, 1781

Every child of the Saxon race is educated to wish to be first. It is our system; and a man comes to measure his greatness by the regrets, envies, and hatreds of his competitors.

RALPH WALDO EMERSON, 1850

The best education in the world is that got by struggling to get a living.

WENDELL PHILLIPS, 1863

All the powers [of the child] must be developed to resist misfortune and wrong. Capital, therefore, should weigh the cost of the mob and the tramp against the expense of universal and sufficient education.　　ALLAN K. TATEM, 1877

Skilled labor teaches something not to be found in books or in colleges.

HARRIET ROBINSON, 1883

Had they gone into active work during the years spent at college they would have been better educated men in every true sense of that term. The fire and energy have been stamped out of them, and how to so manage as to live a life of idle-

ness and not a life of usefulness has become the chief question with them.

ANDREW CARNEGIE, 1902

The commercial class has always mistrusted verbal brilliancy and wit, deeming such qualities, perhaps with some justice, frivolous and unprofitable.　　DOROTHY NEVILL, 1907

An exaggerated competitive attitude is inculcated into the student, who is trained to worship acquisitive success as a preparation for his future career.　　ALBERT EINSTEIN, 1949

Education for full employment really means education that develops the general qualities of persons rather than specific skills.

JAMES RUSSELL, 1965

A lot of fellows nowadays have a B.A, M.D., or Ph.D. Unfortunately, they don't have a J.O.B.

FATS DOMINO, 1966

Economists report that a college education adds many thousands of dollars to a man's lifetime income—which he then spends sending his son to college.　　BILL VAUGHN, 1971

The university, which once merely reflected the status system of the society, has now become the arbiter of class position. As the gatekeepers, it has gained a quasi-monopoly in determining the future stratification of society.

DANIEL BELL, 1972

[The] real villain of the oil crisis is the Harvard Business School. . . . Almost every Arab sheik now in charge of his country's oil policy was trained at Harvard.　　ART BUCHWALD, 1973

The ladder was there, "from the gutter to the university," and for those stalwart enough to ascend it, the schools were a boon and a path out of poverty.　　DIANE RAVITCH, 1974

Although there are countless alumni of the school of hard knocks, there has not yet been a move to accredit that institution.

SONYA RUDIKOFF, 1974

The big advantage of getting your college money in cash now is that you can invest it in something that has a higher return than a diploma.

CAROLINE BIRD, 1975

I oppose federal aid to education because no one has been able to prove the need for it.

RONALD REAGAN, 1981

Employment

Employment is nature's physician, and is essential to human happiness.

GALEN, C. A.D. 170

Employment is so essential to human happiness that indolence is justly considered the mother of misery. ROBERT BURTON, 1621

The number of useful and productive laborers is everywhere in proportion to the quantity of capital stock which is employed in setting them to work and to the particular way in which it is so employed. ADAM SMITH, 1776

A man willing to work, and unable to find work, is perhaps the saddest sight that fortune's inequality exhibits under this sun.

THOMAS CARLYLE, 1839

Improvements in production and emigration of capital to the more fertile soils and unworked mines of the uninhabited or thinly peopled parts of the globe, do not, as appears to a superficial view, diminish the gross produce and the demand for labor at home, but, on the contrary, are what we have chiefly to depend on for increasing both, and are even necessary conditions for any great or prolonged augmentation of either. JOHN STUART MILL, 1848

A man who accepts Adam Smith's statement that a workman is kept honest by fear of losing his employment is in an entirely damned state of soul. JOHN RUSKIN, 1862

The course characteristic of modern industry, of periods of average activity, production at high pressure, crisis and stagnation, depend on the constant formation, the greater or less absorption and the reformation of the industrial reserve army or surplus population. In their turn the various phases of the industrial cycle recruit the surplus population, and become one of the most energetic agents of its reproduction.

KARL MARX, 1883

The only effective remedy for unemployment is a continuous adjustment of means to ends, in such a way that credit can be based on the solid foundation of fairly accurate forecasts; and that reckless inflations of credit—the chief cause of all economic malaise—may be kept within narrower limits.   ALFRED MARSHALL, 1890

A man who has no office to go to—I don't care who he is—is a trial of which you can have no conception.   GEORGE BERNARD SHAW, 1905

No other technique for the conduct of life attaches the individual so firmly to reality as laying emphasis on work; for his work at least gives him a secure place in a portion of reality, in the human community.   SIGMUND FREUD, 1914

When more and more people are thrown out of work unemployment results.
     CALVIN COOLIDGE, 1916

Any man who has a job has a chance.
     ELBERT HUBBARD, 1923

Unemployment, the precarious life of the worker, the disappointment of expectation, the sudden loss of savings, the excessive windfalls to individuals, the speculator, the profiteer—all proceed, in large measure, from the instability of the standard of value.
     JOHN MAYNARD KEYNES, 1923

In order to mitigate unemployment attending business depression, we urge the enactment of legislation authorizing that construction and repair of public works be initiated in periods of acute unemployment.
     DEMOCRATIC PARTY PLATFORM, 1924

It is worse, in an impoverished world, to provoke unemployment than to disappoint the rentier.   JOHN MAYNARD KEYNES, 1924

If the unemployed could eat plans and promises they would be able to spend the winter on the Riviera.   W. E. B. DU BOIS, 1931

I have known people to stop and buy an apple on the corner and then walk away as if they had solved the whole unemployment problem.
     HEYWOOD BROUN, 1933

Given the propensity to consume and the rate of new investment, there will be only one level of employment consistent with equilibrium.
     JOHN MAYNARD KEYNES, 1936

With a given organization, equipment and technique, real wages and the volume of output (and hence of employment) are uniquely correlated, so that, in general, an increase in employment can only occur to the accompaniment of a decline in the rate of real wages.
     JOHN MAYNARD KEYNES, 1936

There must be sufficient unemployment to keep us so poor that our consumption falls short of our income by not more than the equivalent of the physical provision for future consumption which it pays to produce today.
     JOHN MAYNARD KEYNES, 1936

As a matter of theory, the continuance in any country of a substantial volume of unemployment . . . is in itself proof that the price being asked for labor as wages is too high for the conditions of the market; demand for and supply of labor are not finding the appropriate price of meeting.   ANEURIN BEVAN, 1944

Full employment is the device by which we flourish; and so the old curse of Adam, that he must work in order to live, now becomes a goal to be struggled for, just because we have the means to produce a surplus, cause of all our woes.   PAUL GOODMAN, 1947

Charity separates the rich from the poor; aid raises the needy and sets him on the same level with the rich.   EVA PERON, 1949

Wage rates tend to be among the least flexible prices. In consequence, an incipient deficit that is countered by a policy of permitting or forcing prices to decline is likely to produce unemployment rather than, or in addition to, wage decreases. . . . This is clearly a highly inefficient method of adjusting to external changes.

MILTON FRIEDMAN, 1953

It's a recession when your neighbor loses his job; it's a depression when you lose yours.

HARRY S TRUMAN, 1958

The rise in the total of those employed is governed by Parkinson's Law and would be much the same whether the volume of work were to increase, diminish, or even disappear.

C. NORTHCOTE PARKINSON, 1958

When you have 7 percent unemployed, you have 93 percent working.

JOHN F. KENNEDY, 1962

Have you ever told a coal miner in West Virginia or Kentucky that what he needs is individual initiative to go out and get a job when there isn't any?   ROBERT F. KENNEDY, 1964

Full employment may be said to mean that the number of vacant jobs at prevailing wages is as large as the number employed and that the labor market is so organized that everyone who is able, willing, and seeking to work already has a job or can obtain one after a brief search or after undergoing some training.

ARTHUR BURNS, 1964

[Unemployment insurance] provides prepaid vacations for a segment of our society which has made it a way of life.

RONALD REAGAN, 1966

The social hygiene of full employment.

ABBA P. LERNER, 1967

A structuralist is correctly defined as a Keynesian who believes that changes in the structure of the economy can have an independent effect on the levels of employment and unemployment.

CHARLES C. KILLINGSWORTH, 1969

Hitler had already found how to cure unemployment before Keynes had finished explaining why it occurred.   JOAN ROBINSON, 1972

Unemployment is rarely considered desirable except by those who have not experienced it.

JOHN KENNETH GALBRAITH, 1976

There are a lot of jobs available that some people now call "menial." Maybe we need to get back to the Depression mentality, where there were no menial jobs. A job was a job, and anyone who got one felt lucky.

RONALD REAGAN, 1976

It is much harder to find a job than to keep one.

JULES BECKER, 1978

The reason for the high rate of unemployment is Henry Kissinger. Every time a new job opens up, Kissinger grabs it before anybody else can apply.   RUSSELL BAKER, 1980

Ethics

Prefer a loss to a dishonest gain: the one brings pain at the moment, the other for all time.

CHILON, C. 560 B.C.

The quest for riches darkens the sense of right and wrong. ANTISTHENES, C. 390 B.C.

No man should so act as to make a gain out of the ignorance of another.

CICERO, C. 63 B.C.

The door will not open to words, and it is only a well-filled palm that should do the knocking.

TIBULLUS, C. 25 B.C.

Bribes, believe me, buy both gods and men.

OVID, C. 1 B.C.

For what is a man profited, if he shall gain the whole world, and lose his own soul.

MATTHEW 16:26, C. A.D. 80

For your selling ought not to be a work that is within your own power and will without law or limit, as though you were a god and beholden to no one; but because this selling of yours is a work that you perform toward your neighbor, it must be so governed by law and conscience that you do it without harm and injury to your neighbor. MARTIN LUTHER, 1524

Make yourself a seller when you are buying, and a buyer when you are selling, and then you will sell and buy justly.

ST. FRANCIS DE SALES, 1606

Let me have no lying; it becomes none but tradesmen.

WILLIAM SHAKESPEARE,
The Winter's Tale (IV, iii), 1615

That for which all virtue now is sold,
And almost ever vice—almighty gold.

BEN JONSON, 1616

To refuse with the right and take with the left.

JOHN CLARKE, 1639

He that will be rich before night may be hanged before noon. ROGER L'ESTRANGE, 1692

A friend that you buy with presents will be bought from you. THOMAS FULLER, 1732

Honor sinks where commerce long prevails.

OLIVER GOLDSMITH, 1765

People of the same trade seldom meet together but the conversation ends in a conspiracy against the public, or in some diversion to raise prices.

ADAM SMITH, 1776

I'm called away by particular business.
But I leave my character behind me.

RICHARD B. SHERIDAN, 1782

The darker hour in the history of any young man is when he sits down to study how to get money without honestly earning it.

HORACE GREELEY, 1782

I have noticed that in this world people invariably sacrifice the esteem of honest men in order to get their own way, and sacrifice peace of mind for celebrity.

SÉBASTIEN R. N. CHAMFORT, 1794

We must hold a man amenable to reason for the choice of his daily craft or profession. It is not an excuse any longer for his deeds, that they are the custom of his trade. What business has he with an evil trade.

RALPH WALDO EMERSON, 1841

Goodness is the only investment that never fails.

HENRY DAVID THOREAU, 1854

Moral principle is a looser bond than pecuniary interest.

ABRAHAM LINCOLN, 1856

For the merchant, even honesty is a financial speculation.

CHARLES BAUDELAIRE, 1867

A crowded court docket is the surest of all signs that trade is brisk and money plenty.

MARK TWAIN, 1872

How many men are there who fairly earn a million dollars?

HENRY GEORGE, 1879

Ninety-eight out of 100 of the rich men of America are honest. That is why they are rich.

RUSSELL CONWELL, 1881

When I want to buy up any politicians I always find the anti-monopolists the most purchaseable. They don't come so high.

WILLIAM H. VANDERBILT, 1882

Mercantile morality is really nothing but a refinement of piratical morality.

FRIEDRICH NIETZSCHE, 1883

Good will is the one and only asset that competition cannot undersell or destroy.

MARSHALL FIELD, 1887

The nature of business is swindling.

AUGUST BEBEL, 1892

He who has money has in his pocket those who have none.

LYOF N. TOLSTOY, 1895

No one can earn a million dollars honestly.

WILLIAM JENNINGS BRYAN, 1896

Rich men without convictions are more dangerous in modern society than poor women without chastity.

GEORGE BERNARD SHAW, 1898

The greatest nations, like the greatest individuals, have often been the poorest; and with wealth comes often what is more terrible than poverty—corruption.

OLIVE SCHREINER, C. 1899

Barring some piece of luck I have seen but few men get rich rapidly except by means that would make them writhe to have known in public.

CHARLES DUDLEY WARNER, 1899

Golden Rule principles are just as necessary for operating a business profitably as are trucks, typewriters, or twine.

JAMES CASH PENNEY, 1902

There are very honest people who do not think that they have had a bargain unless they have cheated a merchant.

ANATOLE FRANCE, 1904

Don't steal; thou'lt never thus compete Successfully in business. Cheat.

AMBROSE BIERCE, 1907

Every great man of business has got somewhere a touch of the idealist in him.
WOODROW WILSON, 1913

All business sagacity reduces itself in the last analysis to a judicious use of sabotage.
THORSTEIN VEBLEN, 1919

You will find out, if you want to make any money, that it is not always wise to be disturbed by what we call evil, though its existence must be admitted.　ARTHUR BRISBANE, 1925

Our whole business system would break down in a day if there was not a high sense of moral responsibility in our business world.
HERBERT HOOVER, 1929

When we see what people we like will do for money, it is best to be sad and say nothing.
LOGAN PEARSALL SMITH, 1934

It is a mistake to think that they [businessmen] are more immoral than politicians. If you work them into the surly, obstinate, terrified mood, of which domestic animals, wrongly handled, are so capable, the nation's burdens will not get carried to market; and in the end, public opinion will veer their way.
JOHN MAYNARD KEYNES, 1938

It is difficult but not impossible to conduct strictly honest business.　MOHANDAS GANDHI, 1946

Two thirds of the people who can make money are mediocre; and at least one half of them are morally at a low level.
ALFRED NORTH WHITEHEAD, 1947

Men are more often bribed by their loyalties and ambitions than by money.
ROBERT H. JACKSON, 1951

If their cheating, their theft, their lies, were of colossal proportions, if it were successful, they met with praise, not blame.
DOROTHY DAY, 1952

Money is only money, beans tonight and steak tomorrow. So long as you can look yourself in the eye.　MERIDEL LE SUEUR, 1955

Do you know that the tendrils of graft and corruption have become mighty interlacing roots so that even men who would like to be honest are tripped and trapped by them.
AGNES SLIGH TURNBULL, 1955

It is good business men that are corrupting our bad politicians.　JOSEPH W. FALK, 1956

A man who makes a one-dollar profit on his expense account is dishonest. A man who loses five cents on one is a damned fool.
GENE FOWLER, 1958

The central or classical tradition of economics was more than an analysis of economic behavior and a set of rules for economic polity. It also had a moral code.
JOHN KENNETH GALBRAITH, 1958

The philosophers, I am sure, have somewhat the impression that the economists are avoiding what they regard as the basic issue, namely, the value judgements that affect and enter into private and public policy. And by value judgements, the philosophers do not mean relative exchange value. They mean "moral" or "ethical" values. The philosophers in my opinion are correct.
MILTON FRIEDMAN, 1966

The man who damns money has obtained it dishonorably; the man who respects it has earned it.　AYN RAND, 1966

Where large sums of money are concerned it is advisable to trust nobody.
AGATHA CHRISTIE, 1967

Capitalism was doomed ethically before it was doomed economically, a long time ago.
ALEKSANDR SOLZHENITSYN, 1968

It is no secret that organized crime in America takes in over forty billion dollars a year. This is quite a profitable sum, especially when one considers that the Mafia spends very little for office supplies.
WOODY ALLEN, 1974

People will swim through shit if you put a few dollars in it.
PETER SELLERS, 1975

There are no new forms of financial fraud; in the last several hundred years, there have only been small variations on a few classic designs.
JOHN KENNETH GALBRAITH, 1976

If one offers money to a government to influence it, that is corruption. But if someone receives money for services afterward, that is a commission.
ADNAN KHASHOGGI, 1976

To me, this concern about business credibility is only a part of a much wider concern I have about general morality today. It occurs at all levels . . . a lack of concern for other people, an attempt to get away with all that you think you can get away with. I see this in every facet of society.
WALTER A. HAAS, JR., 1976

Ethics is not a branch of economics.
YERACHMIEL KUGEL, 1977

Nothing is illegal if one hundred businessmen decide to do it.
ANDREW YOUNG, 1978

That the love of money is the root of all evil can, conceivably, be disputed. What is not in doubt is that the pursuit of money, or an enduring association with it, is capable of inducing not only bizarre but ripely perverse behavior.
JOHN KENNETH GALBRAITH, 1979

Fiscal Policy

The budget should be balanced, the Treasury should be refilled, public debt should be reduced, the arrogance of officialdom should be tempered and controlled, and the assistance to foreign lands should be curtailed lest Rome become bankrupt.
CICERO, C. 63 B.C.

The public is a debtor, whom no man can oblige to pay.
DAVID HUME, 1755

The only good budget is a balanced budget.
ADAM SMITH, 1776

Like an improvident spendthrift, whose pressing occasions will not allow him to wait for the regular payment of his revenue, the state is in the constant practice of borrowing of its own factors and agents and of paying interest for the use of its own money.
ADAM SMITH, 1776

By lending money to government, they do not even for a moment diminish their ability to carry on their trade and manufactures. On the contrary, they commonly augment it . . . The merchant or monied man makes money by lending money to government, and instead of diminishing, increases his trading capital.

ADAM SMITH, 1776

No nation ought to be without a debt. A national debt is a national blessing.

THOMAS PAINE, 1776

As a very important source of strength and security, cherish public credit. One method of preserving it is to use it as sparingly as possible.

GEORGE WASHINGTON, 1796

Of all the modes in which a government can employ its surplus revenues, none is more permanently beneficial than that of internal improvement. Fixed to the soil, it becomes a durable part of the land itself, diffusing comfort, and activity, and animation on all sides.

HENRY CLAY, 1806

It is incumbent on every generation to pay its own debts as it goes—a principle which, if acted on, would save one-half the wars of the world.

THOMAS JEFFERSON, 1820

Among the maxims of political economy which the stewards of the public moneys should never suffer without urgent necessity to be transcended is that of keeping the expenditures of the year within the limits of its receipts.

JOHN QUINCY ADAMS, 1827

Public credit means the contracting of debts which a nation never can pay.

WILLIAM COBBETT, 1829

He [Albert Gallatin] smote the rock of the national resources and abundant streams of revenue gushed forth. He touched the dead corpse of Public Credit, and it sprung upon its feet.

DANIEL WEBSTER, 1831

In case of war our credit must be our chief resource, at least for the first year, and this would be greatly impaired by having contracted a large debt in time of peace.

JAMES BUCHANAN, 1858

The great advantage of citizens being creditors as well as debtors with relation to the public debt is obvious. Men readily perceive that they cannot be much oppressed by a debt which they owe to themselves.

ABRAHAM LINCOLN, 1864

As all men desire to leave to their heirs unincumbered estates, so should it be the ambition of the people of the United States to relieve their descendents of this national mortgage.

HUGH MCCULLOCH, 1865

The only part of the so-called national wealth that actually enters into the collective possessions of modern peoples is their National Debt.

KARL MARX, 1867

Loans enable the government to meet extraordinary expenses, without the taxpayers feeling it immediately, but they necessitate, as a consequence, increased taxes. On the other hand, the rising of taxation, caused by the accumulation of debts contracted one after another, compels the government always to have recourse to new loans for new extraordinary expenses. . . . Overtaxation is not an incident, but rather a principle.

KARL MARX, 1873

Extravagant expenditure of public money is an evil not to be measured by the value of that money to the people who are taxed for it.

CHESTER A. ARTHUR, 1882

[Government] money is being spent without new taxation, and appropriation without accompanying taxation is as bad as taxation without representation.   WOODROW WILSON, 1888

The retirement of bonds in the future before maturity should be a matter of convenience, not of compulsion. We should not collect revenue for that purpose, but only use any casual surplus.   BENJAMIN HARRISON, 1892

We are slowly emerging from the crash of '93, and the cuckoos are cocksure that a country fairly bursting with wealth was saved from the demnition bowwows by the blessed expedient of going into debt.
        WILLIAM COWPER BRANN, 1895

The budget is the skeleton of the state stripped of all misleading ideologies.
        RUDOLF GOLDSCHEID, 1918

Public credit has been utilized in increasing measure not only because modern business life lays continually more stress on credit, but also because under the dynamic conditions of a rapidly augmenting national wealth the weight of a given public debt tends gradually to diminish. Public credit is not only a natural, but within bounds a salutary phenomenom.
        EDWIN SELIGMAN, 1921

. . . the Central Bank is the conductor of the orchestra and sets the tempo.
        JOHN MAYNARD KEYNES, 1925

It [the national debt] is a menace to our credit. It is the greatest weakness in our line of national defense. It is the largest obstacle in the path of our economic development. It should be retired as fast as possible under a system of reasonable taxation. This can be done only by continuing the policy of rigid Government economy.
        CALVIN COOLIDGE, 1927

In national affairs, a million is only a drop in the budget.   BURTON RASCOE, 1928

Prosperity cannot be restored by raids upon the public treasury.   HERBERT HOOVER, 1930

"Sound" finance may be right psychologically; but economically it is a depressing influence.
        JOHN MAYNARD KEYNES, 1932

Let us have the courage to stop borrowing to meet continuing deficits. Stop the deficits.
        FRANKLIN D. ROOSEVELT, 1932

At this time, above all, when private spending is at its lowliest, is the time to expand public spending. Just as we saved our way into depression, we must squander our way out of it.
        VIRGIL JORDAN, 1932

Any government, like any family, can for a year spend a little more than it earns. But you and I know that a continuance of that habit means the poorhouse.
        FRANKLIN D. ROOSEVELT, 1932

A nation is not in danger of financial disaster merely because it owes itself money.
        ANDREW MELLON, 1933

I lay overwhelming emphasis on the increase of national purchasing power resulting from government expenditure which is financed by loans.   JOHN MAYNARD KEYNES, 1933

Our analysis leads us to believe that recovery is sound only if it does come of itself. For any revival which is merely due to artificial stimulus leaves part of the work of depressions undone and adds, to an undigested remnant of maladjustment, new maladjustments of its own.
        JOSEPH A. SCHUMPETER, 1934

Whilst, therefore, the enlargement of the functions of government, involved in the task of adjusting to one another the propensity to consume and the inducement to invest, would seem to a nineteenth-century publicist or to a contemporary American financier to be a terrible encroachment on individualism, I defend it, on the contrary, both as the only practicable means of avoiding the destruction of existing economic forces in their entirety and as the condition of the successful functioning of individual initiative.   JOHN MAYNARD KEYNES, 1936

I desire to go on record as predicting that we will never pay our public debt in full.
                              LEWIS H. HANEY, 1938

When the public sector collects more taxes from the private sector and uses the revenue for increased outlays, total employment will be increased exactly by an amount corresponding to the increase in outlays. This at least holds true when the marginal propensity to consume as well as productivity in the private sector are unaffected.   JÖRGEN GELTING, 1941

A public debt, internally held, is not like a private debt. It has none of the essential earmarks of a private debt. The public debt is an instrument of public policy. It is a means to control the national income and, in conjunction with the tax structure, to regulate the distribution of income.   ALVIN HANSEN, 1941

The purpose of taxation is never to raise money but to leave less in the hands of the taxpayer.
                              ABBA P. LERNER, 1944

Borrowing is an anti-inflation measure, not a proper means for financing reflationary spending. Borrowing is properly a means for curtailing purchasing power, private and governmental. To use it for injecting purchasing power is like burning the fire engine for heating purposes when there is an abundance of good fuel to be had free.   HENRY SIMONS, 1944

Ah, for those good old days when Uncle Sam lived within his income—and without most of yours.   BARCLAY BRADEN, 1948

The modern government budget is, and must be, the balance wheel of the economy. Its very size is such that if it were permitted to fluctuate up and down with the rest of the economy, instead of counter to the swings of economic activity, it would so exaggerate booms and depressions as to be disasterous.
                              DOUGLAS C. ABBOTT, 1949

The Keynesians tear the economic system out of its social context and treat it as though it were a machine to be sent to the repair shop there to be overhauled by an engineer state.
                              PAUL M. SWEEZY, 1956

The proper guide to cyclical management of the debt should not be economic stabilization. More long-term debt should be issued in recessions, more short-term debt in booms. This would hold down the Federal interest burden, reduce fluctuations in long-term interest rates and leave to monetary policy the responsibility for helping to stabilize total monetary expenditures through influencing the supply of money, supply of liquid assets, asset values and interest rates.
                              HERBERT STEIN, 1958

Everyone is always in favor of general economy and particular expenditure.
                              ANTHONY EDEN, 1959

American law, like the law of other capitalist democracies, has accepted the view that prolonged depressions and inflations threaten the fabric of society far too gravely to be tolerated.
                              EUGENE V. ROSTOW, 1959

Our true choice is not between tax reduction, on the one hand, and the avoidance of large Federal deficits on the other. It is increasingly clear that no matter what party is in power, so long as our national security needs keep rising, an economy hampered by restrictive tax rates will never produce enough jobs or enough profits. Surely the lesson of the last decade is that budget deficits are not caused by wild-eyed spenders but by slow economic growth and periodic recessions—and any new recession would break all deficit records.

JOHN F. KENNEDY, 1962

The myth persists that federal deficits create inflation and budget surpluses prevent it. Yet sizeable budget surpluses after the war did not prevent inflation and persistent deficits for the last several years have not upset our basic price stability. Obviously deficits are sometimes dangerous and so are surpluses. But honest assessment plainly requires a more sophisticated view than the old and automatic cliché that deficits automatically bring inflation.

JOHN F. KENNEDY, 1962

Macro-economics: a laudable attempt to explain how large parts (or the whole) of an economy work, without pretending to know how the component parts work.

RALPH HARRIS, 1964

The largest determining factor of the size and content of this year's budget is last year's budget.

AARON WILDAVSKY, 1964

From a Keynesian standpoint, the 1930s simply proved that fiscal policies which are too timid, too wavering, and too often contradicted by other measures with quite different tendencies will not expand employment and income by the amount requisite to restore prosperity.

ROBERT LEKACHMAN, 1966

Gross National Product is our Holy Grail.

STEWART L. UDALL, 1968

There is every plausible reason in terms of experience, in terms of rarified neo-classical theory, for the velocity of circulation to be a systematic and increasing function of the rate of interest; and the minute you believe that, you have moved from the right of the spectrum—that of monetarism—to that noble eclectic position which I hold, the post-Keynesian position.

PAUL A. SAMUELSON, 1969

Man does not live by GNP alone.

PAUL A. SAMUELSON, 1970

How can a national government make an economic plan with any confidence if a board of directors meeting 5,000 miles away can, by altering its pattern of purchasing and production, affect in a major way the country's economic life?

GEORGE BALL, 1971

Each period of emergency—each war, each depression, each epoch of enhanced concern over poverty and equality—expands the activity of government. After each emergency is over, expenditures never seem to go back to previous levels.

PAUL A. SAMUELSON, 1973

I believe that he [F. D. Roosevelt] saved the capitalist system by deliberately forgetting to balance the books, by transferring the gorgeous resources of credit from the bankers to the government.

ALISTAIR COOKE, 1973

Virtually everything is under federal control nowadays except the federal budget.

HERMAN TALMADGE, 1975

Thrift should be the guiding principle in our government expenditure.

MAO ZEDONG, 1976

Although the relative roles of fiscal policy and monetary policy in affecting aggregate demand remain a subject of debate among economists, it is probably prudent in analysis as well as in policy to assume that both have significant influence. HERBERT STEIN, 1976

We used to think that you could just spend your way out of a recession and increase employment by cutting taxes and raising government spending. I tell you, in all candor, that that option no longer exists, and that it only worked on each occasion since the war by injecting bigger doses of inflation into the economy, followed by higher levels of unemployment as the next step. JAMES CALLAGHAN, 1976

The only way to cut government spending is not to give them the money to spend in the first place. HOWARD JARVIS, 1978

Any jackass can draw up a balanced budget on paper. LANE KIRKLAND, 1980

I will err on the side of public use versus preservation. We will use the budget system to be the excuse to make major policy decisions. JAMES WATT, 1981

As far as paying off debt is concerned, there are very few instances in history when any government has ever paid off debt. WALTER WRISTON, 1982

Deficits allow our representatives to vote for spending without having to vote taxes to pay for it, and that creates irresponsibility. MILTON FRIEDMAN, 1984

Forecasting

Dreams and Predictions ought to serve but for winter talk by the fireside. FRANCIS BACON, 1597

To count is a modern practice, the ancient method was to guess; and when numbers are guessed they are always magnified. SAMUEL JOHNSON, 1775

The laws of probability, so true in general, so fallacious in particular. EDWARD GIBBON, 1794

Statistics are no substitute for judgement. HENRY CLAY, 1842

We are employed in narrowing the circle within which the final truths must lie, rather than in an attempt at once to seize them. STATISTICAL SOCIETY, 1849

A statistician says a man stands sixteen chances to be killed by lightning to one of being worth a million of money. MARTIN F. TUPPER, 1867

There are three kinds of lies—lies, damned lies, and statistics. BENJAMIN DISRAELI, 1867

To ultimately expect from political economy results of such certainty and exactness, that it can present the legislator with numerical predictions . . . is by no means hopeless.

SIMON NEWCOMB, 1885

Nearly all dealings in commodities that are not very perishable, are affected by the calculation of the future. ALFRED MARSHALL, 1890

It is a capital mistake to theorize before one has data. ARTHUR CONAN DOYLE, 1891

Statistics are mendacious truths.

LIONEL STRACHEY, 1904

He uses statistics as a drunken man uses lampposts—for support rather than illumination.

ANDREW LANG, 1904

All business proceeds on beliefs or judgements of probabilities, and not on certainties.

CHARLES W. ELIOT, 1910

The economists are generally right in their predictions but generally a good deal out in their dates. SIDNEY WEBB, 1924

Statistics are like alienists—they will testify for either side. FIORELLO H. LA GUARDIA, 1933

More zeal and energy, more fanatical hope, and more intense anguish have been expended over the past century in efforts to "forecast" the stock market than in almost any other single line of human action.

RICHARD DANA SKINNER, 1937

The statistician with his plotted graph showing where we will arrive ten years hence is not as convincing as he was of yore. I have seen too many fine ascending projections dip into the cellar these past few years.

J. A. DAFOE, 1938

In economics it is often possible to specify the necessary conditions required for prices to move in one direction or the other. But this exercise is only useful if we are as a result enabled to make some estimate of the probability of the event. In this case there does not appear to be any such possibility. I. F. PEARCE, 1952

The only relevant test of the validity of a hypothesis is comparison of its predictions with experience. MILTON FRIEDMAN, 1953

The impossibility of prediction in economics follows from the fact that economic change is linked to change in knowledge and future knowledge cannot be gained before its time.

L. M. LACHMANN, 1959

Business, more than any other occupation, is a continual dealing with the future; it is a continual calculation, an instinctive exercise in foresight. HENRY R. LUCE, 1960

If one could divine the nature of the economic forces in the world, one could foretell the future. ROBERT L. HEILBRONER, 1960

One of the difficulties of economics is that it is too easy to explain after a particular event has happened, why it should have happened; and too easy to explain before it happens, why it should not happen. M. G. KENDALL, 1960

It is now proved beyond a shadow of a doubt that smoking is one of the leading causes of statistics. FLETCHER KNEBEL, 1961

Never make forecasts, especially about the future. SAMUEL GOLDWYN, 1961

If successful prediction were the sole criterion of a science, economics should long have ceased to exist as a serious intellectual pursuit.

R. CLOWER, 1964

The average professional . . . economic forecaster is a bit like the average weather fore-

caster; he gives you a 40% chance of precipitation and a 40% chance there will be no rain. The extra 20% is your problem and the forecaster is right either way.
                              JOHN W. DAY, 1969

Dropouts are simply anticipating future economic trends.   RICHARD NEVILLE, 1970

With seasonally adjusted temperatures, you could eliminate winter in Canada.
                       ROBERT L. STANSFIELD, 1971

Incompatible data are useless data.
                         WASSILY LEONTIEF, 1971

The "testing hypotheses" is frequently merely a euphemism for obtaining plausible numbers to provide ceremonial adequacy for a theory chosen and defended on a priori grounds.
                        HARRY G. JOHNSON, 1971

An extrapolation of the trends of the 1880s would show today's cities buried under horse manure.   NORMAN MACRAE, 1972

I think the greatest error in forecasting is not realizing how important are the probabilities of events other than those everyone is agreeing upon.   PAUL A. SAMUELSON, 1974

It does not follow that because something *can* be counted it therefore *should* be counted.
                        HAROLD L. ENARSON, 1975

The economist doll: You wind it up, ask it to forecast, and it shrugs its shoulders.
                       EUGENE A. BIRNBAUM, 1977

Economists state their GNP growth projections to the nearest tenth of a percentage point to prove they have a sense of humor.
                         EDGAR R. FIEDLER, 1977

I could prove God statistically.
                          GEORGE GALLUP, 1979

Thinking rosy futures is as biological as sexual fantasy.   LIONEL TIGER, 1979

It wasn't raining when Noah built the ark.
                          HOWARD RUFF, 1980

Free Enterprise

He who works for his own interests will arouse much animosity.   CONFUCIUS, C. 479 B.C.

That which is common to the greatest number has the least care bestowed upon it. Every one thinks chiefly of his own, hardly at all of the common interest; and only when he is himself concerned as an individual.
                         ARISTOTLE, C. 336 B.C.

It remains true that the greatest injustices proceed from those who pursue excess, not from those who are driven by necessity.
                         ARISTOTLE, C. 336 B.C.

Do not hold the delusion that your advancement is accomplished by crushing others.
                            CICERO, C. 58 B.C.

A horse never runs so fast as when he has other horses to catch up and outpace.
OVID, C. A.D. 8

Is it not lawful for me to do what I will with mine own? MATTHEW 20:15, c. A.D. 80

In general Zeus has so created the nature of the rational animal, that he can attain nothing good for himself, unless he contributes some service to the community. So it turns out that to do everything for his own sake is not unsocial.
EPICTETUS, c. 138

At the king's court, my brother,
Each man for himself, there is none other.
GEOFFREY CHAUCER, 1387

You must obey this, now, for a law—that "he that will not work shall not eat."
JOHN SMITH, 1624

Everyone wishes to be rich, and most persons work night and day in order to become so; men must never be expected to supply products to others as a result of their liberality or prudence.
PIERRE DE BOISGUILBERT, 1707

Laisser-faire, laissez-passer.
FRANÇOIS QUESNAY, 1758

[The rich] are led by an invisible hand to make nearly the same distribution of the necessaries of life, which would have been made had the earth been divided into equal portions among all its inhabitants; and thus, without intending it, without knowing it, advance the interest of the society, and afford means to the multiplication of the species. ADAM SMITH, 1759

Every one might consider the interest of his country in a different light than their own, and many might join in the ruin of it, by endeavoring to promote its advantages. Were a rich merchant to begin and sell his goods without profit, what would become of trade? . . . Were people to feed all who would ask charity, what would become of industry? JAMES STEUART, 1767

Man we find acting uniformly in all ages, in all countries, and in all climates, from the principles of self-interest, expediency, duty, or passion. In this he is alike, in nothing else.
JAMES STEUART, 1767

By directing that industry in such a manner as its produce may be of the greatest value, an individual intends only his own gain, and he is in this . . . led by an invisible hand to promote an end which has no part of his intention. . . . By pursuing his own interest he frequently promotes that of the society more effectually than when he really intends to promote it.
ADAM SMITH, 1776

The desire of bettering our condition comes with us from the womb and never leaves us until we go to the grave. ADAM SMITH, 1776

It is not from the benevolence of the butcher, the brewer, or the baker that we expect our dinner, but from their regard to their interest. We address ourselves, not to their humanity, but to their self-love, and never talk to them of our own necessities but of their advantages.
ADAM SMITH, 1776

It is true, that commerce, the principal object of that office, flourishes most when it is left to itself. Interest, the great guide of commerce, is not a blind one. EDMUND BURKE, 1780

It is by competition only, by unlimited liberty, and equality of the laws of buying and selling, that the general welfare can be obtained.
MOSES MENDELSSOHN, 1782

Inequality of property will exist as long as liberty exists. ALEXANDER HAMILTON, 1788

Agriculture, manufactures, commerce and navigation, the four pillars of our prosperity, are the most thriving when left most free to individual enterprise.   THOMAS JEFFERSON, 1801

A man will fight harder for his interests than his rights.   NAPOLEON BONAPARTE, 1815

Private initiative would give to the laboring poor neither education nor employment, for the children of commerce have been trained to direct all their facilities to buy cheap and sell dear; and consequently, those who are the most expert and successful in this wise and noble art are, in the commercial world, deemed to possess foresight and superior achievements, while such an attempt to improve the moral habits and increase the comfort of those whom they employ are termed wild enthusiasts.
    ROBERT OWEN, 1821

Merchants are occupied solely with crushing each other: such is the effect of free competition.
    CHARLES FOURIER, 1822

By competition the total amount of the supply is increased, and by increase of the supply a competition in the sale ensues, and this enables the consumer to buy at lower rates. Of all human powers operating on the affairs of mankind, none is greater than that of competition.
    HENRY CLAY, 1832

Now it is clear that the production in which no appropriated natural agent has concurred, is the only production which has been made under circumstances of perfectly equal competition. And how few are the commodities of which the production has in no stage been assisted by peculiar advantages of soil, or situation or by extraordinary talent of body or mind, or by processes generally unknown or protected by law from imitation.   NASSAU SENIOR, 1836

Self-interest, . . . spurring to action by hopes and fears, caused all those disorders amongst men which required the remedy of civil society.
    HENRY WARBURTON, 1837

"A bargain," said the son, "here's the rule for bargains—'Do other men for they would do you.' That's the true business precept. All others are counterfeit."   CHARLES DICKENS, 1841

The opening of vast prospects of wealth to the multitude of men has stirred up a fierce competition, a wild spirit of speculation, a feverish, insatiable cupidity, under which fraud, bankruptcy, distrust, distress are fearfully multiplied, so that the name American has become a by-word beyond the ocean.
    WILLIAM ELLERY CHANNING, 1841

Laissez-faire, Supply-and-Demand—one begins to be weary of all that. Leave all to egoism, to ravenous greed of money, of pleasure, of applause:—it is the Gospel of Despair!
    THOMAS CARLYLE, 1843

It is only in a very imperfect state of the world's arrangements that any one can best serve the happiness of others by the absolute sacrifice of his own.   JOHN STUART MILL, 1848

Thou shalt not covet; but tradition
Approves all forms of competition.
    ARTHUR H. CLOUGH, 1859

It's them as take advantage that get advantage i' this world.   GEORGE ELIOT, 1859

The man who accepts the laissez-faire doctrine would allow his garden to run wild, so that the roses might fight it out with the weeds and the fittest might survive.   JOHN RUSKIN, 1862

That some should be rich, shows that others may become rich, and hence is just encouragement to industry and enterprise.
    ABRAHAM LINCOLN, 1864

The men I see before me are owners and managers of colossal capital. You are, doubtless in some degree, clinging to the illusion that you are working for yourselves, but it is my pleasure to claim that you are working for the public. While you are scheming for your own selfish ends, there is an over-ruling and wise Providence directing that the most of all you do should inure to the benefit of the people. Men of colossal fortunes are in effect, if not in fact, trustees for the public. SAMUEL TILDEN, 1873

Save possibly in education effects, cooperation can produce no general results that competition will not produce. HENRY GEORGE, 1879

Poverty is uncomfortable; but nine times out of ten the best thing that can happen to a young man is to be tossed overboard and compelled to sink or swim. JAMES A. GARFIELD, 1880

The growth of a large business is merely a survival of the fittest.
JOHN D. ROCKEFELLER, 1882

Capitalism will kill competition.
KARL MARX, 1883

Whatever is not nailed down is mine. Whatever I can pry loose is not nailed down.
COLLIS P. HUNTINGTON, 1884

The gospel of wealth advocates leaving free the operation of laws of accumulation.
ANDREW CARNEGIE, 1886

In view of the helplessness of the individual, the slogan of the liberal school, "Laissez-faire, laissez-passer," becomes almost a mockery.
FRIEDRICH VON WIESER, 1889

There is no such thing as a purely private enterprise, and we may perhaps say, also, that there is no such thing as a purely public enterprise. Certainly in the vast majority of the enterprises with which we are familiar, private and public activities are combined in varying proportions.
RICHARD T. ELY, 1889

Industrial giants impelling incessant speculation create a restlessness and haste among the skilled and unskilled masses of laborers that drive them in search of chances from town to town. Senseless competition keeps them in a state of constant migration from place to place, from street to street, from house to house.
HENRY W. CHEROUNY, 1900

Even those who emphasize most clearly what self-interest has done for political and industrial progress are compelled to recognize that it will not do everything. Its successes have been great, but they have not been unmixed with failures. It is a powerful stimulant, but it is by no means that panacea for social ills which so many economists and moralists have considered it.
ARTHUR T. HADLEY, 1901

The "economic man" whose only interest is the self-regarding one and whose only human trait is prudence, is useless for the purposes of modern industry. THORSTEIN VEBLEN, 1904

The more modern nations detest each other the more meekly they follow each other; for all competition is in its nature only a furious plagiarism. GILBERT K. CHESTERTON, 1906

The truth is, we are all caught in a great economic system which is heartless.
WOODROW WILSON, 1912

American industry is not free, as once it was free; American enterprise is not free; the man with only a little capital is finding it harder to get into the field, more and more impossible to compete with the big fellow.
WOODROW WILSON, 1913

Under a state which accurately distinguishes between the economic and uneconomic ways of getting wealth, and effectively suppresses all the latter, it follows of necessity that every individual will be forced, with respect to wealth, to act in his own self-interest precisely as he would if he were animated by the most completely altruistic motives and patriotic sentiment.

THOMAS NIXON CARVER, 1915

The idea that to make a man work you've got to hold gold in front of his eyes is a growth, not an axiom. We've done that for so long that we've forgotten there's any other way.

F. SCOTT FITZGERALD, 1920

If the spirit of business adventure is dulled, this country will cease to hold the foremost position in the world.　　ANDREW MELLON, 1923

The pulse of modern life is economic and the fundamental principle of economic production is individual independence.

CH'EN TU-HSIU, 1923

It is Enterprise which builds and improves the world's possessions. . . . If Enterprise is afoot, wealth accumulates whatever may be happening to Thrift; and if Enterprise is asleep, Wealth decays, whatever Thrift may be doing.

JOHN MAYNARD KEYNES, 1925

The whole record of civilization is a record of the failure of money as a higher incentive. The enormous majority of men never make any serious effort to get rich. The few who are sordid enough to do so easily become millionaires with a little luck, and astonish the others by the contrast between their riches and their stupidity.

GEORGE BERNARD SHAW, 1928

The American system of rugged individualism.

HERBERT HOOVER, 1928

The cold truth is that the individualist creed of everybody for himself and the devil take the hindmost is principally responsible for the dis-

tress in which Western civilization finds itself—with investment racketeering at one end and labor racketeering at the other.

CHARLES AND MARY BEARD, 1931

Most prudent people hesitate to do business with their relatives. When the necessity arrives, the results are seldom a stimulant of family affection. Each kinsman expects the other by reason of his kin to make kindly concessions.

WALTER FENTON, 1932

In a sense, the financial conflict is more bitter and ruthless than war itself; in war, friend and foe can be distinguished.

B. F. WINKELMAN, 1932

When it comes to selling the business system, we get as drab as a crutch, as unexciting as a chorus girl in a flannel nightgown.

WALTER B. WEISENBURGER, 1933

As a matter of fact all argument in favor of free competition rests on one tacit assumption, which, however, corresponds but little to reality, namely that from the beginning all men are equal. . . . But if all conditions are basically unequal, if some people have good hands from the beginning and others hold only low cards, free competition does nothing to stop the former from winning every trick while the latter pay the table.

KNUT WICKSELL, 1934

After I asked him what he meant, he replied that freedom consisted of the unimpeded right to get rich, to use his ability, no matter what the cost to others, to win advancement.

NORMAN THOMAS, 1934

Our whole evolutionary thinking leads us to the conclusion that economic independence lies at the very foundation of social and moral well-being.　　FELIX FRANKFURTER, 1936

We have always known that heedless self-interest was bad morals; we now know that it is bad economics. FRANKLIN D. ROOSEVELT, 1937

Private enterprise is ceasing to be free enterprise. FRANKLIN D. ROOSEVELT, 1938

In business, the competition will bite you if you keep running; if you stand still, they will swallow you. WILLIAM KNUDSEN, 1939

Capital which overreaches for profits; labor which overreaches for wages, or a public which overreaches for bargains, will all destroy each other. There is no salvation for us on that road. OWEN D. YOUNG, 1939

The only type of economic system in which government is free and in which the human spirit is free is one in which commerce is free.
THURMAN WESLEY ARNOLD, 1942

It would be madness to let the purposes or the methods of private enterprise set the habits of the age of atomic energy.
HAROLD J. LASKI, 1945

The pursuit of business advantage in a competitive market takes the form of reductions in price, improvements in quality, and a constant search for cost reductions and innovations.
M. A. ADELMAN, 1948

In contrast to conflict, which aims to destroy or banish the opponent, competition simply aims to out-do the competitor in achieving some mutually desired goal. . . . The rules are so arranged that the ends must be obtained by other methods than fraud or physical force.
KINGSLEY DAVIS, 1949

Today's challenge, today's dire necessity is to sell—to resell if you will—to free Americans the philosophy that has kept us and our economy free. WILLIAM H. WHYTE, 1950

There's no resting place for an enterprise in a competitive economy.
ALFRED P. SLOAN, 1954

I don't meet competition, I crush it.
CHARLES REVSON, 1958

Call it what you will, incentives are what get people to work harder.
NIKITA KHRUSHCHEV, 1959

The dynamo of our economic system is self-interest which may range from mere petty greed to admirable types of self-expression.
FELIX FRANKFURTER, 1960

In the race for money some men may come first, but man comes last. MARYA MANNES, 1964

Competition brings out the best in products and the worst in people. DAVID SARNOFF, 1964

The cosmetics industry is the nastiest business in the world. ELIZABETH ARDEN, 1966

In spite of its intricacy, the basic idea of a free market economy is very simple. It is the idea of decentralizing control of the economy down to units of manageable proportions, coupled with a stupendously efficient method for conveying information among the decentralized units, and a highly effective method of motivating the units to perform their appropriate tasks efficiently.
ROBERT DORFMAN, 1967

Material welfare and the "higher" humanism are complimentary, not competing, things. The civilized sensibilities flourish where there is economic plenty; and the more the better, even when it is devoted in part to automobiles and television sets. SCOTT GORDON, 1968

The consumer, so it is said, is the king . . . each is a voter who uses his money as votes to get the things done that he wants done.
PAUL A. SAMUELSON, 1970

And no matter how radical Ralph Nader may sound, his is a highly conventional view of the "system." Indeed, his are the values of our oldest tradition: populism. Nader believes in economic performance above all; he makes it the central touchstone of a good society.

PETER DRUCKER, 1971

Nothing could be less appropriate than to consider the giant firm a private enterprise. General Motors is as much a public enterprise as the U.S. Post Office Department, . . . wholly dependent for its survival during every second of its operations on a vast network of laws, protection, services, inducements, constraints, and coercions provided by innumerable governments, federal, state, local, foreign.

ROBERT DAHL, 1972

The idea that egotism is the basis of the general welfare is the principle on which competitive society has been built.   ERICH FROMM, 1973

International business is a real law of the jungle. We watch what they do. The more sophisticated we become, the more we realize in how many areas they can take money out of our pockets. They have their tricks, so we have to have our tricks.

ABOL GESSAM KHERADJOU, 1974

It is ridiculous to call this an industry. This is rat eat rat, dog eat dog. I'll kill 'em, and I'm going to kill 'em before they kill me. You're talking about the American way of survival of the fittest.   RAY KROC, 1975

Going into business for yourself, becoming an entrepreneur, is the modern-day equivalent of pioneering on the old frontier.

PAULA NELSON, 1975

Competition, you know, is a lot like chastity. It is widely praised, but alas, too little practiced.

CAROL TUCKER, 1977

Officially we revere free enterprise, initiative and individuality. Unofficially we fear it.

GEORGE LOIS, 1977

The pursuit of gain is the only way in which men can serve the needs of others whom they do not know.   FRIEDRICH A. HAYEK, 1978

One of the aspects of the free enterprise system is that you should be allowed to succeed, and you should also be allowed to fail.

REGINALD JONES, 1979

The free-enterprise system has gone to hell.

LEE A. IACOCCA, 1979

The most important feature of a liberal, market-oriented economy's industrial policy is that it has an effective and objective way to sort out winners and losers. If something new brought to the marketplace is preferred by customers, it prevails, and the old fades out.

PAUL MCCRACKEN, 1981

America cannot survive half rich, half poor; half suburb, half slum. If the country wakes up it will not do so by way of laissez-faire.

FELIX ROHATYN, 1983

The competition is like horse manure. It's everywhere.   R. WAYNE OLDHAM, 1984

Gold and Silver

Of all the activities I know, silver mining is the only one in which expansion arouses no envy. . . . If there are more coopersmiths, for example, copperwork becomes cheap and the coppersmiths retire. The same is true in the iron trade. . . . But an increase in the amount of the silver ore . . . brings more people into this industry.   XENOPHON, C. 450 B.C.

When Gold argues the cause, eloquence is impotent.
     PUBLILIUS SYRUS, first century B.C.

Accursed thirst for gold! what dost thou not compel mortals to do?   VERGIL, 19 B.C.

Gold will buy the highest honors; and gold will purchase love.   OVID, A.D. 8

Not Philip, but Philip's gold, took the cities of Greece.   PLUTARCH, C. A.D. 100

Gold is treasure, and he who possesses it does all he wishes to in this world, and succeeds in helping souls into paradise.
     CHRISTOPHER COLUMBUS, 1496

The tongue hath no force when gold speaketh.
     MARCO GUAZZO, 1536

How quickly nature falls into revolt
When gold becomes her object!

For this the foolish over-careful fathers
Have broke their sleep with thoughts, their brains with care,
Their bones with industry.
     WILLIAM SHAKESPEARE,
     Henry IV, Part II (IV,v), 1600

Bell, book, and candle shall not drive me back,
When gold and silver becks me to come on.
     WILLIAM SHAKESPEARE,
     King John (III, iii), 1616

My gold has burnt this twelve months in my pocket.   JAMES SHIRLEY, 1637

Gold is the soul of all civil life, that can resolve all things into itself, and turn itself into all things.   SAMUEL BUTLER, 1660

Gold gives an appearance of beauty even to ugliness: but with poverty everything becomes frightful.   NICHOLAS BOILEAU, 1668

When we have gold we are in fear; when we have none we are in danger.
     JOHN RAY, 1670

Mankind, having consented to put an imaginary value upon gold and silver . . . have made them by general consent the common pledges whereby men are assured . . . to receive equally valuable things . . . for any quantity of these metals.   JOHN LOCKE, 1692

Though money has hitherto been called the measure of trade, yet mankind may agree to set up any other thing in this room; and whatever it be . . . it may serve their turn as well as gold and silver.   CHARLES DAVENANT, 1698

O cursed lust of gold! when, for thy sake,
The fool throws up his interest in both worlds,
First starved in this, then damned in that to come.
                                        ROBERT BLAIR, 1734

The lust of gold succeeds the rage of conquest;
The lust of gold, unfeeling and remorseless!
The last corruption of degenerate man.
                                        SAMUEL JOHNSON, 1748

Gold is everything; without gold there's nothing!   DENIS DIDEROT, 1749

Princes and sovereign states have frequently fancied that they had a temporary interest to diminish the quantity of pure metal contained in their coins; but they seldom have fancied that they had any to augment it. The quantity of metal contained in the coins, I believe, of all nations, has, accordingly, been almost continually diminishing, and hardly ever augmenting.
                                        ADAM SMITH, 1776

To attempt to increase the wealth of any country by introducing or by detaining in it an unnecessary quantity of gold and silver, is as absurd as it would be to attempt to increase the good cheer of private families by obliging them to keep an unnecessary number of kitchen utensils.   ADAM SMITH, 1776

The gold and silver money which circulates in any country may very properly be compared to a highway, which, while it circulates and carries to market all the grass and corn of the country, produces itself not a single pile of either.
                                        ADAM SMITH, 1776

Gold and silver, like all other commodities, are valuable only in proportion to the quantity of labor necessary to produce them and bring them to market. Gold is about fifteen times dearer than silver . . . solely because fifteen times the quantity of labor is necessary to procure a given quantity of it.   DAVID RICARDO, 1809

Gold and silver, having been chosen for the general medium of circulation, they are, by the competition of commerce, distributed in such proportions amongst the different countries of the world as to accommodate themselves to the natural traffic which would take place if no such metals existed and the trade between countries were purely a trade of barter.
                                        DAVID RICARDO, 1817

Any great accumulation of the public monies . . . if consisting of gold and silver accumulated in the Treasury chest . . . is an active capital taken from the people and rendered unproductive.   ALBERT GALLATIN, 1841

We find that the development of all nations was analogous to this extent, that capital was everywhere able to develop its economic power strongly only after the introduction and widespread use of metallic money and to reveal its more extensive power only at higher levels of civilization.   KARL KNIES, 1853

By common consent of the nations, gold and silver are the only true measure of value. They are the necessary regulators of trade. I have myself no more doubt that these metals were prepared by the Almighty for this very purpose, than I have that iron and coal were prepared for the purposes in which they are being used.
                                        HUGH MCCULLOCH, 1865

Nothing precipitates and solidifies this gold so readily as contact with human flesh heated by passion.   MARK TWAIN, 1866

Although gold and silver are not by nature money, money is by nature gold and silver.
                          KARL MARX, 1867

Gold and silver! They are the legal tender of Commerce and the Constitution . . . the legal tender of God Almighty, who has made it precious.   SAMUEL COX, 1870

The first chief function of money is to supply commodities with the material for the expression of their values, or to represent their values as magnitudes of the same denomination, qualitatively equal, and quantitatively comparable. It thus serves as a universal measure of value. And only by virtue of this function does gold, the equivalent commodity par excellence, become money.   KARL MARX, 1873

O God! how poor a man may be
With nothing in this world but gold!
                     JOAQUIN MILLER, 1873

I believe gold and silver coin to be the money of the Constitution. No power was conferred on Congress to declare that either metal should not be money.   JAMES G. BLAINE, 1878

Like liberty, gold never stays where it is undervalued.   J. S. MORRILL, 1878

You shall not press down upon the brow of labor this crown of thorns—you shall not crucify mankind upon a cross of gold!
                WILLIAM JENNINGS BRYAN, 1896

Of course bullion of itself is useless, but men desire useless things because they confer distinction. Men are not actuated by "utility" but a desire to outshine neighbors, and that is true of nations as well, and they want to have the feeling of superiority which the possession of plenty of money, whether it can be turned into goods or not, gives.   WILLIAM CARLILE, 1901

The possession of gold has ruined fewer men than the lack of it.
                THOMAS BAILEY ALDRICH, 1903

In very truth, gold is god today and rules with pitiless sway in the affairs of men.
                     EUGENE V. DEBS, 1918

Gold is the spirit of society.
                        PAUL VALÉRY, 1921

The value of the yellow metal, originally chosen as money because it tickled the fancy of savages, is clearly a chancy and irrelevant thing on which to base the value of our money and the stability of our industrial system.
                 DENNIS H. ROBERTSON, 1922

You have to chose [as a voter] between trusting to the natural stability of gold and the honesty and intelligence of members of our government. And with due respect for these gentlemen, I advise you, as long as the capitalist system lasts, to vote for gold.
                GEORGE BERNARD SHAW, 1928

I am for gold dollars as against baloney dollars. I am for experience against experiment.
                     ALFRED E. SMITH, 1933

Gold is not necessary. I have no interest in gold. We'll build a solid state, without an ounce of gold behind it. Anyone who sells above the set prices, let him be marched off to a concentration camp. That's the bastion of money.
                        ADOLF HITLER, 1942

The modern mind dislikes gold because it blurts out unpleasant truths.
                 JOSEPH A. SCHUMPETER, 1947

The production of shell money in the Pacific for the sake of being piled up in the house of a chief . . . is [not] more futile than the labor spent on the mining of gold for the sake of being able to buy it once more in the vaults of Fort Knox.

PAUL EINZIG, 1948

Even during the period when Rome lost much of her ancient prestige, an Indian traveller observed that trade all over the world was operated with the aid of Roman gold coins which were accepted and admired everywhere.

PAUL EINZIG, 1949

People fight the gold standard because they want to substitute national autarchy for free trade, war for peace, totalitarian government omnipotence for liberty.

LUDWIG VON MISES, 1949

When the world went off gold in the early Thirties, a great economic change occurred. It took about ten years before the politicians of the new world fully appreciated what a powerful tool was placed in their hands, but now they all fully realize it. The masses in every country will not take deflation. Deflation means the elimination of the party in power.

ROBERT WOOD, 1950

There can be no doubt that the international gold standard, as it evolved in the 19th century, provided the growing industrial world with the most efficient system of adjustment for balance of payments which it was ever to have, either by accident or by conscious planning.

W. M. SCAMMELL, 1965

There can be no other criterion, no other standard than gold. Yes, gold which never changes, which can be shaped into ingots, bars, coins, which has no nationality and which is eternally and universally accepted as the unalterable fiduciary value par excellence.

CHARLES DE GAULLE, 1965

It is unthinkable that modern countries individually or collectively would surrender sover-

eignty over their full employment policy, growth policy, stabilization policies to the vagaries of gold production, Russian gold sales, and the whims of gold hoarders.

GOTTFRIED HABERLER, 1968

There are about three hundred economists in the world who are against gold, and they think that gold is a barbarous relic—and they might be right. Unfortunately, there are three billion inhabitants of the world who believe in gold.

JANOS FEKETE, 1973

Gold-hoarding goes against the American grain; it fits better with European pessimism than with America's traditional optimism.

PAULA NELSON, 1975

Gyrations in gold's prices today are today's symptoms of happenings in finance, not causes.

PAUL A. SAMUELSON, 1977

The gold standard was never the perfect machine for untended economic evenhandedness that a somewhat romantic view would impute to it. . . . There were both serious unemployment and pronounced inflations in England and the United States when the classic gold standard prevailed.   ROY JOHNSON, 1977

It is interesting to note that the average earnings of an English worker in 1900 came to half an ounce of gold a week and that in 1979 after two world wars, a world slump, and a world inflation, the British worker has average earnings of half an ounce of gold a week.

WILLIAM REES MOGG, 1979

Regardless of the dollar price involved, one ounce of gold would purchase a good-quality man's suit at the conclusion of the Revolutionary War, the Civil War, the presidency of Franklin Roosevelt, and today.   PETER A. BUSHRE, 1981

Government

A democracy is a government in the hands of men of low birth, no property, and vulgar employments.   ARISTOTLE, C. 336 B.C.

I see it is impossible for the King to have things done as cheap as other men.
                                        SAMUEL PEPYS, 1662

And having looked to government for bread, on the very first scarcity, they will turn and bite the hand that fed them.   EDMUND BURKE, 1768

Civil government, so far as it is instituted for the security of property, is in reality instituted for the defense of the rich against the poor, or of those who have some property against those who have none at all.   ADAM SMITH, 1776

The whole, or almost the whole public revenue, is in most countries employed in maintaining unproductive hands.   ADAM SMITH, 1776

The man who has half a million dollars in property . . . has a much higher interest in the government than the man who has little or no property.   NOAH WEBSTER, 1796

Government always harms industry when it mixes in its affairs; it harms it even in instances where it makes an effort to encourage it.
                              CLAUDE HENRI SAINT-SIMON, 1814

Were we directed from Washington when to sow and when to reap, we should soon want bread.
                                        THOMAS JEFFERSON, 1826

Government is emphatically a machine: to the discontented a "taxing machine," to the contented a "machine for securing property."
                                        THOMAS CARLYLE, 1829

Nothing is so galling to a people, not broken in from the birth, as a paternal or, in other words, meddling government, a government which tells them what to read and say and eat and drink and wear.   THOMAS MACAULEY, 1833

It is to be regretted that the rich and powerful too often bend the acts of government to their selfish purposes.   ANDREW JACKSON, 1837

The delicate duty of devising schemes of revenue should be left where the Constitution has placed it—with the immediate representatives of the people.
                              WILLIAM HENRY HARRISON, 1840

Were I to define the State, I should prefer to think of it as the poor man's bank.
                                        LOUIS BLANC, 1840

Bureaucracy is a giant mechanism operated by pygmies.   HONORÉ DE BALZAC, 1844

The State lives in a glasshouse, we see what it tries to do, and all its failures, partial or total, are made the most of. But private enterprise is sheltered under opaque bricks and mortar. The public rarely knows what it tries to do, and only hears of failures when they are gross and patent to all the world.   THOMAS H. HUXLEY, 1878

The state, so far from being the source of innumerable evils, has always been not only the absolutely essential condition of human progress, but also one of the most important, if not, indeed, the most important factor, in the economic evolution of society itself.

EDMUND JANES JAMES, 1886

Political causes alone seldom produce serious discontent, unless they affect injuriously the economic condition of the people.

WILFRID LAURIER, 1888

You have got to have the same interest in public affairs as in private affairs, or you cannot keep this country what this country should be.

THEODORE ROOSEVELT, 1903

It is an axiom enforced by all the experience of the ages, that they who rule industrially will rule politically.   JAMES CONNOLLY, 1905

Politics is economics in action.

ROBERT M. LA FOLLETTE, 1906

I niver knew a pollytician to go wrong ontil he's been contaminated by contact with a business man.   FINLEY PETER DUNNE, 1910

The labor unions shall have a square deal, and the corporations shall have a square deal, and in addition, all private citizens shall have a square deal.   THEODORE ROOSEVELT, 1912

The way to stop financial "joy-riding" is to arrest the chauffeur, not the automobile.

WOODROW WILSON, 1912

Those who have economic power have civil power also.   GEORGE W. RUSSELL, 1913

The masters of the government of the United States are the combined capitalists and manufacturers of the United States.

WOODROW WILSON, 1913

Political institutions are a superstructure resting on an economic foundation.

NIKOLAI LENIN, 1917

A Lobbyist is a person that is supposed to help a Politician to make up his mind, not only help him but pay him.   WILL ROGERS, 1919

Every new industry and every new commercial connection is equivalent to battalions. All politics are economic politics.

WALTER RATHENAU, 1920

I have said to the people we mean to have less Government in business as well as more business in Government.

WARREN G. HARDING, 1921

Bureaucracy, as it is, is a direct negation of mass self-activity.

ALEKSANDRA KOLLONTAI, 1921

There is nowhere a realization that only as the Government strips itself can the people clothe themselves. There is still a lurking desire to have the government do more rather than less.

IRVING T. BUSH, 1922

We must realize that the democratic form of government is bound to penetrate our industrial life as well. It cannot be confined merely to our political institutions.

SIDNEY HILLMAN, 1924

This is a business country . . . and it wants a business government. I do not mean a government by business nor a government for business, but I do mean a government that will understand business. CALVIN COOLIDGE, 1925

The business of government is to keep the government out of business—that is, unless business needs government aid.
WILL ROGERS, 1927

If the government was as afraid of disturbing the consumer as it is of disturbing business, this would be some democracy.
FRANK MCKINNEY HUBBARD, 1929

The political problem of mankind is to combine three things: economic efficiency, social justice, and individual liberty.
JOHN MAYNARD KEYNES, 1936

Nobody who has wealth to distribute ever omits himself. LEON TROTSKY, 1937

Government with all its power can't control even the Mississippi River, much less the tides of American business or sentiment. Government money policies, if constructive, can help a bull market, but can't stop a bear market.
ROBERT RHEA, 1937

Under our present system, the chief duty of the governor of Alabama is running an employment agency. FRANK DIXON, 1938

That businessmen should from time to time direct candid criticism toward our Government is not only understandable but salutary in a free democracy. CLARENCE B. RANDALL, 1938

As a society becomes more complicated, as its division of labor ramifies more widely, as its commerce extends, as technology takes the place of handicrafts and local self-sufficiency, the functions of government increase in number and in their vital relationships to the fortunes of society and individuals.
CHARLES A. BEARD, 1940

Bureaucracy is not an obstacle to democracy but an inevitable complement to it.
JOSEPH A. SCHUMPETER, 1942

The dilemma of the politics of economic control comes from the fact that governments must keep in check the pressures of particularism, yet at the same time governments derive their power in no small degree from the support of particularistic interest. V. O. KEY, 1944

Where distinction and rank is achieved almost exclusively by becoming a civil servant of the state . . . it is too much to expect that many will long prefer freedom to security.
FRIEDRICH A. HAYEK, 1944

It is logical that the United States should do whatever it is able to do to assist in the return of full economic health in the world without which there can be no political stability and no assured peace. GEORGE MARSHALL, 1947

What the New Deal shows is . . . that when a country has fallen so low as the United States fell from 1929 to 1933 only the most drastic measures will suffice to get it up again.
W. ARTHUR LEWIS, 1949

In no other period of American history [1789–1800] has the government been so active in financing and actually promoting, owing and controlling banks and public works including turnpikes, bridges, canals, and railroads.
GEORGE R. TAYLOR, 1951

It's a terribly hard job to spend a billion dollars and get your money's worth.
GEORGE HUMPHREY, 1954

The inherent tendency will always be for public services to fall behind private production.
JOHN KENNETH GALBRAITH, 1958

Money is the mother's milk of politics.
JESSE UNRUH, 1958

From the standpoint of the employee, it is coming to make less and less practical difference to him what his country's official ideology is and whether he happens to be employed by a government or commercial corporation.

ARNOLD J. TOYNBEE, 1958

Economists have paid much attention to the formulation of theories that examine the problems of consumer households, business firms, cooperatives, trade unions and other decision-making units in the economy. While much remains to be done, we can boast of a fairly adequate framework in which to explore these matters. No such success can be claimed for occasional attempts to develop a corresponding theory of the public sector.

RICHARD A. MUSGRAVE, 1959

I mean business on economy. Of course I have some trouble in my own Administration. My cabinet consists of nine salesmen and one credit manager.   LYNDON B. JOHNSON, 1963

It is clear to the most obtuse observer that there is a much more distant relationship between business and government leadership in the United States, than, say, in Britain, France, or the Netherlands. . . . A British businessman can say, "Some of my best friends are civil servants," and really mean it. This would be rare in the United States.   EDWARD S. MASON, 1963

No class of Americans, so far as I know, has ever objected . . . to any attempt of governmental meddling if it appeared to benefit that particular class.   CARL BECKER, 1964

The most important current problem facing the United States economy is also a very old problem. This is the continued "cold war" between business and government, with organized labor and agriculture running interference for both, and increasing the noise level.

KENNETH E. BOULDING, 1964

You talk about capitalism and communism and all that sort of thing, but the important thing is the struggle everybody is engaged in to get better living conditions and they are not interested too much in the form of government.

BERNARD BARUCH, 1964

Increasingly, it will be recognized that the mature corporation, as it develops, becomes part of the larger administrative complex associated with the state. In time the line between the two will disappear.

JOHN KENNETH GALBRAITH, 1967

At the risk of sounding just a bit partisan, let me point out that my administration makes no bones about being business-oriented.

RONALD REAGAN, 1967

When we buy an automobile we no longer buy an object in the old sense of the word, but instead we purchase a three-to-five year lease for participation in the state-recognized private transportation system, a highway system, a traffic safety system, an industrial parts-replacement system, a costly insurance system.

JACK BURNHAM, 1968

Government expands to absorb revenue and then some.   TOM WICKER, 1968

In our democracy we must have a partnership of labor, of business and of government.

CHARLES H. PERCY, 1969

The only possible way to keep open the economic opportunities for new activities is for a "third force" to protect their weak and still incipient interests. Only government can play this economic role.   JANE JACOBS, 1969

Everyone else is represented in Washington by a rich and powerful lobby, it seems. But there is no lobby for the people.

SHIRLEY CHISHOLM, 1970

The most difficult issues of political economy are those where goals of efficiency, freedom of choice and quality conflict.

JAMES TOBIN, 1970

As matters currently stand, the government does not even deserve to be called the executive committee of the bourgeoisie. Rather, it is . . . a subsidiary branch of the corporate community.

ANDREW HACKER, 1971

Judged by its contribution to solving social welfare, to solving the big social problems, fiscal-monetary policy can be regarded as trivial and perhaps somewhat obsolete.

ARTHUR M. OKUN, 1972

Administrative [government] interventionism allows the traditional employing class to invoke liberalism to make its profits and socialization to cushion its losses.

JEAN-JACQUES SERVAN-SCHREIBER, 1972

I don't really ask companies to do a single thing that isn't profitable. But political forces are just as real as market forces, and business must respond to them, which means it often must be content with optimizing and not maximizing immediate profits.   NEIL JACOBY, 1973

We are not just here to manage capitalism but to change society and to define its finer values.

TONY BENN, 1975

The only thing that saves us from the bureaucracy is its inefficiency.

EUGENE MCCARTHY, 1975

We find ourselves in an adversary relationship with the bureaucracy. We must find a way of making government a partner with business.

IRVING S. SHAPIRO, 1975

The best minds are not in government. If any were, business would hire them away.

RONALD REAGAN, 1976

You've got to distinguish between a politician using economics and using economists.

CHARLES L. SCHULTZE, 1976

To get the government off your back, get your hands out of the government's pocket.

GARY HART, 1977

Anything that the private sector can do, government can do it worse.   DIXIE LEE RAY, 1977

Government is nothing but who collects the money and how do they spend it.

GORE VIDAL, 1977

Folklore has it that the oldest profession is prostitution. I always thought it was lobbying.

CHUCK LIPSEN, 1977

Bureaucracy defends the status quo long past the time when the quo has lost its status.

LAURENCE J. PETER, 1978

What's good politics is bad economics; what's bad politics is good economics.

EUGENE W. BAER, 1978

Inability to get results back at the plant doesn't seem to matter anymore. Nowadays, to get results you go to Washington. . . . What is it in the Washington air that restores the energies of these once dynamic American manufacturers?

RUSSELL BAKER, 1980

If you're a public employee and your job depends on public officials, you have to be in politics.   RACHEL HOROWITZ, 1980

There is one common denominator in all this so-called reindustrialization. Every measure would try to assist American industry. And each measure would do so by using federal resources. Reindustrialization would strengthen American business by using the federal taxing, spending, and lending power to do so.

WILLIAM PROXMIRE, 1980

The failures of national governments to force economic life to do their bidding suggest that nations are essentially irrelevant to promoting economic success.   JANE JACOBS, 1984

Greed

The avarice of mankind is insatiable.

ARISTOTLE, C. 336 B.C.

Poverty wants much; but avarice, everything.

PUBLILIUS SYRUS, first century B.C.

If you wish to remove avarice you must remove its mother, luxury.   CICERO, C. 46 B.C.

What good does this weight of gold and silver, if fear forces you to bury it secretly in the ground?   HORACE, 35 B.C.

Accursed greed for gold,
To what dost thou not drive the heart of man?

VERGIL, 19 B.C.

It is not the man who has little, but he who desires more, that is poor.   SENECA, C. A.D. 40

Pride, envy, avarice—these are the sparks
Have set on fire the hearts of all men.

DANTE ALIGHIERI, 1322

Can one desire too much of a good thing?

WILLIAM SHAKESPEARE,
As You Like It (IV, i), 1613

No wealth can satisfy the covetous desire of wealth.   JEREMY TAYLOR, 1650

Greed is the source of all our actions—in addition, of course, to human nature!

BLAISE PASCAL, 1656

Poverty wants some, luxury many, avarice all things.   ABRAHAM COWLEY, 1661

Avarice is more opposed to economy than liberality is.

FRANÇOIS DE LA ROCHEFOUCAULD, 1664

Riches have made men more covetous Men, than Covetousness hath made rich Men.

THOMAS FULLER, 1732

Avarice, or the desire of gain, is a universal passion, which operates at all times, at all places, and upon all persons.   DAVID HUME, 1754

The selfish spirit of commerce knows no country, and feels no passion or principle but that of gain.   THOMAS JEFFERSON, 1809

I am rich beyond the dreams of avarice.

GEORGE EDWARD MOORE, 1922

Economics is the science of greed.
F. V. MEYER, 1933

The world has enough for everyone's needs, but not enough for everyone's greed.
MOHANDAS GANDHI, 1937

Suppose everybody cared enough, everybody shared enough? There is enough in the world for everyone's need but not for everyone's greed.
FRANK BUCHMAN, 1938

People who are greedy have extraordinary capacities for waste—they must, they take in too much.
NORMAN MAILER, 1968

What kind of society isn't structured on greed? The problem of social organization is how to set up an arrangement under which greed will do the least harm; capitalism is that kind of a system.
MILTON FRIEDMAN, 1973

Avarice walks among us disguised as ambition.
EZRA J. MISHAN, 1974

In their greed the robber barons gave us the great railroads and giant steel mills; had government checked their greed more effectively it would have curbed much of their creativity.
FRIEDRICH A. HAYEK, 1979

Growth

The opinion of those who maintain that the high wages in the United States must, for a long time yet, retard the progress of manufactures, is practically refuted by the number of flourishing establishments, which are constantly springing up in every part of the country.
FRANCIS J. GRUND, 1837

In poor nations the people are comfortable; in rich nations they are generally poor.
DESTUTT DE TRACY, 1839

It must always have been seen, more or less distinctly, by political economists, that the increase of wealth is not boundless; that at the end of what they term the progressive state lies the stationary state, that all progress in wealth

is but a postponement of this, and that each step in advance is an approach to it.
JOHN STUART MILL, 1848

It is in vain to suppose that a free trade system will be beneficial to a new and struggling colony which has nothing to export but raw materials. It is rather calculated to enrich an old commonwealth, whose people by their skill and labor make such raw materials valuable, and return them for consumption.
ABRAHAM GESNER, 1849

All is well since all grows better.
ANDREW CARNEGIE, 1889

The number of members of the possessing classes is today not smaller but larger. The enormous increase of social wealth is not accompanied by a decreasing number of large capitalists, but by an increasing number of capitalists of all degrees.   EDUARD BERNSTEIN, 1899

Few problems are more fascinating, more important, or more neglected than the rates at which development proceeds in successive generations in different countries.
                    WESLEY C. MITCHELL, 1927

I helped make Mexico safe for American oil interests in 1914. I helped make Haiti and Cuba a decent place for the National City Bank boys to collect revenue in. I helped purify Nicaragua for the international banking house of Brown Brothers.   GENERAL SMEDLEY BUTLER, 1931

Without development there is no profit, without profit, no development.
                    JOSEPH A. SCHUMPETER, 1934

Prosperity has no fixed limits. It is not a finite substance to be diminished by division. On the contrary, the more of it that other nations enjoy, the more each nation will have for itself.
                    HENRY MORGENTHAU, 1944

Industrialization is the only hope of the poor.
                    C. P. SNOW, 1949

An undeveloped country is poor because it has no industry, and an underdeveloped country has no industry because it is poor.
                    H. W. SINGER, 1949

Incomes in underdeveloped countries today are from about one-sixth to one-third of the per capita incomes of the developed countries a century ago.   COLIN CLARK, 1954

We will never question whether we want a big or a little pie of national wealth to divide, or deviate from our conviction that the big pie is always the easiest to split.
                    WALTER REUTHER, 1955

The rate of technical progress and the rate of increase of the labor force . . . govern the rate of growth of output of an economy that can be permanently maintained at a constant rate of profit.   JOAN ROBINSON, 1956

Progress might have been all right once but it has gone on too long.   OGDEN NASH, 1957

From a dollar-and-cents point of view it is quite obvious that over a period of years, even those who find themselves at the short end of inequality have more to gain from faster growth than from any conceivable income redistribution.
                    ROGER M. BLOUGH, 1957

It is the resentment aroused by spiritual humiliation that gives rise to an irrational response to rational exploitation. The apparently unreasonable, and certainly unprofitable, resistance of many of the world's underdeveloped countries today to Western business enterprise makes sense only in this context.   DAVID LANDES, 1958

Foreign economic aid, far from contributing to rapid economic development along democratic lines, is likely to retard improvement in the well-being of the masses, to strengthen the government sector at the expense of the private sector, and to undermine democracy and freedom.
                    MILTON FRIEDMAN, 1958

Industrialized economies have never relied on increased physical effort by workers for economic growth.   VAN D. KENNEDY, 1960

In an era in which economic progress depends so much on scientific research, such chronic underemployment of technical knowledge might have, in the long run, an even more deleterious

effect on the rate of economic growth than idle capital or unemployed labor.
WASSILY LEONTIEF, 1960

It is very much easier for a rich man to invest and grow richer than for the poor man to begin investing at all. And this is also true of nations.
BARBARA WARD, 1962

Every country has peasants—ours have money.
GLORIA STEINEM, 1964

If the criteria of the International Monetary Fund had governed the United States in the nineteenth century, our own economic development would have taken a great deal longer. In preaching fiscal orthodoxy to developing nations, we were somewhat in the position of the prostitute who, having retired on her earnings, believes that public virtue requires the closing down of the red-light district.
ARTHUR SCHLESINGER, JR., 1965

Imperialism was born when the ruling class in capitalist production came up against national limits to its economic expansion.
HANNAH ARENDT, 1966

The primary conflict, I think, is between people whose interests are with already well-established economic activities, and those whose interests are with the emergence of new economic activities.
JANE JACOBS, 1969

For many years economic growth has been treated as an end in itself. Somewhere along the line economists forgot that increased GNP is a means.
ARTHUR CORDELL, 1970

The idea of progress is not merely a dream unfulfilled but an inherent absurdity.
PHILIP SLATER, 1970

If you think the United States has stood still, who built the largest shopping center in the world?
RICHARD M. NIXON, 1972

Growth tends to threaten traditional middle-class values: it is felt to be disruptive and unpleasant precisely because it turns minority privileges into majority ones—because it means crowded roads, crowded beaches, and so on.
RUDOLF KLEIN, 1972

The era of low cost energy is almost dead. Popeye has run out of cheap spinach.
PETER PATERSON, 1972

Economic growth is not only unnecessary, but ruinous.
ALEKSANDR SOLZHENITSYN, 1973

Economic growth has been a political solvent. While growth invariably raises expectations, the means of financing social welfare expenditures and defense without reallocating income (always a politically difficult matter) or burdening the poor (which has become an equally difficult affair) has come essentially from economic growth.
DANIEL BELL, 1974

There is an absolute limit to the ability of the earth to support or tolerate the process of industrial activity, and there is reason to believe that we are now moving toward the limit very rapidly.
ROBERT L. HEILBRONER, 1974

There's a limit to the good things we have in this country. We're coming up against those limits.
JERRY BROWN, 1975

In an underdeveloped country don't drink the water; in a developed country, don't breathe the air.
JONATHAN RABAN, 1976

Transnational enterprises have been powerful instruments of modernization both in industrial nations and in the developing countries where there is often no substitute for their ability to marshal capital, management skills, technology and initiative. Thus the controversy over their role and conduct is itself an obstacle to economic development.
HENRY KISSINGER, 1976

Development in the Third World usually means the over-development of objects and the under-development of people.   RICHARD GOTT, 1976

We have learned that more is not necessarily better, that even our great nation has its recognized limits, and that we can neither answer all questions nor solve all problems. We cannot afford to do everything.   JIMMY CARTER, 1977

What the Arabs cleverly have done is to put the New York banks in the front row of risk. In other words, if Zaire goes kaput, Chase Manhattan is in trouble.   PAUL ERDMAN, 1977

Watch the developing countries. It's a trillion dollar race.   HERMAN KAHN, 1978

The people of the United States must be content to watch the standard of living rise more slowly.   JIMMY CARTER, 1979

We don't have a desperate need to grow. We have a desperate desire to grow.   MILTON FRIEDMAN, 1979

Income

If we did not see it with our own eyes, could we ever imagine the extraordinary disproportion created between men by a larger or smaller degree of wealth.   JEAN DE LA BRUYÈRE, 1688

The riches of the several members of a community contribute to increase my riches, whatever profession I may follow. They consume the produce of my industry, and afford me the produce of theirs in return. Nor need any state entertain apprehensions that their neighbors will improve to such a degree in every art and manufacture as to have no demand from them.   DAVID HUME, 1739

The distribution of wealth not only regulates and decides the channels in which the industry of every country is embarked, and, of course, the articles in the production of which it excels; but a proper distribution of wealth insures the increase of opulence, by sustaining a regular progressive demand in the home market, and still more effectually, by affording to those whose habits are likely to create a desire of supplanting labor, the power of executing it.   LORD LAUDERDALE, 1804

Our incomes are like our shoes; if too small, they gall and pinch us; but if too large, they cause us to stumble and to trip.   CHARLES C. COLTON, 1822

The larger the income, the harder it is to live within it.   RICHARD WHATELY, 1832

The distribution of wealth depends on the laws and customs of society. The rules by which it is determined, are what the opinions and feelings of the ruling portion of the community make them, and are very different in different ages and countries; and might be still more different if mankind so chooses.

JOHN STUART MILL, 1848

The rich and the poor—the have-nots and the haves. EDWARD R. BULWER-LYTTON, 1856

You cannot bring about prosperity by discouraging thrift. You cannot strengthen the weak by weakening the strong. You cannot help the wage earner by pulling down the wage payer. You cannot help the poor by destroying the rich.

ABRAHAM LINCOLN, 1860

As a general rule, nobody has money who ought to have it. BENJAMIN DISRAELI, 1867

What has destroyed every previous civilization has been the tendency to the unequal distribution of wealth and power.

HENRY GEORGE, 1879

The impassable gulf that lies between riches and poverty. ELIZABETH CADY STANTON, 1881

Too long, that some may rest,
Tired millions toil inblest.

WILLIAM WATSON, 1907

Income, n. The natural and rational gauge and measure of respectability, the commonly accepted standards being artificial, arbitrary and fallacious. AMBROSE BIERCE, 1911

Since the income available for distribution is limited, and since, therefore, when certain limits have been passed, what one group gains another group must lose, it is evident that if the relative incomes of different groups are not to be determined by their functions, there is no method other than mutual self-assertion which is left to determine them.

RICHARD H. TAWNEY, 1920

The contribution made by any one person to the total demand for goods is, in the long run, bound to be just equal to his income, no more no less. FRED M. TAYLOR, 1921

Maybe they call it take-home pay because there is no other place you can afford to go with it.

FRANKLIN P. JONES, 1924

It is still imagined by many that inequalities of income coincide broadly with inequalities of merit. HUGH DALTON, 1925

God must love the poor, said Lincoln, or he wouldn't have made so many of them. He must love the rich, or he wouldn't divide so much mazuma among so few of them.

H. L. MENCKEN, 1927

Indeed, I thought, slipping the silver into my purse, it is remarkable, remembering the bitterness of those days, what a change of temper a fixed income will bring about.

VIRGINIA WOOLF, 1929

There are several ways in which to apportion the family income, all of them unsatisfactory.

ROBERT BENCHLEY, 1930

A man's income [is] the maximum amount which he can consume during a week, and still expect to be as well off at the end of the week as he was at the beginning. JOHN R. HICKS, 1939

There is nothing more demoralizing than a small but adequate income.

EDMUND WILSON, 1950

A radically unequal distribution of income has been characteristic of the American social structure since at least 1910, and despite minor year-to-year fluctuations in the shares of the income-tenths, no significant trend toward income equality has appeared.

GABRIEL KOLKO, 1962

Middle income: that means, if.you steal, you can pay the rent.

GODFREY CAMBRIDGE, 1964

All social values—liberty and opportunity, income and wealth, and the bases of self-respect—are to be distributed equally unless an unequal distribution of any, or all, of these values is to everyone's advantage.

JOHN RAWLS, 1971

People of privilege will always risk their complete destruction rather than surrender any material part of their advantage.

JOHN KENNETH GALBRAITH, 1977

Inflation

Though the wages of the workman are commonly paid to him in money, his real revenue, like that of all other men, consists, not in money, but in the money's worth, not in the metal pieces, but in what can be got for them.

ADAM SMITH, 1776

The power of the laborer to support himself . . . does not depend on the quantity of money which he may receive for wages, but on the quantity of food, necessaries, and conveniences become essential to him from habit, which that money will purchase.   DAVID RICARDO, 1817

Ordinary tyranny, oppression, excessive taxation, these bear lightly on the happiness of the mass of the community, compared with fraudulent currencies and the robberies committed by depreciated paper.   DANIEL WEBSTER, 1832

All variations in the value of the circulating medium are mischievous: they disturb existing contracts and expectations, and the liability to such changes renders every pecuniary engagement of long date entirely precarious. The person who buys for himself, or gives to another, an annuity of £100, does not know whether it will be equivalent to £200 or to £50 a few years hence.   JOHN STUART MILL, 1848

The whole civilized world is now eager to know whether in the future the high cost of living is to advance further, recede or remain stationary. Opinions are plentiful but data supporting them are few.   IRVING FISHER, 1912

I think some folks are foolish to pay what it costs to live.

FRANK MCKINNEY HUBBARD, 1916

Inflation is repudiation.

CALVIN COOLIDGE, 1922

No economist has ever held that the general level of prices can be exactly stabilized. There will always be fluctuations of the general level up and down, even with the most perfect stabilization of prices. What is really meant by stabilization of prices is in fact merely the stabilization of "the general credit situation," so as to avoid only the excessive peaks and excessive slumps of the general price level.

JOHN R. COMMONS, 1925

It is an economic axiom as old as the hills that goods and services can be paid for only with goods and services.

ALBERT JAY NOCK, 1928

Inflation might also be called legal counterfeiting.

IRVING FISHER, 1928

It's a great country, but you can't live in it for nothing.

WILL ROGERS, 1929

I haven't heard of anybody who wants to stop living on account of the cost.

FRANK MCKINNEY HUBBARD, 1929

What this country needs is a good five-cent nickel.

FRANKLIN P. ADAMS, 1932

With old inflation riding the headlines, I have read till I'm bleary-eyed, and I can't get head from tails of the whole thing. We are living in an age of explanations, and plenty of them, too, but no two things that's been done to us has been explained twice the same way—by even the same man.

WILL ROGERS, 1934

Whilst workers will usually resist a reduction of money-wages, it is not their practice to withdraw their labor whenever there is a rise in the price of wage-goods. It is sometimes said that it would be illogical for labor to resist a reduction of money-wages but not to resist a reduction of real wages. . . . But, whether logical or illogical, experience shows that this is how labor in fact behaves.

JOHN MAYNARD KEYNES, 1936

The cost of living has gone up another dollar a quart.

W. C. FIELDS, 1937

An individual cannot by saving more protect himself from the consequences of inflation if others do not follow his example; just as he cannot protect himself from accidents by obeying the rule of the road if others disregard it.

JOHN MAYNARD KEYNES, 1940

A severe inflation is the worst kind of revolution.

THOMAS MANN, 1942

Increased wages, higher pensions, more unemployment insurance, all are of no avail if the purchasing power of money falls faster.

BERNARD M. BARUCH, 1954

Actually we are slaves to the cost of living.

CAROLINE MARIA DE JESUS, 1955

Inflation is like sin; every government denounces it and every government practices it.

FREDERICK LEITH-ROSS, 1957

One of the main factors in the inflation that we have had since the end of World War II is that many consumers, businessmen, and trade union leaders expected prices to rise and therefore acted in ways that helped to bring about this result.

ARTHUR F. BURNS, 1957

Inflation is a bigger danger than Russia, a bigger danger than recession, a bigger danger than anything this country has encountered in the last several years.

WILLIAM E. UMSTATTD, 1958

Prices are going up by the elevator and wages are going up by the stairs.

ROBERT A. BEER, 1965

Inflation in the Sixties was a nuisance to be endured, like varicose veins or French foreign policy.

BERNARD LEVIN, 1970

Inflation is always and everywhere a monetary phenomenon.   MILTON FRIEDMAN, 1970

The rules of economics are not working in quite the way they used to. Despite extensive unemployment in our country, wage rate increases have not moderated. Despite much idle industrial capacity, commodity prices continue to rise rapidly.   ARTHUR F. BURNS, 1971

Wage increases are the result of inflation, and not the cause.   MILTON FRIEDMAN, 1971

Inflation is the one form of taxation that can be imposed without legislation.
          MILTON FRIEDMAN, 1973

The first few months or years of inflation, like the first few drinks, seem just fine. Everyone has more money to spend and prices aren't rising quite as fast as the money that's available. The hangover comes when prices start to catch up. And, of course, some people are hurt worse than others by inflation. Some people aren't hurt at all. And others profit enormously.
          MILTON FRIEDMAN, 1973

All major crises have been caused by previous inflation, which is far from being isolated and which, sooner or later, leads to collapse.
          FRIEDRICH A. HAYEK, 1974

The real causes of inflation lie deeper than monetary factors. They nonetheless are not unalterable. The present widespread concern about inflation gives hope that people will indeed demand changes in economic structure and policy that will bring down inflation.

          HENRY WALLICH, 1974

I offer my opinion that inflation is greatly exaggerated as a social evil. Even while prices are rising year after year, the economy is producing more and more of the goods, services and jobs that meet people's needs. That, after all, is its real purpose.   JAMES TOBIN, 1974

During the recent boom, some carelessness crept into our financial system, as usually happens in a time of inflation.   ARTHUR F. BURNS, 1974

We all have a stake in this economy. Everybody is hurt by inflation. If you really wanted to examine percentage-wise who was hurt most in their income, it was Wall Street brokers.
          ALAN GREENSPAN, 1974

Inflation is bringing us true democracy. For the first time in history, luxuries and necessities are selling at the same price.
          ROBERT ORBEN, 1975

Inflation does lubricate trade but by rescuing traders from their errors of optimism or stupidity.   JOHN KENNETH GALBRAITH, 1975

Inflation is just a high-priced depression.
          BETTE LOWREY, 1975

In Latin America a rise of prices under 10 percent is regarded as deflation.
          GOTTFRIED HARBERLER, 1975

Inflation, generalized and permanent, arbitrarily redistributes wealth in no relation to work and productivity.   NELLO CELIO, 1975

We have a love-hate relationship with inflation. We hate inflation, but we love everything that causes it.   WILLIAM SIMON, 1975

Inflation is a great conservatizing issue.
          GEORGE WILL, 1977

There's only one place where inflation is made: that's in Washington.
          MILTON FRIEDMAN, 1977

I've got all the money I'll ever need if I die by four o'clock.   HENNY YOUNGMAN, 1977

Inflation has not found its Keynes. I personally think the Keynes of inflation will not be an economist. He will be a political, philosophical or moral leader inspiring people to do without the excess consumption so prominent in the developed countries.   PIERRE TRUDEAU, 1977

There's nothing wrong with the Republican Party that double-digit inflation won't cure.
RICHARD SCAMMON, 1978

Inflation is like a crowd at a football game. No one is willing to be the first to sit down.
JIMMY CARTER, 1978

The fight against inflation must be on the basis of the equality of sacrifice, not the sacrifice of equality.   GEORGE MEANY, 1979

The standard of living of the average American has to decline.   PAUL A. VOLCKER, 1979

Since money is the base line for any discussion of American society, inflation has accelerated the aging process of The Good Old Days.
CALVIN TRILLIN, 1979

Inflation is like a dictator. It must be fought before it becomes established or it is too late.
OTMAR EMMINGER, 1979

We know now that inflation results from all that deficit spending.   RONALD REAGAN, 1981

The government fighting inflation is like the Mafia fighting crime.
LAURENCE J. PETER, 1982

Interest

Nothing is esteemed a more certain sign of the flourishing condition of any nation than the lowness of interest.   DAVID HUME, 1754

No law can reduce the common rate of interest below the lowest ordinary market rate at the time when that law is made.
ADAM SMITH, 1776

The lowest ordinary rate of interest must, in the same manner, be something more than sufficient to compensate the occasional losses to which lending, even with tolerable prudence, is

exposed. Were it not more, charity or friendship could be the only motives for lending.
ADAM SMITH, 1776

It may be laid down as a maxim, that wherever a great deal can be made by the use of money, a great deal will commonly be given for the use of it.   ADAM SMITH, 1776

To ascertain how far the desires of obtaining loans at the bank may be expected at any time to be carried, we must inquire into the subject of the quantum of profit likely to be derived from borrowing there under the existing circumstances. This is to be judged of by considering two points: the amount, first, of interest to be paid on the sum borrowed; and, secondly, of the mercantile or other gain to be obtained by the employment of the borrowed capital.

HENRY THORNTON, 1802

We have heard it said that five percent is the natural interest of money.

THOMAS MACAULEY, 1830

Under a more favorable distribution of property, there cannot be a doubt that such a demand for produce, agricultural, manufacturing and mercantile, might have been created, as to have prevented for many, many years the interest on money from falling below 3 percent.

THOMAS MALTHUS, 1836

The fact is, in my opinion, that we often buy money very much too dear.

WILLIAM MAKEPEACE THACKERAY, 1857

Interest works night and day, in fair weather and in foul. It gnaws at a man's substance with invisible teeth.

HENRY WARD BEECHER, 1873

The sweet simplicity of three per cents.

BENJAMIN DISRAELI, 1880

It is always better policy to earn an interest than to make a thousand pounds.

ROBERT LOUIS STEVENSON, 1887

That surplus benefit which a person gets in the long run by postponing enjoyment, and which is measured by the rate of interest, is the reward of waiting.   ALFRED MARSHALL, 1890

There are three forms of usury: interest on money, rent of land and houses, and profit in exchange. Whoever is in receipt of any of these is a usurer.   BENJAMIN R. TUCKER, 1893

The rate of interest at which the demand for loanable capital and the supply of savings exactly agree, and which more or less corresponds to the expected yield on newly created capital, will then be the normal or natural real rate.

KNUT WICKSELL, 1898

The truth is that the rate of interest is not a narrow phenomenom applying only to a few business contracts, but permeates all economic relations. It is a link which binds man to the future and by which he makes all his far-reaching decisions.   IRVING FISHER, 1907

In the early days there was often much discussion as to what should be paid for the use of money. Many people protested that the rate of 10 per cent was outrageous, and none but a wicked man would exact such a charge. I was accustomed to argue that money was worth what it would bring—no one would pay 10 per cent, or 5 per cent, or 3 per cent unless the borrower believed that at this rate it was profitable to employ it.   JOHN D. ROCKEFELLER, 1909

The theory [of interest] is one of investment opportunity and human impatience as well as exchange.   IRVING FISHER, 1911

To the trader the high rate of interest presents itself in the first instance as an expense to be subtracted from his profits, but behind this initial loss looms the far more serious menace of a difficulty in borrowing, which will affect not merely himself but those to whom he hopes to sell.   R. G. HAWTREY, 1919

Usury is the taking of any interest whatever upon an unproductive loan.

HILAIRE BELLOC, 1921

The great bulk of what I call automatic saving will scarcely be affected by a fall in the rate of interest except in so far as this reduces the aggregate unearned incomes. Some sort of conscious thrift, aiming to make a definite provision of income for old age or other future contingency, may even be stimulated, instead of depressed, by a falling rate of interest which demands a larger volume of saving to yield the required income.   JOHN A. HOBSON, 1923

All the stability that the world of business has so far enjoyed and is capable of is the gift of the natural stability of interest.
                          JOHN A. HOBSON, 1925

Man was lost if he went to a usurer, for the interest ran faster than a tiger upon him.
                          PEARL S. BUCK, 1933

The rate of interest is the reward for parting with liquidity for a specified period.
                          JOHN MAYNARD KEYNES, 1936

A boom is a situation in which over-optimism triumphs over a rate of interest which, in a cooler light, would be seen to be excessive.
                          JOHN MAYNARD KEYNES, 1936

The actual amount investors will actually invest will depend on the rate of interest. They will invest up to the point where they feel that the likely return on their capital will be equal to the market rate of interest.
                          JOHN MAYNARD KEYNES, 1936

The interest rate is not only an expression of the force of nature: it also depends on the wisdom of men.   PIERRE MASSÉ, 1962

Investment

All men's gains are the fruit of venturing.
                          HERODOTUS, fifth century B.C.

No gain is possible without attendant outlay, but there will be no profit if the outlay exceeds the receipts.   PLAUTUS, C. 218 B.C.

Nothing is to be had for nothing.
                          EPICTETUS, C. a.d. 138

A citizen should never hesitate to increase his property for fear it will be taken away from him, or to open a business for fear of taxes.
                          NICCOLÒ MACHIAVELLI, 1513

Be not penny-wise; riches have wings, and sometimes they fly away of themselves, sometimes they must be sent flying to bring in more.
                          FRANCIS BACON, 1625

You must lose a fly to catch a trout.
                          GEORGE HERBERT, 1640

Now it cannot be rationally expected, but that where the venture is great, and the gains small, many will choose rather to hoard up their money, than venture it abroad on such terms.
                          JOHN LOCKE, 1692

To hazard much to get much has more of avarice than wisdom.   WILLIAM PENN, 1693

Every noble acquisition is attended with its risks; he who fears to encounter the one must not expect to obtain the other.

PIETRO METASTASIO, 1722

Many of the questions both in morals and politics seem to be of the nature of the problems de maximis et minimis in fluxions; in which there is always a point where a certain effect is the greatest, while on the either side of this point it gradually diminishes.

THOMAS MALTHUS, 1814

Through life's dark road his sordid way he
     wends,
An incarnation of fat dividends.

CHARLES SPRAGUE, 1841

People do not grow rich by keeping their money unused . . . they must be willing to spend in order to gain.   JOHN STUART MILL, 1848

Ah, but a man's reach should exceed his grasp
Or what's a heaven for?

ROBERT BROWNING, 1861

Our great father has a big safe, and so have we. The hill is our safe. . . . We want seventy million dollars for the Black Hills. Put the money away some place at interest so we can buy livestock. That is the way the white people do.

MATO GLESKA (SPOTTED BEAR), c. 1875

The man who makes no mistakes does not usually make anything.

EDWARD JOHN PHELPS, 1899

More money has been made in real estate than in all industrial investments combined.

ANDREW CARNEGIE, 1902

Remember, my son, that any man who is a bear on the future of this country will go broke.

J. PIERPONT MORGAN, 1908

We are all dependent upon the investment of capital.   WILLIAM H. TAFT, 1908

No one could suspect that times were coming . . . when the man who did not gamble would lose all the time, even more surely than he who gambled.   CHARLES PÉGUY, 1912

The discrepancy which discourages business men is a discrepancy between that nominal capitalization which they have set their hearts upon through habitation in the immediate past and that actual capitalizable value of their property which its current earning capacity will warrant. But where the preconceptions of the business men engaged have, as commonly happens, in great part, been fixed and legalized in the form of interest-bearing securities, this malady of the affections becomes extremely difficult to remedy.

THORSTEIN VEBLEN, 1915

If managers succeed beyond their expectations, their very success evokes the law of capitalization and leads to an increase in the value of the investments upon which in the future they are expected to pay dividends. Thus success, instead of bringing relief, merely renews the slavery.   WALTON H. HAMILTON, 1918

If the sources of capital investment are dried up, the flow of all income may eventually cease.

ANDREW MELLON, 1924

Inequality of foresight produces overinvestment during rising prices and relative stagnation during falling prices. In the former case society is trapped into devoting too much investment of productive energies for future return, while in the contrary case, underinvestment is the rule.

IRVING FISHER, 1930

Partly on reasonable and partly on instinctive grounds our desire to hold money as a store of wealth is a barometer of the degree of our distrust of our own calculations and conventions concerning the future. The possession of money lulls our disquietude; the premium which we require to make us part with money is a measure of the degree of our disquietude.

JOHN MAYNARD KEYNES, 1930

The chances of success of a given investment (whether of capital or labor) depend on the efficiency with which all those who work in the same firm cooperate with the factor in question.

JOHN R. HICKS, 1931

Hard work is the best investment a man can make.   CHARLES M. SCHWAB, 1931

Don't be afraid to take a big step when one is indicated. You can't cross a chasm in two small jumps.   DAVID LLOYD GEORGE, 1936

Businessmen play a mixed game of skill and chance, the average results of which to the players are not known by those who take a hand. If human nature felt no temptation to take a chance, no satisfaction (profit apart) in constructing a factory, a railway, a mine or a farm, there might not be much investment merely as a result of cold calculation.

JOHN MAYNARD KEYNES, 1936

If we speak frankly, we have to admit that our basis of knowledge for estimating the yield ten years hence of a railway, a copper mine, a textile factory, the goodwill of a patent medicine, an Atlantic liner, and a building in the City of London amounts to little and sometimes to nothing; or even five years hence.

JOHN MAYNARD KEYNES, 1936

There is no clear evidence from experience that the investment policy which is socially advantageous coincides with that which is most profitable.   JOHN MAYNARD KEYNES, 1936

The amount of current investment will depend, in turn, on what we shall call the inducement to invest; and the inducement to invest will be found to depend on the relation between the schedule of marginal efficiency of capital and the complex of interest rates on loans of various maturities and risks.

JOHN MAYNARD KEYNES, 1936

In investing money, the amount of interest you want should depend on whether you want to eat well or sleep well.

J. KENFIELD MORLEY, 1937

No one is likely to challenge the statement that foreign investment will in the next fifty years play an incomparably smaller role than was the case in the nineteenth century.

ALVIN HANSEN, 1938

Take calculated risks. That is quite different from being rash.   GEORGE S. PATTON, 1944

A greater amount of fixed capital should be invested so long as the annual interest on the capital plus the annual cost of repair, depreciation, etc., is less than the price of any additional output expected from the investment plus the price of any existing prime factors which it is expected to save, minus the price of any additional prime factor which it is expected to take on as a result of the investment.

J. E. MEADE, 1944

Long-range investing under rapidly changing conditions, especially under conditions that change or may change at any moment under the impact of new commodities and technologies, is like shooting at a target that is not only indistinct but moving and moving jerkily at that.

JOSEPH A. SCHUMPETER, 1947

Dollars do better if they are accompanied by sense.   EARL RINEY, 1951

Behold the turtle. He makes progress only when he sticks his neck out.
          JAMES BRYANT CONANT, 1953

Never invest your money in anything that eats or needs repairing.   BILLY ROSE, 1957

The fundamental difficulty of uncertainty cannot really be dodged; and since it cannot be faced, it must simply be ignored.
          ROBERT M. SOLOW, 1963

What is the worth of a market average . . . which works except when it doesn't work.
          DAVID L. HOFFMAN, 1967

Economists are agreed that an important factor in causing income and employment to fluctuate is fluctuations in investment. Whether we are to face a situation of inflationary bidding up of prices or shall live in a frigid state of mass unemployment can depend upon the level of investment.   PAUL A. SAMUELSON, 1970

You can't expect to hit the jackpot if you don't put a few nickels in the machine.
          FLIP WILSON, 1971

To understand uncertainty and risk is to understand the key business problem—and the key business opportunity.
          DAVID B. HERTZ, 1972

Americans want action for their money. They are fascinated by its self-reproducing qualities if it's put to work.   PAULA NELSON, 1975

Capital formation is shifting from the entrepreneur who invests in the future to the pension trustee who invests in the past.
          PETER DRUCKER, 1977

Oil is a wasting asset, and if you don't invest [its revenues] in profitable assets, you'll be left with nothing.   DENZIL DAVIES, 1980

The higher the monkey climbs, the more he shows his ass.   THOMAS WATSON, SR., 1982

Labor

More will be accomplished, and better, and with more ease, if every man does what he is best fitted to do, and nothing else.
          PLATO, C. 374 B.C.

The herd of hirelings.   PLAUTUS, C. 200 B.C.

We ought not to treat living creatures like shoes or household belongings, which when worn with use we throw away.   PLUTARCH, C. A.D. 90

I wonder why an employee should have to be subservient to his employer, and should have to please and praise him.

          JOSEPH IBN PAKUDA, 1040

He that labors and thrives spins gold.
GEORGE HERBERT, 1640

Labor is the father and active principle of wealth, as lands are the mother.
WILLIAM PETTY, 1662

Alexander the Great, reflecting on his friends degenerating into sloth and luxury, told them that it was a most slavish thing to luxuriate, and a most royal thing to labor.
ISAAC BARROW, 1669

Men in business are in as much danger from those at work under them as from those that work against them.
MARQUESS OF HALIFAX, c. 1680

I think it will be but a very modest computation to say, that of the products of the earth useful to the life of man, 9/10 are the effects of labor.
JOHN LOCKE, 1681

Labor makes the far greatest part of the value of things.
JOHN LOCKE, 1689

The greatest part of mankind are given up to labor, whose lives are worn out only in the provisions for living.
JOHN LOCKE, 1691

The wealth of all nations arises from the labor and industry of the people.
CHARLES DAVENANT, 1698

Everything in the world is purchased by labor.
DAVID HUME, 1754

When bad men combine, the good must associate, else they will fall, one by one, an unpitied sacrifice in a contemptible struggle.
EDMUND BURKE, 1770

The whole produce of labor does not always belong to the laborer. He must in most cases share it with the owner of the stock which employs him.
ADAM SMITH, 1776

In the original state of things which precedes both the accumulation of land and the accumulation of stock, the whole produce of labor belongs to the laborer. He has neither landlord nor master to share with him.
ADAM SMITH, 1776

The man whose whole life is spent in performing a few simple operations, of which the effects are perhaps always the same, or very nearly the same, has no occasion to exert his understanding or to exercise his invention in finding out expedients for removing difficulties which never occur. He naturally loses, therefore, the habit of such exertion, and generally becomes as stupid and ignorant as it is possible for a human creature to become.
ADAM SMITH, 1776

What are the common wages of labor, depends everywhere upon the contract usually made between those two parties [master and workman], whose interests are by no means the same. . . . It is not, however, difficult to foresee which of the two parties must, upon all ordinary occasions have the advantage in the dispute and force the other into a compliance with their terms.
ADAM SMITH, 1776

Labor . . . is the real measure of the exchangeable value of all commodities.
ADAM SMITH, 1776

The price of the necessaries of life is, in fact, the cost of producing labor.
THOMAS MALTHUS, 1815

Such hath it been—shall be—beneath the sun:
The many still must labor for the one.
LORD BYRON, 1817

It is not to be understood that the natural price of labor, estimated even in food and necessities, is absolutely fixed and constant. It varies at different times in the same country, and very materially differs in different countries. It essentially depends on the habits and customs of the people.   DAVID RICARDO, 1817

Labor in this country is independent and proud. It has not to ask the patronage of capital, but capital solicits the aid of labor.
DANIEL WEBSTER, 1824

There is more danger that capital will swallow up the profits of labor, than that labor will confiscate capital.   GEORGE BANCROFT, 1834

When a workman is unceasingly and exclusively engaged in the fabrication of one thing, he ultimately does his work with singular dexterity; but at the same time he loses the general faculty of applying his mind to the direction of the work. He every day becomes more adroit and less industrious; so that it may be said of him that in proportion as the workman improves, the man is degraded.
ALEXIS DE TOCQUEVILLE, 1839

Labor is discovered to be the grand conqueror, enriching and building up nations more surely than the proudest battles.
WILLIAM ELLERY CHANNING II, 1847

There can be little doubt that the relations of masters and work people will be gradually superceded by partnerships in one or two forms; in some cases, association of the laborers with the capitalists; in others, and perhaps finally in all, association of laborers among themselves.
JOHN STUART MILL, 1848

The proletarians have nothing to lose but their chains. They have a world to win. Workers of the world, unite!
KARL MARX AND FRIEDRICH ENGELS, 1848

Economic perfection lies in the absolute independence of the workers, just as political perfection consists in the absolute independence of the citizens.
PIERRE JOSEPH PROUDHON, 1858

I believe it can be easily shown that the laborer is placed at a disadvantage if he attempts simply as an individual to arrange his bargain, and I further believe that laborers must show that they have the power of combining, in order at all times to be able to sell their labor on the best possible terms.   HENRY FAWCETT, 1865

Labor—the expenditure of vital effort in some form—is the measure, nay, it is the maker of values.   JOSIAH G. HOLLAND, 1865

Eight hours for work,
Eight hours for sleep,
Eight hours for what you will.
SLOGAN, NATIONAL LABOR UNION
OF THE UNITED STATES, 1866

The value of labor power is the value of the means of subsistence necessary for the maintenance of the laborer.   KARL MARX, 1867

The machinery of labor strikes down the laborer.   KARL MARX, 1867

It is in the absolute interest of every capitalist to press a given quantity of labor out of a smaller rather than a greater number of laborers, if the cost is about the same.   KARL MARX, 1867

The methods by which a trade union can alone act are necessarily destructive; its organization is necessarily tyrannical.
HENRY GEORGE, 1879

The very last thing the ordinary industrial worker wants is to have to think about his work.
GEORGE BERNARD SHAW, 1882

We denounce the importation of contract labor, whether from Europe or Asia, as an offense against the spirit of American institutions.
REPUBLICAN NATIONAL PLATFORM, 1884

Labor is the capital of our working man.
GROVER CLEVELAND, 1885

Trade unionism has enabled skilled artisans and even many classes of unskilled workers, to enter into negotiations with their employers with the same gravity, self-restraint, dignity and fore-thought as are observed in the diplomacy of great nations. It has led them to recognize that a simply aggressive policy is a foolish policy, and that the chief use of military resources is to preserve an advantageous peace.
ALFRED MARSHALL, 1890

The laborer is at no disadvantage in bargaining with the employer, who is tied to his machines, which he must keep fully employed, or perish financially.
T. S. CREE, 1891

And you prate of the wealth of nations, as if it
    were bought and sold,
The wealth of nations is men, not silk and cot-
    ton and gold.
RICHARD HOVEY, 1892

Men do not compare themselves with their ancestors, but with their contemporaries. You cannot appease a restless workman by telling him how much better off he is than his simian progenitor. What he feels is his dependence on his fellowman, who is growing richer every day upon the fruits of his poorly paid toil.
JOHN R. COMMONS, 1894

The industrial field is littered with more corpses or organizations destroyed by the damning influences of partisan political action than from all other causes combined.
SAMUEL GOMPERS, 1896

The man who is employed for wages is as much a businessman as his employer.
WILLIAM JENNINGS BRYAN, 1896

A scab in labor unions is the same as a traitor to his country.
EUGENE V. DEBS, 1897

For labor a short day is better than a short dollar.
WILLIAM MCKINLEY, 1900

Pure and simple trade unionism means the ideological subordination of the workers to the bourgeoisie.
NIKOLAI LENIN, 1902

Composed as it is of the men of muscle rather than the men of intelligence, and commanded by leaders who are at heart disciples of revolution, it is not strange that organized labor stands for principles that are in direct conflict with the natural laws of economics.
DAVID PARRY, 1903

In an English ship, they say, it is poor grub, poor pay, and easy work; in an American ship, good grub, good pay, and hard work. And this is applicable to the working populations of both countries.
JACK LONDON, 1903

A man is a worker. If he is not that he is nothing.
JOSEPH CONRAD, 1906

Labor, n. One of the processes by which A acquires property for B.
AMBROSE BIERCE, 1906

We all belong t' th' union when it come t' wantin' more money and less work.
FRANK MCKINNEY HUBBARD, 1906

With all their faults, trade-unions have done more for humanity than any other organization of men that ever existed.
CLARENCE DARROW, 1909

After God had finished the rattlesnake, the toad, the vampire, He had some awful substance left with which He made a scab.
                                    JACK LONDON, 1910

A demand for commodities is not a demand for labor. The demand for labor is determined by the amount of capital directly devoted to the remuneration of labor: the demand for commodities simply determines in what direction labor shall be employed.
                    MILLICENT GARRETT FAWCETT, 1911

America . . . cannot develop citizens unless the workingmen possess industrial liberty; and industrial liberty is impossible if the right to organize be denied.   LOUIS D. BRANDEIS, 1912

Labor cannot on any terms surrender the right to strike.   LOUIS D. BRANDEIS, 1913

What labor is demanding all over the world today is not a few material things like more dollars and fewer hours of work, but the right to a voice in the conduct of industry.
                                    SIDNEY HILLMAN, 1918

There is no right to strike against the public safety by anybody, anywhere, anytime.
                                    CALVIN COOLIDGE, 1919

To say that a working man loses his individualism or his sovereignty in joining a union of labor is begging the question entirely. The fact of the matter is as soon as a man enters an industrial plant he loses his individuality and becomes a cog in a great revolving machine.
                                    SAMUEL GOMPERS, 1919

The trade agreement has become a rather distinct feature of the American labor movement. . . . It is based on the idea that labor shall accept the capitalist system of production and makes terms of peace with it.
                                    MARY RITTER BEARD, 1920

The organized labor movement is the advance guard. It is the militant expression of the desires of all the workers.   SAMUEL GOMPERS, 1920

Never forget that men who labor cast the votes, set up and pull down governments.
                                    ELIHU ROOT, 1921

The strike is the weapon of the industrial jungle.   SIDNEY HILLMAN, 1921

Unionism seldom, if ever, uses such power as it has to insure better work; almost always it devotes a large part of that power to safeguarding bad work.   H. L. MENCKEN, 1922

Industry must manage to keep wages high and prices low. Otherwise it will limit the number of its customers. One's own employees should be one's best customers.
                                    HENRY FORD, 1922

Fight labor's demands to the last ditch and there will come a time when it seizes the whole of power, makes itself sovereign and takes what it used to ask.   WALTER LIPPMANN, 1922

Where there is most labor there is not always most life.   HAVELOCK ELLIS, 1923

Of what use is culture to a laborer?
                                    EMANUEL SHINWELL, 1923

Show me the country in which there are no strikes and I'll show you that country in which there is no liberty.   SAMUEL GOMPERS, 1924

Not a penny off the pay; not a minute on the day.   A. J. COOK, 1925

Neither the common law nor the Fourteenth Amendment confers the absolute right to strike.
                                    LOUIS D. BRANDEIS, 1926

Facts show that politically independent trade unions do not exist anywhere. There have never been any. Experience and theory say that there never will be any.   LEON TROTSKY, 1929

I am a friend of the working man, and I would rather be his friend than be one.
                                 CLARENCE DARROW, 1929

So long as the thoughts of a worker do not, and cannot, go beyond the near implications of his labor bargain, and his sense of cooperation is confined to his trade union, it is idle to suppose that the more general problems of our economic system can be rightly solved.
                                 JOHN A. HOBSON, 1929

If business be unprofitable on account of bad management, want of enterprise or out-worn methods, that is not a just reason for reducing the wages of its workers.
                                 POPE PIUS XI, 1931

Had the employers of the past generation dealt fairly with men, there would have been no trade unions.   STANLEY BALDWIN, 1931

The American worker is merely a capitalist without money.   GEORGE SOKOLSKY, 1934

Pappenhacker says that every time you are polite to a proletarian you are helping bolster up the capitalist system.   EVELYN WAUGH, 1938

We gain nothing by trading the tyranny of capital for the tyranny of labor.
                                 LOUIS D. BRANDEIS, 1941

You can't dig coal with bayonets.
                                 JOHN L. LEWIS, 1942

The Taft-Hartley Statute is the first ugly, savage thrust of fascism in America. It came into being through an alliance between industrialists and the Republican majority in Congress, aided and abetted by those Democratic legislators who still believe in the institution of human slavery.
                                 JOHN L. LEWIS, 1947

Trade unions arose as a spontaneous and necessary consequence of capitalism, established as an economic system.   POPE PIUS XII, 1949

Laymen and economists alike tend, in my view, to exaggerate greatly the extent to which labor unions affect the structure and level of wage rates. This fact is one of the most serious obstacles to a balanced judgement about appropriate public policies toward unions.
                                 MILTON FRIEDMAN, 1951

Don't condescend to unskilled labor. Try it for half a day first.   BROOKS ATKINSON, 1951

Strikes are a crime. . . . This is the law of jungles and primitive societies.
                                 FRANCISCO FRANCO, 1951

Never confuse socialism with trade unionism.
                                 ANEURIN BEVAN, 1952

Every day, I have a matutinal indisposition that emanates from the nauseous effluvia of that oppressive slave statute [Taft-Hartley Act].
                                 JOHN L. LEWIS, 1953

Anybody who has any doubt about the ingenuity or the resourcefulness of a plumber never got a bill from one.   GEORGE MEANY, 1954

If capitalism is fair then unionism must be. If men have a right to capitalize their ideas and the resources of their country, then that implies the right of men to capitalize their labor.
                                 FRANK LLOYD WRIGHT, 1955

If the building of a bridge does not enrich the awareness of those who work on it, then that bridge ought not to be built.
                                 FRANTZ FANON, 1961

To the extent that leadership views on bargaining demands and strategy differ from those of the rank and file, it is usually the leaders who are more moderate. Increasing union democracy is therefore likely to lead unions to make larger economic demands and to press grievances that have little merit.

ALBERT REES, 1962

If the job rights won for workers by unions are not conceded by the rest of society simply because they are just, they should be conceded because they help to protect the minimum consensus that keeps our society stable. In my judgement, the economic losses imposed by unions are not too high a price to pay for their successful performance of this role.

ALBERT REES, 1962

Unions have . . . not only harmed the public at large and workers as a whole by distorting the use of labor; they have also made the incomes of the working class more unequal by reducing the opportunities available to the most disadvantaged workers.

MILTON FRIEDMAN, 1962

But you gotta admit we're ahead of the Russians in one thing—strikes. . . . I haven't seen so many people walking off their jobs since I asked for a menu in Little Rock.

DICK GREGORY, 1962

We must recognize that some strikes are simply part of the price we pay for free collective bargaining. If you tell people they are not allowed to strike or, in the case of management, take a strike, then they are simply not free to pursue their interests as they see those interests. It is just one of the costs that goes with the gain of having a free system.

GEORGE P. SHULTZ, 1963

Purely material transformations in the conditions of labor are insufficient. . . . The true problem is psychological. The worker is confronted by cut and dried procedures that must be carried out in unvarying sequence in order that work be systematic, rational and efficient . . . he is bored, slowed down and psychologically constrained.

JACQUES ELLUL, 1964

He who considers his work beneath him will be above doing it well.

ALEXANDER CHASE, 1966

Unions would be better off if their membership was voluntary.

RONALD REAGAN, 1966

Over any extended period of time the effect which unions have on the general wage level is undoubtedly limited, but over shorter periods and in particular circumstances they may exert a much stronger influence.

FRANK PIERSON, 1967

On the evening bus, the tense, pinched faces of young file clerks and elderly secretaries tell us more than we care to know.

STUDS TERKEL, 1973

The chief leverage of the strikers, in securing capitulation to their demands, was the amount of hardship and suffering they were able to inflict, not directly on the employers, but primarily on the public.

HENRY HAZLITT, 1973

The blunt truth is that labor unions cannot raise the real wages of all workers. . . . The actual policies that labor unions have systematically followed . . . have in fact reduced the real wages of the workers as a whole below what they would otherwise have been.

HENRY HAZLITT, 1973

How do I stop eleven million people from buying the grape?

DOLORES HUERTA, 1975

When people move from a low-productivity country to a high one, world real GNP presumably goes up. Those already in the rich country, taken as a whole, benefit from the infusion of new labor.

PAUL A. SAMUELSON, 1975

The whole history of unionism has been a history in which unions wield their most specific influence in determining how industries in decline are accelerated toward their extinction.
PAUL A. SAMUELSON, 1975

If people outside Italy have the impression that Italy is always on strike, that is because it is.
TINA ANSELMI, 1976

I am a man, not a consignment of goods to be bought and sold.   CURT FLOOD, 1978

Dammit, the law is the law, and the law says they cannot strike. If they [air-traffic controllers] strike, they quit their jobs.
RONALD REAGAN, 1981

Encouraging worker ideas and participation in decision making is no longer just an option for American business. It is a necessity. Employees come to the workplace today with expectations that their recommendations will be given serious consideration.   ROGER B. SMITH, 1982

Leisure

The goal of war is peace; of business, leisure.
ARISTOTLE, C. 336 B.C.

He who does not know how to use leisure makes more business of it than there is business in business itself.   QUINTUS ENNIUS, C. 190 B.C.

Remember that even though work stops, nevertheless the expenses continue to mount up.
MARCUS CATO, C. 184 B.C.

Cessation of work is not accompanied by cessation of expenses.
MARCUS CATO, C. 184 B.C.

Six hours are enough for work; the others say to men, "Live!"   LUCIEN, C. 1st C. B.C.

The bow cannot possibly always stand bent, nor can human nature or human frailty subsist without some lawful recreation.
MIGUEL DE CERVANTES, 1585

If all the year were playing holidays,
To sport would be as tedious as to work.
WILLIAM SHAKESPEARE,
Henry IV, Part I (I, ii), 1598

Gold that buys health can never be ill spent
Nor hours laid out in harmless merriment.
JOHN WEBSTER, 1607

All work and no play makes Jack a dull boy.
JAMES HOWELL, 1659

He that will make a good use of any part of his life must allow a large part of it to recreation.
                    JOHN LOCKE, 1690

He that is busy is tempted by but one devil; he that is idle, by a legion.
                    THOMAS FULLER, 1732

Few people do business well who do nothing else.   LORD CHESTERFIELD, 1749

When man was placed in the garden of Eden, he was placed there to cultivate it; which proves that mankind are not created to be idle.
                    VOLTAIRE, 1759

Great labor, either of mind or body, continued for several days together, is in most men naturally followed by a great desire of relaxation, which, if not restrained by force or by some strong necessity, is almost irresistible.
                    ADAM SMITH, 1776

Hackneyed in business, wearied at that oar,
Which thousands, once fast chained to, quit no more.   WILLIAM COWPER, 1785

Leisure for men of business, and business for men of leisure, would cure many companies.
                    ESTHER L. S. THRALE, 1788

In proportion as the labor and ingenuity of man exercised upon the land have increased this surplus produce, leisure has been given to a greater number of persons to employ themselves in all the inventions which embellish civilized life.
                    THOMAS MALTHUS, 1798

Let me caution persons grown old in active business, not lightly, nor without weighing their own resources, to forego their customary employment all at once, for there may be danger in it.   CHARLES LAMB, 1823

Ah, why Should life all labor be?
                    ALFRED TENNYSON, 1832

Rest is not quitting the busy career; rest is the fitting of self to its sphere.
                    JOHN S. DWIGHT, 1843

Men cannot labor on always. They must have recreation.   ORVILLE DEWEY, 1844

They talk of the dignity of work. Bosh. The dignity is in leisure.   HERMAN MELVILLE, 1849

When a man's busy, why, leisure
Strikes him as wonderful pleasure;
'Faith, and at leisure once is he?
Straightway he wants to be busy.
                    ROBERT BROWNING, 1855

To continue much longer overwhelmed by business cares and with most of my thought wholly upon the way to make more money in the shortest time, must degrade me beyond hope of permanent recovery. I will resign business at thirty-five.   ANDREW CARNEGIE, 1868

We have had somewhat too much of the "gospel of work." It is time to preach the gospel of relaxation.   HERBERT SPENCER, 1882

Abstention from labor is the conventional evidence of wealth and is therefore the conventional mark of social standing; and this insistence on the meritoriousness of wealth leads to a more strenuous insistence on leisure.
                    THORSTEIN VEBLEN, 1899

Pensioner: A kept patriot.
                    H. L. MENCKEN, 1916

Thus far in our industrial development the workers have not evidenced any particular desire for a vacation.   GEORGE EASTMAN, 1919

As a rule, from what I've observed, the American captain of industry doesn't do anything out of business hours. When he has put the cat out and locked up the office for the night, he just relapses into a state of coma from which he emerges only to start being a captain of industry again. P. G. WODEHOUSE, 1925

The best test of the quality of a civilization is the quality of its leisure. IRWIN EDMAN, 1929

To be able to fill leisure intelligently is the last product of civilization. BERTRAND RUSSELL, 1930

The thing that I should wish to obtain from money would be leisure with security. BERTRAND RUSSELL, 1935

Be temperate in your work, but don't carry the practice over into your leisure hours. MONTY WOOLLEY, 1939

The overworked, driven person or class is seldom creative, while leisure, even wasteful leisure, may end creatively. BERNARD BERENSON, 1942

Vacation is time off, to remind employees that the business can get along without them. EARL WILSON, 1949

There are . . . other business societies—England, Holland, Belgium and France, for instance. But ours [America] is the only culture now extant in which business so completely dominates the national scene that sports, sex, death, philanthropy and Easter Sunday are money-making propositions. MARGARET HALSEY, 1952

More free time means more time to waste. The worker who used to have only a little time in which to get drunk and beat his wife now has time to get drunk, beat his wife—and watch TV. ROBERT HUTCHINS, 1954

Work is becoming suffused with leisure values. Executives on an expense account hardly know whether they are at leisure or at work; they assume it must be the latter since they are getting paid for what they do. AUGUST HECKSCHER, 1957

To retire is the beginning of death. PABLO CASALS, 1958

Retirement is the ugliest word in the language. ERNEST HEMINGWAY, 1960

Work is less boring than pleasure. JAY PIEPER, 1963

Few men of action have been able to make a graceful exit at the appropriate time. MALCOLM MUGGERIDGE, 1966

Five days shalt thou labor, as the Bible says. The seventh day is the Lord thy God's. The sixth day is for football and spreading the word and punishing and suchlike. ANTHONY BURGESS, 1968

Leisure tends to corrupt, and absolute leisure corrupts absolutely. EDGAR A. SHOAFF, 1971

A good retirement is about two weeks. ALEX COMFORT, 1976

Modern industry having reduced most jobs to a routine, games take on added meaning in our society. CHRISTOPHER LASCH, 1979

Management

What a man dislikes in his superiors, let him not display in the treatment of his inferiors.

TSANG SIN, fifth century B.C.

He that defraudeth a laborer of his hire is a bloodshedder.

ECCLESIASTICUS 34, c. 210 B.C.

We tend to meet any new situation by reorganizing and a wonderful method it can be for creating the illusion of progress while producing inefficiency and demoralization.

PETRONIUS, C. A.D. 65

Who is more busy than he who hath least to do?

JOHN CLARKE, 1660

It is easier to appear worthy of a position one does not hold, than of the office which one fills.

FRANÇOIS DE LA ROCHEFOUCAULD, 1664

A good horse should be seldom spurred.

THOMAS FULLER, 1732

Drive thy business or it will drive thee.

BENJAMIN FRANKLIN, 1757

It is wonderful when a calculation is made, how little the mind is actually employed in the discharge of any profession.

SAMUEL JOHNSON, 1761

The man who occupies the first place seldom plays the principal part.

JOHANN WOLFGANG GOETHE, 1774

The great requisite for the prosperous management of ordinary business is the want of imagination.

WILLIAM HAZLITT, 1806

Men are never very wise and select in the exercise of a new power.

WILLIAM ELLERY CHANNING, 1841

Captains of Industry.

THOMAS CARLYLE, 1843

There are people who are socialists and rebels today and company directors tomorrow. Examples of reincarnation.

FRIEDRICH HEBBEL, 1846

The number of persons fitted to direct and superintend any industrial enterprise, or even to execute any process which cannot be reduced almost to an affair of memory and routine, is always far short of the demand; as is evident from the enormous difference between the salaries paid to such persons, and the wages of ordinary labor.

JOHN STUART MILL, 1848

There is always room at the top.

DANIEL WEBSTER, 1851

I am never satisfied unless I either do everything myself or personally superintend everything done even to an entry in the books. This I cannot help.   J. PIERPONT MORGAN, 1862

No man can be a pure specialist without being, in a strict sense, an idiot.
                                    GEORGE BERNARD SHAW, 1882

The man who gives me employment, which I must have or suffer, that man is my master, let me call him what I will.
                                    HENRY GEORGE, 1883

The most valuable executive is one who is training somebody to be a better man than he is.
                                    ROBERT G. INGERSOLL, 1883

The Forgotten Man works and votes—generally he prays—but his chief business in life is to pay.   WILLIAM G. SUMNER, 1883

If you want work well done, select a busy man—the other kind has not time.
                                    ELBERT HUBBARD, 1896

The captains of industry, like the kings of yore, are honestly unable to understand why their personal power should be interfered with, and kings and captains alike have never found any difficulty in demonstrating that its maintenance was indispensable to society.
                                    SIDNEY AND BEATRICE WEBB, 1898

The employer generally gets the employees he deserves.   WALTER GILBEY, 1901

Boss your boss just as soon as you can; try it on early. There is nothing he will like so well if he is the right kind of boss; if he is not, he is not the man for you to remain with.
                                    ANDREW CARNEGIE, 1902

Titles distinguish the mediocre, embarrass the superior, and are disgraced by the inferior.
                                    GEORGE BERNARD SHAW, 1903

The relation of superior to inferior excludes good manners.   GEORGE BERNARD SHAW, 1903

Except during nine months before he draws his first breath, no man manages his affairs as well as a tree does.
                                    GEORGE BERNARD SHAW, 1903

Every successful enterprise requires three men—a dreamer, a businessman, and a son-of-a-bitch.
                                    PETER MCARTHUR, 1904

The best executive is the one who has sense enough to pick good men to do what he wants done, and self-restraint enough to keep from meddling with them while they do it.
                                    THEODORE ROOSEVELT, 1907

Mistrust a subordinate who never finds fault with his superior.
                                    JOHN CHURTON COLLINS, 1908

The ability to deal with people is as purchasable a commodity as sugar or coffee. And I pay more for that ability than for any other under the sun.
                                    JOHN D. ROCKEFELLER, 1908

What is worth doing is worth the trouble of asking somebody to do it.
                                    AMBROSE BIERCE, 1911

One captain of industry is worth a good many of the rank and file.
                                    WILLIAM PETERSON, 1911

Good management consists in showing average people how to do the work of superior people.
                                    JOHN D. ROCKEFELLER, 1913

Next to knowing all about your own business, the best thing is to know all about the other fellow's business.
                                    JOHN D. ROCKEFELLER, 1913

Lots of folks confuse bad management with destiny.   ELBERT HUBBARD, 1915

To be a leader of men one must turn one's back on men.   HAVELOCK ELLIS, 1917

The business man has the same fundamental psychology as the artist, inventor, and states-man. He has set himself at a certain work and the work absorbs and becomes himself. It is the expression of his personality: he lives in its growth and perfection according to his plans.
                              FRANK KNIGHT, 1921

The outstanding mistake of the employer is his failure to realize that he is dealing with human material.   ROGER WARD BABSON, 1923

The self-made manager in business is nearing the end of his road. Despite his own blind faith in the "practical" he is already hiring profes-sionally trained engineers, chemists, account-ants and hygienists. . . . He must himself turn to professional education, or surrender control to those who do.   RICHARD J. WALSH, 1924

Most people like hard work. Particularly when they are paying for it.
                         FRANKLIN P. JONES, 1924

Personnel selection is decisive. People are our most valuable capital.
                            JOSEPH STALIN, 1928

A professional is one who does his best work when he feels the least like working.
                         FRANK LLOYD WRIGHT, 1932

Our captains of industry are mainly engaged not in making a living but in playing a great game; and it need make little difference whether the evidence of having played well be diamonds and sables on one's wife or a prominent place in the list of contributors under the income tax. Be-sides—and this may be emphasized—the mere privilege of exercising power is no mean prize for the successful enterpriser.
                             HENRY SIMONS, 1938

I don't want any yesmen around me. I want everyone to tell me the truth—even though it costs him his job.   SAMUEL GOLDWYN, 1939

The modern businessman, whether entrepre-neur or mere managing administrator, is of the executive type. . . . Whether a stockholder or not, his will to fight and to hold on is not and cannot be what it was with the man who knew ownership and its responsibilities in the full-blooded sense of these words.
                         JOSEPH A. SCHUMPETER, 1942

We have seen that the industrialist and mer-chant, as far as they are entrepreneurs, also fill a function of leadership. But economic leader-ship of this type does not readily expand, like the medieval lord's military leadership, into the leadership of nations. On the contrary, the ledger and the cost calculation absorb and confine.
                         JOSEPH A. SCHUMPETER, 1942

Never tell people how to do things. Tell them what to do and they will surprise you with their ingenuity.   GEORGE S. PATTON, 1944

Management itself is rapidly becoming a profession, attracting a new type of individual, one who tries to reconcile his business ethics with his social obligations. The rate at which this type has grown in the past few years is promising for the future.   OSWALD KNAUTH, 1948

Nothing is so embarrassing as watching your boss do something you assured him couldn't be done.   EARL WILSON, 1949

The most difficult part of getting to the top of the ladder is getting through the crowd at the bottom.   ARCH WARD, 1951

If you're the chief executive you get more blame than you deserve, and you also get more credit than you deserve. If you want one, you've got to accept the other too.   K. T. KELLER, 1952

No matter how lofty you are in your department, the responsibility for what your lowliest assistant is doing is yours.
BESSIE ROWLAND JAMES, 1952

The average vice-president is a form of executive fungus that attaches itself to a desk. On a boat this growth would be called a barnacle.
FRED ALLEN, 1954

Take my assets—but leave me my organization and in five years I'll have it all back.
ALFRED P. SLOAN, JR., 1954

The business executive is by profession a decision maker. Uncertainty is his opponent. Overcoming it is his mission.
JOHN MCDONALD, 1955

Economic independence doesn't set anyone free. Or it shouldn't, for the higher up you go, the more responsibilities become yours.
BERNARD F. GIMBEL, 1956

A decision is the action an executive must take when he has information so incomplete that the answer does not suggest itself.
ARTHUR W. RADFORD, 1957

Corporate executives as individuals are not capitalists seeking profit. They are men seeking careers, in a structure offering rewards of power and position rather than profit or great wealth.
ADOLF A. BERLE, 1958

By working faithfully eight hours a day, you may eventually get to be a boss and work twelve hours a day.
ROBERT FROST, 1961

The mark of a true executive is usually illegible.
LEO J. FARRELL, JR., 1962

The leader must know, must know that he knows, and must be able to make it abundantly clear to those about him that he knows.
CLARENCE B. RANDALL, 1964

Rarely, if ever, has a new basic institution, a new leading group, emerged as fast as has management since the turn of this century. Rarely in human history has a new institution proven indispensable so quickly; and even less often has a new institution arrived with so little opposition, so little disturbance, so little controversy.
PETER DRUCKER, 1964

The task of management is not to apply a formula but to decide issues on a case-by-case basis. No fixed, inflexible rule can ever be substituted for the exercise of sound business judgement in the decision-making process.
ALFRED P. SLOAN, JR., 1964

The most important thing I have ever learned about management is that the work must be done by other men.
ALFRED P. SLOAN, JR., 1964

Few great men could pass Personnel.
PAUL GOODMAN, 1965

My mistake was buying stock in the company. Now I worry about the lousy work I'm turning out.
MARVIN TOWNSEND, 1968

He's fair. He treats us all the same—like dogs.
HENRY JORDAN, 1968

In a hierarchy, every employee tends to rise to his level of incompetence.
LAURENCE J. PETER, 1969

Only mediocrities rise to the top in a system that won't tolerate wavemaking.
LAURENCE J. PETER, 1969

A manager develops people. Through the way he manages he makes it easy or difficult for them to develop themselves. He directs people or misdirects them. He brings out what is in them or he stifles them.
PETER DRUCKER, 1970

Nobody should be chief executive of anything for more than five or six years. By then he's stale, bored, and utterly dependent on his own clichés—though they may have been revolutionary ideas when he first brought them to the office.   ROBERT TOWNSEND, 1970

We have yet to find a significant case where the company did not move in the direction of the chief executive's home.   KEN PATTON, 1971

Today the large organization is lord and master, and most of its employees have been desensitized much as were the medieval peasants who never knew they were serfs.

RALPH NADER, 1972

I am constantly intrigued by the idea that men who receive a salary of two hundred and fifty thousand dollars a year need some extra incentive to do their job well.

IRVING BLUESTONE, 1972

The first myth of management is that it exists. The second myth of management is that success equals skill.   ROBERT HELLER, 1972

The question of justice arises when those on top can convert their authority positions into large, discrepant, material and social advantages.

DANIEL BELL, 1973

Robot executives who cling to this-is-the-way-it's-always-been-done conformity are not only stifling their own careers but are precipitating a case of hardening of the arteries throughout U.S. industry.   LOUIS WOLFSON, 1974

I like players to be married and in debt. That's the way you motivate them.

ERNIE BANKS, 1976

Industrial relations are like sexual relations. It's better between two consenting parties.

VIC FEATHER, 1976

These men of the technostructure are the new and universal priesthood. Their religion is business success; their test of virtue is growth and profit.   JOHN KENNETH GALBRAITH, 1977

So much of what we call management consists in making it difficult for people to work.

PETER DRUCKER, 1978

The road to the board room leads through the locker room.   DAVID RIESMAN, 1978

The longer the title, the less important the job.

GEORGE MCGOVERN, 1979

An M.B.A.'s first shock could be the realization that companies require experience before they hire a chief executive officer.

ROBERT HALF, 1980

Delegating work works, provided the one delegating works too.   ROBERT HALF, 1980

One uncooperative employee can sabotage an entire organization because bad spirit is more contagious than good spirit.

ROBERT HALF, 1980

Marketing

The market is the place set apart where men may deceive each other.

ANACHARSIS, c. 600 B.C.

Small opportunities are often the beginning of great enterprises.

DEMOSTHENES, c. 343 B.C.

There's always chance to fear, and many a slip
Makes for anxiety in salesmanship.

GEOFFREY CHAUCER, 1382

He that makes use of another's fancy or necessity to sell ribbon or cloth dearer to him than to another man at the same time, cheats him.

JOHN LOCKE, 1695

A tradesman behind his counter must have no flesh and blood about him, no passions, no resentment; he must never be angry—no, not so much as seem to be so.

DANIEL DEFOE, 1725

All our wants, beyond those which a very moderate income will supply, are purely imaginary.

HENRY ST. JOHN, 1743

Commerce consists in making superfluous things useful and useful things necessary.

C. S. MONTESQUIEU, 1748

We are not here to sell a parcel of boilers and vats, but the potentiality of growing rich beyond the dreams of avarice.

SAMUEL JOHNSON, 1752

When great inequality of fortune prevails, the demand for labor employed in giving forms adapted to the taste of the luxurious and the rich, encourages that species of industry.

LORD LAUDERDALE, 1804

Things, as such, become goods as soon as the human mind recognizes them as means suitable for the promotion of human purposes.

CARL MENGER, 1871

The salesman knows nothing of what he is selling save that he is charging a great deal too much for it.

OSCAR WILDE, 1882

Every one lives by selling something.

ROBERT LOUIS STEVENSON, 1882

I am the world's worst salesman, therefore, I must make it easy for people to buy.

F. W. WOOLWORTH, 1888

The surest foundation of a manufacturing concern is quality. After that, and a long way after, comes cost.

ANDREW CARNEGIE, 1902

All competition is in its nature only a furious plagiarism.   GILBERT K. CHESTERTON, 1906

Twenty percent of the customers account for 80% of the turnover, 20% of the components account for 80% of the cost, and so forth.   VILFREDO PARETO, 1911

Nothing is as irritating as the fellow that chats pleasantly while he's overcharging you.   FRANK MCKINNEY HUBBARD, 1911

In all minor discussions between Statler employees and Statler guests, the employee is dead wrong.   E. M. STATLER, 1921

It's no trick to be a successful salesman if you have what the people want. You never hear the bootleggers complaining about hard times.   BOB EDWARDS, 1922

He was nimble in the calling of selling houses for more than people could afford to pay.   SINCLAIR LEWIS, 1922

People will buy anything that's one to a customer.   SINCLAIR LEWIS, 1922

The changes in new models should be so novel and attractive as to create dissatisfaction with past models. Automobile design is not, of course, pure fashion, but the laws of Paris dressmakers have come to be a factor in the automobile industry. Woe to the company which ignores them.   ALFRED P. SLOAN, JR., 1922

It is considered good manufacturing practice, and not bad ethics, occasionally to change designs so that old models will become obsolete and new ones will have to be bought. . . . Our principle of business is precisely to the contrary. We cannot conceive how to serve the customer unless we make for him something that, as far as we can provide, will last forever.   HENRY FORD, 1923

Our old friend, the "economic man," is becoming very self-conscious and bafflingly non-committal. Instead of introducing himself to his readers with his old-time freedom, he says: "I may behave one way and I may behave another, but what is that to you? You must take my choices as you find them: I choose as I choose and that is all you really need to know."   JOHN MAURICE CLARK, 1936

More great Americans were failures than they were successes. They mostly spent their lives in not having a buyer for what they had for sale.   GERTRUDE STEIN, 1937

Whether under monopoly or so-called competitive conditions, markets are intrinsically unfair models of distribution.   JOHN A. HOBSON, 1938

It is taken for granted that by lunchtime the average man has been so beaten down by life that he will believe anything.   CHRISTOPHER MORLEY, 1939

The best mental effort in the game of business is concentrated on the major problem of securing the consumer's dollar before the other fellow gets it.   STUART CHASE, 1941

Man does not only sell commodities, he sells himself and feels himself to be a commodity.   ERICH FROMM, 1941

The customer is an object to be manipulated, not a concrete person whose aims the businessman is interested to satisfy.   ERICH FROMM, 1941

In the case of retail trade the competition that matters arises not from additional shops of the same type, but from the department store, the chain store, the mail-order house and the supermarket.   JOSEPH A. SCHUMPETER, 1942

In the U.S., doing good has come to be, like patriotism, a favorite device of persons with something to sell. H. L. MENCKEN, 1949

There are always thousands of people on the verge of buying a car, held back only by some secret caution. E. B. WHITE, 1949

The first mark of a good business is the ability to deliver. To deliver its product or service on time and in the condition which the client was led to expect.
MICHAEL J. T. FERGUSON, 1951

In an economy, such as that of the United States of America, where leisure is barely moral, the problem of creating sufficient wants . . . to absorb productive capacity may become chronic in the not too distant future.
W. BECKERMAN, 1956

There is no such thing as "soft sell" and "hard sell." There is only "smart sell" and "stupid sell." CHARLES BROWER, 1958

Salesmanship consists of transferring a conviction by a buyer to a seller.
PAUL G. HOFFMAN, 1960

Salesmanship is an American specialty. It typifies the competitive spirit of our economy. Nowhere else in the world have so many executives come up through the selling ranks.
ROBERT A. WHITNEY, 1963

The commercial process consists of sensing the existence of latent needs and exploiting them, i.e., converting them into conscious wants by marketing and advertising appropriate products. ROBIN MORRIS, 1964

In the factory we make cosmetics; in the drugstore we sell hope. CHARLES REVSON, 1967

To continue to regard the market, in an affluent and growing economy, as primarily a "want-satisfying" mechanism is to close one's eyes to the more important fact that it has become a "want-creating" mechanism.
E. J. MISHAN, 1967

Business has only two functions—marketing and innovation. PETER DRUCKER, 1970

Successful salesman: someone who has found a cure for the common cold shoulder.
ROBERT ORBEN, 1971

Minicars produce miniprofits.
HENRY FORD II, 1972

One illusion is that you can industrialize a country by building factories. You don't. You industrialize it by building markets.
PAUL G. HOFFMAN, 1974

Inequality of knowledge is the key to a sale.
DEIL O. GUSTAFSON, 1974

The diffuse and inchoate consumer interest has been no match for the sharply focused, articulate and well-financed efforts of producer groups. WALTER A. HELLER, 1975

The meek have to inherit the earth—they sure don't know how to market it.
JENO F. PAULVECI, 1976

The decent thing for an inanimate object in America to do is wear out. Most inanimate objects understand and do their duty. Light bulbs are particularly good about it.
RUSSELL BAKER, 1977

Contrary to popular opinion, the hustle is not a new dance step—it is an old business precedure.
FRAN LEBOWITZ, 1979

Money

Money is life to us wretched mortals.

HESIOD, eighth century B.C.

The love of money is the mother of all evil.

PHOCYLIDES, sixth century B.C.

Money lays waste cities; it sets men to roaming from home; it seduces and corrupts honest men and turns virtue to baseness; it teaches villainy and impiety. SOPHOCLES, c. 441 B.C.

All things that are exchanged must be somehow comparable. It is for this end that money has been introduced, and it becomes in a sense an intermediate; for it measures all things.

ARISTOTLE, c. 340 B.C.

Wine maketh merry: but money answereth all things. ECCLESIASTES 10:19, c. 210 B.C.

That man is admired above all men who is not influenced by money. CICERO, c. 60 B.C.

The love of money grows as the money itself grows. JUVENAL, c. A.D. 120

Love of money is the disease which makes men most groveling and pitiful.

LONGINUS, c. 270

A fool and his money are soon parted.

GEORGE BUCHANAN, 1570

For they say, if money go before, all ways do lie open.

WILLIAM SHAKESPEARE,
Merry Wives of Windsor (II, ii), 1602

Money makes a man laugh.

JOHN SELDOM, c. 1650

The beautiful eyes of my money-box!
He speaks of it as a lover of his mistress.

MOLIÈRE, 1668

Honor, without money, is a mere malady.

JEAN RACINE, 1677

Money speaks sense in a language all nations understand. APHRA BEHN, 1682

They who are of opinion that money will do everything may very well be expected to do everything for money.

GEORGE SAVILE, 1693

But it is pretty to see what money can do.

SAMUEL PEPYS, 1699

No man will take counsel, but every man will take money: therefore money is better than counsel. JONATHAN SWIFT, 1706

Money is the life blood of the nation.

JONATHAN SWIFT, 1706

Man was made the standing jest of Heav'n,
And gold but sent to keep the fools in play,
For some to heap and some to throw away.
ALEXANDER POPE, 1735

Make money your god, it will plague you like
the devil.   HENRY FIELDING, 1743

Remember that time is money.
BENJAMIN FRANKLIN, 1757

Money is not, properly speaking, one of the
subjects of commerce; but only the instrument
which men have agreed upon to facilitate the
exchange of one commodity for another. It is
none of the wheels for another. It is none of the
wheels of trade: It is the oil which renders the
motion of the wheels more smooth and easy.
DAVID HUME, 1762

"Nothing comes out of nothing," is as true of
life as in physics: money is the seed of money,
and the first guinea is sometimes more difficult
to acquire than the second million.
JEAN-JACQUES ROUSSEAU, 1762

There are few ways in which a man can be more
innocently employed than in getting money.
SAMUEL JOHNSON, 1775

No complaint . . . is more common than that
of a scarcity of money.   ADAM SMITH, 1776

Money never made a man happy yet, nor will
it. There is nothing in its nature to produce
happiness.   BENJAMIN FRANKLIN, 1779

It is much easier to get goods than money.
JEREMY BENTHAM, 1789

Money, and not morality, is the principle of
commercial nations.
THOMAS JEFFERSON, 1810

They say that knowledge is power. I used to think
so, but I now know that they meant money.
LORD BYRON, 1811

In the use of money, everyone is a trader.
DAVID RICARDO, 1817

Money without honor is a disease.
HONORÉ DE BALZAC, 1843

What I as a human being cannot do, in other
words, what all my individual faculties cannot
do, I can do by means of money. Hence money
makes every one of these faculties into something which it is not in itself, i.e., turns it into
its opposite.   KARL MARX, 1844

Money plays the largest part in determining the
course of history.   KARL MARX, 1848

Money alone is absolutely good, because it is
not only a concrete satisfaction of one need in
particular; it is an abstract satisfaction of all.
ARTHUR SCHOPENHAUER, 1851

Money is human happiness in the abstract: he,
then, who is no longer capable of enjoying human happiness in the concrete devotes himself
utterly to money.
ARTHUR SCHOPENHAUER, 1851

Money is everything in this world to some people and more than the next to other poor souls.
AUGUSTA EVANS, 1859

I haven't got as much money as some folks, but
I've got as much impudence as any of them, and
that's the next thing to money.
JOSH BILLINGS, 1865

Building one's life on a foundation of gold is
just like building a house on foundations of
sand.   HENRIK IBSEN, 1867

Money is economical power.

WALTER BAGEHOT, 1873

Money, which represents the prose of life, and which is hardly spoken of in parlors without an apology, is, in its effects and laws, as beautiful as roses.   RALPH WALDO EMERSON, 1876

The purse strings tie us to our kind.

WALTER BAGEHOT, 1879

Money is the alienated essence of man's work and existence; this essence dominates him and he worships it.   KARL MARX, 1884

Money is indeed the most important thing in the world; and all sound and successful personal and national morality should have this fact for its basis.   GEORGE BERNARD SHAW, 1884

Young people, nowadays, imagine that money is everything, and when they grow older they know it.   OSCAR WILDE, 1895

If I were honest, I would admit that money is one half of happiness; it makes it so much more attractive!   MARIE LÉNERU, 1898

Money is a great dignifier.

PAUL LAURENCE DUNBAR, 1898

It's good to have money and the things that money can buy, but it's good, too, to check up once in a while and make sure that you haven't lost the things that money can't buy.

GEORGE HORACE LORIMER, 1902

What is the use of money if you have to work for it?   GEORGE BERNARD SHAW, 1903

Money—money, like everything else—is a deception and a disappointment.

H. G. WELLS, 1905

Money talks.   O. HENRY, 1905

Money, n. A blessing that is of no advantage to us excepting when we part with it.

AMBROSE BIERCE, 1911

Money is like a sixth sense without which you cannot make a complete use of the other five.

SOMERSET MAUGHAM, 1915

The reason you have no money is because you don't love it for itself alone. Money won't ever surrender to such a flirt.

FINLEY PETER DUNNE, 1919

He . . . knew now, more than ever, that money was everything, the wall that stood between all he loathed and all he wanted.

WILLA CATHER, 1920

Make money, and the whole nation will conspire to call you a gentleman.

BOB EDWARDS, 1920

Thus, money, which is a source of so many blessings to mankind, becomes also, unless we can control it, a source of peril and confusion.

DENNIS H. ROBERTSON, 1922

Money is only important for what it will procure.   JOHN MAYNARD KEYNES, 1924

Money is like love; it kills slowly and painfully the one who withholds it, and it enlivens the other who turns it upon his fellow man.

KAHLIL GIBRAN, 1926

When a man says money can do anything, that settles it: he hasn't any.   E. W. HOWE, 1926

Money is one of those concepts which, like a teaspoon or an umbrella, but unlike an earthquake or buttercup, are definable primarily by the use or purpose which they serve.

RALPH G. HAWTREY, 1928

The love of money as a possession—as distinguished from the love of money as a means to the enjoyments and realities of life—will be recognized for what it is, a somewhat disgusting morbidity, one of those semicriminal, semipathological propensities which one hands over with a shudder to the specialists in mental disease.

JOHN MAYNARD KEYNES, 1930

There is no problem about money, except who has it.　　　MONTAGU NORMAN, 1931

Money is like an arm or a leg—use it or lose it.

HENRY FORD, 1931

Life shouldn't be printed on dollar bills.

CLIFFORD ODETS, 1937

With money I'll throttle the beast-blind world between my fingers. Without it I am strapped; weakened, my life is a curse and a care.

THOMAS WOLFE, 1938

Money doesn't make you happy, but it quiets the nerves.　　　SEAN O'CASEY, 1939

My boy . . . always try to rub up against money, for if you rub up against money long enough, some of it may rub off on you.

DAMON RUNYON, 1939

Some folks seem to get the idea that they're worth a lot of money just because they have it.

SETH PARKER, 1941

I don't like money actually, but it quiets my nerves.　　　JOE LOUIS, 1948

The chief value of money lies in the fact that one lives in a world in which it is overestimated.

H. L. MENCKEN, 1949

Money buys everything except love, personality, freedom, immortality, silence, peace.

CARL SANDBURG, 1952

The only reason to have money is to tell any s.o.b. in the world to go to hell.

HUMPHREY BOGART, 1954

But Jesus, when you don't have any money, the problem is food. When you have money, it's sex.　　　J. P. DONLEAVY, 1955

I think money is on the way out.

ANITA LOOS, 1956

Money is what you'd get on beautifully without if only other people weren't so crazy about it.

MARGARET C. HARRIMAN, 1958

Come back next Thursday with a specimen of your money.　　　GROUCHO MARX, 1959

Money, it turned out, was exactly like sex, you thought of nothing else if you didn't have it and thought of other things if you did.

JAMES BALDWIN, 1961

European society . . . automatically assumes its superiority to Americans whether they have money or not, but money tends to blur the sharpness of the distinction.

VIRGILIA PETERSON, 1961

Money is the barometer of a society's virtue.

AYN RAND, 1962

Money for me has only one sound: liberty.

GABRIELLE CHANEL, 1962

Money doesn't talk, it swears.

BOB DYLAN, 1967

To most people money is a serious thing. They expect financial architecture to reflect this quality.　　　JOHN KENNETH GALBRAITH, 1967

Money is like manure. You have to spend it around or it smells.　　　J. PAUL GETTY, 1967

A fool and his money are soon parted. What I want to know is how they got together in the first place.   CYRIL FLETCHER, 1969

Money brings some happiness. But, after a certain point, it just brings more money.
NEIL SIMON, 1970

So you think that money is the root of all evil. Have you ever asked what is the root of money?
AYN RAND, 1971

Money won't buy happiness, but it will pay the salaries of a large research staff to study the problem.   BILL VAUGHN, 1971

Money as money is nothing.
H. L. HUNT, 1975

Folks are serious about three things—their religion, their family, and most of all, their money.
BERT LANCE, 1976

Not having to worry about money is almost like not having to worry about dying.
MARIO PUZO, 1976

I do everything for a reason. Most of the time the reason is money.   SUZY PARKER, 1978

What's worth doing is worth doing for money.
JOSEPH DONOHUE, 1978

Monopoly

The holder of a monopoly is a sinner and offender.   MOHAMMED, c. 610

For whenever men consult for the public good, as far as the advancement of trade, wherein all are concerned, they usually esteem the immediate interest of their own to be the common measure of good and evil.
DUDLEY NORTH, 1691

The masters, being fewer in number, can combine more easily; and the law besides, authorizes, or at least does not prohibit their combinations, while it prohibits those of the workmen.   ADAM SMITH, 1776

All the original sources of revenue, the wages of labor, the rent of land, and the profits of stock, the monopoly renders much less abundant then they otherwise would be. To promote the little interest of one little order of men in one country, it hurts the interest of all other orders of men in that country, and of all men in all other countries.   ADAM SMITH, 1776

Monopoly . . . is a great enemy to good management.   ADAM SMITH, 1776

The price of monopoly is upon every occasion the highest which can be got.
ADAM SMITH, 1776

Monopolies are sacrifices of the many to the few. JAMES MADISON, 1788

It is better to abolish monopolies in all cases than to do it in any. THOMAS JEFFERSON, 1788

By the concentration of fortunes in the hands of a small number of owners, the internal market is all the time shrinking, and industry is more and more reduced to looking for outlets in foreign markets. SIMONDE DE SISMONDI, 1819

Monopoly, in all its forms, is the taxation of the industrious for the support of indolence, if not of plunder. JOHN STUART MILL, 1848

When, therefore, a business of real public importance can only be carried on advantageously upon so large a scale as to render the liberty of competition almost illusory, . . . It is much better to treat it at once as a public function; and if it be not such as the government itself could beneficially undertake, it should be made over entire to the company or association which will perform it on the best terms for the public. JOHN STUART MILL, 1848

Rent is the effect of a monopoly. JOHN STUART MILL, 1848

We do not ride on the railroad; it rides upon us. HENRY DAVID THOREAU, 1854

It may be said generally that businesses which are in their nature monopolies are properly part of the functions of the state, and should be assumed by the state. HENRY GEORGE, 1879

Rent, in short, is the price of monopoly. HENRY GEORGE, 1879

Rings and bosses are rising to the top in the evolution of industry as in that of politics. . . . A few individuals are becoming rich enough to control almost all the great markets, including the legislatures. HENRY DEMAREST LLOYD, 1882

Trusts are largely private affairs. JAMES G. BLAINE, 1888

We declare our opposition to all combinations of capital, organized as trusts or otherwise. REPUBLICAN NATIONAL PLATFORM, 1888

At one extreme are world markets in which competition acts directly from all parts of the globe; and at the other those secluded markets in which all direct competition from afar is shut out, though indirect and transmitted competition may make itself felt even in these; and about midway between these extremes lie the greater majority of the markets which the economist and the business man have to study. ALFRED MARSHALL, 1890

Monopoly is business at the end of its journey. HENRY DEMAREST LLOYD, 1890

The trusts and combinations—the communism of self. GROVER CLEVELAND, 1894

When a trust becomes a monopoly the state has an immediate right to interfere. THEODORE ROOSEVELT, 1900

In a community in which every man had been trained to his highest efficiency the evils of monopoly and poverty would be alike impossible. WILLIAM H. MAXWELL, 1905

Mr. Morgan buys his partners: I grow my own. ANDREW CARNEGIE, 1906

A trust is known by the companies it keeps. ELLIS O. JONES, 1909

Mere size is no sin against the law. WILLIAM H. TAFT, 1911

A trust does not bring efficiency to the aid of business; it buys efficiency out of business.

WOODROW WILSON, 1912

The greatest monopoly in this country is the monopoly of big credits. So long as that exists, our old variety and freedom and individual energy of development are out of the question.

WOODROW WILSON, 1913

It may indeed be said that in the main competitive and monopoly theory do not diverge, that the supply and demand analysis applies without change to competition to monopoly and that monopoly differs from competition only in the fact that in monopoly the volume of supply is under centralized control, while in competition the limit of supply is found in marginal cost of production.   HERBERT J. DAVENPORT, 1913

Monopoly has generally evolved into state monopoly.   NIKOLAI LENIN, 1917

No one can argue that a monopolist is impelled by "an invisible hand" to serve the public interest.   RICHARD H. TAWNEY, 1920

Competitors are free—except to combine.

JOHN MAURICE CLARK, 1926

The difference between the Standard Oil Company in its prime and the little corner grocery is quantitative rather than qualitative.

EDWARD H. CHAMBERLIN, 1929

We find in comparing a world of monopolized industries with a world of imperfect competition that there may be very considerable improvements in the technique of production when the unit of control in industry increases in size. But we find that the increase in the size of the unit of control will lead to an increase in the inequality of the distribution of wealth.

JOAN ROBINSON, 1933

In so far as consumers really want the variety of product, . . . the ideal competitive equilibria of traditional theory would not adequately meet their wants. What would appear to be monopolistic exploitation according to the familiar criterion turns out to be a symptom of greater precison in the satisfaction of wants.

DONALD H. WALLACE, 1936

The theory of oligopoly has been aptly described as a ticket of admission to institutional economics.   EDWARD S. MASON, 1939

The real significance of the traditional monopoly case—the singleness of the seller—is to identify a form with an industry and thus to substitute for the shifting demand curve of the former the stable demand curve of the latter. It is in this sense that monopoly means the absence of competition.   ROBERT TRIFFIN, 1940

The superior efficiency of large establishments has not been demonstrated; the advantages that are supposed to destroy competition have failed to manifest themselves in many fields. Nor do the economics of size, where they exist, invariably necessitate monopoly.

CLAIRE WILCOX, 1940

The monopoly racket, like that of tariffs and subsidies, works only so long as it is exceptional—works only to advantage minorities relatively, with overall diseconomy and loss.

HENRY SIMONS, 1948

It is the ability of monopolies to protect themselves from capital losses that is injurious to the economy. They try to postpone investment until existing equipment is sufficiently depreciated, and thus new technical devices are financed from depreciation reserves, therefore failing to create investment opportunities for outside savings.

EVSEY D. DOMAR, 1948

To suppose that there are grounds for antitrust prosecution wherever three, four or a half dozen firms dominate a market is to suppose that the very fabric of American capitalism is illegal.

JOHN KENNETH GALBRAITH, 1952

The comparative importance of a small number of great corporations in the American economy cannot be denied except by those who have a singular immunity to statistical evidence or striking capacity to manipulate it.

JOHN KENNETH GALBRAITH, 1952

It is relatively easy to fix prices that are already fixed.   JOHN KENNETH GALBRAITH, 1952

Not only do 500 corporations control two-thirds of the non-farm economy but within each of that 500 a still smaller group has the ultimate decision-making power. This is, I think, the highest concentration of economic power in recorded history.   ADOLPH A. BERLE, 1962

The statistical evidence is sketchy and not very reliable; yet such as there is all tends to show that the degree of concentration in the ownership of property is quite as great in the poor or semi-developed countries of the Middle East, Asia, or Latin America, as in the countries of advanced capitalism.   N. KALDOR, 1964

Equilibrium for the firm under perfect competition can only occur when the marginal cost of the firm is rising at and near equilibrium output. Equilibrium under monopoly can occur whether marginal costs are rising, falling or constant.

ALFRED STONIER AND
DOUGLAS HAGUE, 1964

When economic tests alone are applied, the case for antitrust is not that it does much good, but rather that it probably does little harm.

DONALD DEWEY, 1966

A plausible hypothesis, though one very hard to confirm, is that the price leaders act like monopolists on behalf of the entire industry.

ROBERT DORFMAN, 1967

Every sovereign is aware that a multinational corporate group which is able to provide export markets for the host country is also capable of withholding such markets and cutting off the jobs that depend on such exports. . . . Along similar lines, a multinational group that can provide foreign capital to the host government's economy is also thought capable of draining capital away for use elsewhere.

RAYMOND VERNON, 1967

Like many businessmen of genius he learned that free competition was wasteful, monopoly efficient.   MARIO PUZO, 1969

In the Communist countries, as in the capitalist world, oligopoly stands as the principal barrier to the achievement of better economic performance.   JOHN BLAIR, 1973

The fact that a business is large, efficient and profitable does not mean it takes advantage of the public.   CHARLES CLORE, 1974

A fair price for oil is whatever you can get plus ten percent.   ALI AHMED ATTIGA, 1974

Philanthropy

The man who first invented the art of supporting beggars made many wretched.

MENANDER, C. 310 B.C.

The only wealth which you keep forever is the wealth which you have given away.

MARTIAL, C. A.D. 80

If a thief helps a poor man out of the spoils of his thieving, we must not call that charity.

DANTE ALIGHIERI, 1314

In charity, there is no excess.

FRANCIS BACON, 1597

What is called generosity is usually only the vanity of giving; we enjoy the vanity more than the thing given.

FRANÇOIS DE LA ROCHEFOUCAULD, 1665

Plenty of people despise money, but few know how to give it away.

FRANÇOIS DE LA ROCHEFOUCAULD, 1665

He who bestows his goods upon the poor,
Shall have as much again, and ten times more.

JOHN BUNYAN, 1678

It is impossible to make great largesses to the people without great extortion.

C. S. MONTESQUIEU, 1748

A decent provision for the poor is the true test of civilization.　　SAMUEL JOHNSON, 1749

Giving is the business of the rich.

JOHANN WOLFGANG GOETHE, 1797

Our charity begins at home,
And mostly ends where it begins.

HORACE SMITH, 1812

He is one of those wise philanthropists who, in a time of famine, would vote for nothing but a supply of toothpicks.

DOUGLAS JERROLD, 1839

Philanthropies and charities have a certain air of quackery.

RALPH WALDO EMERSON, 1842

We do not forgive a giver. The hand that feeds us is in some danger of being bitten.

RALPH WALDO EMERSON, 1844

Generosity during life is a very different thing from generosity in the hour of death; one proceeds from genuine liberality and benevolence, the other from pride or fear.

HORACE MANN, 1852

Much is required of them to whom much is given.　　THOMAS C. HALIBURTON, 1853

As for doing good, that is one of the professions that are full.   HENRY DAVID THOREAU, 1854

Philanthropy is almost the only virtue which is sufficiently appreciated by mankind.
HENRY DAVID THOREAU, 1854

One must be poor to know the luxury of giving.
GEORGE ELIOT, 1872

In this world, it is not what we take up, but what we give up, that makes us rich.
HENRY WARD BEECHER, 1873

The preaching in England used all to be done to the poor—that they ought to be contented with their lot and respectful to their betters. Now the greatest part of the preaching in America consists in injunctions to those who have taken care of themselves to perform their assumed duty to take care of others.
WILLIAM GRAHAM SUMNER, 1883

Do not give, as many rich men do, like a hen that lays her eggs and then cackles.
HENRY WARD BEECHER, 1887

The man who dies rich dies disgraced.
ANDREW CARNEGIE, 1889

There is but one right mode of using enormous fortunes—namely, that the possessions from time to time during their own lives should so administer these as to promote the permanent good of the communities from which they were gathered.   ANDREW CARNEGIE, 1889

With one hand I take thousands of rubles from the poor, and with the other I hand back a few kopecks.   LYOF N. TOLSTOY, 1891

Money-getters are the benefactors of our race. To them . . . are we indebted for our institutions of learning, and of art, our academies, colleges and churches.   P. T. BARNUM, 1891

Remember the poor—it costs nothing.
MARK TWAIN, 1898

Pauperism exists only because of charity and would soon pass away if almsgiving ceased.
JOHN J. KELSO, 1905

All philanthropy . . . is only a savory fumigation burning at the mouth of a sewer.
ELLEN KEY, 1909

Philanthropist, n. A rich old gentleman who has trained himself to grin while his conscience is picking his pocket.   AMBROSE BIERCE, 1911

Business pays. Philanthropy begs.
W. E. B. DU BOIS, 1911

Pity the poor millionaire—for the way of the philanthropist is hard.
ANDREW CARNEGIE, 1913

It's better to give than to lend, and it costs about the same.   PHILIP GIBBS, 1923

Luxury feeds more poor people than philanthropy.   JUDAH LAZEROV, 1928

Suspicion of one's own motives is especially necessary for the philanthropist and the executive.   BERTRAND RUSSELL, 1930

Charity is injurious unless it helps the recipient to become independent of it.
JOHN D. ROCKEFELLER, JR., 1936

Charity deals with symptoms instead of causes.
HERBERT SAMUEL, 1937

Money giving is a very good criterion, in a way, of a person's mental health. Generous people are rarely mentally ill people.
KARL MENNINGER, 1937

I rather think there is an immense shortage of Christian charity among so-called Christians.
HARRY S TRUMAN, 1947

Philanthropy is commendable, but it must not cause the philanthropist to overlook the circumstances of economic injustice which make philanthropy necessary.
MARTIN LUTHER KING, JR., 1963

We'd all like a reputation for generosity and we'd all like to buy it cheap.
MIGNON MCLAUGHLIN, 1963

There is no anonymous giver, except perhaps the guy who knocks up your daughter.
LENNY BRUCE, 1963

The poor don't know that their function in life is to exercise our generosity.
JEAN-PAUL SARTRE, 1964

Social work is a band-aid on the festering wounds of society.   ALEXANDER CHASE, 1966

Being very rich as far as I am concerned is having a margin. The margin is being able to give.
MAY SARTON, 1973

What am I supposed to do with the money I earn? Give it back?   ROD STEWART, 1975

Planning

Which of you, intending to build a tower, sitteth not down first, and counteth the cost.
LUKE 14:28, C. A.D. 80

Method goes far to prevent trouble in business; for it makes the task easy, hinders confusion, saves abundance of time, and instructs those who have business depending, what to do and what to hope.   WILLIAM PENN, 1694

There is nothing more requisite in business than dispatch.   JOSEPH ADDISON, 1712

Take time to deliberate, but when the time for action has arrived, stop thinking and go in.
NAPOLEON BONAPARTE, 1815

I leave this rule for others when I'm dead. Be always sure you're right—then go ahead.
DAVID CROCKETT, 1832

What people say you cannot do, you try and find that you can.
HENRY DAVID THOREAU, 1854

There is no reason to fear the tyranny of planning since everyone would be motivated by a desire to cooperate. This does not mean government ownership of the factors of production. It merely means that all who own or produce, work toward the same end.
SIMON N. PATTEN, 1902

That industries like coal and electric power, transport and banking, the supply of meat and the provision of houses, should be left to the hazards of private enterprise will appear as unthinkable to a future generation as it is unthinkable to our own that the army of the State should be left to private hands.

HAROLD J. LASKI, 1925

The existence of some sort of parliament is no guarantee against planned economy being developed into dictatorship. On the contrary, experience has shown that representative bodies are unable to fulfill all the multitudinous functions connected with economic leadership without becoming more and more involved in the struggle between competing interests, with the consequence of a moral decay ending in party— if not individual—corruption.

GUSTAV CASSEL, 1934

I expect to see the state . . . taking an ever greater responsibility for directly organizing investment; since it seems likely that the fluctuations in the market estimation of the marginal efficiency of capital . . . will be too great to be offset by any practicable changes in the rate of interest.   JOHN MAYNARD KEYNES, 1936

An organized functioning society requires a planned economy. The more complex the society the greater the demand for planning. Otherwise there results a haphazard and inefficient method of social control, and in the absence of planning, the law of the jungle prevails.

JOSEPH P. KENNEDY, 1936

The more the state "plans" the more difficult planning becomes for the individual.

FRIEDRICH A. HAYEK, 1944

In a directed economy, where the authority watches over the ends pursued, it is certain that it would use its powers to assist some ends and to prevent the realization of others. Not our own

view, but somebody else's, of what we ought to like or dislike would determine what we should get.   FRIEDRICH A. HAYEK, 1944

The plans and the prices system should be pushing in the same direction and not against each other.   JOHN JEWKES, 1948

I do not believe government can run any business as efficiently as private enterprise and the victim of every such experiment is the public.

THOMAS DEWEY, 1948

A main element of every national development plan is a decision to increase the total amount of investment, aimed at raising the productive powers of the country, and to procure the capital formation necessary for this purpose.

GUNNAR MYRDAL, 1957

Fundamentally, there are only two ways of coordinating the economic activities of millions. One is central direction involving the use of coercion—the technique of the army and of the modern totalitarian state. The other is voluntary cooperation of individuals—the technique of the market place. . . . Exchange can bring about coordination without coercion.

MILTON FRIEDMAN, 1962

There is simply no other choice than this: either to abstain from interference in the free play of the market, or to delegate the entire management of production and distribution to the government. Either capitalism or socialism: there exists no middle way.

LUDWIG VON MISES, 1962

A completely planned economy ensures that when no bacon is delivered, no eggs are delivered at the same time.   LEO FRAIN, 1965

The talent that once went into governing Britain now goes more and more into clothes design.   ANTHONY LEWIS, 1966

The persistent breakdowns of the capitalist economy, whatever their immediate precipitating factors, can all be traced to a single underlying cause. This is the anarchic or planless character of capitalist production.

ROBERT HEILBRONER, 1966

The size of General Motors is in the service not of monopoly or the economies of scale but of planning. And for this planning—control of supply, control of demand, provision of capital, minimization of risk—there is no clear upper limit to the desirable size.

JOHN KENNETH GALBRAITH, 1967

The basic notions of the Keynesian theory are so simple that once they are grasped it is difficult to realize the desperate intellectual struggle by which they were evolved. The basic concept is that of the Gross National Product—the total value measured in constant prices; of all goods and services produced.

KENNETH E. BOULDING, 1968

It is unrealistic today to contend that business must be free to pursue its own goals without reference to the broader needs and aims of the total society. All of us in business must recognize and accept the necessity for an expanded government role in our economic life. We must make the most of the situation by cooperating fully in setting the new ground rules.

ARJAY MILLER, 1972

For government to get increasingly into economic planning and intervention is not necessarily the right direction. It's the inevitable direction.   JOHN KENNETH GALBRAITH, 1974

In developing our industrial strategy for the period ahead, we have had the benefit of much experience. Almost everything has been tried at least once.   TONY BENN, 1974

But make no mistake about it; this economy is already "planned," although not in a rational or coherent way.   HUBERT HUMPHREY, 1975

Sooner or later the Government plan, if it is going to serve any purpose at all, is going to mandate a different mix of goods and services than the free market would spontaneously provide. In other words, inevitably someone—maybe all us us—would lose our freedom.

THOMAS A. MURPHY, 1975

People in politics tend to think in two-year, four-year, or six-year cycles, depending on the office they hold or serve. But industry cannot operate in such a framework. Business planning must run in different, usually longer, cycles, up to ten years, even longer.

NELSON ROCKEFELLER, 1975

Our economic understanding and models are simply not powerful enough to handle such a large and complex economic system better than the marketplace.

C. JACKSON GRAYSON, 1975

Implied in the argument for government planning of industrial and commercial activity is the belief that government would be in a better position to predict the future needs of consumer goods, materials, and productive equipment than individual firms. But is it really seriously contended that some government office would be more likely to foresee correctly the effects of future changes in taste . . . ?

FRIEDRICH A. HAYEK, 1976

Despite the myth of a free market, all capitalist economies are planned—and have been, to a greater or lesser degree, since at least World War I.   MICHAEL HARRINGTON, 1984

Poverty

In a country well governed poverty is something to be ashamed of.   CONFUCIUS, c. 500 B.C.

It is plain poverty, no doubt, to need a thing and not to have the use of it.
XENOPHON, c. 415 B.C.

The real disgrace of poverty is not in owning to the fact but in declining the struggle against it.
THUCYDIDES, c. 410 B.C.

Poverty is the parent of revolution and crime.
ARISTOTLE, c. 335 B.C.

It is the nature of the poor to hate and envy men of property.   PLAUTUS, c. 200 B.C.

A generous and noble spirit cannot be expected to dwell in the breasts of men who are struggling for their daily bread.
DIONYSIS, c. 20 B.C.

Poverty urges us to do and suffer anything that we may escape from it, and so leads us away from virtue.   HORACE, c. 19 B.C.

The prosperous cannot easily form a right idea of misery.   QUINTILIAN, c. A.D. 75

They do not easily rise whose abilities are repressed by poverty at home.
DECIMUS JUNIUS JUVENALIS, c. A.D. 120

Cheerless poverty has no harder trial than this, that it makes men the subject of ridicule.
DECIMUS JUNIUS JUVENALIS, c. A.D. 120

The bread that you store up belongs to the hungry; the cloak that lies in your chest belongs to the naked; and the gold that you have hidden in the ground belongs to the poor.
ST. BASIL, c. 375

The beggar fears no reverse of fortune.
BHARTRIHARI, c. 625

No man should commend poverty but one who is poor.
ST. BERNARD OF CLAIRVAUX, c. 1153

Beggars should be no choosers.
JOHN HEYWOOD, 1546

Well, whiles I am a beggar I will rail
And say there is no sin but to be rich;
And being rich, my virtue then shall be
To say there is no vice but beggary.
WILLIAM SHAKESPEARE,
King John (II, i), 1594

Poverty is no vice, but an inconvenience.
JOHN FLORIO, 1603

He must have a great deal of godliness who can find any satisfaction in being poor.
MIGUEL DE CERVANTES, 1605

If the poor are too well off they will be disorderly.   RICHELIEU, 1617

The right time to dine—for a rich man, when he is hungry; for a poor man, when he has something to eat.   LUIS VÉLEZ DE GUEVARA, 1641

Beggars breed and rich men feed.
JOHN RAY, 1670

It is a reproach to religion and government to suffer so much poverty and excess.
WILLIAM PENN, 1688

Poverty palls the most generous spirits; it cows industry, and casts resolution itself into despair.
JOSEPH ADDISON, 1712

Beg from beggars and you'll never be rich.
JAMES KELLY, c. 1721

Poverty is not a shame, but the being ashamed of it is.   THOMAS FULLER, 1732

The pleasures of the rich are bought with the tears of the poor.   THOMAS FULLER, 1732

The poor man is never free; he serves in every country.   VOLTAIRE, 1755

Every country where begging is a profession is ill-governed.   VOLTAIRE, 1762

Nobody has occasion for pride but the poor; everywhere else it is a sign of folly.
THOMAS GRAY, 1769

I never could teach the fools of this age that the indigent world could be clothed out of the trimmings of the vain.
OLIVER GOLDSMITH, 1773

No society can surely be flourishing and happy, of which the far greater part of the members are poor and miserable.   ADAM SMITH, 1776

Virtue is the compensation to the poor for the want of riches.   HORACE WALPOLE, 1778

What we are told about the great sums got by begging is not true: the trade is overstocked.
SAMUEL JOHNSON, 1779

Poverty is a great enemy to human happiness; it certainly destroys liberty, and it makes some virtues impracticable, and others extremely difficult.   SAMUEL JOHNSON, 1782

Poverty, of course, is no disgrace, but it is damned annoying.   WILLIAM PITT, 1784

But poverty, with most who wimper forth
Their long complaints, is self-inflicted woe;
The effect of laziness, or sottish waste.
WILLIAM COWPER, 1785

Wealth rarely begets sedition; that baneful production generally springs from poverty, vice and disappointment. There are characters which find interest in fishing in troubled waters. We have, perhaps, no instance of a nation ruined by its merchants.   PELATIAH WEBSTER, 1791

The people must comprehend that they are themselves the cause of their own poverty.
THOMAS MALTHUS, 1798

The rude inelegance of poverty.
ROBERT BLOOMFIELD, 1800

Poverty is no disgrace to a man, but it is confoundedly inconvenient.
SYDNEY SMITH, 1800

The poor man commands respect; the beggar must always excite anger.
NAPOLEON BONAPARTE, 1815

It is not poverty so much as pretense that harasses a ruined man—the struggle between a proud mind and an empty purse—the keeping up of a hollow show that must soon come to an end. WASHINGTON IRVING, 1819

He is not expected to become bail or surety for anyone. No man troubleth him with questioning his religion or politics. He is the only free man in the universe. CHARLES LAMB, 1822

Wherever there is excessive wealth, there is also in the train of it excessive poverty; as where the sun is brightest the shade is deepest.
WALTER SAVAGE LANDOR, 1829

To be poor and independent is very nearly an impossibility. WILLIAM COBBETT, 1830

Respectable means rich, and decent means poor. I should die if I heard my family called decent.
THOMAS L. PEACOCK, 1831

The poor are everywhere more liberal, more obligin' and more hospitable according to their means, than the rich are.
THOMAS C. HALIBURTON, 1838

None can be an impartial or wise observer of human life but from the vantage ground of what we should call voluntary poverty.
HENRY DAVID THOREAU, 1854

Poverty destroys pride. It is difficult for an empty bag to stand upright.
ALEXANDRE DUMAS, *fils*, 1857

The greatest man in history was the poorest.
RALPH WALDO EMERSON, 1860

Of all the preposterous assumptions of humanity over humanity, nothing exceeds most of the criticisms made on the habits of the poor by the well-housed, well-warmed, and well-fed.
HERMAN MELVILLE, 1860

Pauperism is the hospital of the labor army.
KARL MARX, 1867

You cannot sift out the poor from the community. The poor are indispensable to the rich.
HENRY WARD BEECHER, 1873

Looking comprehensively at the matter . . . the general truth will stand that no man in this land suffers from poverty unless it be more than his fault—unless it be his *sin*.
HENRY WARD BEECHER, 1877

Poverty is the openmouthed relentless hell which yawns beneath civilized society.
HENRY GEORGE, 1879

Let every man be sober, industrious, prudent, and wise, and bring up his children to be so likewise, and poverty will be abolished in a few generations.
WILLIAM GRAHAM SUMNER, 1883

Beggars should be abolished. It annoys one to give to them, and it annoys one not to give to them. FRIEDRICH NIETZSCHE, 1885

Poverty comes pleading, not for charity, for the most part, but imploring us to find a purchaser for its unmarketable wares.
OLIVER WENDELL HOLMES, SR., 1891

There is only one class in the community that thinks more about money than the rich and that is the poor. The poor can think of nothing else.
OSCAR WILDE, 1898

The notion there is necessarily any causal connection between opulence and poverty is too crude to require serious refutation.
F. S. BALDWIN, 1899

The prevalent fear of poverty among the educated classes is the worst moral disease from which our civilization suffers.
WILLIAM JAMES, 1902

We despise anyone who elects to be poor in order to simplify and save his inner life. If he does not join the general scramble and pant with the money-making street, we deem him spiritless and lacking in ambition.   WILLIAM JAMES, 1902

One of the strangest things about life is that the poor, who need money the most, are the very ones that never have it.
FINLEY PETER DUNNE, 1902

Poverty keeps together more homes than it breaks up.   HECTOR HUGH MUNRO, 1902

To be a poor man is hard, but to be a poor race in a land of dollars is the very bottom of hardships.   W. E. B. DU BOIS, 1903

Beggar, n. One who has relied on the assistance of his friends.   AMBROSE BIERCE, 1906

The honest poor can sometimes forget poverty. The honest rich can never forget it.
GILBERT K. CHESTERTON, 1908

Poverty is the strenuous life—without brass bands, or uniforms.   WILLIAM JAMES, 1908

Most of our realists and sociologists talk about a poor man as if he were an octopus or an alligator.   GILBERT K. CHESTERTON, 1909

There is one advantage of being poor—a doctor will cure you faster.
FRANK MCKINNEY HUBBARD, 1915

It's no disgrace t' be poor, but it might as well be.   FRANK MCKINNEY HUBBARD, 1915

We shall probably discover that the poor are even less ready to part with their neuroses than the rich, because the hard life that awaits them when they recover has no attraction, and illness in them gives them more claim to the help of others.   SIGMUND FREUD, 1924

I thank fate for having made me born poor. Poverty taught me the true value of the gifts useful to life.   ANATOLE FRANCE, 1924

We are nearer today to the ideal of the abolition of poverty and fear from the lives of men and women than ever before in any land.
HERBERT HOOVER, 1928

I've worked myself up from nothing to a state of extreme poverty.   GROUCHO MARX, 1931

I've known what it is to be hungry, but I always went right to a restaurant.
RING LARDNER, 1932

Poverty annihilates the future. Within certain limits, it is actually true that the less money you have, the less you worry.
GEORGE ORWELL, 1933

If you aren't rich, you should always look useful.   LOUIS-FERDINAND CÉLINE, 1934

Only the rich preach content to the poor.
HOLBROOK JACKSON, 1934

Those who know the normal life of the poor, its haunting sense of impending disaster, its fitful search for beauty which perpetually eludes, will realize well enough that, without economic security, liberty is not worth having.
HAROLD J. LASKI, 1937

Poverty is an awful, eventually a degrading thing, and it is rare that anything good comes from it. We rise, old friend, in spite of adversity, not because of it.   THOMAS WOLFE, 1938

The line between hunger and anger is a thin line.   JOHN STEINBECK, 1939

Modern poverty is not the poverty that was blest in the Sermon on the Mount.
GEORGE BERNARD SHAW, 1941

It's a kind of spiritual snobbery that makes people think they can be happy without money.
ALBERT CAMUS, 1942

It was clear . . . that poverty and disease formed a vicious circle. Men and women were sick because they were poor; they became poorer because they were sick, and sicker because they were poorer.
C. E. A. WINSLOW, 1951

The first and strategic step in an attack on poverty is to see that it is no longer self-perpetuating.
JOHN KENNETH GALBRAITH, 1958

If the population density in some of Harlem's worst blocks pertained in the rest of New York City, the entire population of the United States could fit into three of New York's boroughs.
U.S. CIVIL RIGHTS COMMISSION, 1959

Anyone who has ever struggled with poverty knows how extremely expensive it is to be poor.
JAMES BALDWIN, 1960

The problems of abolishing want is not a problem in division, as the politicians so often aver; it is a problem in multiplication.
HENRY M. WRISTON, 1960

Poverty is a culture.
MICHAEL HARRINGTON, 1963

Poverty is expensive to maintain.
MICHAEL HARRINGTON, 1963

If a free society cannot help the many who are poor, it cannot save the few who are rich.
JOHN F. KENNEDY, 1963

Wealth is conspicuous, but poverty hides.
JAMES RESTON, 1964

Poor people have more fun than rich people, they say; and I notice it's the rich people who keep saying it.
JACK PAAR, 1965

That men and women actually starved in the great cities was known; while deplorable, that fact was not enough in itself to shake the old conceptions of responsibility.
OSCAR HANDLIN, 1966

The poor don't even have a unity of their own. Those who manage to escape the condition of poverty rarely look back, and those at the bottom of the heap live in almost total isolation of each other.
JOSEPH P. LYFORD, 1966

The rich man may never get into heaven, but the pauper is already serving his term in hell.
ALEXANDER CHASE, 1966

The conspicuously wealthy turn up urging the character-building value of privation for the poor.
JOHN KENNETH GALBRAITH, 1977

The best way to help the poor is not to become one of them.
LAING HANCOCK, 1977

The war on poverty that began in 1964 has been won.
MARTIN ANDERSON, 1978

Those who have some means think that the most important thing in the world is love. The poor know that it is money.
GERALD BRENAN, 1978

Generally speaking, the poorer person summers where he winters.
FRAN LEBOWITZ, 1981

Price

A thing is worth whatever the buyer will pay for it.   PUBLILIUS SYRUS, first century B.C.

The price of an article is changed according to difference in location, time or risk to which one is exposed in carrying it from one place to another or in causing it to be carried. Neither purchase nor sale according to this principle is unjust.   THOMAS AQUINAS, c. 1264

Things of greatest profit are set forth with least price.   JOHN LYLY, 1579

It doesn't help to remember the price of yesterday's roast beef.   BEN JONSON, 1637

The "value" or "worth" of a man is as of all other things, his price; that is to say, so much as would be given for the use of his power.
     THOMAS HOBBES, 1647

What is worth in anything
But so much money as 'twill bring?
     SAMUEL BUTLER, 1664

The greatest of all gifts is the power to estimate things at their true worth.
     FRANÇOIS DE LA ROCHEFOUCAULD, 1665

Made them pay for it most unconscionable and through the nose.   ANDREW MARVELL, 1672

The price of any commodity rises or falls by the proportion of the number of buyers and sellers.
     JOHN LOCKE, 1692

Every man has his price.
     ROBERT WALPOLE, 1734

The duties felt least by the people are those on merchandise, because they are not demanded of them in form. They may be so prudently managed that the people themselves shall hardly know they pay them. For this purpose it is of the utmost consequence that the person who sells the merchandise should pay the duty. He is very sensible that he does not pay it for himself; and the consumer, who pays it in the main, confounds it with the price.
     C. S. MONTESQUIEU, 1748

Value is a relation between persons.
     FERDINANDO GALIANI, 1750

It seems a maxim almost self-evident that the price of everything depends on the proportion between commodities and money.
     DAVID HUME, 1752

The actual price at which any commodity is commonly sold is called its market price. It may either be above, or below, or exactly the same with its natural price.   ADAM SMITH, 1776

Rent, it is to be observed, therefore, enters into the composition of the price of commodities in a different way from wages and profit. High or low wages and profit, are the causes of high or low price; high or low rent is the effect of it.

ADAM SMITH, 1776

Wages, profit, and rent, are the three original sources of all revenue as well as of all exchangeable value. All other revenue [interest, taxes, etc.] is ultimately derived from some one or other of these.   ADAM SMITH, 1776

Nothing is more useful than water: but it will purchase scarce any thing. . . . A diamond, on the contrary, has scarce any value in use; but a very great quantity of other goods may frequently be had in exchange for it.

ADAM SMITH, 1776

The market price of every particular commodity is regulated by the proportion between the quantity which is actually brought to market and the demand of those who are willing to pay the natural price of the commodity.

ADAM SMITH, 1776

What we obtain too cheaply we esteem too lightly; it is dearness only which gives everything its value.   THOMAS PAINE, 1786

The price of commodities in the market is formed by means of a certain struggle which takes place between the buyers and the sellers.

HENRY THORNTON, 1802

If any one commodity could be found which now and at all other times required precisely the same amount of labor to produce it, that commodity would be of an unvarying value, and would be eminently useful as a standard by which the variations of other things might be measured.

DAVID RICARDO, 1817

Possessing utility, commodities derive their exchangeable value from two sources: from their scarcity, and from the quantity of labor required to obtain them.

DAVID RICARDO, 1817

The natural price of all commodities, excepting raw produce and labor, has a tendency to fall in the progress of wealth and population; for though, on one hand, they are enhanced in real value, from the rise in the natural price of the raw material of which they are made, this is more than counterbalanced by the improvements in machinery, by the better division and distribution of labor, and by the increasing skill, both in science and art, of the producers.

DAVID RICARDO, 1817

A cheap article ain't always the best; if you want a real right down first chop, *genuwine* thing, you must pay for it.

THOMAS C. HALIBURTON, 1838

The value of a thing means the quantity of some other thing, or things in general, which it exchanges for.   JOHN STUART MILL, 1848

The cost of a thing is the amount of what I will call life which is required to pay for it.

HENRY DAVID THOREAU, 1854

As values, all commodities are only definite masses of congealed labor time.

KARL MARX, 1867

Price in any particular instance will be greater or less according as it is the buyer or seller who is best in a position to take advantage of the other's necessities.   W. T. THORNTON, 1870

There is no such thing as cheapness in the universe. Everything costs its own cost, and one of our best virtues is a just desire to pay it.

JOHN RUSKIN, 1884

The timid man yearns for full value and demands a tenth. The bold man strikes for double value and compromises on par.

MARK TWAIN, 1897

No matter how eagerly the products of one country may be demanded by another country . . . no appreciable difference of prices can persist when there is a free interchange of goods.

KNUT WICKSELL, 1906

Price, n. Value, plus a reasonable sum for the wear and tear of conscience in demanding it.

AMBROSE BIERCE, 1911

The price of an article is exactly what it will fetch.   MARCUS SAMUEL, 1911

Though no precise boundary between economic and non-economic welfare exists, yet the test of accessibility to a money measure serves well enough to set up a rough distinction.

A. C. PIGOU, 1920

We may conclude that, as a general rule, the shorter the period which we are considering, the greater must be the share of our attention which is given to the influence of demand on value; and the longer the period, the more important will be the influence of cost of production on value.   ALFRED MARSHALL, 1920

Price is simply the expression in terms of money of the equation at which a given faculty and a given desire, under given conditions, consent to unite and generate exchange value.

BEATRICE POTTER WEBB, 1926

We are not in a position to weigh the satisfactions for similar persons of Pharoah's slaves against Fifth Avenue's motor cars, or dear fuel and cheap ice to Laplanders against cheap fuel and dear ice to Hottentots.

JOHN MAYNARD KEYNES, 1930

The generalizations of the Theory of Value are as applicable to the behavior of isolated man or the executive authority of a communist society, as to the behavior of man in an exchange economy.   LIONEL ROBBINS, 1932

The price system will fulfill [its] function only if competition prevails, that is, if the individual producer has to adapt himself to price changes and cannot control them.

FRIEDRICH A. HAYEK, 1944

The exchange relation is the fundamental social relation.   LUDWIG VON MISES, 1949

Nothing is intrinsically valuable; the value of everything is attributed to it, assigned to it from outside the thing itself, by people.

JOHN BARTH, 1956

Your father used to say, "Never give away your work. People don't value what they don't have to pay for."   NANCY HALE, 1957

A general definition of intrinsic value would be "that value which is justified by the facts, e.g., assets, earnings, dividends, [and] definite prospects, including the factor of management." The primary objective in using the adjective "intrinsic" is to emphasize the distinction between value and current market price, but not to invest this "value" with an aura of performance.

BENJAMIN GRAHAM, 1962

Of all the possible business strategies open to the firm, price strategy is the easiest [for competitors] to detect, to counteract, and hence to defeat.   JESSE W. MARKHAM, 1963

Economy implies valuations; and valuation is peculiarly and essentially relative. The prices with which rigorous economics deal are pure relations; and relatives cannot be summated into meaningful totals. Market prices afford only the most meager clues to the "value" of *all* goods produced and services rendered.

HENRY C. SIMONS, 1965

The value of anything is not what you get paid for it, nor what it cost to produce, but what you can get for it at an auction.

WILLIAM LYON PHELPS, 1969

There's no such thing as a free lunch.

MILTON FRIEDMAN, 1974

One person's price is another person's income.

WALTER W. HELLER, 1975

The real cost of any action is the value of the alternative opportunity that must be sacrificed in order to take the action.

HALL HEYNE, 1976

If you pay peanuts, you get monkeys.

JAMES GOLDSMITH, 1979

My introduction to the theory of money and exchange occurred when the San Diego Chargers sold me to the Buffalo Bills for $100.

JACK KEMP, 1982

Production

A nation wherein are eight millions of people is more than twice as rich as the same scope of land wherein are but four.

WILLIAM PETTY, 1662

The greatest improvement in the productive powers of labor and the greater part of the skill, dexterity, and judgement with which it is anywhere directed, or applied, seem to have been the effects of the division of labor.

ADAM SMITH, 1776

Men, like all other animals, naturally multiply in proportion to the means of their subsistence.

ADAM SMITH, 1776

All trades, arts, and handiworks have gained by division of labor. . . . Where the different kinds

of work are not distinguished and divided, where everyone is a jack-of-all-trades, there manufactures remain still in the greatest barbarism.

IMMANUEL KANT, 1785

There is no amount of capital which may not be employed in a country, because demand is only limited by production. No man produces but with a view to consume or sell, and he never sells, but with an intention to purchase some other commodity.

DAVID RICARDO, 1817

The increase of net incomes, estimated in commodities, which is always the consequence of improved machinery, will lead to new savings and accumulations . . . and the demand for labor will be as great as before.

DAVID RICARDO, 1817

We have every reason to hope that with the progress of society population and wealth will increase together and that more human beings will be supported in greater comfort than heretofore.   MOUNTIFORT LONGFIELD, 1834

An object of art creates a public capable of finding pleasure in its beauty. Production, therefore, not only produces an object for the subject, but also a subject for the object.
                                    KARL MARX, 1844

Man produces in order to consume.
                                    FRÉDÉRIC BASTIAT, 1847

It is only in the backward countries of the world that increased production is still an important object. In those most advanced what is economically needed is better distribution.
                                    JOHN STUART MILL, 1848

The power of producing wealth is, therefore, infinitely more important than wealth itself; it insures not only the possession and the increase of what has been gained, but also the replacement of what has been lost.
                                    FREDERICK LIST, 1856

The method of production of the material things of life generally determines the social, political and spiritual currents of life.
                                    KARL MARX, 1859

The production of surplus-value, or the extraction of surplus labor, is the specific end and aim, the sum and substance, of capitalist production.
                                    KARL MARX, 1867

It is not the increase of food that has caused this increase of men; but the increase of men that has brought about the increase of food. There is more food simply because there are more men.   HENRY GEORGE, 1879

As it is with an individual, so it is with a nation. One must produce to have, or one will become a have-not.   HENRY GEORGE, 1879

The development of capitalist production makes it constantly necessary to keep increasing the amount of capital laid out in a given industrial undertaking, and competition makes the immanent laws of capitalist production to be felt by each capitalist as external coercive laws.
                                    KARL MARX, 1883

In almost all of the mechanic arts the science which underlies each act of each workman is so great and amounts to so much that the workman who is best suited to actually doing the work is incapable of fully understanding this science, without the guidance and help of those who are working with him or over him.
                                    FREDERICK W. TAYLOR, 1894

Anybody can cut prices, but it takes brains to make a better article.
                                    ALICE HUBBARD, 1899

I will build a motorcar for the great multitudes.
                                    HENRY FORD, 1909

No great man can (with the old system of personal management) hope to compete with a number of ordinary men who have been properly organized so as efficiently to cooperate.
                                    FREDERICK W. TAYLOR, 1911

Along about April 1, 1913, we first tried the experiment of an assembly line.
                                    HENRY FORD, 1922

Economic efficiency consists of making things that are worth more than they cost.
                                    JOHN MAURICE CLARK, 1923

It is not the employer who pays wages. He only handles the money. It is the product that pays wages and it is the management that arranges the production so that the product may pay the wages.   HENRY FORD, 1926

Mass production is the focusing upon a manufacturing product of the principles of power, accuracy, economy, system, continuity and speed . . . and the normal result is a productive organization that delivers in quantities a useful commodity of standard material, workmanship and design at minimum cost.
HENRY FORD, 1926

Every minute, there's another Ford.
HAMILTON FISH ARMSTRONG, 1937

The capitalist achievement does not typically consist in providing more silk stockings for queens but in bringing them within reach of factory girls in return for steadily decreasing amounts of effort.
JOSEPH A. SCHUMPETER, 1942

Productive power is the foundation of a country's economic strength.
STAFFORD CRIPPS, 1948

Production is the goose that lays the golden egg. Payrolls make consumers.
GEORGE HUMPHREY, 1954

Knowledge is the only instrument of production that is not subject to diminishing returns.
JOHN MAURICE CLARK, 1957

One cannot defend production as satisfying wants if that production creates its own wants.
JOHN KENNETH GALBRAITH, 1958

Production only fills a void that it has itself created.   JOHN KENNETH GALBRAITH, 1958

Production is not the application of tools to materials, but logic to work.
PETER DRUCKER, 1965

The more advanced the specialization in production and the more complex the economy, the costlier it will be to undertake all the transactions necessary to make any given good reach its ultimate user by using barter.
BORIS P. PESEK, 1967

In places like the textile mills, where superhuman production rates are set, the people have to take speed (amphetamines) in order to keep up production.   KATHY KAHN, 1974

When a country gains new manpower from the excess of births over deaths or from immigration and increased female participation, its same land and complement of capital assets can produce a larger social pie.
PAUL A. SAMUELSON, 1978

A company cannot increase its productivity. People can.   ROBERT HALF, 1980

Profit

To gain without another's loss is impossible.
PUBLILIUS SYRUS, C. 43 B.C.

The smell of profit is clean
And clean, whatever the source.
JUVENAL, C. A.D. 120

Nothing is less profitable than to spend much labor on that which one profits little.
JOHN OF SALISBURY, c. 1165

Measure not dispatch by the times of sitting, but by the advancement of the business.
FRANCIS BACON, 1597

The primary and sole foundation of virtue or of the proper conduct of life is to seek our own profit.
BENEDICT DE SPINOZA, 1675

Men must have profits proportionable to their expense and hazard.
DAVID HUME, 1754

In reality high profits tend much more to raise the price of work than high wages. . . . Our merchants and master manufacturers complain much of the bad effects of high wages in raising the price and thereby lessening the scale of their goods both at home and abroad. They say nothing concerning the bad effects of high profits.
ADAM SMITH, 1776

The increase in stock which raises wages, tends to lower profits when the stock of many rich merchants are turned to the same trade. Their mutual competition naturally tends to lower profit.
ADAM SMITH, 1776

It is only for the sake of profit that any man employs a capital in the support of industry; and he will always, therefore, endeavor to employ it in the support of that industry of which the produce is likely to be of the greatest value.
ADAM SMITH, 1776

A business with an income at its heels.
WILLIAM COWPER, 1788

When wages are low, profits must be high.
DAVID RICARDO, 1817

Profits depend on high or low wages, wages on the price of necessaries, and the price of necessaries chiefly on the price of food.
DAVID RICARDO, 1817

Nothing contributes so much to the prosperity and happiness of a country as high profits.
DAVID RICARDO, 1817

A profit is made, not because the industry produces more than it costs, but because it fails to

give the workman sufficient compensation for his toil. Such an industry is a social evil.
SIMONDE DE SISMONDI, 1819

A trade won't be followed long that ain't a profitable one, that's a fact.
THOMAS C. HALIBURTON, 1840

There is at every time and place some particular rate of profit, which is the lowest that will induce the people of that country and time to accumulate savings and to employ those savings productively.
JOHN STUART MILL, 1848

The cause of profit is, that labor produces more than is required for its support.
JOHN STUART MILL, 1848

Commerce is like war. Its result is patent. Do you make money or do you not make it? There is as little appeal from figures as from battle.
WALTER BAGEHOT, 1867

I would like to see a fair division of profits between capital and labor, so that the toiler could save enough to mingle a little June with the December of his life.
ROBERT G. INGERSOLL, 1883

At the beginning of his undertaking, and at every successive stage, the alert business man strives to modify his arrangements so as to obtain better results with a given expenditure, or equal results with less expenditure.
ALFRED MARSHALL, 1890

The worst crime against working people is a company which fails to operate at a profit.
SAMUEL GOMPERS, 1908

That I should make him that steals my coat a present of my cloak—what would become of business?
KATHERINE LEE BATES, 1921

Profits and prostitution—upon these empires are built and kingdoms stand.
ADELA PANKHURST, 1921

Businesses planned for service are apt to succeed; businesses planned for profit are apt to fail.
NICHOLAS M. BUTLER, 1923

Not all those who are attempting to conduct successful businesses are profiteers.
CALVIN COOLIDGE, 1924

The rate of return over cost is always that rate which, employed in computing the present worth of all the costs and the present worth of all the returns, will make these two equal.
IRVING FISHER, 1930

In business, the earning of profit is something more than an incident of success. It is an essential condition of success. It is an essential condition of success because the continued absence of profit itself spells failure.
LOUIS D. BRANDEIS, 1930

If you count all your assets you always show a profit.
ROBERT QUILLEN, 1938

Modern economic activity is immediately animated and guided, not by the quest of satisfactions, but by the quest of profits. Therefore, business cycles are distinctly phenomena of a pecuniary as opposed to an industrial character.
WESLEY C. MITCHELL, 1941

Profit is merely the index, the proof that production was for use.
GUSTAV STOLPER, 1942

The trouble with the profit system has always been that it was highly unprofitable to most people.
E. B. WHITE, 1944

Profit is the ignition system of our economic engine.
CHARLES SAWYER, 1950

It is a socialist idea that making profits is a vice; I consider the real vice is making losses.
                                   WINSTON CHURCHILL, 1951

The elementary basis of our economy is that . . . there can be no lasting profit in the exchange unless the exchange is profitable to both.
                                   WALTER LIPPMANN, 1954

Denial of profit by socialism and recognition of profit by capitalism has never served as the feature distinguishing socialism from capitalism. The difference is in the way profit is formed, appropriated and used.   YEVSEI LIBERMAN, 1963

When someone asked me, which do you put first in your mind, service or profits, I said naturally I put service first, but we can only serve by earning money.   FREDERICK R. KAPPEL, 1964

Profitability is the sovereign criterion of the enterprise.   PETER DRUCKER, 1965

Profits are part of the mechanism by which society decides what it wants to see produced.
                                   HENRY C. WALLICH, 1967

Does the modern industrial corporation maximize profits? Probably not rigorously and singlemindedly, and for much the same reason that Dr. Johnson did not become a philosopher—because cheerfulness keeps breaking in.
                                   ROBERT SOLOW, 1967

The next guy who talks to me about tonnage is going to get his salary in tons, and we'll see how he converts that into dollars.
                                   JOHN C. LOBB, 1967

If one has not made a reasonable profit, one has made a mistake.   LI XIANNIAN, 1968

There's no question that excessive labor costs add to inflation. But if you want to put first things first, have a look at the role of profits.
                                   JAMES TOBIN, 1971

Rising corporate profits are needed more than ever by the poor.   SPIRO T. AGNEW, 1971

The only way to keep score in business is to add up how much money you make.
                                   HARRY B. HELMSLEY, 1973

Profits are to a corporation what breathing is to human life. We cannot live in a private enterprise system without profits. But breathing is not the sole purpose of life, and profits are not the sole purpose of the adventure that we call business management.   FLETCHER BYROM, 1974

And I have one last rule: Obey Friedman's law and make a profit. That will create jobs, and that is the most revolutionary concept there is.
                                   THORNTON F. BRADSHAW, 1974

Businessmen commit a fraud when they say they're interested in anything but profit.
                                   JIM BROOKS, 1976

The bottom line is in heaven.
                                   EDWIN HERBERT LAND, 1977

If an exchange between two parties is voluntary, it will not take place unless both believe they will benefit from it. Most economic fallacies derive from the neglect of this simple insight, from the tendency to assume that there is a fixed pie, that one party can gain only at the expense of another.
                                   MILTON FRIEDMAN, 1981

People who think only of profit in the next twenty years won't make any profit.
                                   PAUL BOUGENAUX, 1982

Money in itself doesn't interest me. But you must make money to go on building the business.
                                   RUPERT MURDOCH, 1984

Property

If we all seized the property of our neighbors and grabbed from one another what we could make use of, the bonds of human society would necessarily crumble.   CICERO, c. 65 B.C.

And call not anything your own, but let everything be common property.
                        ST. AUGUSTINE, 397

The reason why men enter into society is the preservation of their property.
                        JOHN LOCKE, 1690

Where there is no property, there is no injustice.
                        JOHN LOCKE, 1690

I have heard of a man who had a mind to sell his house, and therefore carried a piece of brick in his pocket, which he showed as a pattern to encourage purchasers.
                        JONATHAN SWIFT, 1724

The first man to fence in a piece of land, saying "This is mine," and who found people simple enough to believe him, was the real founder of civil society.
                        JEAN-JACQUES ROUSSEAU, 1754

It should be remembered that the foundation of the social contract is property; and its first condition, that every one should be maintained in the peaceful possession of what belongs to him.
                        JEAN-JACQUES ROUSSEAU, 1758

Without that sense of security which property gives, the land would still be uncultivated.
                        FRANÇOIS QUESNAY, 1758

The spirit of property doubles a man's strength.
                        VOLTAIRE, 1764

The rent of land is a monopoly price. It is not at all proportioned to what the landlord may have laid out upon the improvement of the land, or to what he can afford to take, but to what the farmer can afford to give.
                        ADAM SMITH, 1776

Wherever there is great property there is great inequality. For one very rich man there must be at least five hundred poor, and the affluence of the few supposes the indigence of the many.
                        ADAM SMITH, 1776

There is a disadvantage belonging to land, compared with money. A man is not so much afraid of being a hard creditor as of being a hard landlord.   SAMUEL JOHNSON, 1783

Private property . . . is a Creature of Society, and is subject to the Calls of that Society, whenever its Necessities shall require it, even to its last Farthing.   BENJAMIN FRANKLIN, 1783

The small landholders are the most precious part of a state.   THOMAS JEFFERSON, 1785

The most common and durable source of faction has been the various and unequal distribution of property.   JAMES MADISON, 1788

Those who hold and those who are without property have ever formed distinct interests in society.   JAMES MADISON, 1788

Property and law are born together, and die together. Before laws were made there was no property; take away laws, and property ceases.   JEREMY BENTHAM, 1789

Some people talk of morality, and some of religion, but give me a little snug property.   MARIA EDGEWORTH, 1804

The interest of the landlord is always opposed to that of the consumer and manufacturer.   DAVID RICARDO, 1817

Rent is in all cases a portion of the profits previously obtained on the land. It is never the creation of new revenue, but always a part of the revenue already created.   DAVID RICARDO, 1817

[Property] is a patent entitling one man to dispose of another man's labor.   THOMAS MALTHUS, 1827

The natural tendency of every society in which property enjoys tolerable security is to increase in wealth.   THOMAS B. MACAULEY, 1835

An acre in Middlesex is better than a principality in Utopia.   THOMAS MACAULEY, 1837

Property has its duties as well as its rights.   THOMAS DRUMMOND, 1838

Rent: all income secured without personal exertion solely in virtue of possession.   KARL RODBERTUS, 1839

Property is theft.   PIERRE JOSEPH PROUDHON, 1840

Private property was never
Made by nature. . . .
With no pockets in our skins, we
Every one the world first entered.   HEINRICH HEINE, 1841

I am amused to see from my window here how busily man has divided and staked off his domain. God must smile at his puny fences running hither and thither everywhere over the land.   HENRY DAVID THOREAU, 1842

The first thing the student has to do is to get rid of the idea of absolute ownership. Such an idea is quite unknown to the English law.   JOSHUA WILLIAMS, 1845

What we call real estate—the solid ground to build a house on—is the broad foundation on which nearly all the guilt of this world rests.   NATHANIEL HAWTHORNE, 1851

Equity . . . does not permit property in land.   HERBERT SPENCER, 1851

That low, bestial instinct which men call the right of property.   LYOF TOLSTOY, 1852

In a free and just community, property rushes from the idle and imbecile, to the industrious, brave and persevering.   RALPH WALDO EMERSON, 1860

No land is bad, but land is worse. If a man owns land, the land owns him. Now let him leave home, if he dare.   RALPH WALDO EMERSON, 1860

Whereas it has long been known and declared that the poor have no right to the property of the rich, I wish it also to be known and declared that the rich have no right to the property of the poor. JOHN RUSKIN, 1862

Political economy confuses on principle two very different kinds of private property, of which one rests on the producers' own labor, the other on the employment of the labor of others. KARL MARX, 1867

No state shall . . . deprive any person of life, liberty, or property without due process of law. FOURTEENTH AMENDMENT, U. S. CONSTITUTION, 1868

Private property is at once the consequence and the basis of the state. MIKHAIL A. BAKUNIN, 1871

The essential principle of property being to assure to all persons what they have produced by their labor and accumulated by their abstinence. JOHN STUART MILL, 1875

One does not sell the earth upon which the people walk. TASHUNKA WITKO (CRAZY HORSE), c. 1875

For as labor cannot produce without the use of land, the denial of the equal right to use of land is necessarily the denial of the right of labor to its own produce. HENRY GEORGE, 1879

Property is the strongest, deepest, most universal interest of mankind. It is the most fundamental condition of the struggle for existence. WILLIAM GRAHAM SUMNER, 1883

No man should be allowed to own any land that he does not use. ROBERT G. INGERSOLL, 1883

When we have two or three times as many voters as now and few owners of property in proportion to the whole, there may be troubles which will upset the whole scheme and make it necessary to establish one or more strong governments with large standing armies. CHARLES ELLIOTT PERKINS, 1886

Where all of the man is what property he owns, it does not take long to annihilate him. HENRY WARD BEECHER, 1887

If property had simply pleasures, we could stand it; but its duties make it unbearable. In the interest of the rich we must get rid of it. OSCAR WILDE, 1889

The tendency of careful economic study is to base the rights of property, not on any abstract principles, but on the observations that in the past they have been inseparable from solid progress; and therefore it is the part of responsible men to proceed cautiously and tentatively in abrogating or modifying even such rights as may seem to be inappropriate to the ideal conditions of social life.

ALFRED MARSHALL, 1890

It is immoral to use private property to alleviate the horrible evils that result from the institution of private property. It is both immoral and unfair. OSCAR WILDE, 1895

[Land] gives one position, and prevents one from keeping it up. OSCAR WILDE, 1899

The instinct of ownership is fundamental in man's nature. WILLIAM JAMES, 1902

Property, n. Any material thing, having no particular value, that may be held by A against the cupidity of B. AMBROSE BIERCE, 1906

Of all obstacles to that complete democracy of which we dream, is there a greater than property? DAVID GRAYSON, 1907

Property is necessary, but it is not necessary that it should remain forever in the same hands.

REMY DE GOURMONT, 1910

The house was more covered with mortgages than with paint.

GEORGE ADE, 1912

There is something that governments care far more for than human life, and that is the security of property.

EMMELINE PANKHURST, 1914

The fundamental issue . . . is not between scales of ownership, but between ownership of different kinds; not between the large farmer or master and the small, but between property which is used for work and property which yields income without work.

RICHARD H. TAWNEY, 1920

Property is the most ambiguous of categories. It covers a multitude of rights which have nothing in common except that they are exercised by persons and enforced by the State.

RICHARD H. TAWNEY, 1921

No one supposes, that the owner of urban land, performs qua owner, any function. He has a right of private taxation; that is all.

RICHARD H. TAWNEY 1921

Property is merely the art of democracy. It means that every man should have something that he can shape in his own image.

GILBERT K. CHESTERTON, 1922

The fellow that owns his own home is always just coming out of a hardware store.

FRANK MCKINNEY HUBBARD, 1923

Lots of fellows think a home is only good to borrow money on.

FRANK MCKINNEY HUBBARD, 1923

The purpose of promoting the Individual was to depose the Monarch and the Church; the effect—through the new ethical significance attached to contract—was to buttress Property and Prescription.   JOHN MAYNARD KEYNES, 1926

Revolution is a transfer of property from class to class.   LEON SAMSON, 1930

The only dependable foundation of personal liberty is the personal economic security of private property.   WALTER LIPPMANN, 1934

Private property began the instant somebody had a mind of his own.   E. E. CUMMINGS, 1951

In America, the classical theory of natural right [to property] is so deeply embedded in popular thought that the spokesmen of big business sometimes repeat the familiar phrases although their manner of doing so often betrays that they are not aware of the contradictions between the classical doctrine and the institutions which they uphold.   RICHARD SCHLATTER, 1951

The best investment on earth is earth.

LOUIS GLICKMAN, 1957

In most countries, people grow fiercely possessive of their property. It is a bastion of conservatism.   GORDON ALLPORT, 1960

Once you sink that first stake, they'll never make you pull it up.   ROBERT MOSES, 1968

Real estate is the closest thing to the proverbial pot of gold.   ADA LOUISE HUXTABLE, 1970

The world is a fairly untidy place and the most valuable thing one can give to one's children is land. That's the only security.

BERNARD BERENSON, 1972

It is clear enough that income from property is not the reward of waiting but the reward of employing a good stockbroker.
JOAN ROBINSON, 1972

I think nobody owns land until their dead are in it.
JOAN DIDION, 1978

What marijuana was to the Sixties, real estate is to the Seventies.
RON KOSLOW, 1980

Rent—a waste of money. It's so much cheaper to buy.
FRAN LEBOWITZ, 1981

Prosperity

In prosperity there is never any dearth of friends.
EURIPIDES, C. 426 B.C.

Happiness seems to require a modicum of external prosperity.
ARISTOTLE, C. 360 B.C.

One must now apologize for any success in business as if it were a violation of the moral law, so that today it is worse to prosper than to be a criminal.
ISOCRATES, C. 340 B.C.

We are all proud or humble, according as our business prospers or fails.
TERENCE, C. 165 B.C.

In prosperity let us most carefully avoid pride, disdain, and arrogance.
CICERO, C. 65 B.C.

Prosperity makes friends, adversity tries them.
PUBLILIUS SYRUS, first century B.C.

How much does great prosperity overspread the mind with darkness.
SENECA, C. A.D. 35

The remembrance of past wants makes present prosperity more pleasant.
ST. JOHN CHRYSOSTOM, C. 388

Prosperity doth best discover vice; but adversity doth best discover virtue.
FRANCIS BACON, 1597

Every man is the maker of his own fortune.
RICHARD STEELE, 1711

If a nation could not prosper without the enjoyment of perfect liberty and perfect justice, there is not in the world a nation which could ever have prospered.
ADAM SMITH, 1776

To be a success in business, be daring, be first, be different.
HENRY MARCHANT, 1789

Progress in industry depends very largely on the enterprise of deep-thinking men, who are ahead of the times in their ideas.
WILLIAM ELLIS, 1818

Prosperity is a great teacher; adversity is a greater.   WILLIAM HAZLITT, 1839

The hope, and not the fact, of advancement is the spur to industry.   HENRY TAYLOR, 1847

Social prosperity means man happy, the citizen free, the nation great.   VICTOR HUGO, 1862

Prosperity is the surest breeder of insolence I know.   MARK TWAIN, 1867

Can anybody remember when the times were not hard, and money not scarce?
                    RALPH WALDO EMERSON, 1870

Failure seems to be regarded as the one unpardonable crime, success as the all-redeeming virtue, the acquisition of wealth as the single worthy aim of life.   CHARLES FRANCIS ADAMS, 1872

Watch lest prosperity destroy generosity.
                    HENRY WARD BEECHER, 1873

So long as all the increased wealth which modern progress brings goes to build up great fortunes, to increase luxury, and make sharper the contrast between the House of Have and the House of Want, progress is not real and cannot be permanent.   HENRY GEORGE, 1879

Success is counted sweetest
By those who ne'er succeed.
                    EMILY DICKINSON, 1886

Prosperity is the best protector of principle.
                    MARK TWAIN, 1893

Few of us can stand prosperity. Another man's, I mean.   MARK TWAIN, 1897

The Full Dinner Pail.
                    WILLIAM MCKINLEY,
                    campaign slogan, 1900

Keep away from people who try to belittle your ambitions. Small people always do that, but the really great make you feel that you, too, can become great.   MARK TWAIN, 1903

After you are dead it doesn't matter if you were not successful in a business way. No one has yet had the courage to memorialize his wealth on his tombstone.   CORRA MAY HARRIS, 1910

I'll say this fer adversity—people seem to be able to stand it, an' that's more'n I can say fer prosperity.
                    FRANK MCKINNEY HUBBARD, 1912

Success achieved by the most contemptible means cannot but destroy the soul. . . . It helps to cover up the inner corruption and gradually dulls one's scruples so that those who begin with some high ambition cannot, even if they would, create anything out of themselves.
                    EMMA GOLDMAN, 1914

It's pretty hard to tell what does bring happiness; poverty and wealth have both failed.
                    FRANK MCKINNEY HUBBARD, 1919

A society is rich when material goods, including capital, are cheap, and human beings dear.
                    RICHARD H. TAWNEY, 1921

If money is your hope for independence you will never have it. The only real security that a man can have in this world is a reserve of knowledge, experience and ability.
                    HENRY FORD, 1926

Prosperity is only an instrument to be used, not a deity to be worshipped.
                    CALVIN COOLIDGE, 1928

For the first time since his creation man will be faced with his real, his permanent problem—how to use his freedom from pressing economic cares, how to occupy the leisure which science and compound interest will have won for him, to live wisely and agreeably and well.

JOHN MAYNARD KEYNES, 1931

A car in every garage and two chickens in every pot.   HERBERT HOOVER, 1931

Prosperity is just around the corner.

REPUBLICAN CAMPAIGN SLOGAN, 1932

Armaments, universal debt and planned obsolescence—those are the three pillars of Western prosperity.   ALDOUS HUXLEY, 1932

We're on a permanent plateau of prosperity. There's never been anything like it before. It's America.   REBECCA WEST, 1935

Success or failure in business is caused more by mental attitude even than by mental capacities.

WALTER DILL SCOTT, 1941

The man who makes an appearance in the business world, the man who creates personal interest, is the man who gets ahead. Be liked and you will never want.   ARTHUR MILLER, 1949

Often when economic pressure is lifted, a man must pump back into himself a feeling of must.

ALEXANDER F. OSBORN, 1952

Whenever an individual or a business decides that success has been attained, progress stops.

THOMAS J. WATSON, 1952

In the tiny space of twenty years, we have bred a whole generation of working Americans who take it for granted that they will never be out of a job or go a single year without a salary increase.   K. K. DUVALL, 1956

Financial success improves people who are good and debases people who are bad.

JOHN OSBORNE, 1966

I don't know the key to success, but the key to failure is trying to please everybody.

BILL COSBY, 1967

If success is corrupting, failure is narrowing.

STEPHEN SPENDER, 1969

The price of an affluent society may be that by the time one is well enough off to turn the dirty work over to someone else there will be no one willing to do it.   W. WILLARD WIRTZ, 1969

Nothing recedes like success.

WALTER WINCHELL, 1970

Sudden money is going from zero to two hundred dollars a week. The rest doesn't count.

NEIL SIMON, 1971

The sole reason we can now feel concerned about the quality of life instead of worrying where the next meal is coming from is that through our great industries we have, as a society, built up immense material wealth.

PHILIP SADLER, 1972

The trick is to make sure you don't die waiting for prosperity to come.

LEE A. IACOCCA, 1973

It takes brains not to make money. Any fool can make money. . . . But what about people with talent and brains.   JOSEPH HELLER, 1973

Success has become a lobotomy to my past.

NORMAN MAILER, 1974

To succeed it is necessary to accept the world as it is and rise above it.

MICHAEL KORDA, 1975

Affluence does not buy morale, a sense of community, even a quiescent conformity. Indeed, it may only permit large numbers of people to express political and social dissatisfaction because they are no longer crushed by the burdens of the economic struggle.

ROBERT HEILBRONER, 1976

Sometimes I worry about being a success in a mediocre world.   LILY TOMLIN, 1977

The happy hooker stands in place of Horatio Alger as the prototype of personal success.

CHRISTOPHER LASCH, 1979

Regulation

Unnecessary laws are not good laws, but traps for money.   THOMAS HOBBES, 1651

We must consider in general, that as wiser Physicians tamper not excessively with their Patients, rather observing and complying with the motions of nature, then contradicting it with vehement Administrations of their own; so in Politics and Economics the same must be used.

WILLIAM PETTY, 1662

'Tis in vain, therefore, to go about effectually to reduce the price of interest by law; and you may as rationally hope to set a fixed rate of interest upon the hire of houses, or ships, as of money.

JOHN LOCKE, 1692

Trade is in its nature free, finds its own channel, and best directs its own course: and all laws to give it rules and directions, and to limit and circumscribe it, may serve the particular ends of private men, but are seldom advantageous to the public.   CHARLES DAVENANT, 1696

It is very usual, in nations ignorant of the nature of commerce, to prohibit the exportation of commodities, and to preserve among themselves whatever they think valuable and useful. They do not consider that in this prohibition they act directly contrary to their intention; and that the more is exported of any commodity, the more will be raised at home, of which they themselves will always have the first offer.

DAVID HUME, 1762

Whenever the legislature attempts to regulate differences between masters and their workmen, its counselors are always the masters. When the regulation, therefore, is in favor of the workmen, it is always just and equitable; but it is sometimes otherwise when in favor of the masters.   ADAM SMITH, 1776

The proposal of any new law or regulation of commerce which comes from [those who live by profit] ought always to be listened to with great precaution. . . . It comes from an order of men, whose interest is never exactly the same with that of the public, who have generally an interest to deceive and even to oppress the public, and who accordingly have, upon many occasions, both deceived and oppressed it.

ADAM SMITH, 1776

Regulating the prices of goods in general would be an endless task, and no legislator has ever been weak enough to think of attempting it.

JEREMY BENTHAM, 1787

The chain of a free and universal commercial intercourse being once broken, by any one nation, every other nation included in the circle of correspondence, is laid under obligation thereby to secure their own interests, and retain their just share of advantages.

TENCH COXE, 1789

The superiority antecedently enjoyed by nations which have preoccupied and perfected a branch of industry, constitutes a more formidable obstacle . . . to the introduction of the same branch into a country in which it did not before exist. To maintain, between the recent establishments of one country, and the long-matured establishments of another country, a competition upon equal terms, both as to quality and price, is, in most cases, impracticable. The disparity, in the one or the other, or in both, must necessarily be so considerable, as to forbid success rivalship, without the extraordinary aid and protection of government. ALEXANDER HAMILTON, 1791

The laws which regulate this distribution [of labor and profits] is the principle problem in Political Economy. DAVID RICARDO, 1817

I like a smuggler. He is the only honest thief. He robs nothing but the revenue, an abstraction I never particularly cared about.

CHARLES LAMB, 1818

There are persons who constantly clamor. They complain of oppression, speculation, and pernicious influence of wealth. They cry out loudly against all banks and corporations, and a means by which small capitalists become united in order to produce important and beneficial results. They carry on mad hostility against all established institutions. They would choke the foundations of industry and dry all streams.

DANIEL WEBSTER, 1838

People say law but they mean wealth.

RALPH WALDO EMERSON, 1841

The only case in which, on mere principles of political economy, protecting duties can be defensible, is when they are imposed temporarily (especially in a young and rising nation) in hopes of naturalizing a foreign industry, in itself perfectly suitable to the circumstances of the country. JOHN STUART MILL, 1848

The smuggler is a check upon the extravagance of governments and the increase of taxation. Any government that raises its tariffs too high, or increases its taxation too far, will be kept in check by smugglers. JOSEPH HOWE, 1865

Social forces cannot be created by enactment, and when dealing with the production, distributing, and commercial activities of the community, legislation can do little more than interfere with their natural courses.

E. L. YOUMANS, 1874

Has not the tendency ever since the adoption of the protective tariff of 1824 been for many great bodies of the people to think they could better their conditions either by attaining high wages, by shortening the hours of labor, or by some other artificial method, through an appeal to the Legislature to pass every kind of act for regulating the direction of labor, the hours of work, the rate of interest, and the methods of life at every point? EDWARD ATKINSON, 1877

Those who cared to be protected at all, wanted all the protection they could get. They were like the squaw who said of whiskey, that "a little too much was just enough."

JOHN A. MACDONALD, 1878

The tariff is the mother of trusts.

HENRY OSBORNE HAVEMEYER, 1892

We may lay it down as a general principle that, as society becomes dependent upon the individuals in control of an industry, it protects itself by State activity.   RICHARD T. ELY, 1893

Well, I don't know as I want a lawyer to tell me what I cannot do. I hire him to tell me how to do what I want to do.

J. PIERPONT MORGAN, 1897

For if there is one thing that protection *cannot* do, it is to cure unemployment.

JOHN MAYNARD KEYNES, 1923

The title of ownership or the possession of physical property is empty as a business asset if the owner is deprived of his liberty to fix a price on the sale of the product of that property . . . not merely physical things are objects of property but the expected earning power of those things is property; and property is taken from the owner, not merely under the power of eminent domain, which takes title and possession, but also under the police power, which takes its exchange value.   JOHN R. COMMONS, 1924

The law, in its majestic equality, forbids the rich as well as the poor to sleep under bridges.

ANATOLE FRANCE, 1924

Subject to compensation when compensation is due, the legislature may forbid or restrict any business when it has a sufficient force of public opinion behind it.

OLIVER WENDELL HOLMES, JR., 1926

German capitalism, which would like to be freed of the power of the state, and which seeks to push back state intervention as far as possible, is constructed exclusively upon the most thorough intervention of the state.

M. J. BONN, 1931

If you destroy a free market you create a black market. If you have ten thousand regulations you destroy all respect for the law.

WINSTON CHURCHILL, 1931

European countries . . . treat timber as a crop. We treat timber resources as if they were a mine.   FRANKLIN D. ROOSEVELT, 1933

If we do not halt this steady process of building commissions and regulatory bodies and special legislation like huge inverted pyramids over every one of the simple constitutional provisions, we shall soon be spending billions of dollars more.

FRANKLIN D. ROOSEVELT, 1934

If this country ever gets a system of government regulation, labor will suffer most.

WILLIAM GREEN, 1936

In the name of justice (fair wages, fair prices, parity prices, and other derivatives of the medieval conception), we are preventing and destroying the free enterprise, free market, and competitive free trade which are essential to representative government and to orderly political life on a large scale.

HENRY C. SIMONS, 1938

Imposition of tariffs will act similarly to cheap money policy: It creates margins which would not otherwise exist and therefore calls forth enterprise and secondary expansion that may be a source of troubles.

JOSEPH A. SCHUMPETER, 1939

Tariff legislation is politically the first step in the degeneration of popular government into the warfare of each group against all. Its significance for political morality is, moreover, quite patent. Against the tariffs, all other forms of "patronage" and "pork-barrel legislation" seem of minor importance.

HENRY C. SIMONS, 1948

It is in this sense that economists criticize policies from the point of view of the ends aimed at. If an economist calls minimum wage rates a bad policy, what he means is that its effects are contrary to the purpose of those who recommend their application.

LUDWIG VON MISES, 1949

The characteristic of European businessmen as a class as distinguished from Americans is their complacency, their timidity, and their instinctive looking to each other and to government for protection against the rude shocks of the contemporary world. And the thing they fear most is price competition.

CLARENCE RANDALL, 1952

The creeping notion that additives are badditives.   CHARLES MORTIMER, 1960

The trend toward bureaucratic rigidity is not inherent in the evolution of business. It is an outcome of government meddling with business.

LUDWIG VON MISES, 1962

High tariff "protectionism" and "featherbedding" come down to the same thing—which is giving artificial respiration to a job that is economically dead—and making the consumer pay the price for it.   W. WILLARD WIRTZ, 1962

Economists may not know how to run the economy, but they do know how to create shortages or gluts simply by regulating prices below the market, or artificially supporting them above it.

MILTON FRIEDMAN, 1962

In a world in which the flow of a large segment of international transactions is slowed by import duties and quantitative restrictions, it is by no means certain that the imposition of similar restraints also on the remaining segment would lower the efficiency of resource allocation.

TIBOR SCITOVSKY, 1966

Mining is like a search-and-destroy mission.

STEWART L. UDALL, 1968

What the economist regards as rational is to seek, not total or maximum, cleansing of the environment—prohibitions tend to be prohibitively expensive—but an optimum arising out of a careful matching of the "bads" that we overcome and the "goods" that we forego in the process.

WALTER HELLER, 1969

When Ralph Nader tells me that he wants my car to be cheap, ugly and slow, he's imposing a way of life on me that I'm going to resist to the bitter end.   TIMOTHY LEARY, 1969

If all I'm offered is a choice between monopolistic privilege with regulation and monopolistic privilege without regulation, I'm afraid I have to opt for the former.

NICHOLAS JOHNSON, 1971

In the West, our desire to conquer nature often means simply that we diminish the probability of small inconveniences at the cost of increasing the probability of very large disasters.

KENNETH E. BOULDING, 1972

The problem in America is not that the top 100 corporation presidents are violating the laws, though God knows they are; the problem is they're writing the laws.

NICHOLAS JOHNSON, 1972

Even 60,000 bureaucrats backed by 300,000 volunteers plus widespread patriotism were unable during World War II to cope with the ingenuity of millions of people in finding ways to get around price and wage controls that conflicted with their individual sense of justice.

MILTON FRIEDMAN, 1972

Two hundred and ten million persons each with a separate incentive to economize or 210 million persons dragooned by men with guns to cut

down their use of oil—can there be any doubt which is the better system?
MILTON FRIEDMAN, 1973

"Environment" and "safety" are fine objectives, but they have become sacred cows about which it is almost heresy to ask whether the return justifies the cost.
MILTON FRIEDMAN, 1974

All of us have opted for environmental damage, albeit unwittingly, by voting for convenience with our dollars.   RUSSELL W. PETERSON, 1975

One man's conservation is all too frequently another man's unemployment.
MIKE MCCORMACK, 1977

The subterranean economy, like black markets throughout the world, was created by government rules and restrictions. It is a creature of the income tax, of other taxes, of limitations on the legal employment of certain groups and of prohibitions on certain activities. It exists because it provides goods and services that are either unavailable elsewhere or obtainable only at higher prices.   PETER GUTMANN, 1977

During my tenure at Treasury I watched with incredulity as businessmen ran to the government in every crisis, whining for handouts or protection from the very competition that has made this system so productive. . . . And always, such gentlemen proclaimed their devotion to free enterprise and their opposition to the arbitrary intervention into our economic life by the state.   WILLIAM SIMON, 1978

Regulation is the substitution of error for chance.   FRED J. EMERY, 1979

Just as no society operates entirely on the command principle, so none operates entirely through voluntary cooperation.
MILTON FRIEDMAN, 1979

Without the environmental regulation of recent years, much of this continent would look, smell, and taste like an unflushed toilet in the men's room at Yankee Stadium toward the end of the second game of a doubleheader.
NICHOLAS VON HOFFMAN, 1979

Wage and price controls are a military solution to an economic problem.
IRVING KRISTOL, 1979

Don't just stand there—undo something.
MURRAY WEIDENBAUM, 1980

[Nuclear energy] must not be thwarted by a tiny minority opposed to economic growth which often finds friendly ears in regulatory agencies for its obstructionist campaigns.
RONALD REAGAN, 1980

Environmental extremists wouldn't let you build a house unless it looked like a bird's nest.
RONALD REAGAN, 1980

The EPA has rules that would practically shut down the economy if they were put into effect.
DAVID STOCKMAN, 1980

Environmentalism is the demand for more goods and services (clean air, water and land) that does not differ from other consumption demands except that it can only be achieved collectively.
LESTER THUROW, 1980

Egalitarian sentiment often consists of people who were born smart but not rich urging government to eliminate all the advantages of being born rich while preserving all the advantages of being born smart.
MICHAEL KINGSLEY, 1981

We are locked into a system of "fouling our own nest," so long as we behave as independent, rational free-enterprisers.
GARRETT HARDIN, 1982

Blind opposition to all regulation detracts from the valid complaints business may have about the excesses of regulation.

HYMAN G. RICKOVER, 1982

Imperfect products should be available because consumers have different preferences for defect avoidance.   JAMES MILLER, 1982

Religion

He that serves God for money will serve the Devil for better wages.   ROGER L'ESTRANGE, 1702

By doing good with his money, a man, as it were, stamps the image of God upon it, and makes it pass current for the merchandise of heaven.

JOHN RUTLEDGE, 1784

God has always been hard on the poor, and He always will be.   JEAN-PAUL MARAT, 1790

For religion must necessarily produce both industry and frugality and these cannot but produce riches. But as riches increase so will pride, anger, and love of the world in all its branches. How then is it possible that Methodism, that is, a religion of the heart, though it flourishes now as a green bay tree, should continue in this state?   JOHN WESLEY, 1820

The fundamental evil of the world arose from the fact that the good Lord had not created money enough.   HEINRICH HEINE, 1828

Money is the god of our time, and Rothschild is his prophet.   HEINRICH HEINE, 1832

We do not believe there can be a single person found east of the mountains who ever thanked God for permission to work in a cotton mill.

SETH LUTHER, C. 1835

Who has the right to charge for the use of the soil, for the wealth that was not made by man? To whom is due the rent of the land? To the producer of that land, of course. Who made it. God. In that case, landlord, you may withdraw.

PIERRE-JOSEPH PROUDHON, 1840

All true work is religion.

THOMAS CARLYLE, 1843

Merchants throughout the world have the same religion.   HEINRICH HEINE, 1844

God gives every bird its food, but he does not throw it into the nest.

JOSIAH GILBERT HOLLAND, 1859

Money degrades all the gods of man and converts them into commodities.

KARL MARX, 1867

The economical laws of human nature through their general effects upon the wellbeing of society, manifest the contrivance, the wisdom and beneficence, of the Deity, just as clearly as do the marvellous arrangements of the natural universe, or the natural means provided for the enforcement of the moral law and the punishment of crime. FRANCIS BOWEN, 1870

A church debt is the devil's salary.
HENRY WARD BEECHER, 1873

God is making commerce his missionary.
JOSEPH COOK, 1880

The England Established Church . . . will more readily pardon an attack on 38 of its 39 articles than on 1/39 of its income.
KARL MARX, 1883

Riches, n. A gift from Heaven signifying, "This is my beloved son, in whom I am well pleased."
JOHN D. ROCKEFELLER, 1898

The materialist is a Calvinist without a God.
EDUARD BERNSTEIN, 1899

The rights and interests of the laboring man will be protected and cared for—not by labor agitators, but by the Christian men to whom God in His infinite wisdom has given the control of the property interests of the country.
GEORGE F. BAER, 1902

Business underlies everything in our national life, including our spiritual life. Witness the fact that in the Lord's Prayer the first petition is for daily bread. No one can worship God or love his neighbor on an empty stomach.
WOODROW WILSON, 1912

God shows his contempt for wealth by the kind of person he selects to receive it.
AUSTIN O'MALLEY, 1914

Puritanism carried the ethos of the rational organization of capital and labor. It took over from the Jewish ethic only what was adapted to this purpose. MAX WEBER, 1920

Capitalism was the social counterpart of Calvinist theory. RICHARD H. TAWNEY, 1926

The summum bonum of this [Puritan] ethic is the earning of more and more money combined with the strict avoidance of all enjoyment.
MAX WEBER, 1930

Economic life must be inspired by Christian principles. POPE PIUS XI, 1931

The oldest and greatest monopolist of all, Holy Church herself, the monopolist in God, had to be assailed if the new middle men, the soldiers of the market, were to grow and prosper.
JOHN STRACHEY, 1932

If you would know what the Lord God thinks of money, you have only to look at those to whom he gives it. MAURICE BARING, 1936

Counting is the religion of this generation. It is its hope and its salvation.
GERTRUDE STEIN, 1937

Selfish employers of labor have flattered the Church by calling it the great conservative force, and then called upon it to act as a police force while they paid but a pittance of wages to those who worked for them.
GEORGE W. MUNDELEIN, 1938

If a religion cuts at the very fundamentals of economics it is not a true religion but only a delusion. MOHANDAS GANDHI, 1946

Clement Attlee often observed that British Socialism owed more to Christ than Marx.
HENRY R. LUCE, 1956

When the businessman of sixteenth and seventeenth century Geneva, Amsterdam or London looked into his inmost heart, he found that God had planted there a deep respect for the principle of private property.
CHRISTOPHER HILL, 1966

Put God to work for you and maximize your potential in our divinely ordered capitalist system.   NORMAN VINCENT PEALE, 1967

Money is God in action.
REVEREND IKE, 1971

Work is the Protestant ethic? I think of it as Jewish.   EDWARD KOCH, 1975

To the degree that organized religion has decayed and the attachment to the Judeo-Christian tradition has become weaker, to that degree capitalism has become uglier and less justifiable.   IRVING KRISTOL, 1979

As capitalism rose, the idea of the poor being dear to God changed to the idea of the poor having lost favor with God.
S. PRAKASH SETHI, 1980

Savings

Men are divided between those who are thrifty as if they would live forever, and those who are as extravagant as if they were going to die the next day.   ARISTOTLE, C. 360 B.C.

Misers take care of property as if it belonged to them, but derive no more benefit from it than if it belonged to others.
BION, second century B.C.

What greater evil could you wish a miser, than long life?
PUBLILIUS SYRUS, first century B.C.

Frugality is misery in disguise.
PUBLILIUS SYRUS, C. 50 B.C.

What is the difference whether you squander all you have, or never use your savings?
HORACE, C. 35 B.C.

Economy is the science of avoiding unnecessary expenditure, or the art of managing our property with moderation.   SENECA, C. A.D. 40

Frugality, when all is spent, comes too late.
SENECA, C. A.D. 40

It's very well to be thrifty, but don't amass a hoard of regrets.
CHARLES D'ORLÉANS, 1465

Frugality is a handsome income.
DESIDERIUS ERASMUS, 1509

I live from hand to mouth, content to have enough for my ordinary expenses. As to extraordinary contingencies, not all the scrimping in the world would suffice.
MICHEL DE MONTAIGNE, 1588

Riches come rather from management than from revenue.   MICHEL DE MONTAIGNE, 1588

Once you have decided to keep a certain pile, it is no longer yours; for you can't spend it.
MICHEL DE MONTAIGNE, 1588

Taking it all in, I find it is more trouble to watch after money than to get it.
MICHEL DE MONTAIGNE, 1588

Penny wise and pound foolish.
WILLIAM CAMDEN, 1605

A mere madness, to live like a wretch and die rich.   ROBERT BURTON, 1621

Those . . . who know the true use of money, and regulate the measure of wealth according to their needs, live contented with few things.
BENEDICT DE SPINOZA, 1660

Misers mistake gold for good, whereas it is only a means of obtaining it.
FRANÇOIS DE LA ROCHEFOUCAULD, 1662

Misers are neither relations, nor friends, nor citizens, nor Christians, nor perhaps even human beings.   JEAN DE LA BRUYÈRE, 1688

A penny sav'd's a penny got.
WILLIAM SOMERVILLE, 1727

Misers put their back and their belly into their pockets.   THOMAS FULLER, 1732

Frugality is necessary even to complete the pleasure of expense.   SAMUEL JOHNSON, 1750

Without frugality none can be rich and with it very few would be poor.
SAMUEL JOHNSON, 1752

Misers are very good people; they amass wealth for those who wish their death.
STANISLAUS LESZCYNSKI, 1763

The revenue, then, properly speaking, is the groundwork of the expense. It is necessary that the revenue should be expended; for every saving in the revenue occasions a diminution of expenditure, and, by direct consequence, of production and of future revenue.
VICTOR DE MIRABEAU, 1763

The spirit of economy in a nation tends to augment incessantly the sum of its capitals, to increase the number of lenders, to diminish the borrowers. The habit of luxury has precisely the contrary effect.   A. R. J. TURGOT, 1768

Frugality is founded on the principle that all riches have limits.   EDMUND BURKE, 1769

What is annually saved is as regularly consumed as what is annually spent, and nearly in the same time, too; but it is consumed by a different set of people.   ADAM SMITH, 1776

Capitals are increased by parsimony, and diminished by prodigality and misconduct.
ADAM SMITH, 1776

It is not a custom with me to keep money to look at.   GEORGE WASHINGTON, 1780

Mere parsimony is not economy. . . . Expense, and great expense, may be an essential part of true economy.   EDMUND BURKE, 1796

Capital is saved from profits.
DAVID RICARDO, 1817

The principle of saving, pushed to excess, would destroy the motive to production. If every person were satisfied with the simplest food, the poorest clothing, and the meanest houses, it is certain that no other sort of food, clothing and lodging would be in existence.

THOMAS MALTHUS, 1820

He lives poor, to die rich, and is the mere jailor of his house, and the turnkey of his wealth.

CHARLES C. COLTON, 1822

If the prodigal quits life in debt to others, the miser quits it still deeper in debt to himself.

CHARLES C. COLTON, 1825

Economy, the poor man's mint.

MARTIN TUPPER, 1838

Saving, in short, enriches, and spending impoverishes, the community along with the individual.   JOHN STUART MILL, 1848

It is easier to make money than to save it; one is exertion, the other self-denial.

THOMAS C. HALIBURTON, 1853

Economy, in the estimation of common minds, often means the absence of all taste and comfort.   SYDNEY SMITH, 1855

Put not your trust in money, but put your money in trust.

OLIVER WENDELL HOLMES, SR., 1857

Economy is a savings bank, into which men drop pennies, and get dollars back.

JOSH BILLINGS, 1865

Any young man with good health and a poor appetite can save up money.

JAMES MONTGOMERY BAILEY, 1873

You're worth what you saved, not the millions you made.   JOHN BOYLE O'REILLY, 1878

Large enterprises make the few rich, but the majority prosper only through the carefulness and detail of thrift.

THEODORE T. MUNGER, 1882

I had rather be a beggar and spend my last dollar like a king, than be a king and spend my money like a beggar.

ROBERT G. INGERSOLL, 1883

The way to become rich is to make money, my dear Edna, not to save it.

KATE CHOPIN, 1889

Simple rules for saving money: To save half, when you are fired by an eager impulse to contribute to a charity, wait and count forty. To save three-quarters, count sixty. To save it all, count sixty-five.   MARK TWAIN, 1893

But to recommend thrift to the poor is both grotesque and insulting. It is like advising a man who is starving to eat less.

OSCAR WILDE, 1895

Money is like the reputation for ability—more easily made than kept.

SAMUEL BUTLER, 1896

Thrift is the great fortune-maker. It draws the line between the savage and the civilized man.

ANDREW CARNEGIE, 1900

Gentlemen, it is the first hundred dollars saved which tells.   ANDREW CARNEGIE, 1902

Economy, n. Purchasing the barrel of whiskey that you do not need for the price of the cow that you cannot afford.

AMBROSE BIERCE, 1906

Don't a fellow feel good after he gets out of a store where he nearly bought something?

FRANK MCKINNEY HUBBARD, 1918

It's not making money first that's important, it's making it last.   BOB EDWARDS, 1920

Economy is the art of making the most of life. The love of economy is the root of all virtue.
                    GEORGE BERNARD SHAW, 1921

Economy is going without something you do want in case you should, some day, want something you probably won't want.
                    ANTHONY HOPE HAWKINS, 1927

This guy Marx, why, he was one of these efficiency experts. He could explain to you how you could save a million dollars, yet he couldn't save enough himself to eat on.
                            WILL ROGERS, 1929

We shall mean by Savings the sum of the differences between the money-incomes of individuals and their money-expenditures on current consumption.
                    JOHN MAYNARD KEYNES, 1930

Whenever you save five shillings, you put a man out of work for a day.
                    JOHN MAYNARD KEYNES, 1933

"What could you buy with a hundred dollars?" she asked fretfully. "Nothing, nothing at all," said their father, "a hundred dollars is just something you put in the bank."
                    KATHERINE ANNE PORTER, 1936

Practically all business savings which, in turn, constitute the greater part of total saving—is done with a specific investment in view.
                    JOSEPH A. SCHUMPETER, 1939

The world is perishing from an orgy of self-sacrificing.   AYN RAND, 1943

Unequal distribution of income is an excessively uneconomic method of getting the necessary saving done.   JOAN ROBINSON, 1947

No nation is so poor that it could not save 12 percent of its national income if it wanted to; poverty has never prevented nations from launching upon wars, or from wasting their substance in other ways. . . . Productive investment is not small because there is no surplus [above subsistence]; it is small because the surplus is used to maintain unproductive hordes of retainers, and to build pyramids, temples and other durable consumer goods, instead of to create productive capital.
                    W. ARTHUR LEWIS, 1955

The rich man who deludes himself into behaving like a medicant may conserve his fortune although he will not be very happy.
                    JOHN KENNETH GALBRAITH, 1962

When one has had to work so hard to get money, why should he impose on himself the further handicap of trying to save it?
                            DON HEROLD, 1962

Simply by not owning three medium-sized castles in Tuscany I have saved enough money in the last 40 years on insurance premiums alone to buy a medium-sized castle in Tuscany.
                        GEORGE MIKES, 1974

The principle of economy is one of the basic principles of socialist economies.
                            MAO ZEDONG, 1976

Anything left over today will be needed tomorrow to pay an unexpected bill.
                        BETTY CANARY, 1976

There is a certain Buddhistic calm that comes from having . . . money in the bank.
                        TOM ROBBINS, 1976

Socialism

What's mine is yours, and what is yours is mine.
WILLIAM SHAKESPEARE,
Measure for Measure (V, i), 1604

When our people were fed out of the common store, and labored jointly together, glad was he could slip from his labor, or slumber over his task he cared not how, nay, the most honest among them would hardly take so much true pains in a week, as now for themselves they will do in a day. JOHN SMITH, 1624

The best way to make every one poor is to insist on equality of wealth.
NAPOLEON BONAPARTE, 1817

What is a Communist? One who hath yearnings
For equal division of unequal earnings.
Idler or bungler, or both, he is willing,
To fork out his copper and pocket your shilling.
EBENEZER ELLIOTT, 1831

There are people who are socialists and rebels today and company directors tomorrow. Examples of reincarnations.
FRIEDRICH HEBBEL, 1839

The theory of Communism may be summed up in one sentence: Abolish all private property.
KARL MARX AND FRIEDRICH ENGELS, 1848

You are horrified at our intending to do away with private property. But in your existing society private property is already done away with for nine-tenths of the population; its existence for the few is solely due to its non-existence in the hands of those nine-tenths.
KARL MARX AND FRIEDRICH ENGELS, 1848

From each according to his ability, to each according to his needs. KARL MARX, 1867

In economics all roads lead to Socialism, though in nine cases out of ten, so far, the economist does not recognize his destination.
GEORGE BERNARD SHAW, 1884

The economic side of the democratic ideal is . . . socialism itself. SIDNEY WEBB, 1889

When it is understood that instead of working and saving you may vote yourself that earnings and savings of other people, industry will lose some of its charm. GOLDWIN SMITH, 1891

Socialism is the legitimate heir of Liberalism, not only chronologically, but also spiritually.
EDUARD BERNSTEIN, 1899

The most important element in the foundation of Marxism is the materialistic interpretation of history. With it Marxism stands or falls.
EDUARD BERNSTEIN, 1899

I am a firm believer in socialism and I know that the quicker you have monopoly in this country the quicker you will have socialism.

CHARLES STEINMETZ, 1910

God was feeling mighty good when He created 'Gene Debs, and He didn't have anything else to do all day.

JAMES WHITCOMB RILEY, 1910

Now the boss works for the capitalist. Under Socialism, he will work for you. You will elect him and if he isn't satisfactory, you will fire him and get another.   A. W. RICKES, 1914

That which is called Socialism, Marx named the first, or the lower, phase of Communism.

NIKOLAI LENIN, 1917

Socialism is the society which grows directly out of capitalism.   NIKOLAI LENIN, 1917

The whole society will have become a single office and a single factory with equality of work and equality of pay.   NIKOLAI LENIN, 1917

Socialism is nothing but the capitalism of the lower classes.   OSWALD SPENGLER, 1923

This land would not be a land of opportunity, America would not be America, if the people were shackled with government monopolies.

CALVIN COOLIDGE, 1924

How can I adopt a creed which, preferring the mud to the fish, exalts the boorish proletariat above the bourgeois and the intelligentsia who, with whatever faults, are the quality of life and surely carry the seeds of all human advancement?

JOHN MAYNARD KEYNES, 1925

Leninism is a combination of two things which Europeans have kept for some centuries in dif-

ferent compartments of the soul—religion and business.   JOHN MAYNARD KEYNES, 1926

There are three practical ways of providing for the production of commodities and exchange of services in civilized communities. These three are private property, collectivism and communism. . . . In all modern states the three are in operation side by side, but as collectivism and communism are purposely restricted to those departments of industry in which the private property system is practically impossible, the predominating and characteristic method of organizing the industry of the world is at present non-socialist.

GEORGE BERNARD SHAW, 1928

Communism to me is one-third practice and two-thirds explanation.   WILL ROGERS, 1929

Socialism is the abolition of rational economy.

LUDWIG VON MISES, 1935

The question is not merely whether the State owns and controls the means of production. It is also who owns and controls the State.

RICHARD H. TAWNEY, 1935

Socialism, long misrepresented and misunderstood under the violent propaganda of Marxism, has been fairly obliterated in the public mind by the Jewish-Russian nightmare, Bolshevism.

CHARLOTTE PERKINS GILMAN, 1935

Marxian economics is essentially the economics of capitalism, while "capitalist" economics is in a very real sense the economics of socialism.

PAUL M. SWEEZY, 1935

In a country where the sole employer is the State, opposition means death by slow starvation. The old principle: who does not work shall not eat, has been replaced by a new one: who does not obey shall not eat.   LEON TROTSKY, 1937

To the ordinary working man, the sort you would meet in any pub on a Saturday night, Socialism does not mean much more than better wages and shorter hours and nobody bossing you about. GEORGE ORWELL, 1937

The typical socialist . . . a prim little man with a white-collar job, usually a secret teetotaller and often with vegetarian leanings. GEORGE ORWELL, 1937

Socialism is not an economic policy for the timid. OSCAR LANGE, 1938

The Communist party is the biggest corporation of all. JOHN DOS PASSOS, 1939

Enterprise does not have to be private in order to be enterprise. HERBERT MORRISON, 1942

Socialism might be the only means of restoring social discipline. JOSEPH A. SCHUMPETER, 1942

The economy of Communism is an economy which grows in an atmosphere of misery and want. ELEANOR ROOSEVELT, 1947

Corrupt, stupid grasping functionaries will make at least as big a muddle of socialism as stupid, selfish and acquisitive employers can make of capitalism. WALTER LIPPMANN, 1955

Marxism flourishes but in countries where capitalism is least successful. JOAN ROBINSON, 1955

If modern Marxism gives the wrong answers, at least it asks the right questions. DENYS MUNBY, 1956

There is a popular cliché, deeply beloved by conservatives, that socialism and communism are the cause of a low standard of living. It is much more nearly accurate to say that a low and simple standard of living makes socialism and communism feasible. JOHN KENNETH GALBRAITH, 1957

The salient economic assumptions of liberalism are socialist. WILLIAM F. BUCKLEY, JR., 1959

Strike down ignorance, poverty, and disease, and Communism without its allies will wither and die. LYNDON B. JOHNSON, 1961

I can't understand Karl Marx, so how can I be a Communist? CHARLES CHAPLIN, 1964

To be a Marxist does not mean that one becomes a Communist party member. There are as many varieties of Marxists as there are of Protestants. HELEN FOSTER SNOW, 1967

The inherent danger of socialism is that in establishing a social machinery for economic direction it creates a concentration of power—the coercive power of the State and the power of a focused economy—far beyond anything capitalism dreamed of and makes men far more dependent than free. ERAZIM V. KOHAK, 1971

Communists are frustrated Capitalists. ERIC HOFFER, 1973

While private ownership is an instrument that by itself largely determines the ends for which it can be employed, public ownership is an instrument the ends of which are undetermined and need to be consciously chosen. E. F. SCHUMACHER, 1975

If "socialism" is defined as "ownership of the means of production by the workers" then the

United States is the first truly "Socialist" country. Through their pension funds, employees of American business today own at least 25 percent of its equity capital, which is more than enough for control.   PETER DRUCKER, 1976

A Marxist has never written a good novel.
ISAAC BASHEVIS SINGER, 1978

The Marxist analysis has nothing to do with what happened in Stalin's Russia. It's like blaming Jesus for the Inquisition in Spain.
TONY BENN, 1980

In a socialist country you can get rich by providing necessities, while in a capitalist country you can get rich by providing luxuries.
NORA EPHRON, 1983

Social Welfare

People at present think that five sons are not too many and each son has five sons also, and before the death of the grandfather there are already 25 descendants. Therefore people are more and wealth is less; they work hard and receive little.   HAN FEI-TZU, C. 500 B.C.

O health, health! The blessing of the rich! the riches of the poor! who can buy thee at too dear a rate?   BEN JONSON, 1605

To give aid to the poor man is far beyond the reach and power of each man . . . care of the poor is incumbent on society as a whole.
BENEDICT DE SPINOZA, 1665

Health without wealth is half a sickness.
THOMAS FULLER, 1732

Pity the sorrows of a poor old man,
Whose trembling limbs have brought him to your door.
THOMAS MOSS, 1769

It will also be said . . . that were a workman to receive an increase of wages daily, he would not save it against old age nor be much the better for it in the interim. Make the Society the treasurer to guard it for him in a common fund.
THOMAS PAINE, 1792

There is one right, which man is generally thought to possess, which I am confident he neither does, nor can, possess, a right to subsistence when his labor will not fairly purchase it.
THOMAS MALTHUS, 1798

It is only when the rich are sick that they feel fully the impotence of wealth.
CHARLES C. COLTON, 1825

The right of the state to require the services of its members, even to the jeopardizing of their lives, in the common defense, establishes a right in the people . . . to public support, when, from any cause, they may be unable to support themselves.   WILLIAM WORDSWORTH, 1835

Man tends to increase at a greater rate than his means of subsistence; consequently he is occasionally subjected to a severe struggle for existence. CHARLES DARWIN, 1871

The more is given, the less the people will work for themselves and the less they work, the more their poverty will increase. LYOF TOLSTOY, 1892

A system of relief is an essential to industrial freedom; economic activity will not reach its maximum until it is so effective that the energy of individuals can be applied to the satisfaction of their own wants. The social surplus is more than sufficient to provide for all the exigencies that persons cannot control. SIMON N. PATTEN, 1902

Subsidy: a formula for handing you back your own money with a flourish that makes you think it's a gift. JO BINGHAM, 1903

The larger the corporation becomes, the greater becomes it responsibilities to the entire community. The corporations of the future must be those that are semi-public servants, serving the public, with ownership widespread among the public, and with labor so fairly and equitably treated that it will look upon its competition as its friend. GEORGE PERKINS, 1908

Society produces the causes of unemployment, and society must meet the problem. HARRY ROGOFF, 1930

The effect of an extension of social services, accompanied by progressive taxation, is to diminish inequality, since it involves, though at present on an extremely modest scale, the transference of wealth from large incomes to small. RICHARD H. TAWNEY, 1931

The Federal government must and shall quit the business of relief. FRANKLIN D. ROOSEVELT, 1935

There is no finer investment for any community than putting milk into babies. Healthy citizens are the greatest asset any country can have. WINSTON CHURCHILL, 1943

There can be no betterment in the standard of living by any distribution of unearned money. Nothing but a distribution of goods needed by humanity can help the standard of living, and these goods must first be brought into being. ARTHUR MEIGHEN, 1943

No social system will bring us happiness, health and prosperity unless it is inspired by something greater than materialism. CLEMENT R. ATTLEE, 1952

It's my absolute opinion that in our complex industrial society, no business enterprise can succeed without sharing the burden of the problems of other enterprises. AYN RAND, 1957

There is the fundamental paradox of the welfare state: that it is not built for the desperate, but for those who are already capable of helping themselves. MICHAEL HARRINGTON, 1962

Few trends could so thoroughly undermine the very foundations of our free society as the acceptance by corporate officials of a social responsibility other than to make as much money for the stockholders as possible. MILTON FRIEDMAN, 1962

Being assured of some, for many people insufficient, funds after retirement, the attainment of adequate funds for one's old age no longer appears an insurmountably difficult task; being closer to the goal stimulates people to work harder to achieve the goal, and therefore collective retirement plans promote individual saving. GEORGE KATONA, 1965

The welfare state has very much softened the harshness of raw capitalism and has played a large part in saving it, till now, from the doom that Marx foresaw a hundred years ago.

JOAN ROBINSON, 1969

The truth is that medical care today goes where the money is.   MICHAEL DE BAKEY, 1970

Poverty programs put very little money into the hands of the poor because middle-class hands are so much more gifted at grasping money— they know better where it is, how to apply for it, how to divert it, how to concentrate it.

PHILIP SLATER, 1970

As far as unwed mothers on welfare are concerned, it seems to me they must be capable of some other form of labor.   AL CAPP, 1971

I believe that the social responsibility of the corporation today is fundamentally the same as it has always been: to earn profits for shareholders by securing consumer wants with maximum efficiency. This is not the whole of the matter, but it is the heart of the matter.

HENRY FORD II, 1971

The Welfare State is often compared to Santa Claus, and that comparison is usually drawn by those who object to presents for poor people. But in fact the Welfare State resembles Santa Claus because he gives more to rich people than to poor ones.   JAN PEN, 1971

We know that poverty in this country is primarily the problem of *all* women—that most women are only a husband away from welfare.

TONI CARABILLO, 1974

Food stamps have become a massive subsidy for some of the exotic experiments in group living you have read about, what the sociologists call the underground culture.

RONALD REAGAN, 1974

The modern welfare state intermingles benefits, dispensations, and transfers to such an extent that it is practically impossible to separate dependents and nondependents.

A. HEIDENHEIMER, 1975

How much health care Americans get should depend not on how much they can afford but on how much they need.

EDWARD M. KENNEDY, 1976

Those old-fashioned values of liberty, equality and fraternity come with massive bills for education, health and social services.

K. NEWTON, 1977

Unemployment insurance is a prepaid vacation plan for freeloaders.

RONALD REAGAN, 1980

Economic performance is no longer enough. Business is properly expected to act in the public interest as well as the shareholders' interest.

REGINALD JONES, 1981

Stock Market

Buy cheap, sell dear. THOMAS LODGE, 1595

If you will talk to them [stockbrokers] about their occupation, there is not a man but will own it is a complete system of knavery; that it is a trade founded in fraud, born of deceit, and nourished by trick, treat, wheedle, forgeries, falsehoods, and all sorts of delusions; coining false news, this way good, that way bad; whispering imaginary terrors, frights, hopes, expectations. DANIEL DEFOE, 1719

A friend in the market is better than money in the chest. THOMAS FULLER, 1732

There is no more mean, stupid, pitiful, selfish, envious, ungrateful animal than the stock-speculating public. It is the greatest of cowards, for it is afraid of itself.

WILLIAM HAZLITT, 1805

The wealth acquired by speculation and plunder is fugacious in its nature, and fills society with the spirit of gambling.

THOMAS JEFFERSON, 1806

If to the Stock Exchange you speed,
To try with bulls and bears your luck,
'Tis odds you soon from gold are freed
And waddle forth a limping duck.

WILLIAM H. IRELAND, 1807

An enlargement of confidence always produces that enlargement of the market which it anticipates. ROBERT TORRENS, 1821

Is it not odd that the only generous person I ever knew, who had money to be generous with, should be a stockbroker.

PERCY BYSSHE SHELLEY, 1822

Every transaction in which an individual buys produce in order to sell it again, is, in fact, a speculation. JOHN R. MCCULLOCH, 1825

Through Life's dark road his sordid way he
    wends,
An incarnation of fat dividends.

CHARLES SPRAGUE, 1829

I do not regard a broker as a member of the human race. HONORÉ DE BALZAC, 1841

A wise man was he who counselled that speculation should have free course, and look fearlessly toward all the thirty-two points of the compass, withersoever and howsoever it listed.

THOMAS CARLYLE, 1843

No warning can save a people determined to grow suddenly rich.

LORD OVERSTONE, 1846

The prices of things are neither so much depressed at one time nor so much raised at another, as they would be if speculative dealers did not exist.   JOHN STUART MILL, 1848

Steal awhile away from Wall Street and every
    worldly care,
And spend an hour about mid-day in humble,
    hopeful prayer.
                            Journal of Commerce, 1857

What do you think of those fellows on Wall Street who are gambling in gold at a time like this? For my part, I wish every one of them had his devilish head shot off.
                            ABRAHAM LINCOLN, 1862

Wall Street owns the country. It is no longer a government of the people, by the people and for the people, but a government of Wall Street, by Wall Street and for Wall Street.
                            MARY LEASE, 1890

With an evening coat and a white tie, even a stockbroker can gain a reputation for being civilized.   OSCAR WILDE, 1891

There are two times in a man's life when he should not speculate: when he can't afford it, and when he can.   MARK TWAIN, 1894

It is very vulgar to talk about one's own business. Only people like stockbrokers do that, and then merely at dinner parties.
                            OSCAR WILDE, 1895

In the course of evolution and a higher civilization we might be able to get along comfortably without Congress, but without Wall Street never.   HENRY CLEWS, 1900

It is as certain as anything in the future that industrial securities will form the principal medium for speculation in this country. The field for the formation of industrial corporations is vast and varying degrees of skill in management coupled with the succession of good times and bad times, will make constant changes in values which will be discounted by movements in the prices of stock.   CHARLES H. DOW, 1900

In most bull markets there comes a time when the public controls fluctuations and the efforts of the largest operators are insufficient to check the rising tide.   CHARLES H. DOW, 1901

A man is robbed on the Stock Exchange, just as he is killed in a war, by people whom he never sees.   ALFRED CAPUS, 1901

Do you know the only thing that gives me pleasure? It's to see my dividends coming in.
                            JOHN D. ROCKEFELLER, 1901

There is scarcely an instance of a man who has made a fortune by speculation and kept it.
                            ANDREW CARNEGIE, 1902

The safest way to double your money is to fold it over once and put it in your pocket.
                            FRANK MCKINNEY HUBBARD, 1907

This is "predatory wealth," and is found in stock markets.   WOODROW WILSON, 1908

There is no moral difference between gambling at cards or in lotteries or on the race track and gambling in the stock-market.
                            THEODORE ROOSEVELT, 1908

I never gamble.   J. PIERPONT MORGAN, 1909

The gambling known as business looks with austere disfavor upon the business known as gambling.   AMBROSE BIERCE, 1911

There is no such thing as an innocent purchaser of stocks.   LOUIS D. BRANDEIS, 1911

All the speculation in the world never raised a bushel of wheat. BOB EDWARDS, 1912

It is more dangerous to be a great prophet or pet than to promote twenty companies for swindling simple folk out of their savings. GEORGE BERNARD SHAW, 1914

A speculator is one who thinks and plans for a future event—and acts before it occurs. And a speculator must always be right. BERNARD BARUCH, 1916

We may not know when we're well off, but investment salesmen get on to it somehow. FRANK MCKINNEY HUBBARD, 1918

Let Wall Street have a nightmare and the whole country has to help get them back in bed again. WILL ROGERS, 1920

On the whole, brokers as a class compare well, mentally and morally, with other business men. They are always patriotic, if for no other reason than that of self-interest, for if the Government went down or suffered from domestic revolt or foreign invasion, the whole structure of Wall Street credits and values would collapse like a house of cards. SERENO PRATT, 1921

Don't gamble; take all your savings and buy some good stock and hold it till it goes up, then sell it. If it don't go up, don't buy it. WILL ROGERS, 1924

The meaning of property, in the business sense of assets, is a shift from things to the expected purchasing power of things by way of expected transactions on the commodity and exchange markets. JOHN R. COMMONS, 1924

I am concerned that credit should not be used in speculation at the expense of industry or at a rate that becomes competitive with commercial rates or interferes with Federal Reserve credit. WALTER W. STEWART, 1926

Gentlemen prefer bonds. ANDREW MELLON, C. 1926

Artificial inflation of stocks must be considered a crime as serious as counterfeiting, which it closely resembles. ANDRÉ MAUROIS, 1926

Stock prices have reached what looks like a permanently high plateau. IRVING FISHER, OCTOBER 15, 1929

It seems probable that stocks have been passing not so much from the strong to the weak as from the smart to the dumb. LEONARD P. AYRES, 1929

Believing that fundamental conditions of the country are sound . . . my son and I have for some days been purchasing sound common stocks. JOHN D. ROCKEFELLER, OCTOBER 29, 1929

Those who voluntarily sell stocks at current prices are extremely foolish. OWEN D. YOUNG, DECEMBER 1, 1929

Speculators may do no harm as bubbles on a steady stream of enterprise. But the position is serious when enterprise becomes a bubble on the whirlpool of speculation. When the capital development of a country becomes a by-product of the activities of a casino, the job is likely to be ill done. JOHN MAYNARD KEYNES, 1930

I claim that this country [America] has been built by speculation, and further progress must be made in that line. RICHARD WHITNEY, 1930

So far as possible, the aim should be to create a condition [so that] fluctuations in security values more nearly approximate fluctuations in the position of the enterprise itself and of general economic conditions—that is, tend to represent what is going on in the business and in our economic life rather than mere speculative or "technical" conditions in the market.

FRANKLIN D. ROOSEVELT, 1932

A broker is a man who runs your fortune into a shoestring. ALEXANDER WOOLLCOTT, 1935

Fortunes come. They are not made.

HENRY FORD, 1938

There is surely no trace of mystic glamour about the businessman, which is what counts in the ruling of men. The stock exchange is a poor substitute for the Holy Grail.

JOSEPH A. SCHUMPETER, 1942

My father dealt in stocks and shares and my mother also had a lot of time on her hands.

HERMIONE GINGOLD, 1945

The market is mostly a matter of psychology and emotion, and all that you find in balance sheets is what you read into them; we're all guessers to one extent or another, and when we guess wrong they say we're crooks.

L. L. B. ANGAS, 1947

You can rest assured that, as long as I am President, the gentlemen in Wall Street are not to control the operations of the International Bank. HARRY S TRUMAN, 1947

The speculators, promoters, investors and moneylenders, in determining the structure of the stock and commodity exchanges and of the money market, circumscribe the orbit within which definite minor tasks can be entrusted to the manager's discretion.

LUDWIG VON MISES, 1949

Too much investment literature and investor thought is devoted to a cyclical approach toward common stocks. The existences of a bull or bear market never can be established beyond reasonable doubt until the trend is far progressed. Few people ever buy near the bottom or sell near the top; and the vast majority who try to do it obtain poorer net results than those realized by not trying too hard.

LUCIEN O. HOOPER, 1953

We all know it's ridiculous. But the stock market reflects every human frailty, and the big one now is greed. Others are fear and stupidity. They'll come a little later.

SIDNEY LURIE, 1953

Cause and effect run from the economy to the stock market, never the reverse.

JOHN KENNETH GALBRAITH, 1955

Of all the mysteries of the stock exchange there is none so impenetrable as why there should be a buyer for everyone who seeks to sell. October 24, 1929, showed that what is mysterious is not inevitable. Often there were no buyers, and only after wide vertical declines could anyone be induced to bid.

JOHN KENNETH GALBRAITH, 1955

To the child, the savage and the Wall Street operator everything seems possible—hence their credibility. ERIC HOFFER, 1955

Repeatedly in my market operations I have sold a stock while it was rising—and that has been one reason why I have held on to my fortune.

BERNARD BARUCH, 1957

If you don't know who you are, the stock market is an expensive place to find out.

GEORGE GOODMAN, 1959

The stock market has called nine of the last five recessions. PAUL A. SAMUELSON, 1960

I was even thinking of dabbling in the stock market, only the broker everybody recommended had a very disturbing word in the name—Lynch! DICK GREGORY, 1962

The thing that most affects the stock market is everything. JAMES PLAYSTED WOOD, 1966

In economics, the majority is always wrong. JOHN KENNETH GALBRAITH, 1968

The most certain mechanism by which men can survive while other men are going under is to bet on the side of the disaster. In a plague, corner the market in coffins; in an earthquake, invest in concrete; in a war, sell guns or oil; in a depression, sell short. KENNETH LAMOTT, 1969

You've got more crooks in Wall Street than in any other industry I've ever seen. LOUIS WOLFSON, 1969

[Learn] how to make money in bear markets, bull markets, and chicken markets. CONRAD W. THOMAS, 1970

Many Wall Street firms have what they call a capital structure, but which more closely resembles a scaffold. DONALD T. REGAN, 1970

I deal in a big floating crap game, one that is played every weekday in the richest and most exclusive casino in the world: the New York Stock Exchange. RICHARD NEY, 1970

Frankly, if I had any money, I'd be buying stocks right now. RICHARD M. NIXON, 1970

Money made by money should be taxed at the same rate as money made by men. GEORGE MCGOVERN, 1972

Do you want to make some money? Next time Mr. Nixon decides he is going to make a speech on economic policy or foreign policy, you buy because the stock market is going to go up. But sell within 48 hours. Get the hell out. . . . The stock market goes up. But then the people—and this includes your big business tycoons . . . they

say, "What the hell did he say?" and they get to reading and analyzing. . . . He didn't say anything. So then the stock market goes down. GEORGE MEANY, 1973

There is a way to make a lot of money in the market; unfortunately it is the same way to lose a lot of money in the market. PETER PASSELL AND LEONARD ROSE, 1974

Any inflation rate which is correctly and universally anticipated by the financial markets should have no effect at all on stock prices. EZRA SOLOMON, 1975

I refuse to believe that trading recipes is silly. Tuna-fish casserole is at least as real as corporate stock. BARBARA GRIZZUTI HARRISON, 1975

Bulls and bears aren't responsible for as many stock losses as bum steers. OLIN MILLER, 1976

In Wall Street the only thing that's hard to explain is—next week. LOUIS RUKEYSER, 1976

Inside every buy there is a sale screaming to get out. ROBERT HELLER, 1977

Like the cosmetics industry, the securities business is engaged in selling illusion. PAUL A. SAMUELSON, 1977

The ceiling on taxation of capital gains reflects the natural belief that speculation is a more worthwhile way to make a living than work. CALVIN TRILLIN, 1978

There are only two emotions in Wall Street: fear and greed. WILLIAM M. LEFEVRE, 1978

Stocks do not move unless they are pushed. S. JAY LEVIN, 1979

It is easier to invest based on current profits rather than trying to figure out who will be successful in ten years. The investor does not have to live with ten years of risk and uncertainty.

LESTER THUROW, 1981

There is an inverse reciprocal between the direction of a stock price and the amount of money you have just invested.

ARTHUR W. SAMANSKY, 1984

Supply and Demand

Good merchandise finds a ready buyer.

PLAUTUS, c. 200 B.C.

It remains true that the quantity of commodities or of merchandise offered for sale compared with the demand or with the number of Buyers, is the basis upon which people fix, or always think they fix, the prevailing Market prices; and that in general these prices do not differ much from the intrinsic value.

RICHARD CANTILLON, 1732

It is the interest of all those who employ their land, labor, or stock, in bringing any commodity to market, that the quantity should never exceed the effectual demand; and it is the interest of all other people that it never should fall short of that demand.   ADAM SMITH, 1776

Say's Law: Supply creates its own demand.

JEAN-BAPTISTE SAY, 1803

No man produces, but with a view to consume or sell, and he never sells, but with an intention to purchase some other commodity.

JEAN-BAPTISTE SAY, 1803

The rich and poor are necessary to each other; it is precisely the fable of the belly and the limbs; without the rich the poor would starve; without the poor the rich would be compelled to labor for their own subsistence.

JANE HALDIMAND MARCET, 1816

In the usual and ordinary course of things, the demand for all commodities precedes their supply.   DAVID RICARDO, 1817

Productions are always bought by productions or by services. Money is only the medium by which the change is effected. Hence the increased production being always accompanied by a corresponding increased ability to get and consume, there is no possibility of overproduction.   DAVID RICARDO, 1817

A glut is an evil. It generally implies production without profit, and sometimes without even the return of the capital employed.

DAVID RICARDO, 1817

I consider the wants and tastes of mankind as unlimited. We all wish to add to our enjoyments or to our power. Consumption adds to our enjoyments, accumulation to our power, and they equally promote demand.

DAVID RICARDO, 1820

The encouragement of mere consumption is no benefit to commerce; for the difficulty lies in supplying the means, not in stimulating the desire of consumption; and we have seen that production alone furnishes those means. Thus, it is the aim of good government to stimulate production, of bad government to encourage consumption.   JEAN-BAPTISTE SAY, 1832

Supply-and-Demand is not the one law of Nature; cash-payment is not the sole nexus of man with man.   THOMAS CARLYLE, 1843

Supply-and-Demand—alas! For what noble work was there ever yet any audible demand in that poor sense? The man of Macedonia, speaking in vision to an Apostle Paul, "Come over and help us," did not specify what rate of wages he would give.   THOMAS CARLYLE, 1843

The level of the sea is not more surely kept, than is the equilibrium of value in society, by the demand and supply: and artifice or legislation punishes itself, by reactions, gluts, and bankruptcies.

RALPH WALDO EMERSON, 1860

The laws which regulate the value of the supply forthcoming from the producers have been almost exhaustively developed in political economy; but the deeper laws which regulate the demand of the consumers, and which give the love of money all its force and all its meaning, have never yet received the regular attention of any school of philosophers.

CLIFFE LESLIE, 1861

Economic activity will be engaged in more energetically the more urgent a person's need for a good and the more difficult it is to procure the good corresponding to that need. The more these two factors (intensity of desire and degree of difficulty of procurement) operate upon one another, the more strongly does the importance of the good enter into the consciousness that guides economic activity.   A. E. F. SCHÄFFLE, 1885

He mocks the people who proposes that the Government shall protect the rich and that they in turn will care for the laboring poor.

GROVER CLEVELAND, 1888

Economics from beginning to end is a study of the mutual adjustments of consumption and production.   ALFRED MARSHALL, 1890

When considering an individual producer, we must couple his supply curve—not with the general demand curve for his commodity in a wide market but—with the particular demand curve of his own special market.

ALFRED MARSHALL, 1890

The price of ability does not depend on merit, but on supply and demand.

GEORGE BERNARD SHAW, 1894

There are those who believe that, if you will only legislate to make the well-to-do prosperous, their prosperity will leak through to those below. The Democratic idea, however, has been that if you legislate to make the masses prosperous, their prosperity will find its way up through every class which rests upon them.

WILLIAM JENNINGS BRYAN, 1896

It is pauperism and a glutted market that lie at the root of the economic distress of the time.

KARL RODBERTUS, 1898

I think people are going to buy quite a passel of these gasoline buggies and they need gasoline to make 'em go. It may be the thing has a future.

FRANK PHILLIPS, 1904

In October, 1913, when England launched the "Queen Elizabeth," first of the cruisers to burn crude oil, I knew then that it was up to me to concern myself with the supply of oil for my country and not with archeology.

T. E. LAWRENCE (OF ARABIA), 1916

That "producer's economy" then beginning to prevail in America, which first creates articles and then attempts to create a demand for them; an economy that has flooded the country with breakfast foods, shaving soaps, poets, and professors of philosophy.

GEORGE SANTAYANA, 1920

I am like any other man. All I do is supply a demand.   AL CAPONE, 1926

The cure for "Materialism" is to have enough for everybody and to spare. When people are sure of having what they need they cease to think about it.   HENRY FORD, 1931

Demand for new supplies of durable goods fluctuates more intensely than demand for the current services these durable goods render.

JOHN MAURICE CLARK, 1934

Adequate distribution of goods makes, unmakes—or remakes—all capital values!

KENNETH GOODE, 1947

Demands in general can be deficient only as supply is withheld.   W. H. HUTT, 1963

The relative prices of goods arise in principle, from the pattern of demand that emerges from the distribution of income.

E. J. MISHAN, 1967

The oilcan is mightier than the sword.

EVERETT DIRKSEN, 1967

Democracy is the greatest system of mutual reinsurance ever invented. When we see a friend in the line of unemployment compensation, we each say, "There but for the grace of supply and demand go I."   PAUL A. SAMUELSON, 1974

It is difficult to believe that there can ever have been another case of a country [America] where the demand of the rest of the world for its products was so urgent and its demand for the products of the world so indifferent.

GEOFFREY CROWTHER, 1975

Those who invented the law of supply and demand have no right to complain when this law works against their interest.

ANWAR SADAT, 1978

There isn't a gasoline shortage. There's a driving surplus.   JOHN O'LEARY, 1979

I do believe in supply-side economics.

RONALD REAGAN, 1981

Waiting for supply-side economics to work is like leaving the landing lights on for Amelia Earhart.   WALTER HELLER, 1982

Taxes

Render therefore unto Caesar the things which are Caesar's.   MATTHEW 22:21, c. A.D. 65

At the beginning of the dynasty, taxation yields a large revenue from small assessments. At the end of the dynasty taxation yields a small revenue from large assessments.
          IBN KHALDUN, fourteenth century

Never will it be that a people overlaid with taxes should ever become valiant and martial.
          FRANCIS BACON, 1597

When the impositions [taxes] are laid upon those things which men consume, every man pays equally for what he uses; Nor is the Commonwealth defrauded by the luxurious waste of private men.   THOMAS HOBBES, 1651

That which angers men most is to be taxed above their neighbors.   WILLIAM PETTY, 1662

It is generally allowed by all, that men should contribute to the public charge but according to the share and interest they have in the public peace; that is, according to their estates or riches.   WILLIAM PETTY, 1662

The art of taxation consists in so plucking the goose as to obtain the largest possible amount of feathers with the smallest possible amount of hissing.   JEAN-BAPTISTE COLBERT, 1665

It is true governments cannot be supported without great charge, and it is fit everyone who enjoys his share of the protection should pay out of his estate his proportion for the maintenance of it.   JOHN LOCKE, 1691

In constitutional states liberty is compensation for the heavy taxation; in despotic states the equivalent of liberty is light taxes.
          C. S. MONTESQUIEU, 1748

Each citizen contributes to the revenues of the State a portion of his property in order that his tenure of the rest may be secure.
          C. S. MONTESQUIEU, 1748

Excise: A hateful tax levied upon commodities, and adjudged not by the common judges of property, but wretches hired by those to whom excise is paid.   SAMUEL JOHNSON, 1752

There is a prevailing maxim among some reasoners, that every new tax creates a new ability in the subject to bear it, and that each increase of public burden increases proportionably the industry of the people.   DAVID HUME, 1754

What is't to us if taxes rise or fall?
Thanks to our fortune, we pay none at all.
          CHARLES CHURCHILL, 1761

To tax and to please, no more than to love and be wise, is not given to man.
                              EDMUND BURKE, 1774

Taxation without representation is tyranny.
                              JAMES OTIS, 1775

Every tax must finally be paid from some one or other of those three different sorts of revenue [rent, profit, or wages], or from all of them indifferently.   ADAM SMITH, 1776

After all the proper subjects of taxation have been exhausted, if the exigencies of the state still continue to require new taxes, they must be imposed upon improper ones.
                              ADAM SMITH, 1776

There is no art which one government sooner learns of another than that of draining money from the pockets of the people.
                              ADAM SMITH, 1776

High taxes, sometimes by diminishing the consumption of the taxed commodities, and sometimes by encouraging smuggling, frequently afford a smaller revenue to government than what might be drawn from more moderate taxes.
                              ADAM SMITH, 1776

The subjects of every state ought to contribute towards the support of the government, as nearly as possible, in proportion to the revenue which they respectively enjoy under the protection of the state.   ADAM SMITH, 1776

All taxes which proceed according to the amount of capital supposed to be employed in a business, or of profits supposed to be made in it, are unavoidably hurtful to industry.
                              ALEXANDER HAMILTON, 1781

Another means of silently lessening the inequality of property is to exempt all from taxation below a certain point, and to tax the higher portions of property in geometric progression as they rise.   THOMAS JEFFERSON, 1785

In this world nothing can be said to be certain, except death and taxes.
                              BENJAMIN FRANKLIN, 1789

All taxes that are of any continuance, must come some how or other out of income: but in the instance of one class of taxes they are forced, and are laid upon the possession of income: in the instance of another class they are voluntary, and derived from the expenditure of it.
                              JEREMY BENTHAM, 1794

No possible contributions or sacrifices of the rich, particularly in money, could for any time prevent the recurrence of distress among the lower orders of society.   THOMAS MALTHUS, 1798

A taxed commodity will not rise in proportion to the tax, if the demand for it diminish, and if the quantity cannot be reduced.
                              DAVID RICARDO, 1817

Taxes which are levied on a country for the purpose of supporting war, or for the ordinary expenses of the state, and which are chiefly devoted to the support of unproductive laborers, are taken from the productive industry of the country; and every saving which can be made from such expense will be generally added to the income, if not to the capital of the contributors.   DAVID RICARDO, 1817

The power to tax involves the power to destroy.
                              JOHN MARSHALL, 1819

Almost all taxes on production fall finally on the consumer.   DAVID RICARDO, 1822

Give us day by day our Real Taxed Substantial Money bought bread; deliver from the Holy Ghost whatever cannot be Taxed; for all is debt & Taxes between Caesar & us & one another.
                              WILLIAM BLAKE, 1827

The widsom of man never yet contrived a system of taxation that would operate with perfect equality.   ANDREW JACKSON, 1832

The moment you abandon the cardinal principle of exacting from all individuals the same proportion of their income or their property, you are at sea without rudder or compass, and there is no amount of injustice or folly you may not commit.   JOHN MCCULLOCH, 1845

What is taken from the rich in taxes, would, if not so taken, have been saved and converted into capital or even expended in the maintenance and wages of servants or any class of unproductive laborers, to that extent the demand for labor is no doubt diminished, and the poor injuriously affected, by the tax on the rich.
                              JOHN STUART MILL, 1848

Unless . . . savings are exempted from income tax, the contributors are twice taxed on what they save, and only once on what they spend.
                              JOHN STUART MILL, 1848

I would suggest the taxation of all property equally whether church or corporation.
                              ULYSSES S. GRANT, 1868

The tax upon land values is the most just and equal of all taxes. It falls upon those who receive from society a peculiar and valuable benefit, and upon them in proportion to the benefit they receive.   HENRY GEORGE, 1879

Taxation must not lead men into temptation, by requiring trivial oaths, by making it profitable to lie, to swear falsely, to bribe or to take bribes.   HENRY GEORGE, 1879

The mode of taxation is, in fact, quite as important as the amount. As a small burden badly placed may distress a horse that could carry with ease a much larger one properly adjusted, so a people may be impoverished and their power of

producing wealth destroyed by taxation, which, if levied another way, could be borne with ease.
                              HENRY GEORGE, 1879

It is beyond the sphere of true governmental power to tax one man to help the business of another. It is taking money from one to give it to another.   FRANK H. HURD, 1881

How much is he [the taxpayer] compelled to labor for other benefit than his own, and how much can he labor for his own benefit? The degree of his slavery varies according to the ratio between that which he is forced to yield up and that which he is allowed to retain; and it matters not whether his master is a single person or a society.   HERBERT SPENCER, 1884

To make a taxpayer pay up, it's practically essential to put him before a gallows.
                              BENITO PÉREZ GÁLDOS, 1886

No tax is a good tax unless it leaves individuals in the same relative position as it finds them.
                              FRANCIS A. WALKER, 1887

That a great reluctance to pay taxes existed in all the colonies, there can be no doubt. It was one of the marked characteristics of the American people long after their separation from England.   G. S. CALLENDER, 1909

The Congress shall have power to lay and collect taxes on incomes, from whatever source derived, without apportionment among the several States, and without regard to any census or enumeration.
            SIXTEENTH AMENDMENT, U.S. CONSTITUTION,
                                                    1913

In levying taxes and in shearing sheep it is well to stop when you get down to the skin.
                              AUSTIN O'MALLEY, 1915

Taxes not only helped to create the state. They helped to form it. The tax system was the organ the development of which entailed the other organs. Tax bill in hand, the state penetrated the private economies and won increasing dominion over them.

JOSEPH A. SCHUMPETER, 1918

The Congress might well consider whether the higher rates of income and profits taxes can in peace times be effectively productive of revenue, and whether they may not, on the contrary, be destructive of business activity and productive of waste and inefficiency. There is a point at which in peace times high rates of income and profits taxes discourage energy, remove the incentive to new enterprise, encourage extravagant expenditures and produce industrial stagnation with consequent unemployment and other attendant evils.

WOODROW WILSON, 1919

The income tax returns would indicate that there is untold wealth in Canada.

BOB EDWARDS, 1920

The Income Tax has made more Liars out of the American people than golf has.

WILL ROGERS, 1924

The first object of taxation is to secure revenue. When the taxation of large incomes is approached with that in view, the problem is to find a rate which will produce the largest returns. Experience does not show that the higher rate produces the larger revenue.

CALVIN COOLIDGE, 1924

Collecting more taxes than is absolutely necessary is legalized robbery.

CALVIN COOLIDGE, 1926

An income tax is the price which the government charges for the privilege of having taxable income. If the price is too low, the government's revenue is not large enough: If the price is too high, the taxpayer, through the many means available, avoids a taxable income, and the government gets less out of a high tax than it would get out of a lower tax.

ANDREW W. MELLON, 1926

When everybody has got money they cut taxes, and when they're broke they raise 'em. That's statesmanship of the highest order.

WILL ROGERS, 1929

Just be glad you're not getting all the government you're paying for.

WILL ROGERS, 1929

The promises of yesterday are the taxes of today.   WILLIAM L. MACKENZIE KING, 1931

A citizen can hardly distinguish between a tax and a fine, except that the fine is generally much lighter.   GILBERT K. CHESTERTON, 1933

Taxes, after all, are the dues that we pay for the privileges of membership in an organized society.   FRANKLIN D. ROOSEVELT, 1936

There is no such thing as a good tax.

WINSTON CHURCHILL, 1937

Men in America were so conditioned that they felt differently about taxes and about prices. The former was an involuntary taking; the latter a voluntary giving. . . . No one observed the obvious fact that in terms of total income of an individual it made no difference whether his money went for prices or taxes.

THURMAN W. ARNOLD, 1937

The case for drastic progression in taxation must be rested on the case against inequality—on the ethical or aesthetic judgment that the prevailing distribution of wealth and income reveals a degree of inequality which is distinctly evil or unlovely.   HENRY C. SIMONS, 1938

Increasing progression means augmenting incomes where saving is impossible and diminishing incomes too large to be used entirely for consumption. Thus, it means diversion of resources from capital-creation to consumption uses.   HENRY C. SIMONS, 1938

It shocks the man with his feet on the ground to see a man with his head in the clouds pay a big income tax.   HENRY S. HASKINS, 1939

The avoidance of taxes is the only intellectual pursuit that still carries any reward.
JOHN MAYNARD KEYNES, 1942

Governments last as long as the undertaxed can defend themselves against the over-taxed.
BERNARD BERENSON, 1944

Unquestionably, there is progress. The average American now pays out almost as much in taxes alone as he formerly got in wages.
H. L. MENCKEN, 1949

Anyone may so arrange his affairs that his taxes shall be low as possible; he is not bound to choose that pattern which will best pay the treasury; there is not even a patriotic duty to increase one's taxes.   LEARNED HAND, 1951

Taxation is a most flexible and effective but also a dangerous instrument of social reform. One has to know precisely what one is doing lest the results diverge greatly from one's intentions.
GUNNAR MYRDAL, 1953

The relative stability of profits after taxes is evidence that the corporation profits tax is in effect almost entirely shifted; the government simply uses the corporation as a tax collector.
KENNETH E. BOULDING, 1953

The hardest thing in the world to understand is the income tax.   ALBERT EINSTEIN, 1953

The point to remember is that what the government gives it must first take away.
JOHN S. COLEMAN, 1954

To produce an income tax return that has any depth to it, any feeling, one must have Lived and Suffered.   FRANK SULLIVAN, 1954

An income tax form is like a laundry list—either way you lose your shirt.   FRED ALLEN, 1954

The Tax Collector's letters are invariably mimeographed, and all they say is that you still haven't paid him.   WILLIAM SAROYAN, 1958

The observation is frequently made that because in the long run the [corporate] tax tends to be included in the price of the product, it is to this extent borne by consumers. This observation misconstrues the nature of the tax. Fundamentally, it is a tax on a factor of production: corporate equity capital.
ARNOLD C. HARBERGER, 1959

The illusion that by some means of progressive taxation the burden can be shifted substantially onto the shoulders of the wealthy has been the chief reason why taxation has increased as fast as it has done and that, under the influence of this illusion, the masses have come to accept a much heavier load than they would have done otherwise. The only major result of the policy has been the severe limitation of the incomes that could be earned by the most successful and thereby gratification of the envy of the less well off.   FRIEDRICH A. HAYEK, 1960

An economy hampered by restrictive tax rates will never produce enough revenues to balance our budget, just as it will never produce enough jobs or enough profits.
JOHN F. KENNEDY, 1962

There is one difference between a tax collector and a taxidermist—the taxidermist leaves the hide.   MORTIMER CAPLAN, 1963

All money nowadays seems to be produced with a natural homing instinct for the Treasury.
DUKE OF EDINBURGH, 1963

We can trace the personal history of a man, and his successes and failures, just by looking at his tax returns from his first job to his retirement.
CHARLES A. CHURCH, 1964

The most damaging thing you can do to any businessman in America is to keep him in doubt, and to keep him guessing, on what our tax policy is.
LYNDON B. JOHNSON, 1964

Although the difference between the before-tax and after-tax distribution of income, in recent years, is not striking, neither is it trivial. There is no evidence that the re-distribution impact of the income tax has been offset by changes in before-tax income shares. Income before tax has become less unequal, and there is reason for believing that the tax has contributed, to a minor extent, to this change.
RICHARD GOODE, 1964

Taxes must in the long run be derived from net annual production. Individuals may acquire goods through gambling, speculation, gifts, and bequests; but these individual gains contribute nothing to that reservoir from which all taxes must be drawn.
HENRY C. SIMONS, 1965

The first nine pages of the Internal Revenue Code define income; the remaining 1,100 pages spin the web of exceptions and preferences.
WARREN G. MAGNUSON, 1966

A surtax is a tax on a tax—which is a case of adding insult to penury.
ROBERT ORBEN, 1967

To suppose that tax officers can be encountered carelessly and addressed frankly is an elementary error, which may create hardship and expense for the unwary and the innocent.
OLIVER STANLEY, 1967

The forgotten American is that fellow living in the suburbs or in a high-rise in the middle of town and is working sixty hours a week to provide the advantages for his family, but is being taxed heavily to take care of some other people's problems.
RONALD REAGAN, 1968

Many of the immediate problems of pollution of the atmosphere or of the bodies of water arise because of the failure of the price system, and many of them could be solved by corrective taxation.
KENNETH E. BOULDING, 1968

Man is not like other animals in the ways that are really significant: animals have instincts, we have taxes.
ERVING GOFFMAN, 1969

People hate taxes the way children hate brushing their teeth—and in the same shortsighted way.
PAUL A. SAMUELSON, 1972

Since the accumulation of a substantial estate is one of the motivations that drive people to work hard, a death tax on saving is indirectly a tax on work.
RICHARD POSNER, 1972

Taxes are not levied for the benefit of the taxed.
ROBERT HEINLEIN, 1973

Youth today must be strong, unafraid, and a better taxpayer than its father.
HARRY V. WADE, 1973

It is silly to say that corporations really pay taxes. In the end it is the shareholder, the consumer or the wage earner who pays those taxes indirectly, depending on whether and how the corporation shifts its tax burden. Taxes are paid by individuals period.
RICHARD A. MUSGRAVE, 1973

Tax reform is when you take the taxes off things that have been taxed in the past and put taxes on things that haven't been taxed before.
ART BUCHWALD, 1974

Income tax returns are the most imaginative fiction being written today.
HERMAN WOUK, 1975

Tax reform means, "Don't tax you, don't tax me. Tax that fellow behind the tree."
RUSSELL B. LONG, 1976

The taxpayer—that's someone who works for the federal government but doesn't have to take a civil service examination.
RONALD REAGAN, 1976

The rich aren't like us, they pay less taxes.
PETER DE VRIES, 1976

The nation should have a tax system which looks like someone designed it on purpose.
WILLIAM E. SIMON, 1977

Why does a slight tax increase cost you $200 and a substantial tax cut save you 30 cents?
PEG BRACKEN, 1978

Of all the deficiencies in our income tax system, for me the most serious is that the laws directly invite us to commit tax evasion and tax cheating. The honesty of Swedes has been a source of pride to me and my generation. Now I have a feeling that we are becoming a nation of hustlers because of bad laws.
GUNNAR MYRDAL, 1979

The last important human activity not subject to taxation is sex.
RUSSELL BAKER, 1980

The entire graduated-income-tax structure was created by Karl Marx.
RONALD REAGAN, 1980

If you are truly serious about preparing your child for the future, don't teach him to subtract—teach him to deduct.
FRAN LEBOWITZ, 1981

Technology

The greatest inventions were produced in times of ignorance; as the use of the compass, gunpowder, and printing; and by the dullest nation, as the Germans.
JONATHAN SWIFT, 1737

It is not the fault of the progress of mechanical science, but the fault of the social order, if the worker, who acquires the power to make in two hours what would take him twelve to make before, does not find himself richer, and consequently does not enjoy more leisure, but on the contrary is doing six times more work than is demanded.
SIMONDE DE SISMONDI, 1803

The progression of physical science is much more connected with your prosperity than is usually imagined. You owe to experimental philosophy some of the most important and peculiar of your advantages. It is not by foreign conquests chiefly that you are become great, but by a conquest of nature in your own country.

HUMPHREY DAVY, 1809

One of my primary objects is to form the tools so the tools themselves shall fashion the work and give to each part its just proportion—which when once accomplished, will give expedition, uniformity and exactness to the whole.

ELI WHITNEY, 1812

The advance and perfecting of mathematics are closely joined to the prosperity of the nation.

NAPOLEON BONAPARTE, 1815

Machinery and labor are in constant competition, and the former can frequently not be employed until labor rises.

DAVID RICARDO, 1817

It might be possible to do almost all the work performed by men with horses, would the substitution of horses in such case, even if attended with a greater produce, be advantageous to the working classes, would it not on the contrary very materially diminish the demand for labor?

DAVID RICARDO, 1817

Every newly observed phenomenon is a discovery, every discovery is property. Touch a man's property and his passions are easily aroused.

JOHANN WOLFGANG GOETHE, 1823

From Avarice thus, from Luxury and War
Sprang heavenly Science; and from Science
Freedom.

SAMUEL TAYLOR COLERIDGE, 1828

In considering this increase of employment, it must be admitted that the two thousand persons thrown out of work are not exactly of the same class as those called into employment by the power looms.   CHARLES BABBAGE, 1832

Man is a tool-using animal. . . . Without tools he is nothing, with tools he is all.

THOMAS CARLYLE, 1843

The mystery of mysteries is to view machinery making machinery.

BENJAMIN DISRAELI, 1844

All our inventions have endowed material forces with intellectual life, and degraded human life into a material force.   KARL MARX, 1856

Machinery is intended to cheapen commodities, and by shortening that proportion of the working day in which the laborer works for himself, to lengthen the other portion that he gives without an equivalent to the capitalists. In short, it is a means of creating surplus value.

KARL MARX, 1867

The instrument of labor, when it takes the form of a machine immediately becomes a competitor of the workman himself.

KARL MARX, 1867

Name the greatest of all inventors. Accident.

MARK TWAIN, 1875

But the second way by which competitive commerce destroys our mental wealth is yet worse: it is by the turning of almost all handicraftsmen into machines.   WILLIAM MORRIS, 1883

Anything that won't sell, I don't want to invent.

THOMAS A. EDISON, 1887

Pioneering does not pay.

ANDREW CARNEGIE, 1888

Results? Why, man, I've gotten a lot of results. I know several thousand things that won't work.   THOMAS A. EDISON, 1900

What we call "progress" is the exchange of one nuisance for another nuisance.

HAVELOCK ELLIS, 1904

I am not saying that all invention had been stopped by the growth of trusts, but I think it is perfectly clear that invention in many fields has been discouraged, that inventors have been prevented from reaping the full fruits of their ingenuity and industry, and that mankind has been deprived of many comforts and conveniences, as well as the opportunity of buying at lower prices.   WOODROW WILSON, 1911

Every industry, every process, is wrought by a hand, or by a super-hand—a machine whose mighty arm and cunning fingers the human hand invents and wields.   HELEN KELLER, 1912

And there is the patent fact that such a thing as a general strike of the technological specialists in industry need involve no more than a minute fraction of one percent of the population; yet it would swiftly bring a collapse of the older order and sweep the timeworn fabric of finance and absentee sabotage into the discard for good and all.   THORSTEIN VEBLEN, 1921

One of my most vivid early recollections is the great trouble that came to the silk weavers when machinery was invented to replace their skill and take their jobs. No thought was given to these men whose trade was gone.

SAMUEL GOMPERS, 1922

I never did anything worth doing by accident, nor did any of my inventions come by accident; they came by work.

THOMAS A. EDISON, 1923

Nothing you can't spell will ever work.

WILL ROGERS, 1924

The task of stimulating demand is never done; for the march of technological improvements is ever increasing our capacity to produce, and before we have learned to distribute and to use what has just been added to our output, new advances have been scored. Hence, the chronic complaints of businessmen that our industries are "over built."

WESLEY C. MITCHELL, 1927

Big industrial inventions may sometimes be important; but it is the decision to exploit inventions that is the active cause of disturbance, and the time and intensity of exploitations are largely determined by the state of business confidence.

A. C. PIGOU, 1927

Bankers regard research as most dangerous and a thing that makes banking hazardous to the rapid changes it brings about in industry.

CHARLES F. KETTERING, 1927

The only way to solve the Traffic problems of the Country is to pass a law that only paid-for Cars are allowed to use the Highways.

WILL ROGERS, 1927

The primary cause which has determined the movement of wages in the United States during the past thirty years has been the introduction of labor-saving machinery. The effect of the substitution of mechanical devices for human skill is the displacement of the skilled mechanic by the unskilled laborer.

SELIG PERLMAN, 1928

The slogan of progress is changing from the full dinner pail to the full garage.

HERBERT HOOVER, 1928

For the scientific acquisition of knowledge is almost as tedious as the routine acquisition of wealth.   ERIC LINKLATER, 1929

The fall of capitalism began when it made razor blades that would get dull in a month instead of those that would easily last 10 years at the same cost.   W. E. B. DU BOIS, 1933

Have you ever thought, not only about the airplane but about whatever man builds, that all of man's industrial efforts, all his computations and calculations, all the nights spent over working drafts and blueprints, invariably culminate in the production of a thing whose sole and guiding principle is the ultimate principle of simplicity?

ANTOINE DE SAINT-EXUPÉRY, 1939

Everything in life is somewhere else, and you get there in a car.   E. B. WHITE, 1944

There is no rate of pay at which a United States pick-and-shovel laborer can live which is low enough to compete with the work of a steam shovel as an excavator.

NORBERT WEINER, 1948

We have created an industrial order geared to automatism, where feeble-mindedness, native or acquired, is necessary for docile productivity in the factory; and where a pervasive neurosis is the final gift of the meaningless life that issues forth at the other end.

LEWIS MUMFORD, 1951

The power that enables the firm to have some influence on price insures that the resulting gains will not be passed on to the public by imitators (who have stood none of the costs of development) before the outlay for development can be recouped. In this way market power protects the incentive to technical development.

JOHN KENNETH GALBRAITH, 1952

But if capitalism had built up science as a productive force, the very character of the new mode of production was serving to make capitalism itself unnecessary.   JOHN D. BERNAL, 1952

One cannot walk through a mass-production factory and not feel that one is in Hell.

W. H. AUDEN, 1953

The industry of discovery is one of the most rapidly expanding industries in the economy.

And it seems destined to grow rapidly for some years to come because its size today is limited, not by the number of problems that are worth studying, but by the supply of skilled personnel.

SUMNER SLICHTER, 1956

It is easy to overlook the absence of appreciable advance in an industry. Inventions that are not made, like babies that are not born, are rarely missed.   JOHN KENNETH GALBRAITH, 1958

We believe that if men have the talent to invent new machines that put men out of work, they have the talent to put those men back to work.

JOHN F. KENNEDY, 1962

History teaches us . . . that by and large workers displaced by technological advance have moved rapidly into other employment, ultimately to better-paying jobs. This is why we have had rising personal incomes rather than mass unemployment as new technology has come into use and productivity has increased.

HENRY FORD II, 1962

The car has become a secular sanctuary for the individual, his shrine to the self, his mobile Walden Pond.   EDWARD MCDONAGH, 1963

Innovators are inevitably controversial.

EVA LE GALLIENNE, 1965

American labor has no illusion that the problems associated with technological change can be solved through collective bargaining alone, without recourse to government action.

WALTER REUTHER, 1965

The big concern has the ability to finance innovation; it does not necessarily do so. There is no clear relationship between size and investment in research.   CLAIR WILCOX, 1966

For over a hundred years technology has been the single most propulsive and revolutionizing force within capitalism, but we still know very little about its workings. Until we do, the power of the machine will continue to be praised and feared in extravagant terms, but not understood.   ROBERT L. HEILBRONER, 1966

Formerly the problem was to invent new forms of labor-saving. Today the reverse is the problem. Now we have to adjust, not to invent. We have to find the environments in which it will be possible to live with our new inventions.
     MARSHALL MCLUHAN, 1967

In a consumer society, the best product you can manufacture is one that must be replaced immediately.   GENE LEES, 1969

The real problem is not whether machines think but whether men do.   B. F. SKINNER, 1969

Automized and computerized industry requires more and more young men and women who have white-collar skills but behave with the docility expected of blue-collar workers.
     STAUGHTON LYND, 1970

America's technology has turned in upon itself; its corporate form makes it the servant of profits, not the servant of human needs.
     ALICE EMBREE, 1970

The economic and technological triumphs of the past few years have not solved as many problems as we thought they would, and, in fact, have brought us new problems we did not foresee.   HENRY FORD II, 1971

In guessing the direction of technology it is wise to ask who is in the best position to profit most.
     BEN H. BAGDIKIAN, 1971

The plight of the ordinary mortal, however, is seemingly inescapable. . . . How can he hold his head up when it is plain beyond doubt that as a producer he does not rate; that nobody

depends on him for anything; that he is but a drone in a world become a buzzing hive of technology.   E. J. MISHAN, 1971

The automobile is the single most wasteful, destructive thing we've done in—and to—this generation.   STEWART L. UDALL, 1973

Mass transportation is doomed to failure in North America because a person's car is the only place where he can be alone and think.
     MARSHALL MCLUHAN, 1975

The worship of science and technology is at least as much in evidence in the present spectrum of advanced socialist nations as it is within the spectrum of capitalist ones.
     ROBERT L. HEILBRONER, 1976

The main impact of the computer has been the provision of unlimited jobs for clerks.
     PETER DRUCKER, 1976

Think about all those people in automobiles, driving about with their debts.
     ELIZABETH HARDWICK, 1979

If it's good, they'll stop making it.
     HERBERT BLOCK, 1979

Technological progress in these last 80 years has occurred almost exclusively in the non-socialist countries, and the former industrially advanced countries that have become socialistic have lost their technological leadership, and are now largely living on what technology they can import from the still market-organized countries.
     FRIEDRICH A. HAYEK, 1980

Right now, the children of the well-to-do are given liberal access to computers. People may very well attribute the success of these children to their computer experience. In reality, these children will have had many other important advantages right from the start. If you want to reduce inequality, the solution is to give the poor money, not computers.

JOSEPH WEIZENBAUM, 1983

No businessman these days dares to embark upon the journey of incorporation without first acquiring a computer so huge and so omniscient as to strike terror into the software of its enemies.   LEWIS H. LAPHAM, 1984

Trade

We maintain that if the merchandise which goes out of England be well and rightly governed, the money that is in England will remain and great plenty of money will come from beyond the sea, that is to say, let not more strange merchandise come within the realm than to the value of the denizen merchandise which passes out of the realm.   RICHARD AYLESBURY, 1382

Trade is the mother of money.

THOMAS DRAXE, c. 1605

Let the foundation of profitable trade be thus laid that the exportation of home commodities be more in value than the importation of foreign, so we shall be sure that the stocks of the Kingdom shall increase, for the balance of trade must be returned in money or bullion.

FRANCIS BACON, 1616

And what has more relation to matters of state, than commerce of merchants? For when trade flourishes, the King's revenue is augmented, lands and rents improved, navigation is increased, the poor employed. But if trade decay, all these decline with it.   EDWARD MISSELDEN, 1622

The ordinary means therefore to increase our wealth and treasure is by Foreign Trade, wherein we must ever observe this rule; to sell more to strangers yearly than we consume of theirs in value . . . because that part of our stock which is not returned to us in wares must necessarily be brought home in treasure.

THOMAS MUN, 1664

The chief end of trade is riches and power which beget each other. Riches consist in plenty of moveables, that will yield a price to foreigners, and are not like to be consumed at home, but especially in plenty of gold and silver. Power consists in numbers of men, and ability to maintain them. Trade conduces to both these by increasing your stock and your people.

JOHN LOCKE, 1674

By means of trade all needs of life are in some way satisfied, without the intervention of charity. Take the citizen of a state which does not admit charity because it bans the true religion. Such a citizen does not fail to live as much in peace, security, and ease as would the member of a republic of saints.

PIERRE NICOLE, 1675

There can be no trade unprofitable to the public; for if any prove so, men leave it off; and whenever the traders thrive, the public, of which they are part, thrives also.

DUDLEY NORTH, 1691

Trade fetches it [gold] away from that lazy and indigent people [Spain], notwithstanding all their artificial and forced contrivances to keep it there. It follows trade, against the rigor of their laws; and their want of foreign commodities makes it openly be carried out at noonday.

JOHN LOCKE, 1692

Trade is in its nature free, finds its own channel, and best directeth its own course: and all Laws to give it rules and directions, and to limit and circumscribe it, may serve the particular ends of private men, but are seldom advantageous to the public. CHARLES DAVENANT, 1697

The usual trade and commerce is cheating all round by consent. THOMAS FULLER, 1732

What war could ravish, commerce could bestow,
And he returned a friend, who came a foe.

ALEXANDER POPE, 1733

Peace is the natural effect of trade. Two nations who traffic with each other become reciprocally dependent; for if one has an interest in buying, the other has an interest in selling; and thus their union is founded on their mutual necessities.

C. S. MONTESQUIEU, 1748

If we consult history, we shall find that, in most nations, foreign trade has preceded any refinement in home manufactures, and given birth to domestic luxury. DAVID HUME, 1772

Nothing dejects a trader like the interruption of his profits. SAMUEL JOHNSON, 1776

The importation of gold and silver is not the principal, much less the sole benefit which a nation derives from its foreign trade. Between whatever places foreign trade is carried on, they all of them derive two distinct benefits from it. It carries out that surplus part of the produce of their land and labor for which there is no demand among them, and brings back in return for it something else for which there is a demand. ADAM SMITH, 1776

If a foreign country can supply us with a commodity cheaper than we ourselves can make it, better buy it of them with some part of the produce of our own industry, employed in a way in which we have some advantage.

ADAM SMITH, 1776

When the exchange between two places, such as London and Paris, is at par, it is said to be a sign that the debts due from London to Paris are compensated by those due from Paris to London. ADAM SMITH, 1776

No nation was ever ruined by trade.

BENJAMIN FRANKLIN, 1779

Trade's proud empire hastes to swift decay.

SAMUEL JOHNSON, 1781

There is, perhaps, nothing more likely to disturb the tranquillity of nations than their being bound to mutual contributions for any common object that does not yield an equal and coincident benefit. For it is an observation, as true as it is trite, that there is nothing men differ so readily about as the payment of money.

ALEXANDER HAMILTON, 1788

In passing along the highway one frequently sees large and spacious buildings, with the glass broken out of the windows, the shutters hanging in ruinous disorder, without any appearance of activity and enveloped in solitary gloom. Upon inquiry what they are, you are almost always informed that they were some cotton or other factory, which their proprietors could no longer keep in motion against the overwhelming pressure of foreign competition.

HENRY CLAY, 1820

Free trade, one of the greatest blessings which a government can confer on a people, is in almost every country unpopular.

THOMAS MACAULEY, 1824

The objects of an old society in promoting colonization seems to be three: first, the extension of the market for disposing of their own surplus produce; secondly, relief from excessive numbers; thirdly, an enlargement of the field for employing capital.

EDWARD G. WAKEFIELD, 1829

The call for free trade is as unavailing as the cry of a spoiled child for the moon. It never has existed; it never will exist.   HENRY CLAY, 1832

One of the greatest benefits which foreign commerce confers, and the reason why it has always appeared an almost necessary ingredient in the progress of wealth, is its tendency to inspire new wants, to form new tastes, and to furnish fresh motives for industry.

THOMAS MALTHUS, 1836

Trade, the calm health of nations.

EDWARD G. BULWER-LYTTON, 1838

Protection and patriotism are reciprocal. This is the road that all great nations have trod.

JOHN C. CALHOUN, 1843

[Protectionism] is . . . the sacrifice of the consumer to the producer—or the ends to the means.   FRÉDÉRIC BASTIAT, 1847

Tariffs only raise the prices of things because they diminish the quantity offered in the market.   FRÉDÉRIC BASTIAT, 1847

A country which prohibits some foreign commodities, does, *ceteris paribus,* obtain those

which it does not prohibit at a lesser price than it would otherwise have to pay.

JOHN STUART MILL, 1848

The only direct advantage of foreign commerce consists in the imports.

JOHN STUART MILL, 1848

The increase of the general riches of the world, when accompanied with freedom of commercial intercourse, improvements in navigation, and inland communication by roads, canals, or railways, tends to give increased productiveness to the labor of every nation in particular, by enabling each locality to supply with its special products so much larger a market, that a great extension of the division of labor in their production is an ordinary consequence.

JOHN STUART MILL, 1848

The relation of international trade to the development of new resources and productive forces is a more significant part of the explanation of the present status of nations, of incomes, prices, well-being, than is the cross-section value analysis of classical economists.

JOHN STUART MILL, 1848

England and the United States are bound together by a single thread of cotton, which, weak and fragile as it may appear, is, nevertheless, stronger than an iron cable.

FRIEDRICH ENGELS, 1857

The greatest meliorator of the world is selfish, huckstering trade.

RALPH WALDO EMERSON, 1870

The most advanced nations are always those who navigate the most.

RALPH WALDO EMERSON, 1870

Free-trade, they concede, is very well as a principle, but it is never quite time for its adoption.

RALPH WALDO EMERSON, 1876

In the pre-capitalist stages of society, commerce rules industry. The reverse is true of modern society. KARL MARX, 1883

Commerce is the great civilizer. We exchange ideas when we exchange fabrics.
ROBERT G. INGERSOLL, 1883

American factories are making more than the American people can use; American soil is producing more than they can consume. Fate has written our policy for us; the trade of the world must and shall be ours.
ALBERT J. BEVERIDGE, 1898

Hands accrost th' sea and into some wan's pocket. FINLEY PETER DUNNE, 1898

If we will not buy, we cannot sell.
WILLIAM MCKINLEY, 1899

[Imperialism is] the endeavor of the great controllers of industry to broaden the channel for the flow of their surplus wealth by seeking foreign markets. JOHN A. HOBSON, 1902

Tariff, n. A scale of taxes on imports designed to protect the domestic producer against the greed of his consumer.
AMBROSE BIERCE, 1906

Dollar Diplomacy.
PHILANDER C. KNOX, 1909

Sooner or later, every war of trade becomes a war of blood. EUGENE V. DEBS, 1916

I believe in the protective tariff policy, and know we will be calling for its saving Americanism again. WARREN G. HARDING, 1920

A protective tariff is a typical conspiracy in restraint of trade. THORSTEIN VEBLEN, 1921

Enduring peace and the welfare of nations are indissolubly connected with friendliness, fairness, equality and the maximum practicable degree of freedom in international trade.
CORDELL HULL, 1937

National income cannot be increased by avoiding imports, since this will result only in diverting resources to the production of articles of domestic consumption, thereby withdrawing them from the most profitable export markets. Nor can domestic employment be increased by reducing imports because this would reduce exports to the same extent.
W. ARTHUR LEWIS, 1949

It is not possible for this nation to be at once politically internationalist and economically isolationist. This is just as insane as asking one Siamese twin to high dive while the other plays piano. ADLAI STEVENSON, 1952

What we call foreign affairs is no longer foreign affairs. It's a local affair. Whatever happens in Indonesia is important to Indiana. Whatever happens in any corner of the world has some effect on the farmer in Dickinson County, Kansas, or on a worker in a factory.
DWIGHT D. EISENHOWER, 1956

We declare war upon the United States in the peaceful field of trade.
NIKITA KHRUSHCHEV, 1957

Our [America's] dominant role in world trade and finance has meant that we could not either prudently or effectively use many of the simpler and most direct types of action by which other countries have sometimes dealt with their payment deficits. Currency devaluation, import restriction, exchange control . . . are all out of the question. DOUGLAS DILLON, 1963

The crux of the problem is whether leaders in both industrial and developing countries have adjusted intellectually and emotionally to this being one interdependent world.
LEE KUAN YEW, 1978

Economists, who are supposed to be a contentious bunch, have generally agreed that the community at large stands to gain in material standard of living from specialization and exchange according to the various nations' comparative advantage.

PAUL A. SAMUELSON, 1980

Backward cities must trade most heavily with other backward cities, or the gulf between what they import and what they can replace with their own production will be too great to be bridged.

JANE JACOBS, 1984

Utility

The value of all wares arise from their use; things of no use, have no value, as the English phrase is, they are good for nothing.

NICHOLAS BARBON, 1690

The sale of any thing depends upon its necessity or usefulness; as convenience or opinion, guided by fancy, or fashion, shall determine. The sale of any commodity comes to be increased, or decreased, as a greater part of the running cash of the nation is designed to be laid out, by several people at the same time, rather in that, than another; as we see in the change of fashions.

JOHN LOCKE, 1692

Utility itself is measured by considerations of eternal life.   LOUIS THOMASSIN, 1697

We never know the worth of water, till the well is dry.   THOMAS FULLER, 1732

The word value . . . has two different meanings and sometimes expresses the utility of some particular object, and sometimes the power of purchasing other goods which the possession of that object conveys. The one may be called "value in use," the other "value in exchange."

ADAM SMITH, 1776

I learnt to see that utility was the test and measure of all virtues.   JEREMY BENTHAM, 1776

A thing is said to be useful when it serves for one of our needs; . . . according to this utility we esteem it more or less. . . . Now, this esteem is what we call value.

E. B. DE CONDILLAC, 1777

Since the dispositions of human minds vary, the value of things varies.

FERDINANDO GALIANI, 1781

Nature has placed mankind under the governance of two sovereign masters, pain and pleasure. It is for them alone to point out what we ought to do, as well as to determine what we shall do. . . . They govern us in all we do.

JEREMY BENTHAM, 1787

By the principle of utility is meant the principle which approves or disapproves of every action whatsoever, according to the tendency which it has to augment or diminish the happiness of the party whose interest is in question; or what is the same thing in other words, to promote or to oppose that happiness.

JEREMY BENTHAM, 1789

That which has no value cannot be wealth. These things are not within the domain of political economy.   JEAN-BAPTISTE SAY, 1803

Pleasure diminishes in a rapidly increasing ratio. . . . Two articles of the same kind will seldom afford twice the pleasure of one, and still less will ten give five times the pleasures of two.

NASSAU SENIOR, 1836

Since use value is always a relation of a thing to man, the use value of every species of goods is determined by the magnitude and rank of the human needs the species of goods satisfies. Where there are no men and no needs, no use value exists.   BRUNO HILDEBRAND, 1848

Labor is not creative of objects, but of utilities. Why should not all labor which produces utility be accounted productive?

JOHN STUART MILL, 1848

The value . . . of an article . . . is determined by the cast of that portion of the supply which is produced and brought to market at the greatest expense.   JOHN STUART MILL, 1848

Thus the magnitudes of the use value of goods depend (a) on the intensity of the human needs they satisfy, and (b) on the intensity with which they satisfy these human needs.

JARL KNIES, 1855

Nothing can have value without being an object of utility.   KARL MARX, 1867

Value is . . . nothing inherent in goods, no property of them, but merely the importance that we first attribute to the satisfaction of our needs.   CARL MENGER, 1871

Cost of production determines supply;
Supply determines final degree of utility;
Final degree of utility determines value.

W. STANLEY JEVONS, 1871

The nature of Wealth and Value is explained by the consideration of indefinitely small amounts of pleasure and pain, just as the Theory of Statics is made to rest upon the equality of indefinitely small amounts of energy.

W. STANLEY JEVONS, 1871

[Economics] is the mechanics of utility and self-interest.   W. STANLEY JEVONS, 1871

A unit of pleasure or pain is difficult even to conceive, but it is the amount of these feelings which is continually prompting us to buying and selling, borrowing and lending, laboring and resting, producing and consuming: and it is from the quantitative effects of the feelings that we must estimate their comparative amounts.

W. STANLEY JEVONS, 1871

A thing is worth precisely what it can do for you, not what you choose to pay for it.

JOHN RUSKIN, 1884

What a man does, as his means increase, is, before anything else, to demand new qualities in the articles that he uses. Often he does not add at all to their number; but he causes them to be made of finer material or to be larger and handsomer. He adds to his wealth for consumption, not new things, but new utilities; and these are mainly attached to things of the kind formerly consumed.   JOHN BATES CLARK, 1886

In every self-contained private economy utility is the highest principle; but, in the business world, wherever the providing of society with goods is in the hands of undertakers who desire to make a gain out of it, and to obtain a remuneration for their services, exchange value takes place. The private undertaker is not concerned to provide the greatest utility for society generally; his aim is rather to obtain the highest value for himself:—which is at the same time his highest utility.   FRIEDRICH VON WIESER, 1889

That part of a thing which he is only just induced to purchase may be called his marginal purchase because he is at the margin of doubt whether it is worth his while to incur the outlay required to obtain it.
                          ALFRED MARSHALL, 1890

The larger the amount of a thing that a person has the less, other things being equal, will be the price which he will pay for a little more of it: or in other words his marginal demand price for it diminishes.   ALFRED MARSHALL, 1890

A stronger incentive will be required to induce a person to pay a given price for anything if he is poor than if he is rich. A shilling is the measure of less pleasure, or satisfaction, of any kind, to a rich man than to a poor one.
                          ALFRED MARSHALL, 1890

If the money measures of the happiness caused by two events are equal, there is not in general any very great difference between the amounts of happiness in the two cases.
                          ALFRED MARSHALL, 1890

And in a money economy, good management is shown by so adjusting the margins of suspense on each line of expenditure that the marginal utility of a shilling's worth of goods on each line shall be the same. And this result each one will attain by constantly watching to see whether there is anything on which he is spending so much that he would gain by taking a little away

from that line of expenditure and putting it on some other line.   ALFRED MARSHALL, 1890

At every stage the cost incurred in making a thing is the relinquished possibility of making other things, and its extent or amount is determined by the value, or marginal significance on the collective scale, which those other things would have had.   PHILIP H. WICKSTEED, 1894

Man's chief interest in life is after all to find life interesting, which is a very different thing from merely consuming a maximum amount of wealth. Change, novelty, and surprise must be given a large consideration as values per se.
                          FRANK KNIGHT, 1921

It was not until the marginal [utility] theory was thoroughly worked out on its psychological side that progressive taxation obtained a really secure basis in principle.   JOSIAH STAMP, 1929

The law of diminishing returns holds good in almost every part of our human universe.
                          ALDOUS HUXLEY, 1937

This is in fact what utility represents: the common essence of all wants into which all wants can be merged.
          NICHOLAS GEORGESCU-ROEGEN, 1954

Utility is a metaphysical concept of impregnable circularity; utility is the quality in commodities that makes individuals want to buy them, and the fact that individuals want to buy commodities shows that they have utility.
                          JOAN ROBINSON, 1962

Diminishing marginal utility is an expression of the "variety is the spice of life" philosophy of most individuals—that people prefer to have one or a few of a lot of different goods and services rather than a great many of only a few goods and services.   WERNER SICHEL, 1974

Wages

Every man shall receive his own reward according to his own labor.
I CORINTHIANS 3:8, c. A.D. 55

It is not that actual greatness of national wealth, but its continual increase which occasions a rise in the wages. ADAM SMITH, 1776

What are the common wages of labor depends every where upon the contract usually made between those two parties, whose interests are by no means the same. The workmen desire to get as much, the masters to give as little as possible. The former are disposed to combine in order to raise, the latter in order to lower the wages of labor. ADAM SMITH, 1776

To fix the minimum of wages, is to exclude from labor many workmen who would otherwise have been employed; it is to aggravate the distress you wish to relieve.
JEREMY BENTHAM, 1780

Take not from the mouth of labor the bread it has earned. THOMAS JEFFERSON, 1801

The natural price of labor is that price which is necessary to enable the laborers, one with another, to subsist and to perpetuate their race, without either increase or diminution.
DAVID RICARDO, 1817

Like all other contracts, wage should be left to the fair and free competition of the market and should never be controlled by the interference of the legislatures. DAVID RICARDO, 1817

There is no other way of keeping profits up but by keeping wages down.
DAVID RICARDO, 1817

The markets of the world are created solely by the remuneration allowed for the industry of the working classes, and those markets are more or less extended and profitable in proportion as these classes are well or ill remunerated for their labor. But the existing arrangements of society will not permit the laborer to be remunerated for his industry, and in consequence all markets fail. ROBERT OWEN, 1817

Universally, then, we may affirm, other things remaining the same, that if the ratio which capital and population bear to one another remains the same, wages will remain the same; if the ratio which capital bears to population increases, wages will rise; if the ratio which population bears to capital increases, wages will fall.
JAMES MILL, 1821

The limitation of the number of births by raising wages, will accomplish every thing which we desire, without trouble and without interference. JAMES MILL, 1821

When a man says he wants to work, what he means is that he wants wages.

RICHARD WHATELY, 1832

The really exhausting and the really repulsive labors, instead of being better paid than others are almost invariably paid the worst of all.

JOHN STUART MILL, 1848

As a general rule, remuneration by fixed salaries does not in any class of functionaries produce the maximum of zeal.

JOHN STUART MILL, 1848

Wages are determined by the bitter struggle between capitalist and worker.

KARL MARX, 1867

It is but a truism that labor is most productive where its wages are largest. Poorly paid labor is inefficient labor, the world over.

HENRY GEORGE, 1879

A few men without employment, and a few employers without souls, are the conditions of a general reduction of wages below the point to which more legitimate causes would reduce them.   JOHN BATES CLARK, 1887

The law of work does seem utterly unfair, but there it is, and nothing can change it: the higher the pay in enjoyment the worker gets out of it, the higher shall be his pay in cash also.

MARK TWAIN, 1889

Large consumption is at the basis of saving in manufacture, and hence high wages contribute their share to progress.

THOMAS B. REED, 1894

No man can claim to be free unless he has a wage that permits him and his family to live in comfort.   SIDNEY HILLMAN, 1918

No business which depends for existence on paying less than living wages to its workers has any right to continue in this country.

FRANKLIN D. ROOSEVELT, 1932

We're overpaying him but he's worth it.

SAMUEL GOLDWYN, 1939

It is difficult to get a man to understand something when his salary depends upon his not understanding it.   UPTON SINCLAIR, 1940

Each worker receives the value of his marginal product under competition. If a minimum wage is effective, it must therefore have one of two effects: first, workers whose services are worth less than the minimum wage are discharged or, second, the productivity of low-efficiency workers is increased.   G. J. STIGLER, 1946

People who work sitting down get paid more than people who work standing up.

OGDEN NASH, 1962

The minimum wage law is an instrument by which the middle-class worker, precisely at the expense of the poor, effects a redistribution of income to his benefit.

WILLIAM F. BUCKLEY, JR., 1966

One man's wage increase is another man's price increase.   HAROLD WILSON, 1970

Wages are the measure of dignity that society puts on a job.   JOHNNIE TILLMON, 1972

Economy: cutting down other people's wages.

JOHN B. MORTON, 1974

The minimum wage has caused more misery and unemployment than anything since the Great Depression.   RONALD REAGAN, 1980

War

The success of war is not so much dependent on arms, as on the possession of money.

THUCYDIDES, C. 410 B.C.

Money: the sinews of war.

CICERO, C. 65 B.C.

It is not the longest sword but the longest purse that conquers.   DANIEL DEFOE, 1702

The great increase of commerce and manufactures hurts the military spirit of a people; because it produces a competition for something else than martial honors—a competition for riches.   SAMUEL JOHNSON, 1773

In the midst of the most destructive foreign war . . . the greater part of manufacturers may frequently flourish greatly; and, on the contrary, they may decline on the return to peace.

ADAM SMITH, 1776

Among the civilized nations of modern Europe, it is commonly computed, that not more than one hundredth part of the inhabitants of any country can be employed as soldiers, without ruin to the country which pays the expense of their service.   ADAM SMITH, 1776

War involves in its progress such a train of unforeseen and unsupposed circumstances that no human being can calculate the end. It has but one thing certain, and that is to increase taxes.

THOMAS PAINE, 1787

War is the national industry of Prussia.

COMTE DE MIRABEAU, 1789

The war demand for the productions of labor having ceased, markets could no longer be found for them; and the revenues of the world were inadequate to purchase that which a power so enormous in its effects did produce: a diminished demand consequently followed.

ROBERT OWEN, 1817

There cannot be a greater security for the continuance of peace than the imposing on ministers the necessity of applying to the people for taxes to support a war.

DAVID RICARDO, 1820

The employment of the poor in roads and public works, and a tendency among landlords and persons of property to build, to improve and beautify their grounds, and to employ workmen and menial servants, are the means most within our power and most directly calculated to remedy the evils arising from that disturbance in the balance of produce and consumption, which has been occasioned by the sudden conversion of

211

soldiers, sailors and various other classes which the war employed, into productive laborers.

THOMAS MALTHUS, 1821

Wars drive up riches in heaps, as winds drive up snow, making and concealing many abysses.

WALTER SAVAGE LANDOR, 1829

The next war criminals will come from the chemical and electronics industries.

ALFRED KRUPP, 1872

"In war," answered the weaver, "the strong make slaves of the weak, and in peace the rich make slaves of the poor."   OSCAR WILDE, 1888

Militarism . . . is one of the chief bulwarks of capitalism, and the day that militarism is undermined, capitalism will fail.

HELEN KELLER, 1903

It is well known, and also it is right and good by law and custom, that when recourse is had to arms the common man pays the cost. He pays it in lost labor, anxiety, privation, blood and wounds.   THORSTEIN VEBLEN, 1904

An inevitable link in a chain of logical sequences: industry, markets, control, navy bases.

ALFRED T. MAHAN, 1908

No worker has any business to enlist in capitalist class war or fight a capitalist class battle. It is our duty to enlist in our own war and fight our own battle.   EUGENE V. DEBS, 1914

The last £100,000,000 will win.

DAVID LLOYD GEORGE, 1914

When that terrible blood-red fog of war burns away we shall see finance still standing firm. We shall see the spectacle of the businessmen of all nations paying to one another their just debts. We shall see the German merchant keeping his

word sacred to the English; and the French to the Turk.   THOMAS W. LAMONT, 1915

The few who profit by the labor of the masses want to organize the workers into an army which will protect the interests of the capitalists.

HELEN KELLER, 1916

The high stage of world-industrial development in capitalistic production finds expression in the extraordinary technical development and destructiveness of the instruments of war.

ROSA LUXEMBURG, 1919

This war [World War I] was a commercial and industrial war. It was not a political war.

WOODROW WILSON, 1919

The war is over—the part you see in the picture papers. But the tax collector will continue his part with relentless fury. Cavalry charges are not the only ones in a real war.

FINLEY PETER DUNNE, 1919

The prosecution of modern wars rests completely upon the operation of labor in mines, mills and factories, so that labor fights there just as truly as the soldiers do in the trenches.

MARY RITTER BEARD, 1920

You believe you are dying for the fatherland— you die for some industrialists.

ANATOLE FRANCE, 1922

I learned that war was a profit-making business and that there are men in the world who stir up war for profit.   HENRY FORD, 1926

The war [World War I] taught us the new possibilities of molding public opinion, improved the machinery and transformed the old-time press agent into the modern public relations counsel, whose clients are colleges, cathedrals, corporations, societies and even nations.

ERNEST E. CALKINS, 1929

I spent 33 years [in the Marines] . . . most of my time being a high-class muscle man for Big Business, for Wall Street and the bankers. In short, I was a racketeer for capitalism.

SMEDLEY BUTLER, 1931

In arguing that capitalism as such is not the cause of war, I must not be taken as arguing that capitalists do not often believe in war, believe that they and their country benefit from it.

NORMAN ANGELL, 1933

War, which perpetrates itself under the form of preparation for war, has once and for all given the State an important role in production.

SIMONE WEIL, 1933

What most people don't seem to realize is that there is just as much money to be made out of the wreckage of a civilization as from the up-building of one.

MARGARET MITCHELL, 1936

A bayonet is a weapon with a worker at each end.   BRITISH PACIFIST SLOGAN, 1940

Where there is money, there is fighting.

MARIAN ANDERSON, 1941

The object of this war [World War II] is to make sure that everybody in the world has the privilege of drinking a quart of milk a day.

HENRY A. WALLACE, 1942

In the long run war and the preservation of the market economy are incompatible. Capitalism is essentially a scheme for peaceful nations.

LUDWIG VON MISES, 1949

When the rich wage war, it's the poor who die.

JEAN-PAUL SARTRE, 1951

In the large sense, the primary cause of the Great Depression was the war of 1914–1918. With-out the war there would have been no depression of such dimensions.

HERBERT HOOVER, 1952

It should never be forgotten that quantitatively the only really new feature of post-World War II capitalism is the vastly increased size of the arms budget. All other government spending is about the same percentage of the Gross National Product as in 1929.

PAUL SWEEZY, 1959

In the councils of government, we must guard against the acquisition of unwarranted influence, whether sought or unsought by the military-industrial complex. The potential for the disastrous rise of misplaced power exists and will persist.   DWIGHT D. EISENHOWER, 1961

Frankly, I'd like to see the government get out of war altogether and leave the whole field to private enterprise.   JOSEPH HELLER, 1961

For Britain, two world wars have meant the outpouring of her wealth on such a scale that from the leading creditor nation of the capitalist world, she has become, at least in short term, a constant and embarrassed debtor.

HAROLD MACMILLAN, 1966

The butter to be sacrificed because of the war always turns out to be the margarine of the poor.   JAMES TOBIN, 1967

Let those who are actually concerned with peace observe that capitalism gave mankind the longest period of peace in history—a period during which there were no wars involving the entire civilized world—from the end of the Napoleonic wars in 1815 to the outbreak of World War I in 1914.   AYN RAND, 1967

War has been the most convenient pseudo-solution for the problems of twentieth-century capitalism. It provides incentives to modernization and technological revolution which the market and the pursuit of profit do only fitfully and by accident.

ERIC J. E. HOBSBAUM, 1968

In the Department of Defense, the leading defense contractors are regarded as subsidiaries that must be protected for the benefit of the whole system.   RICHARD BARNET, 1970

In the final analysis, the morality of armaments boils down to who makes the sale.

SAMUEL CUMMINGS, 1976

The price of any product produced for a government agency will not be less than the square of the initial Firm Fixed-Price Contract.

RAY CONNOLLY, 1978

If sunbeams were weapons of war, we would have had solar energy centuries ago.

GEORGE PORTER, 1980

Wealth

These riches are possess'd, but not enjoy'd!

HOMER, c. 1000 B.C.

Wealthy men are insolent and arrogant; their possession of wealth affects their understanding; they feel as if they had every good thing that exists; wealth becomes a sort of standard of value for everything else, and therefore they imagine there is nothing it cannot buy.

ARISTOTLE, c. 360 B.C.

The sleep of a laboring man is sweet, whether he eat little or much: but the abundance of the rich will not suffer him to sleep.

ECCLESIASTES 5:12, c. 210 B.C.

Virtue, glory, honor, all things human and divine, are slaves to riches.

HORACE, c. 35 B.C.

He who has made his "pile" will be famous, brave and just.   HORACE, c. 35 B.C.

As riches grow, care follows, and a thirst
For more and more.

HORACE, c. 35 B.C.

The populace may hiss me but when I go home and think of my money I applaud myself.

HORACE, c. 35 B.C.

Many a man has found the acquisition of wealth only a change, not an end of miseries.

SENECA, c. A.D. 30

A great fortune is a great slavery.

SENECA, c. A.D. 30

The lust of lucre has so thoroughly seized upon mankind, that their wealth seems rather to possess them, than they to possess their wealth.

PLINY, A.D. 79

Common sense among men of fortune is rare.

JUVENAL, c. a.d. 120

A son can bear with composure the death of his father, but the loss of his inheritance might drive him to despair.

NICCOLÒ MACHIAVELLI, 1517

We are all of us richer than we think we are.

MICHEL DE MONTAIGNE, 1580

For now a few have all, and all have nought.

EDMUND SPENSER, 1589

Happy always was it for the son
Whose father for his hoarding went to hell.

WILLIAM SHAKESPEARE,
Henry VI, Part III (II, ii), 1594

Great riches have sold more men than they have bought. FRANCIS BACON, 1597

Mother, I have given in to wealth: he is my lover, and I his. Thus from pure affection comes a golden stream!

FRANCISCO DE QUEVEDO, 1613

The rich man's follies pass for wise sayings in this world. MIGUEL DE CERVANTES, 1615

Riches are a good handmaiden but the worst mistress. FRANCIS BACON, 1623

They who know all the wealth they have are poor;
He's only rich that cannot tell his store.

JOHN SUCKLING, 1641

And all to leave what with his toil he won,
To that unfeather'd two-legged thing, a son.

JOHN DRYDEN, 1685

Riches may be instrumental to so many good purposes that it is, I think, vanity rather than religion or philosophy to pretend to condemn them. JOHN LOCKE, 1696

Every man of riches is either a rogue or a rogue's heir. LOUIS BOURDALOUE, 1703

There is a burden of care in getting riches; fear in keeping them; temptation in using them; guilt in abusing them; sorrow in losing them; and a burden of account at last to be given up concerning them. MATTHEW HENRY, c. 1705

Nothing is so hard for those who abound in riches, as to conceive how others can be in want. JONATHAN SWIFT, 1729

The embarrassment of riches.

VOLTAIRE, 1731

Great wealth and content seldom live together.

THOMAS FULLER, 1732

The rich follow Wealth and the Poor the Rich.

THOMAS FULLER, 1732

Oh impudence of wealth! with all thy store,
How darest thou let one worthy man be poor?

ALEXANDER POPE, 1738

No modest man ever did or ever will make a fortune. MARY WORTLEY MONTAGU, 1738

Perhaps you will say a man is not young; I answer, he is rich; he is not gentle, handsome, witty, brave, good humored, but he is rich, rich, rich, rich, rich—that one word contradicts everything you can say against him.

HENRY FIELDING, 1743

One man is born with a silver spoon in his mouth, and another with a wooden ladle.

OLIVER GOLDSMITH, 1762

Naturally speaking, the instant a man ceases to be, he ceases to have any dominion: else if he had a right to dispose of his acquisitions one moment beyond his life, he would also have a right to direct their disposal for a million of ages after him; which would be highly absurd and inconvenient.   WILLIAM BLACKSTONE, 1768

His best riches, ignorance of wealth.
                          OLIVER GOLDSMITH, 1770

It is wonderful to think how men of very large estates not only spend their yearly income, but are often actually in want of money.
                          SAMUEL JOHNSON, 1778

It is better to live rich than to die rich.
                          SAMUEL JOHNSON, 1778

I am indeed rich, since my income is superior to my expense, and my expense equal to my wishes.   EDWARD GIBBON, 1779

For as wealth is power, so all power will infallibly draw wealth to itself by some means or other.   EDMUND BURKE, 1780

It is hard to be poor when there are so many rich fools at whose expense one could live.
                          DENIS DIDEROT, 1784

If we command our wealth, we shall be rich and free: if our wealth commands us, we are poor indeed.   EDMUND BURKE, 1797

There are men who gain from their wealth only the fear of losing it.
                          ANTOINE RIVAROLI, 1808

Birth and wealth together have prevailed over virtue and talent in all ages.
                          JOHN ADAMS, 1813

Every man who is worth thirty millions and is not wedded to them is dangerous to the government.   NAPOLEON BONAPARTE, 1815

Wealth is a power usurped by the few, to compel the many to labor for their benefit.
                          PERCY BYSSHE SHELLEY, 1818

The greatest luxury of riches is, that they enable you to escape so much good advice. The rich are always advising the poor, but the poor seldom venture to return the compliment.
                          JULIUS C. HARE, 1827

It requires a great deal of boldness and a great deal of caution to make a great fortune, and when you have got it, it requires ten times as much wit to keep it.
                          MEYER ROTHSCHILD, c. 1830

Wealth hardens the heart faster than boiling water an egg.   LUDWIG BÖRNE, 1832

Riches are gotten with pain, kept with care and lost with grief.   THOMAS FULLER, 1832

As for money, enough is enough; no man can enjoy more.   ROBERT SOUTHEY, 1832

When, in one of our Atlantic cities, it is once known that a man is rich, that "he is very rich," that he is "amazingly rich," that he is "one of the richest men in the country" . . . the whole vocabulary of praise is exhausted and the individual in question is as effectually canonized as the best Catholic saint.
                          FRANCIS J. GRUND, 1839

To be thought rich is as good as to be rich.
                          WILLIAM M. THACKERAY, 1841

It is far more easy to acquire a fortune like a knave than to expend it like a gentleman.
                          CHARLES C. COLTON, 1845

One does not jump, and spring, and shout hurrah! at hearing one has got a fortune, one begins to consider responsibilities, and to ponder business.   CHARLOTTE BRONTË, 1847

Men do not desire to be rich, but to be richer than other men. JOHN STUART MILL, 1848

The man who has been born into a position of wealth comes to look upon it as something without which he could no more live than he could live without air; he guards it as he does his very life; and so he is generally a lover of order, prudent and economical.
ARTHUR SCHOPENHAUER, 1851

A man is rich in proportion to the number of things which he can afford to let alone.
HENRY DAVID THOREAU, 1854

That man is the richest whose pleasures are the cheapest. HENRY DAVID THOREAU, 1854

Why is one man richer than another? Because he is more industrious, more persevering, and more sagacious. JOHN RUSKIN, 1857

A man's learning dies with him; even his virtues fade out of remembrance; but the dividends on the stocks he bequeaths to his children live on and keep his memory green.
OLIVER WENDELL HOLMES, SR., 1858

The art of getting rich consists not in industry, much less in saving, but in a better order, in timeliness, in being at the right spot.
RALPH WALDO EMERSON, 1860

Work and acquire, and thou hast chained the wheel of Chance.
RALPH WALDO EMERSON, 1860

The best condition in life is not to be so rich as to be envied nor so poor as to be damned.
JOSH BILLINGS, 1865

Very few men acquire wealth in such a manner as to receive pleasure from it.
HENRY WARD BEECHER, 1873

The production of wealth is not the work of any one man, and the acquisition of great fortunes is not possible without cooperation of multitudes of men. PETER COOPER, 1876

The King in a carriage may ride,
And the beggar may crawl at his side;
But in the general race,
They are travelling all the same pace.
EDWARD FITZGERALD, 1876

Superior want of conscience . . . is often the determining quality which makes a millionaire out of one who otherwise might have been a poor man. HENRY GEORGE, 1879

Wealth will not bear much accumulation; except in a few unimportant forms it will not keep. HENRY GEORGE, 1879

I am the richest man in the world.
WILLIAM H. VANDERBILT, 1880

I'm opposed to millionaires, but it would be dangerous to offer me the position.
MARK TWAIN, 1881

It is a great mistake to suppose that the enormous inequalities which we see in wealth imply anything wrong in the system which permits them. SIMON NEWCOMB, 1885

Money is power. Every good man and woman ought to strive for power, to do good with it when obtained. I say, get rich, get rich!
RUSSELL H. CONWELL, 1888

Wealth may be an excellent thing, for it means power, it means leisure, it means liberty.
JAMES RUSSELL LOWELL, 1888

The advantages of wealth are greatly exaggerated. LELAND STANFORD, 1889

It will be a great mistake for the community to shoot the millionaires, for they are the bees that make the most honey, and contribute most to the hive even after they have gorged themselves full. . . . Under our present conditions the millionaire who toils on is the cheapest article which the community secures at the price it pays for him, namely, his shelter, clothing, and food.

ANDREW CARNEGIE, 1889

We Americans worship the almighty dollar! Well, it is a worthier god than Heredity Privilege.

MARK TWAIN, 1894

It is better to have a permanent income than to be fascinating.   OSCAR WILDE, 1895

Money is worth nothing to the man who has more than enough.

GEORGE BERNARD SHAW, 1896

You are affluent when you buy what you want, do what you wish and don't give a thought to what it costs.   J. PIERPONT MORGAN, 1897

No man is rich enough to buy back his past.

OSCAR WILDE, 1897

I am richer than [E. H.] Harriman. I have all the money I want and he hasn't.

JOHN MUIR, 1899

We have too many people who live without working, and we have altogether too many who work without living.

CHARLES R. BROWN, 1899

The office of the leisure class in social evolution is to retard the movement and to conserve what is obsolescent.   THORSTEIN VEBLEN, 1899

The rich get richer and the poor get poorer.

ANDREW CARNEGIE, 1900

He was generally looked upon as an embodiment of all the virtues that make the poor respectable and the rich respected.

SAMUEL BUTLER, 1902

I have to talk to millionaires but I wish I didn't. They bore me. . . . They know their own business but the moment they stop talking shop they haven't an idea. Outside of money-making they're dumb.

THEODORE ROOSEVELT, 1903

Riches, n. The savings of many in the hands of one.   EUGENE V. DEBS, 1904

Inherited wealth is a big handicap to happiness. It is as certain death to ambition as cocaine is to morality.   WILLIAM H. VANDERBILT, 1905

I am a millionaire. That is my religion.

GEORGE BERNARD SHAW, 1905

All the ornaments which decorate the apartments of the rich, that gilt work, those sculptures which art and taste seem to have formed solely to delight the mind, are nothing but a sort of magical characters, presenting everywhere this inscription: Admire the extent of my riches.

JOHN RAE, 1905

Affluence means influence.

JACK LONDON, c. 1905

Malefactors of great wealth.

THEODORE ROOSEVELT, 1907

America contained scores of men worth five million or upwards, whose lives were no more worth living than those of their cooks.

HENRY ADAMS, 1907

Short of genius, a rich man can't imagine poverty.   CHARLES PÉGUY, 1910

The desire of one man to live on the fruits of another's labor is the original sin of the world.
JAMES O'BRIEN, 1910

To be clever enough to get all that money, one must be stupid enough to want it.
GILBERT K. CHESTERTON, 1911

What is the matter with the poor is Poverty: what is the matter with the rich is uselessness.
GEORGE BERNARD SHAW, 1912

Few revolutionists would be such if they were heirs to a baronetcy.
GEORGE SANTAYANA, 1913

If one-half of a man's schemes turned out according to his preliminary figures, he would have nothing to do but spend his money.
BOB EDWARDS, 1915

A titan of finance, said Mr. Dooley, is a man that's got more money than he can carry without being disorderly.
FINLEY PETER DUNNE, 1919

The rich man and his daughter are soon parted.
FRANK MCKINNEY HUBBARD, 1919

The contents of his [Sitting Bull's] pockets were often emptied into the hands of small, ragged little boys, nor could he understand how so much wealth should go brushing by, unmindful of the poor.
ANNIE OAKLEY, 1922

The richer your friends, the more they will cost you.
ELISABETH MARBURY, 1923

You can only drink thirty or forty glasses of beer a day, no matter how rich you are.
ALDOLPHUS A. BUSCH, 1924

If a man dies and leaves his estate in an uncertain condition, the lawyers become his heirs.
E. W. HOWE, 1925

Happiness is the deferred fulfillment of a prehistoric wish. That is why wealth brings so little happiness; money is not an infantile wish.
SIGMUND FREUD, 1930

Man's natural right of possessing and transmitting property by inheritance must remain intact and cannot be taken away by the state.
POPE PIUS XI, 1931

The eminently successful man should beware of the tendency of wealth to chill and isolate.
OTTO H. KAHN, 1931

To suppose, as we all suppose, that we could be rich and not behave as the rich behave, is like supposing that we could drink all day and stay sober.
LOGAN PEARSALL SMITH, 1931

It is the wretchedness of being rich that you have to live with rich people.
LOGAN PEARSALL SMITH, 1931

The man who does not work for the love of work but only for money is not likely to make money nor to find much fun in life.
CHARLES M. SCHWAB, 1932

I love money; just to be in the room with a millionaire makes me less forlorn.
LOGAN PEARSALL SMITH, 1934

It is money that we have not earned, the windfall, the magical bonus, that starts us capering.
J B. PRIESTLEY, 1935

One of the most powerful of all our passions is the desire to be admired and respected. As things stand, admiration and respect are given to the man who seems to be rich. This is the chief reason why people wish to be rich. The actual goods purchased by their money play quite a secondary part.
BERTRAND RUSSELL, 1935

A rich man is nothing but a poor man with money.   W. C. FIELDS, 1937

I do want to get rich but I never want to do what there is to do to get rich.
GERTRUDE STEIN, 1937

Fortunes come. They are not made.
HENRY FORD, 1938

The big house on the hill surrounded by mud huts has lost its awesome charm.
WENDELL WILLKIE, 1940

It is an unfortunate human failing that a full pocket book often groans more loudly than an empty stomach.
FRANKLIN D. ROOSEVELT, 1940

I've been rich and I've been poor. Believe me, honey, rich is better.   SOPHIE TUCKER, 1945

Wealth: Any income that is at least $100 more a year than the income of one's wife's sister's husband.   H. L. MENCKEN, 1949

If we permit extremes of wealth for a few and enduring poverty for many, we shall create a social explosiveness and a demand for revolutionary change.
DWIGHT D. EISENHOWER, 1954

Wealth is not without its advantages and the case to the contrary, although it has often been made, has never proved widely pervasive.
JOHN KENNETH GALBRAITH, 1958

In some ways, a millionaire just can't win. If he spends too freely, he is criticized for being extravagant and ostentatious. If, on the other hand, he lives quietly and thriftily, the same people who have criticized him for being profligate will call him a miser.   J. PAUL GETTY, 1963

There is inherited wealth in this country and also inherited poverty.   JOHN F. KENNEDY, 1963

Wealth does not center in any personality. To be celebrated, to be wealthy, to have power requires access to major institutions.
C. WRIGHT MILLS, 1963

The heartless stupidity of those who have never known a great and terrifying poverty.
EDITH SITWELL, 1965

Wealth is the product of man's capacity to think.   AYN RAND, 1966

It is true that money attracts; but much money repels.   CYNTHIA OZICK, 1966

If you can count your money, you don't have a billion dollars.   J. PAUL GETTY, 1966

No grant of feudal privilege has ever equalled for effortless return, that of the grandparent who bought and endowed his descendents with a thousand shares of General Motors or General Electric.   JOHN KENNETH GALBRAITH, 1967

Most of the rich people I've known have been fairly miserable.   AGATHA CHRISTIE, 1967

Let the moment come when nothing is left but life, and you will find that you do not hesitate over the fate of material possessions.
EDDIE RICKENBACKER, 1967

Keep company with the very rich and you'll end up picking up the check.
STANLEY WALKER, 1968

To die rich is to have lived in vain.
JIDDU KRISHNAMURTI, 1968

Gentility is what is left over from rich ancestors after the money is gone.
JOHN CIARDI, 1972

Man is a luxury-loving animal. Take away play, fancies and luxuries and you will turn a man into a dull, sluggish creature, barely energetic enough to obtain a bare subsistence.
ERIC HOFFER, 1973

Now that he was rich he was not thought ignorant any more, but simply eccentric.
MAVIS GALLANT, 1973

Wealth and power are much more likely to be the result of breeding than they are of reading.
FRAN LEBOWITZ, 1974

Beware of inherited wealth. The job of getting is better than spending.
ROBERT R. YOUNG, 1975

Money is better than poverty, if only for financial reasons.
WOODY ALLEN, 1975

No rich man is ugly.
ZSA ZSA GABOR, 1975

I don't want to be a millionaire, I just want to live like one.
TOOTS SHOR, 1977

I believe in inherited wealth. Society needs to have some people who are above it all.
EDWARD DIGBY BALTZELL, JR., 1978

One can accumulate enough wealth to buy a golden bed, but one cannot buy sound sleep with money.
DANIEL ARAP MOI, 1982

Women

It is worthy of particular remark that in general women and children are rendered more useful, and the latter more easily useful, by manufacturing establishments than they otherwise would be.
ALEXANDER HAMILTON, 1791

Many a woman is tempted by her low wages to marry for a home.
VIRGINIA PENNY, 1869

I have always held, with Florence Nightingale, that the woman who works beside men, must expect no favors on account of her sex, and accept none.
FANNY M. BAGBY, 1884

Unpaid work never commands respect; it is the paid worker who has brought to the public mind conviction of woman's worth.
HARRIOT STANTON BLATCH, 1898

The labor of women in the house, certainly, enables men to produce more wealth than they otherwise could; and in this way women are economic factors in society. But so are horses.
CHARLOTTE PERKINS GILMAN, 1898

The women who do the most work get the least money, and the women who have the most money do the least work.
CHARLOTTE PERKINS GILMAN, 1898

Women's work! Housework's the hardest work in the world. That's why men won't do it.
                                    EDNA FERBER, 1924

Some plants have an established policy whereby a girl automatically writes her own resignation when she marries. Such a policy, if it were more general, would enable industry to pay a better wage to the male wage earner as the head of the family.   FRANK B. KIRBY, 1930

Men lose out when women get low wages, for the reason that low wages for women undercut the standards for men too.
                    MARY AGNES HAMILTON, 1941

The woman who climbs to a high post and then wants everybody to know how important she is is the worst enemy of her own sex.
                    CLAIRE GIANNINI HOFFMAN, 1954

Men get their pictures on money but women get their hands on it.   RUTH SHERRILL, 1955

By and large, mothers and housewives are the only workers who do not have regular time off. They are the great vacationless class.
                    ANNE MORROW LINDBERGH, 1955

If a careful calculation of the GNP were made over the last 10,000 years, it would probably be true in most places and times that women produced more than half of the real Gross National Product.   ALVIN HANSEN, 1960

If women didn't exist, all the money in the world would have no meaning.
                    ARISTOTLE ONASSIS, 1967

The boss' secretary can wield great power, like the king's mistress, without any authority at all.
                    ANTONY JAY, 1968

A good secretary can save her boss more time in a year than a business jet plane can.
                    MALCOLM BALDRIDGE, 1968

Men always try to keep women out of business so they won't find out how much fun it really is.   VIVIEN KELLENS, c. 1969

In sheer quantity, household labor, including child care, constitutes a huge amount of socially necessary production.
                    MARGARET LOWE BENSTON, 1969

At present, the support of a family is a hidden tax on the wage earner—his wage buys the labor power of two people.
                    MARGARET LOWE BENSTON, 1969

Women are the true maintenance class. Society is built upon their acquiescence, and upon their small and necessary labors.
                    SALLY KEMPTON, 1970

Automation and unions have led to a continuously shortened day for men but the work day of housewives with children has remained constant.   BEVERLY JONES, 1970

The single working woman past her early twenties is likely to be portrayed in the popular media as embittered, frustrated, forsaken, displacing her real desires for marriage and children to a career—though she may appear as the home-wrecker who infects the world of the virtuous and happy homemaker and whose only hope is for rehabilitation in her own home with her own children.   CYNTHIA FUCHS EPSTEIN, 1970

No laborer in the world is expected to work for room, board, and love—except the housewife.
                    LETTY COTTIN POGREBIN, 1970

The most wasteful "brain drain" in America today is the drain in the kitchen sink.
                    ELIZABETH GOULD DAVIS, 1971

To be successful, a woman has to be much better at her job than a man.
                    GOLDA MEIR, 1971

As economic affluence increased with the growth of the new industrialism and expansion of trade, women's worth declined as producers and increased as consumers. ALICE ROSSI, 1973

Men are never so tired and harassed as when they have to deal with a woman who wants a raise. MICHAEL KORDA, 1973

Many of the bold buccaneers of trade become timid as mice in the presence of any female who is not working for them.
ALEXANDER KING, 1974

If one is rich and one's a woman, one can be quite misunderstood.
KATHARINE GRAHAM, 1974

As soon as a woman crosses the border into male territory, the nature of professional combat changes. FRANÇOIS GIROUD, 1974

If I had to give a definition of capitalism I would say: the process whereby American girls turn into American women.
CHRISTOPHER HAMPTON, 1974

If a man mulls over a decision, they say, "He's weighing the options." If a woman does it, they say, "She can't make up her mind."
BARBARA PROCTOR, 1975

For any woman to succeed in American life she must first do two things: Prepare herself for a profession, and marry a man who wants her to succeed as much as she does.
CATHLEEN DOUGLAS, 1976

You cannot decree women to be sexually free when they are not economically free.
SHERE HITE, 1976

The average secretary in the U.S. is better educated than the average boss.
GLORIA STEINEM, 1978

Work

Toil is sweeter than idleness when men gain what they toil for or know that they will use it.
DEMOCRITUS, c. 400 B.C.

Business or toil is merely utilitarian. It is necessary, but does not enrich or ennoble a human life. ARISTOTLE, c. 360 B.C.

A nation rushing hastily to and fro, busily employed in idleness. PHAEDRUS, c. A.D. 20

If any would not work, neither should he eat.
II THESSALONIANS 3:10, c. A.D. 55

I never tie myself to hours, for the hours are made for man, and not man for the hours.
FRANÇOIS RABELAIS, 1532

To business that we love we rise betime,
And go to't with delight.
WILLIAM SHAKESPEARE,
Antony and Cleopatra (IV, iv), 1616

Where there is no desire, there will be no industry. JOHN LOCKE, 1693

Make all you can, save all you can, give all you can. JOHN WESLEY, 1738

There is no craving or demand of the human mind more constant and insatiable than that for exercise and employment; and this desire seems the foundation of most of our passions and pursuits. DAVID HUME, 1739

Work banishes those three great evils, boredom, vice and poverty. VOLTAIRE, 1759

No man loves labor for itself. SAMUEL JOHNSON, 1769

Few people do business well who do nothing else. LORD CHESTERFIELD, 1774

Most people work the greater part of their time for a mere living; and the little freedom which remains to them so troubles them that they use every means of getting rid of it. JOHANN WOLFGANG GOETHE, 1774

Every country workman who is obliged to change his work and tools every half hour is almost always slothful and lazy. ADAM SMITH, 1776

When death comes for me, he will find me busy. STEPHEN GIRARD, C. 1815

All work, even cotton-spinning, is noble; work is alone noble. THOMAS CARLYLE, 1839

Human labor is not an end but a means. FRÉDÉRIC BASTIAT, 1841

Those who work much do not work hard. HENRY DAVID THOREAU, 1841

Industry is the soul of business and the keystone of prosperity. CHARLES DICKENS, 1841

Men for the sake of getting a living forget to live. MARGARET FULLER, 1844

Go listen to the slavish bell.
That turns an Eden into hell.
ANDREW MCDONALD, 1845

To work is not necessarily to produce anything. PIERRE-JOSEPH PROUDHON, 1846

In order that people may be happy in their work, these three things are needed: They must be fit for it: They must not do too much of it: And they must have a sense of success in it. JOHN RUSKIN, 1851

I cannot afford to waste my time making money. LOUIS AGASSIZ, 1852

Most men would feel insulted if it were proposed to employ them in throwing stones over a wall, and then in throwing them back, merely that they might earn wages. But many are no more worthily employed now. HENRY DAVID THOREAU, 1854

Work and days were offered us, and we chose work. RALPH WALDO EMERSON, 1857

My father taught me to work; he did not teach me to love it. ABRAHAM LINCOLN, 1858

Work and acquire, and thou hast chained the wheel of chance. RALPH WALDO EMERSON, 1862

In the ordinary business of life, industry can do anything which genius can do, and very many things which it cannot. HENRY WARD BEECHER, 1873

Work consists of whatever a body is obliged to do, and Play consists of whatever a body is not obliged to do. MARK TWAIN, 1876

Perpetual devotion to what a man calls his business, is only to be sustained by perpetual neglect of many other things.
ROBERT LOUIS STEVENSON, 1881

I do not like work even when someone else does it. MARK TWAIN, 1883

I like work; it fascinates me. I can sit and look at it for hours. JEROME K. JEROME, 1889

The pride which every honest man takes in acquitting himself well is an important factor of economic efficiency and an important item in every careful estimate of work and wages.
ALFRED MARSHALL, 1890

A day of worry is more exhausting than a day of work. JOHN LUBBOCK, 1894

By native, man is lazy, working only under compulsion; and when he is strong he will always live, as far as he can, upon the labor or the property of the weak.
BROOKS ADAMS, 1895

Work is the refuge of people who have nothing better to do. OSCAR WILDE, 1897

We work to become, not to acquire.
ELBERT HUBBARD, 1899

Do your work with your whole heart and you will succeed—there is so little competition!
ELBERT HUBBARD, 1899

In life, as in a football game, the principle to follow is: Hit the line hard.
THEODORE ROOSEVELT, 1900

Far and away the best prize that life offers is the chance to work hard at work worth doing.
THEODORE ROOSEVELT, 1903

Folks who never do any more than they get paid for, never get paid for any more than they do.
ELBERT HUBBARD, 1907

Let us be grateful to Adam our benefactor. He cut us out of the "blessing" of idleness and won for us the "curse" of labor.
MARK TWAIN, 1910

No man does as much today as he is going to do tomorrow. BOB EDWARDS, 1912

A man who is not interested in his work and does not recognize in it either beauty or utility, is degraded by that work, whether he knows it or not. JOHN A. HOBSON, 1914

The suburbs are merely vast dormitories where a man may sleep in comparatively pure air while his office is being washed.
WILLIAM MCFEE, 1916

The purpose of industry is to provide the material foundation of a good social life.
RICHARD H. TAWNEY, 1920

The average worker, I am sorry to say, wants a job in which he does not have to put forth much physical exertion—above all, he wants a job in which he does not have to think.
HENRY FORD, 1922

In my business hours I avoid fatigue. I do this by not doing too much work—the only trustworthy recipe. EDMUND VALPY KNOX, 1922

Nobody works as hard for his money as the man who marries it.
FRANK MCKINNEY HUBBARD, 1923

Work is a great blessing; after evil came into the world, it was given as an antidote, not as a punishment. ARTHUR S. HARDY, 1923

Work is the only occupation yet invented which mankind has been able to endure in any but the smallest possible doses.

C. E. M. JOAD, 1928

There has never been any 30-hour week for men who had anything to do.

CHARLES F. KETTERING, 1934

The first duty of a human is to assume the right functional relationship to society—more briefly, to find your real job, and do it.

CHARLOTTE PERKINS GILMAN, 1935

Anyone can do any amount of work, provided it isn't the work he is supposed to be doing at the moment.   ROBERT BENCHLEY, 1936

Like every man of sense and good feeling, I abominate work.   ALDOUS HUXLEY, 1936

A great many people have come up to me and asked how I manage to get so much work done and still keep looking so dissipated.

ROBERT BENCHLEY, 1938

The drive for relentless work was one of the fundamental productive forces, no less important for the development of our industrial system than steam and electricity.

ERICH FROMM, 1941

The world is full of willing people, some willing to work, the rest willing to let them.

ROBERT FROST, 1949

There is dignity in work only when it is work freely accepted.   ALBERT CAMUS, 1953

The brain is a wonderful organ; it starts working the moment you get up in the morning and does not stop until you get into the office.

ROBERT FROST, 1954

This new attitude towards effort and work as an aim in itself may be assumed to be the most important psychological change which has happened to man since the end of the Middle Ages.

ERICH FROMM, 1955

Work expands so as to fill the time available for its completion.

C. NORTHCOTE PARKINSON, 1958

Work provides an artificial world of things. Within its borders each individual life is housed while this world itself is meant to outlast and transcend them all.   HANNAH ARENDT, 1959

Most people spend most of their days doing what they do not want to do in order to earn the right, at times, to do what they may desire.

JOHN MASON BROWN, 1960

Seldom, except in time of emergency or peril, do any job holders, managers, clerks and coil winders, exert themselves fully. If an employer who measures with slide rule and stop watch what workers *can* do and then asserts that these instruments determine what workers *should* do, he confounds descriptive measurement with a prescriptive imperative of personal judgement.

IVAR BERG AND JAMES KUHN, 1962

Work is a necessity for man. Man invented the alarm clock.   PABLO PICASSO, 1964

I have never liked working. To me a job is an invasion of privacy.

DANNY MCGOORTY, 1966

There's only one way to work—like hell.

BETTE DAVIS, 1965

I didn't want to work. It was as simple as that. I distrusted work, disliked it. I thought it was a very bad thing that the human race had unfortunately invented for itself.

AGATHA CHRISTIE, 1967

"Jobs" represent a relatively recent pattern of work. From the fifteenth century to the twentieth century, there is a steady progress of fragmentation of the stages of work that constitute "mechanization" and "specialism." These procedures cannot serve for survival or sanity in this new time.   MARSHALL MCLUHAN, 1967

All we can say in general is that the idea of work as a source of legitimate pride, as a source of gratification, forms no part of the ethos of an industrial civilization.   E. J. MISHAN, 1967

I never forget that work is a curse—which is why I've never made it a habit.
BLAISE CENDRARS, 1968

Work is accomplished by those employees who have not yet reached their level of incompetence.   LAURENCE J. PETER, 1969

Work is the only dirty four-letter work in the language.   ABBIE HOFFMAN, 1970

Nobody should work all the time. Everyone should have some leisure, but I believe the early morning hours are best for this—the five or six hours when you're asleep.
GEORGE ALLEN, 1971

Times have changed. Forty years ago people worked 12 hours a day and it was called economic security. Now they work 14 hours a day, and it's called moonlighting.
ROBERT ORBEN, 1972

In a society which prides itself on its democratic system of freedom for the individual and rejection of dictatorial rule, the workplace stands as an island of authoritarianism.
IRVING BLUESTONE, 1973

Work is the greatest thing in the world, so we should always save some of it for tomorrow.
DON HEROLD, 1974

Work is a form of nervousness.
DON HEROLD, 1974

Work is the only kind of property many people have in America.
EUGENE J. MCCARTHY, 1975

A business civilization regards work as a means to an end, not as an end to itself. The end is profit, income, consumption, economic growth, or whatever; but the act of labor itself is regarded as nothing more than an unfortunate necessity to which we must submit to obtain this end.   ROBERT HEILBRONER, 1976

If not controlled, work will flow to the competent man until he submerges.
CHARLES BOYLE, 1979

No ethic is as ethical as the work ethic.
JOHN KENNETH GALBRAITH, 1980

Hard work without talent is a shame, but talent without hard work is a tragedy.
ROBERT HALF, 1980

Source Index

In the case of some names for which no complete biographical information has been found, I have indicated the century in which the person flourished, and in some cases, his or her nationality and occupation. In these instances, n.d. means no date, and contemp. means contemporary.

MICHAEL JACKMAN

Abbott, Douglas C. (1899–   ), Can. lawyer, 80

Acheson, Dean (1893–1971), Am. cab. off., 68

Adams, Brooks (1848–1927), Am. hist., 225

Adams, Charles Francis (1807–1886), Am. lawyer, dipl., 164

Adams, Franklin P. (1881–1960), Am. journ., 107

Adams, Henry (1838–1918), Am. hist., 218

Adams, Henry Carter (1851–1921), Am. pol. econ., 46

Adams, James Randolph (1898–1956), Am. adv. exec., 4, 17

Adams, John (1735–1826), 2nd Am. pres., 11, 216

Adams, John Quincy (1767–1848), 6th Am. pres., 53, 78

Addison, Joseph (1672–1719), Eng. poet, 11, 59, 142, 146

Ade, George (1866–1944), Am. humorist, 162

Adelman, M. A. (1917–   ), Am. econ., 89

Adler, Mortimer (1902–   ), Am. philos., 43

Aftalion, Albert (1874–1956), Fr. econ., 21

Agassiz, Louis (1807–1873), Sw. naturalist, 224

Agnew, Spiro T. (1918–   ), Am. polit., vice-pres., 158

Aldrich, Thomas Bailey (1836–1907), Am. writer, 93

Aliber, Robert (1930–   ), Am. econ., 57

Alinsky, Saul (1909–1972), Am. polit. activist, 29

Allen, Fred (1894–1956), Am. comed., 4, 18, 127, 195

Allen, George (1922–   ), Am. football coach, 227

Allen, Woody (1935–   ), Am. comed., film prod., 65, 77, 221

Allport, Gordon (1897–1967), Am. psychol., 162

Ambrose, Saint (340?–397), bish. of Milan, 39

Anacharsis (6th c. B.C.), Scyth. philos., 129

Anderson, Marian (1902–   ), Am. singer, 213

Anderson, Martin (1936–   ), Am. econ., 149

Anderson, Sherwood (1876–1941), Am. writer, 9

Angas, L. L. B. (1893–1973), Am.,186

Angell, Norman (1872–1967), Eng. writer, 213

Anselmi, Tina (1924–   ), Ital. polit., 121

Antisthenes (444?–370 B.C.), Gr. philos., 74

Aquinas, Saint Thomas (1225–1274), Ital. theol., 150

Arden, Elizabeth (1878–1966), Am. cosmetics exec., 89

Arendt, Hannah (1906–1975), Am. (Ger.-born) pol. sci., 68, 103, 226

Aristotle (384–322 B.C.), Gr. philos., 34, 58, 62, 84, 95, 100, 121, 145, 163, 173, 214, 223

Armstrong, Hamilton Fish (1893–1973), Am. ed., 155

Arnold, Thurman Wesley (1891–1969), Am. lawyer, 89, 194

Arthur, Chester A. (1829–1886), 21st Am. pres., 78

Ash, Roy L. (1918–   ), Am. bus. exec., 47

Atkinson, Brooks (1894–   ), Am. dram. crit., 28, 119

Atkinson, Edward (1827–1905), Am. cotton magnate, 54, 167

Attiga, Ali Ahmed (1931–   ), S. Arab. bus., 139

Attlee, Clement R. (1883–1967), Eng. polit., 181

Aubrey, Henry G. (1906–1970), Am. econ., 57

Auden, Wystan Hugh (1907–1973), Am. poet, 9, 200

Auerbach, Berthold (1812–1882), Ger. nov., 31

Augustine, Saint (354–430), bish. of Hippo, 14, 59, 159

Austen, Jane (1775–1817), Eng. nov., 15

Aylesbury, Richard (13th c.), Eng. treas., 202

Ayres, Leonard P. (1879–1946), Am. bus. exec., 185

Babbage, Charles (1792–1871), Eng. econ., 198

Key Word Index

ability:
  a. to deal with people, 125
accident:
  a. the greatest of inventors, 198
  banking system grew by a., 13
accomplished:
  more is a. if man does what best fitted for, 114
accountant:
  ever hear of a kid playing a., 32
accounting:
  success in manufacturing a perfect system of a., 17
  success knowing what not to believe in a., 12
accumulation:
  a. of land and a. of stock, 115
  a. of public monies . . . is active capital rendered un-
    productive, 92
acquire:
  work to become, not to a., 225
acquisition:
  a. of knowledge as tedious as a. of wealth, 199
  every a. attended with its risks, 112
acquisitions:
  no man divulges his revenue, everyone publishes his a.,
    39
  right to dispose of a., 216
acquisitiveness:
  instinct of a. has more perverts than sex, 43
action:
  cost of a. is value of opportunity sacrificed, 153
activity:
  our innate urge to a. makes the wheels go round, 64
ad:
  one a. more than forty Editorials, 3
adman:
  few people of 19th century needed a., 5

administrator:
  to estimate . . . , employ . . . , buy . . . in short, the
    ability of the a., 26
advancement:
  delusion that a. accomplished by crushing others, 84
advantage:
  them as take a. get a., 86
advantages:
  a. of wealth greatly exaggerated, 217
  wealth is not without its a., 220
adventure:
  if spirit of business a. dulled, country will cease to hold
    foremost position, 88
adversity:
  a.—people able to stand it, 164
advertise:
  good times people want to a., bad times they have
    to, 4
  man who on trade relies must a., 3
advertisement:
  promise the soul of a., 3
advertisements:
  . . . a. covertly pornographic, 5
  a. gain attention by promises and eloquences, 3
  a. only truths in a newspaper, 3
  tell ideals of nation by its a., 4
advertisin':
  braggin' saves a., 3
affluence:
  a. means influence, 218
  a. of few the indigence of many, 159
  a. . . . permit[s] people to express dissatisfaction, 166
  farmer . . . rising from a. to poverty, 7
affluent:
  price of a. society, 165

251

no worker any business to enlist in c. class war, 212

now the boss works for c., 178

production of surplus the aim of c., 154

show me a c., I'll show you a bloodsucker, 29

wages determined by struggle between c. and worker, 210

worker a c. without money, 119

capitalistic:

c. production finds expression in war, 212

capitalists:

as c. increase, profits by employing them diminish, 23

association of laborers with c., 116

c. believe that they benefit from [war], 213

Communists are frustrated C., 179

increase of social wealth accompanied by increasing number of c., 102

masters of the government of the U.S. the combined c. and manufacturers, 96

organize workers into army [to] protect c., 212

capitalist society:

c. left unchecked make rich richer and poor poorer, 27

capitalist system:

c. saved by transferring credit from bankers to government, 81

defects of c. are threatening its existence, 27

I advise you as long as the c. lasts, to vote for gold, 93

capitalization:

discrepancy between nominal c. and actual capitalizable value of property, 112

if managers succeed, success evokes law of c., 112

capitals:

c. increased by parsimony, 174

capital stock:

number of laborers in proportion to quantity of c. employed in setting them to work, 71

captain of industry:

c. doesn't do anything out of business, 122

c. playing great game, 126

c. unable to understand, 125

one c. worth many rank and file, 125

car:

c. a secular sanctuary for individual, 200

career:

banking a c. no man recovers from, 13

student trained to worship acquisitive success as preparation for c., 70

cash:

amount of c. small compared with credit which rests upon it, 49

c. is virtue, 49

c. Payment the only nexus between man and man, 49

too great a quantity of c. in circulation is a greater evil than too small, 52

caution:

c. is life of banking, 12

celebrity:

people sacrifice peace of mind for c., 75

Central Bank:

C. conductor of orchestra and sets tempo, 79

central bankers:

inflations marked by subjection of c. to political pressures, 56

central banking:

great inventions: fire, the wheel, c., 12

certified public accountant:

is c. upper lower or lower upper middle class?

character:

I'm called away but leave my c. behind me, 75

sign of improved c. if you like paying debts, 59

charities:

c. have air of quackery, 140

charity:

c. deals with symptoms, 141

c. ends where it begins, 140

c. injurious unless helps independence, 141

c. separates rich from poor, 72

if thief helps poor, not c., 140

in c., no excess, 140

pauperism exists because of c., 141

poverty pleading not for c., 147

shortage of Christian c., 142

when fired by impulse to c., wait, 175

Chase National Bank:

Republican candidate for President nominated by C., 13

cheap:

c. ain't always best, 151

cheapest:

advertising c. way of selling goods, 4

cheapness:

no such thing as c., 151

cheat:

don't steal; . . . . C., 75

cheated:

people do not think they had a bargain unless they c. a merchant, 75

cheating:

c. if successful met with praise, 76

commerce school of c., 14

check:

every one . . . pays much by c. more lightheartedly than he pays little in specie, 50

I care who picks up c., 18

cheque:

don't let your mouth write no c. your tail can't cash, 61

children:

c. rarely in position to lend interesting sum of money, 51

circulates:

money which c. compared to highway, 92

competitors:
  c. are free, 138
  man measures greatness by regrets, envies, hatreds of c.,
    70
complementary:
  material welfare and "higher" humanism c., not com-
    peting things, 89
computer:
  impact of c. the provision of jobs for clerks, 201
computerized:
  c. industry requires men [with] white-collar skills, 201
conclusion:
  if all economists were laid end to end, they would not
    reach a c., 67
conference:
  c. gathering of important people who singly can do
    nothing, 18
  no grand idea born in c., 17
confidence:
  cause of [depressions] is a want of c., 20
  credit enduring testimonial to man's c. in man, 50
confusion:
  advertising 85% c., 4
Congress:
  C. shall have power to lay taxes, 193
  might be able to get along without C., 184
  right and duty of C. to create money, 56
conqueror:
  labor the grand c., 116
conscience:
  a corporation has no c., 45
  selling must be governed by law and c., 74
conservatism:
  property . . . a bastion of c., 162
conservatizing:
  inflation a c. issue, 108
conspicuous consumption:
  c. a means of reputability to gentleman of leisure, 42
conspiracy:
  people of same trade meet in c. against public, 74
consultant:
  c.: ordinary guy more than fifty miles from home, 32
consultants:
  c. borrow your watch and tell you what time it is, 32
consume:
  honest man one who knows he can't c. more than he has
    produced, 44
  if men ceased to c., they would cease to produce, 40
  man produces to c., 154
  marginal propensity to c. weaker in a wealthy commu-
    nity, 43
  when people come into contact with superior goods, the
    propensity to c. is shifted upward, 43
consumer:

a c. is born every ten seconds, 44
advertising exhorting c. to buy now, 6
c. interest no match, 131
c. is king, 89
c. is the victim of the manufacturer, 43
c. not a moron, 5
each successive addition to the population brings a c. and
  a producer, 41
if government was as afraid of disturbing c. as it is of
  disturbing business, this would be democracy, 97
in c. society, best product must be replaced immediately,
  201
the American c. is not notable for his imagination, 44
the dynamic c. purchases goods that will serve him in
  the future, 44
consumer cooperatives:
  development of c. follows the straight line of numerical
    progression, 43
consumer's:
  divorce between production and consumption almost
    destroyed c. capacity for measuring quality, 42-43
consumers:
  c. have different preferences, 171
  c. want variety of product, 138
  corporate tax borne by c., 195
  future occupation of moppets is to be skilled c., 43
  laws which regulate demand of c., 189
  payrolls make c., 155
  women's worth declined as producers and increased as
    c., 223
consumer society:
  in a c. there are two kinds of slaves: prisoners of addic-
    tion and of envy, 44
consumes:
  for every man who c. more than he creates, another man
    has to consume less than he creates, 41
consuming:
  the act of buying and c. has become a compulsive irra-
    tional aim, 44
consuming power:
  lifetime c. anticipations are best expressed in terms of
    wealth and the wage rate, 43
consumption:
  c. adds to our enjoyments, 189
  large c. the basis of saving in manufacture, 210
  sufficient unemployment to keep us so poor that c. falls
    short of income, 72
contract:
  c. between master and workman, 115
  wages of labor depends on c., 209
control:
  for employees freedom and security . . . is to have ef-
    fective c. over the job, 46
controls:

credit unions:
   c. do good for people, 13
creeping socialism:
   fearful of stumbling capitalism as of c., 28
crime:
   debt mother of c., 59
criminals:
   next war c. from industries, 212
crises:
   business c. wrecked industries of the nation, 20
   c. promote inequalities in distribution of wealth, 20
   commercial c. a matter of the mind, 20
   commercial countries subject to commercial c., 19
   major c. caused by previous inflation, 108
   reason for c. poverty and restricted consumption of the
      masses, 20
crisis:
   c. disturbance of equilibrium between demand and sup-
      ply, 20
   capitalism is itself a c., 26
   the more promptly c. can be seen, the less community
      will suffer, 19
culture:
   NY business center of American c., 10
   poverty a c., 149
   what use c. to laborer, 118
currency:
   finance art of passing c. until it disappears, 18
curse:
   work a c.—why never made a habit, 227
curves:
   to know public wants, graph it as c., 4
customer:
   c. an object to be manipulated, 130
customers:
   competition obliges bankers be liberal with c., 11
cycle:
   "state of trade" revolves in an established c., 19
cycles:
   agriculture c. no clear relation to c. of business, 7
   c. essence of organism that displays them, 22
   people in politics think in c., 144
   there is a law of c., 19

data:
   incompatible d. are useless d., 84
   mistake to theorize before one has d., 83
day:
   short d. better than short dollar, 117
death:
   when d. comes, he will find me busy, 224
debt:
   few instances when government paid off d., 82
   like players married and in d., 128

more long-term d. in recessions, more short-term d. in
   booms, 80
national d. is national blessing, 78
prodigal quits life in d. to others, 175
some give Men no Rest till they are in their D., 48
debtor:
   d. class not dishonest because in debt, 60
   small debt makes a man your d., 58
debtors:
   forgive us our debts as we forgive our d., 59
debts:
   every generation to pay its own d., 78
   excessive d. precipitate excessive liquidation, 22
   he that dies, pays all d., 59
   people in automobiles driving about with d., 201
   public credit means d. nation never can pay, 78
decisions:
   economics how people make d. Sociology why they don't
      have d. to make, 66
defense:
   d. contractors must be protected, 214
deficits:
   d. allow vote for spending without taxes to pay for it,
      82
   old cliché that d. automatically bring inflation, 81
   stop borrowing to meet continuing d., 79
deficit spending:
   inflation results from d., 109
deflation:
   d. means elimination of the party in power, 94
   rise of prices under 10 percent is d., 108
deliberate:
   take time to d., 142
demand:
   crisis disturbance of equilibrium between d. and supply,
      20
   d. for goods fluctuates more than d. for services, 190
   d. for loans varies more than supply, 19
   d. only limited by production, 153
   d. will be liable to fluctuation, 19
   influence of d. on value, 152
   one person's contribution to total d. for goods equal to
      his income, 105
   quantity never should fall short of d., 188
democracy:
   d. government in hands of men of low birth, 95
   d. the greatest system of reinsurance, 190
   property [an obstacle] to d., 161
   property the art of d., 162
   we've never been in a d.; we've been in a pallocracy,
      33
democratic:
   economic side of d. ideal is socialism, 177
deposits:

dividends *(continued)*

> if ignorance paid d. most Americans could make a fortune, 65
>
> the only pleasure . . . to see d. coming in, 184

division:

> all trades gained by d. of labor, 153

dollar:

> d. became international currency because it met needs more effectively, 57
>
> d. like a hydrant at international convention of dogs, 58
>
> farmer . . . knows strokes of labor d. represents, 7
>
> short day better than short d., 117
>
> size of a d. depends upon how many more you have, 55
>
> to restore the d. will be a painful process, 56
>
> two halves to ivry d. . . . knowing how to make it an' not knowin' how to spend it comfortably, 42

dollars:

> d. do better if accompanied by sense, 114
>
> d. not only count but they rule, 54
>
> I am for gold d. as against baloney d., 93
>
> investment d. are high-powered d., 43
>
> labor demanding not d. but voice, 118
>
> people swim through shit if d. in it, 77
>
> poor in land of d. the bottom of hardships, 148
>
> if we increase the number of dollars . . . prices will be increased, 54-55

door:

> d. will not open to words, only a well-filled palm, 74

dreams:

> founding d. on advertising, 4

dropouts:

> d. anticipating future economic trends, 84

Dunlop, John:

> despite the fact that D. is an economist, I have confidence in him, 69

DuPont:

> General Motors could buy Delaware if D. were willing to sell it, 47

duties:

> d. defensible when imposed temporarily, 167

duty:

> person who sells should pay d., 150

earning:

> the darkest hour . . . to get money without e. it, 75

earnings:

> average e. of English worker half an ounce of gold a week, in 1900 and in 1979, 94

econometrics:

> unification [of statistics, economic theory, and mathematics] constitutes e., 64

economic:

> advertising valuable e. factor, 4
>
> discontent makes people improve their e. status, 4
>
> e. activity guided by quest of profits, 157
>
> e. facts decisive forces in history, 63
>
> e. game rules subject to revisions, 65
>
> e. life inspired by principles, 172
>
> e. movements motivated by crowd psychology, 4
>
> e. perfection lies in independence, 116
>
> e. vice is avarice, waste, 9
>
> no practical questions . . . admit being decided on e. premises alone, 62
>
> our aim to describe man's e. nature and e. wants, 62
>
> profit the ignition system of e. engine, 157
>
> there are no e. ends, 64

economic activities:

> conflict between well-established e. and emergence of new e., 103

economic aid:

> foreign e. . . . likely to . . . undermine democracy and freedom, 102

economical:

> e. laws of human nature, 172

economic analysis:

> the higher study of consumption must come after, and not before, the main body of e., 41

economic development:

> depressing to go back to Adam Smith, especially on e., 68

economic doctrine:

> pessimism of e. of nineteenth century the legacy of Malthus, 67

economic health:

> U.S. should assist return of e. in the world, 97

economic ills:

> erudite men analyze e. of the world and derive a totally different conclusion, 65

economic independence:

> evolutionary thinking leads to conclusion e. foundation of well-being, 88

economic laws:

> e. are schemes of rational action, 64

"economic man":

> e. useless for purposes of modern industry, 87

economic policy:

> problems arise when economics leaves pure science and enters e., 65

economic problem:

> economics only partly an e., 66
>
> ultimate answer to every e. lies in some other field, 65

economics:

> e. a study of adjustments, 189
>
> e. of size necessitate monopoly, 138
>
> e. the mechanics of utility, 207
>
> e. the science of greed, 101
>
> economists own values undoubtedly affect their e., 68
>
> ethics not a branch of e., 77

exchange rates:
  a system of floating e. eliminates the balance of payment problem, 57
exchange value:
  a substance whose public evaluation exempted it from fluctuations of other commodities . . . its e. is based upon its nominal value, 51
excise:
  e. a hateful tax upon commodities, 191
executive:
  best e. is one who has sense, 125
  business e. a decision maker, 127
  chief e. gets more blame, 126
  corporate e. not capitalists, 127
  decision an action e. must take, 127
  e. fungus attaches to desk, 127
  e. least-leisured man in world, 13
  mark of true e. illegible, 127
  most valuable e. is training somebody, 125
  nobody should be chief e., 127
  vice-president a form of e. fungus, 127
executives:
  robot e. stifling careers, 128
executive's:
  company [moves] toward e. home, 128
expansion:
  e. of cycles longer, contractions shorter when trend of prices upward, 22
expenditure:
  e. rises to meet income, 61
  other people's patterns of e. and consumption are highly irrational and slightly immoral, 44
expenditures:
  desire to get superior goods . . . provides a drive to higher e., 43
  maxim of political economy keeping e. within limits of receipts, 78
expense:
  capital should weigh cost of mob and tramp against e. of education, 70
  e. an essential part of true economy, 179
expense account:
  profit on e. dishonest . . . who loses on one is damned fool, 76
expenses:
  beware of little expenses, 40
expensive:
  e. to be poor, 149
expert:
  always believe the e., 30
  e. has made mistakes in very narrow field, 31
explanations:
  we are living in an age of e., 107
exploitation:

society of money and e. never charged . . . with assuring triumph of freedom and justice, 65
exportation:
  usual to prohibit e. of commodities, 166
extravagance:
  the best form of charity is e., 41
  we owe something to e.; thrift and adventure seldom go hand in hand, 42
extravagant:
  e. habits frequent cause of scarcity of capital and high profits, 40

factory:
  whole society will become single f., 178
factories:
  f. making more than people can use, 205
facts:
  economics has two sides: theories and f., 66
  economist can give us the f., 67
  p.r. specialists make flower arrangements of facts, 5
failure:
  f. and panic breed panic and f., 20
  f. from want of energy, 24
  f. the one unpardonable crime, 164
  high f. overleaps bounds of low success, 60
  key to f. is trying to please everybody, 165
  one f. makes many, 20
fairly:
  how many f. earn a million dollars? 75
family:
  support of f. a hidden tax on wage earner, 222
family income:
  ways to apportion f. all unsatisfactory, 105
farm:
  life on f. during Great Depression resembled f. life 2,000 years ago, 8
  state pays owners of f. property not to produce, nothing to f. workers, 8
  to f. well be rich, 7
farmed:
  there ain't no Hell[?] . . . they never f., 7
farmer:
  f. benefited by depreciation of money, 7
  f. buys retail, sells wholesale, pays both ways, 8
  f. handyman with sense of humor, 7
  f. . . . knows strokes of labor [dollar] represents, 7
  f. rich next year, 6
  f. . . . rising from affluence to poverty, 7
  price f. received for commodities sold seemed fixed, 7
farmers:
  American f. welfare addicts, 8
farming:
  country town of f. region flower of self-help and cupidity, 7

generous:
  g. are rarely ill, 141
gifts:
  poverty taught true value of g., 148
Gini coefficients:
  economists work out G., measure income trends, 69
giver:
  no anonymous g., 142
  not forgive a g., 140
giving:
  g. the business of the rich, 140
  money g. criterion of health, 141
  must be poor to know luxury of g., 141
glut:
  g. . . . implies production without profit, 188
GNP:
  economists forgot increased G. a means, 103
  man does not live by G. alone, 81
  when people move, G. goes up, 120
god:
  make money your g., 133
  man stamps image of G. on [his money], 171
gold:
  accursed greed for g., 100
  building life on g., 133
  for which virtue sold, almighty g., 74
  g. that buys health, 121
  g. to keep fools in play, 133
  g. you have hidden belongs to poor, 145
  if a man needs g. he goes to a banker, 12
  only instrument of international payment which has the
    confidence of the public is g., 56
  trade fetches g. from lazy people, 203
Golden Rule:
  G. principles necessary for operating business, 75
gold standard:
  international g. provided most efficient system of adjust-
    ment for balance of payments, 94
  people fight the g. because they want to substitute au-
    tarchy for free trade, 94
  there were unemployment and inflations when classic g.
    prevailed, 94
goodness:
  g. only investment that never fails, 75
goods:
  advertising cheapest way of selling g., if g. are worthless.
    4
  easier to get g. than money, 133
  g. and services paid for only with g. and services, 107
  he who bestows g. upon poor, 140
  things become g., 129
good times:
  g., bad times, always be advertising, 4
good will:

g. asset competition cannot destroy, 75
governed:
  husbandry g. by uncertain winds and tempests, 6
government:
  aim of good g. to stimulate production, 189
  business must accept g. role, 144
  businessman ran to g. for protection, 170
  commerce gives rise to class attached to g., 15
  duty of g. to give protection to bank, 11
  each emergency expands activity of g., 81
  enlargement of functions of g. . . . means of avoiding
    destruction of existing economic forces, 79
  g. fighting inflation like Mafia fighting crime, 109
  g., like family, can spend a little more than it earns, 79
  g. meddling with business, 169
  g. [cannot] run business, 143
  g. draining money from people, 192
  g. in better position to predict future needs, 144
  g. shall protect rich, 189
  if country gets g. regulation, labor will suffer, 168
  income tax the price g. charges for having taxable in-
    come, 194
  inevitable for g., to get in economic planning, 144
  inflation like sin; g. denounces it and g. practices it, 107
  man worth thirty millions dangerous to g., 216
  no g. can afford to be a clipper of coin, 54
  people shackled with g. monopolies, 178
  power has risen in g. greater than the people, 11
  reproach to g. to suffer poverty, 146
  taxpayer works for federal g., 197
governmental:
  beyond g. power to tax one to help another, 193
governments:
  g. last as long as undertaxed can defend themselves, 195
  g. cannot be supported without great charge, 191
  g. care for security of property, 162
graft:
  tendrils of g. and corruption become interlacing roots,
    76
graph:
  to know public wants, g. it as curves, 4
Great Depression:
  G. in the U.S. testament to harm done by mistakes of a
    few men, 56
  life on farm during G. resembled farm life 2,000 years
    ago, 8
greatest:
  g. nations, like g. individuals, often poorest, 75
greatness:
  man measures g. by regrets, envies, hatreds of competi-
    tors, 70
greed:
  stock market reflects g., 186
greenback:

I have lived to see the day when the g. can declare, "I know that my Redeemer liveth," 54

Gross National Product:
   basic concept is G., 144
   G. our Holy Grail, 81
   women produced more than half of G., 222

gross produce:
   improvements in production and emigration of capital . . . do not diminish g., 71

happiness:
   employment essential to human h., 71
   h. requires modicum of prosperity, 163
   inherited wealth a handicap to h., 218
   money brings some h., 136
   money is human h., 133
   money measures of h., 208
   money one half of h., 134
   money won't buy h., 136
   only in imperfect state can one serve h. of others by sacrifice of his own, 86
   poverty a great enemy to h., 146
   wealth brings so little h., 219

happy:
   money doesn't make you h., 135
   money never made man h., 133
   [to] be h. in work, three things needed, 224

Harlem:
   Madison Avenue advertising never done well in H., 5

Harvard Business School:
   villain of oil crisis is H., 70

harvest:
   live within your h., 58

hate:
   business neither love nor h., 16

have-nots:
   rich and poor, h. and haves, 105

haves:
   people divided into H., Have-nots, and Have-Not-Paid-for-What-They-H., 38

Hayek, Friedrich A.:
   the new theories of H. were principal rival of new theories of Keynes, 68

health:
   h. the blessing of the rich, 180

health care:
   h. Americans get should depend on need, 182

hierarchies:
   most h. established by men who now monopolize the upper levels, 33

hirelings:
   the herd of h., 114

history:

h. of all hitherto existing society the h. of class struggles, 35
h. of economics has its heroic ages, 64
money determining course of h., 133
greatest man in h. the poorest, 147

hoarding:
   gold h. goes against the American grain, 94
   [his] father for his h. went to hell, 215

holding company:
   h. where you hand accomplice the goods while policeman searches you, 45

holidays:
   if all the year were h., 121

home:
   h. only good to borrow on, 162

home life:
   h. ceases to be free and beautiful founded on borrowing and debt, 50

homes:
   poverty keeps together more h., 148

honest:
   credit depends on belief most people are h., 50
   difficult, not impossible, to conduct h. business, 76
   rich men of America h., 75

honesty:
   for merchant, even h. a financial speculation, 75

honor:
   h. sinks where commerce prevails, 74
   h. without money, 132
   money without h. a disease, 133

honors:
   gold will buy the highest h., 91

hours:
   h. made for man, not man for h., 223

household management:
   business of h. concerned more with human beings than with property, 62

household:
   h. labor a huge amount of necessary production, 222

house-rent:
   liberality or narrowness of a man's whole expense can be judged by his h., 40

housewife:
   no laborer expected to work for room except h., 222

housewives:
   h. the only workers who don't have time off, 222
   work day of h. has remained constant, 222

housework:
   h. the hardest work in the world, 222

humanity:
   advertising . . . contribution to h. zero, 4

human rights:
   no reason to deprive the child of basic h., 34

price of i. in youth poverty and dependence in old age, 42

industrial:

    i. field littered with corpses, 117

    i. relations like sexual, 128

industrial arts:

    the state of the i. has at no time continued unchanged during the modern era, 64

industrial economy:

    i. prone to cycles of bust and boom, 43

industrial leader:

    i. worthy of historical notice, 18

industrial policy:

    market-oriented i. . . . something preferred prevails, old fades out, 90

industrial régime:

    little in i. . . . The work is another man's work, 35

Industrial Revolution:

    [would] I. have been permitted if franchise had been universal, 25

industrialization:

    i. only hope of the poor, 102

industrialized:

    i. economies never relied on physical effort, 102

industries:

    business crises wrecked the i. of the nation, 20

industry:

    a social class gets what it contributes to the output of i., 36

    captains of i., 124

    every i. is wrought by a hand, 199

    government harms i. when it mixes in its affairs, 95

    hope of advancement spur to i., 164

    i. can do anything genius can, 224

    i. must keep wages high, 118

    i. of discovery one of most rapidly expanding, 200

    i. provide[s] foundation of social life, 225

    i. reduced jobs to routine, 123

    i. the soul of business, 224

    judicious operations of banking can increase i., 11

    labor demanding voice in conduct of i., 118

    poverty cows i., 146

    profit made because i. fails to give workman, 157

    progress in i. the enterprise of men ahead of times, 163

    war the national i. of Prussia, 211

    where there is no desire, no i., 224

industrialists:

    you die for some i., 212

industrialize:

    i. by building markets, 131

industrious:

    let every man be i., 147

inequalities:

still imagined that i. of income coincide with i. of merit, 105

inequality:

    i. of property will exist as long as liberty, 85

    those at short end of i. gain more from faster growth, 102

    to reduce i., give poor money, 202

inflation:

    artificial i. of stocks a crime, 185

    excessive labor costs add to i., 158

    i. rate should have no effect on stock prices, 187

    old cliché that deficits automatically bring i., 81

inflations:

    American law accepted that prolonged depressions and i. threaten fabric of society, 80

    i. marked by subjection of central bankers to political pressures, 56

    reckless i. of credit chief cause of economic malaise, 72

influence:

    America's i. on Europe more food than politics, 8

    mistake to use advertising dollar to i. news, 6

    no detail too trivial to i. public, 4

    [no one] has less i. in country than business, 18

ingenuity:

    people use i. to get into debt and to avoid paying it, 60

inherited:

    i. wealth in this country and i. poverty, 220

initiative:

    ever told a miner what he needs is i. to get a job when there isn't any? 73

injustice:

    i. make[s] philanthropy necessary, 142

    no property, no i., 159

injustices:

    i. from those who pursue excess, not those driven by necessity, 84

inheritance:

    loss of i. might drive him to despair, 215

    natural right of transmitting property by i., 219

inherited:

    I believe in i. wealth, 221

insecurity:

    economic i. can turn freedom into barren and vapid right, 22

instability:

    apart from i. due to speculation is i. due to . . . spontaneous optimism, 22

    i. of economy equaled by i. of economists, 68

    unemployment . . . from i. of standard of value, 72

intellectual:

    man at top of i. pyramid contributes most to those below, . . . but gets no i. bonus from others, 38

intelligence:

    advertising science of arresting i. to get money, 3

no one cleverer than K. nor made less attempt to conceal it, 67

possible to admire K. . . . consider his social vision wrong, his propositions misleading, 67

the new theories of Hayek were principal rival of the new theories of K., 68

Keynesian:

from K. standpoint, 1930's proved timid fiscal policies . . . will not restore prosperity, 81

structuralist a K. who believes changes in structure of economy can have effect on employment and unemployment, 73

Keynesian economics:

K. . . . left unexplained business cycle itself, 22

Keynesians:

K. tear economic system out of social context, 80

we are all K. now, 68

Keynesian theory:

notions of K. are simple, 144

Keynes's:

K. disciples went farther than the master. Widespread view "money does not matter," 68

kindness:

k. valuable part of business, 14

Kissinger, Henry:

reason for high rate of unemployment is K., 73

knowledge:

k. the only instrument of production, 155

run to and fro, k. increased, 14

labor:

abstention from l., evidence of wealth, 122

by improvement of land . . . l. of half the society sufficient, 6

capital still pats l. on th' back, but on'y with an axe, 26

capitalists interested . . . that those who l. for them feel same interest as those who l. on own account, 25

common interest of [capital and l.] is cutting each other's throat, 28

cause of profit is l. produces more than required, 157

commodities are masses of l. time, 151

commodities derive value from l., 151

condescend to unskilled l., 119

desire to live on fruits of another's l., 219

divorce capital from l., capital hoarded, l. starves, 24

effects of division of l., 153

excessive l. costs add to inflation, 158

farmer . . . knows strokes of l. dollar represents, 7

five days shalt thou l., 123

foundation of division of l. separation between town and country, 7

futile l. spend on mining gold to bury it once more in Fort Knox, 93-94

gold and silver valuable in proportion to quantity of l. necessary to produce them, 92

human l. not an end but a means, 224

husbandry not governed by judgement and l., 6

in agriculture, doubling l. does not double produce, 7

l. and capital are antagonistic, 26

l. fights as truly as soldiers in trenches, 212

l. followed by relaxation, 122

l. most productive where wages largest, 210

l. not creative of objects but utilities, 207

l. of man upon the land, 122

l. of women in house enables men to produce, 221

l. the father of wealth, 115

l. the group selling its products, 24

man when strong will live upon l. of the weak, 225

many must l. for the one, 115

men cannot l. always, 122

most l. not always most life, 118

most place limits to conveniences and luxuries they will l. for, 40

most royal thing to l., 115

$^9/_{10}$ the effects of l., 115

no man loves l. for itself, 224

one portion of the community live on the l. of the other, 35

political economy confuses kinds of l., 161

property a patent entitling man to dispose of l., 160

receive own reward according to own l., 209

should life all l. be, 122

there should be no stifling of L. by Capital, or Capital by L., 27

unwed mothers capable of other form of l., 182

you shall not press down upon the brow of l. this crown of thorns, 93

laborer:

he that defraudeth l., 124

l. at disadvantage to bargain, 116

pick-and-shovel l. can [not] compete with steam shovel, 200

produce not always to the l., 115

produce of labor belongs to l., 115

laborers:

conversion of soldiers into productive l., 212

numbers of l. in proportion to quantity of capital stock employed in setting them to work, 71

to enable l. to subsist and perpetuate, 209

laborer's:

Malthus finds no cover laid at Nature's table for the l. son, 66

laboring:

rights of l. man protected, 172

sleep of l. man is sweet, 214

N. shows . . . only drastic measures suffice when country has fallen low, 97

news:

advertising should be news, 3

mistake to use advertising dollar to influence n., 6

newspaper:

advertisements only truths in n., 3

New York:

N.Y. business center of American culture, 10

nickel:

country needs good five-cent n., 107

19th century:

few people of n. needed an adman, 5

growth of n. capitalism depended on justification on moral as well as on political and economic grounds, 28

pessimism of economic doctrine of n. the legacy of Malthus, 67

n. peculiarly the property of economists, 68

1930's:

n. proved timid fiscal policies . . . will not restore prosperity, 81

normality:

n. is a fiction, 23

North America:

N. will continue to be agricultural country. . . . for long time to come, 9

note:

shopkeeper's virtue sacrifices everything to meet n. due, 59

nothing:

n. to be had for n., 111

numbers:

n. guessed are magnified, 82

occupation:

a human being must have o., 31

business person forever apologizing for o., 17

farming not a business; an o., 7

first step in any o., become interested, 31

o. source of happiness and foundation of national greatness, 8

o. that has no basis in sex-determined gifts can now recruit its ranks from twice as many potential artists, 33

serious o. has reference to some want, 30

work the only o. yet invented, 226

occupations:

farming one of finest o. taken in moderation, 7

office:

o. a social center, no place to get work done, 46

man who has no o. to go to is a trial, 72

oil:

o. a wasting asset, 114

fair price for o., 139

oligopoly:

o. barrier to economic performance, 139

o. ticket to institutional economics, 138

open market:

If it wasn't for Abe, I'd still be on the o., 33

opinions:

raising yes Ma'ams in big corporations, no minds of their own, no o., 46

opportunities:

small o., great enterprises, 129

opportunity:

American system gives every one o., 9

opulence:

causal connection between o. and poverty, 147

organization:

capital in great part knowledge and o., 24

disorder, friction, malperformance, evolve by themselves in an o., 46

in life cycle of every o. ability to succeed in spite of itself runs out, 47

large o. is loose organization, 45

large o. is lord, 128

rational o. of capital and labor, 172

what is the use of thinking if after all there is to be o.?, 46

organization man:

emergence of new kind of o.—uncommitted to any organization, 32

organizations:

all o. at least 50 percent waste, 46

organize:

liberty impossible [without] right to o., 118

organized:

o. labor in conflict with economics, 117

o. labor the advance guard, 118

organized crime:

o. in America . . . profitable, spends little for office supplies, 77

owe:

if I o. Smith, and God forgives me, that doesn't pay Smith, 60

I o. you one, 49

to keep friends never o. them anything, 49

to o. is a heroic virtue, 48

owed:

never in the history of human credit has so much been o., 61

owes:

if a man pays what he o. you, you're beholden to him, 48

who o. a little can clear it in a little time, 59

owing:

o. money has never concerned me so long as I know where it could be repaid, 61

ownership:
  get rid of idea of absolute o., 160
  instinct of o. is fundamental, 161
  issue is between o. of different kinds, 162
  private o. determines ends, 179

paid:
  never do more than p. for, 225
panic:
  failure and p. breed p. and failure, 20
  p. denotes fear, 20
  p. species of neuralgia, 20
panics:
  p. have their uses, 19
  with Federal Reserve System, freedom from financial p.,
    21
paper:
  one Ad more to p. than forty Editorials, 3
paper-credit:
  blest p.! last and best supply, 49
  the imaginary riches of p., 49
paper money:
  I am not a believer in any artificial method of making p.
    equal to coin, 54
  if this Colony be flourishing, it is p. . . . that hath ren-
    dered us so, 52
  not necessary that p. be payable in specie to secure its
    value, 53
  p. more like paper, less like money, 58
  public's distrust of p. is too strong, 56
Parkinson's Law:
  rise in total employed governed by P., 73
parsimony:
  more p. is not economy, 174
partner:
  we must find a way of making government a p. with
    business, 99
partners:
  Mr. Morgan buys his p., 137
partnership:
  we must have p. of labor, business, government, 98
partnerships:
  relations of masters superseded by p., 116
patent medicine:
  ønomists' advice] something like p., 68
paternal:
  p. government galling to a people, 95
patriotism:
  p. is no substitute for a sound currency, 54
patronage:
  labor has not to ask p. of capital, 116
pauper:
  p. serving term in hell, 149
pauperism:

p. at root of economic distress, 189
p. the hospital of labor army, 147
pay:
  always p.; you must p. entire debt, 60
  easier not to p. one's mother than not to p. a creditor,
    51
  p. every debt as if God wrote the bill, 60
  p. peanuts, get monkeys, 153
  p. through the nose, 150
  we p. for mistakes of ancestors, fair they leave us money
    to p. with, 60
"pay as you go":
  philosopher's stone that turns everything into gold is p.,
    59
payeth:
  he that p. beforehand shall have his work ill done, 40
paying:
  by not p. bills we can live in the memory of the com-
    mercial classes, 50
payment:
  p. of debts necessary for social order, non-p. equally
    necessary, 61
payment:
  unpardonable sin disposition to evade p. of bills, 60
payments:
  at whatever place people have to make p., at that place
    people must keep money, 54
pays:
  he who p. the piper can call the tune, 40
peace:
  capitalism gave longest p. in history, 213
  manufacturers may decline on return to p., 211
  p. connected with freedom in trade, 205
  p. the natural effect of trade, 203
penny:
  not a p. off pay, 118
  p. wise and pound foolish, 179
pensioner:
  p. a kept patriot, 122
perfection:
  political p. consists in independence, 116
personnel:
  few could pass p., 127
  p. selection decisive, 126
philanthropist:
  suspicion of motives necessary for p., 141
philanthropists:
  p. who vote for toothpicks, 140
philanthropy:
  p. a fumigation of sewer, 141
philosophers:
  less inconvenience from banishment of p. than extinc-
    tion of any common trade, 70
philosophy:

business men in p. are like children, 14

challenge to sell Americans the p. that has kept us free, 89

physical sciences:

economists imitate procedures of p., which may lead to outright error, 68

pirate:

merchant and p. were same person, 16

planets:

p. may prove to be causes of commercial disasters, 20

planned economy:

organized society requires p., 143

p. ensures no bacon delivered, 143

planning:

no reason to fear p., 142

play:

p. whatever a body not obliged to do, 224

plumber:

resourcefulness of p., 119

playthings:

p. of elders called business, 14

pocket book:

full p. often groans more loudly than empty stomach, 220

poetry:

p. of life turned to advertising copy, 4

policy:

failure of economists to guide p. successfully connected with propensity to imitate procedures of physical sciences, 68

political:

p. problem to combine economic efficiency, social justice, individual liberty, 97

political economists:

of all the quacks that ever quacked, p. are the loudest, 67

p. must have seen that increase of wealth not boundless, 101

political economy:

cotton is king; or slavery in the Light of P., 33

decrees in name of P. ratification of existing form of society, 63

difficult issues of p. where goals conflict, 99

fundamentals of p. will be known to . . . society in England, 62

maxim of p. keeping expenditures within limits of receipts, 78

not hopeless to expect results from p., 82-83

p. never pretended to give advice with no lights but its own, 63

p. only one of many subservient Sciences, 66

take as much as I can get, pay no more than I can help . . . p. in a nutshell, 62

while condition of countries is bad, men care for p., 63

competitive capitalism promotes p. because it separates economic power from political power, 28-29

history suggests capitalism a necessary condition for p., 28

political institutions:

modern corporation is a p., 46

democratic form of government cannot be confined to p., 96

p. a superstructure on an economic foundation, 96

politician:

distinguish between p. using economics and using economists, 99

if you forgive a p. why not a business man? 17

politicians:

to buy up p. anti-monopolists most purchaseable, 75

politician's:

economist's "lag" p. catastrophe, 23

politics:

all p. are economic p., 96

America's influence more food than p., 8

p. is economics in action, 96

people in p. think in cycles, 144

pollytician:

p. contaminated by contact with business man, 96

poor:

being p. is a frame of mind, 61

best way to help p. is not become one, 149

care of the p. incumbent on society, 180

despise anyone who elects to be p., 148

God always hard on the p., 171

hard to be p. when there are so many rich fools, 216

he who desires more is p., 100

ice: rich get it in Summer and p. in Winter, 33

if p. are well off they will be disorderly, 146

if p. today, you will always be p., 34

income of the p. must be increased, 40-41

nobody has occasion for pride but the p., 146

p. do everything with their own hands, rich hire hands to do things, 38

p. don't have unity of their own, 149

p. don't know how rich live, and rich don't know how p. live, 38

p. injuriously affected by tax on rich, 193

p. man commands respect; beggar, anger, 146

remember the p., 141

rich will care for laboring p., 189

take rubles from the p., 141

the p. dear to God, 173

the p. indispensable to the rich, 147

the p. man is never free, 146

the p. more liberal than the rich, 147

to be p. and independent an impossibility, 147

to be p. man is hard, 148

virtue the compensation to the p., 146

poor *(continued)*

  wonder is that p. man ever consents to live out of America, 9

  worst country to be p. in is America, 9

poorhouse:

  only nation that ever went to the p. in an automobile, 43

population:

  a prudential restraint on p. is indispensable, 24

  p. increases in geometrical ratio, 6

  ratio which capital and p. bear to one another, 209

pornographic:

  advertisements covertly p., 5

position:

  call that man happy who, however lowly his p. . . . can always hope for more than he has, 41

possesses:

  he who p. gold does all he wishes to in this world, 91

possession:

  preoccupation with p. prevents men from living freely and nobly, 42

possessions:

  call that man happy who, however . . . limited his p., can always hope for more than he has, 41

potentate:

  wisheth he had lived a beggar when he comes to die, 34

poverty:

  America has best-dressed p., 10

  evils of monopoly and p., 137

  farmer . . . rising from affluence to p., 7

  first step in attack on p., 149

  impassable gulf between riches and p., 105

  Marx interpreted needs of mass p. in political terms as uprising . . . for sake of freedom, 68

  modern p. not blest, 148

  p. is uncomfortable, 87

  no better weapon against p. . . . than capitalism, 29

  no man suffers from p. unless his sin, 147

  not p. [but] pretense harasses ruined man, 147

  people cause of their own p., 146

  p. an awful, degrading thing, 148

  p. and wealth failed [to bring happiness], 164

  p. destroys pride, 147

  p. is expensive, 149

  p. never prevented wars, 176

  p. no disgrace, but damned annoying, 146

  p. programs put little into hands of poor, 182

  p. something to be ashamed of, 145

  p. the strenuous life, 148

  reason for crises p. and restricted consumption of the masses, 20

  rich man can't imagine p., 218

  schools were a path out of p., 70

  what is the matter with the poor is p., 219

poverty-stricken:

  wealthy and p. both too preoccupied with finance, 37

power:

  boss' secretary can wield great p., 222

  defense of corporation that its p. does not exist, all p. is surrendered to the market, 47

  money is economical p., 134

  money is p. every man ought to strive for p., 217

  p. goes . . . to those who've got money and those who've got people, 29

  p. will draw wealth to itself, 216

  potential for rise of misplaced p., 213

  socialism creates concentration of p., 179

  the dismal science is the study of p., 66

  those who have economic p. have civil p., 96

  to be wealthy, have power, requires access to institutions, 220

  wealth a p. to compel many to labor, 216

  wealth and p. the result of breeding, 221

PR:

  given right PR, armpit hair could become fetish, 5

practical men:

  p. usually slaves of some defunct economist, 67

prediction:

  if successful p. were criterion, economics should have ceased as serious pursuit, 83

  impossibility of p. in economics . . . future knowledge cannot be gained before its time, 83

predictions:

  dreams and p. fireside talk, 82

  economists right in p., out in dates, 83

  numerical p. from political economy results not hopeless, 82-83

preferred:

  what woman wants common if she can buy p.?, 5

President:

  as long as I am P., Wall Street not to control Bank, 186

price:

  economics the study of the p. and value aspects of human activities and institutions, 65

  every man has his p., 150

  luxuries and necessities selling at same p., 108

  natural p. has tendency to fall, 151

  one man's wage increase another's p. increase, 210

  p. for commodities sold, also supplies bought, fixed, 7

  p. of article is what it will fetch, 152

  p. of labor [not] fixed and constant, 115

  p. of necessaries of life, 115

  remember p. of yesterday's roast beef, 150

  unemployment proof that p. for labor as wages too high, 72

prices:

  anyone can cut p., 154

direct relation between volume of currency and level of p., 55

easy to fix p. that are fixed, 139

expansion longer, contractions shorter, when "trend" of p. upward, 22

inequality of foresight produces overinvestment during rising p., 112

many expected p. to rise and therefore helped bring this result, 107

p. going up by elevator, wages by stairs, 107

regulating p. an endless task, 167

specifying conditions for p. to move only useful to estimate probability of event, 83

stock p. reached high plateau, 185

under steady p. still be booms and depressions, 21

who travels over Europe may see by the p. of commodities, that money has brought itself nearly to a level, 52

price system:

p. . . . determined by pushing additional money into the market, 58

pride:

p. which honest men takes in acquitting himself, 225

priests:

economists the failed p. of our generation, 69

principles:

in U.S. less inclination for p. which threaten laws of property, 8

my p. are to take as much as I can get, pay no more than I can help, 62

private citizen:

corporation, like p., must be held to strict compliance with the will of the people, 45

private enterprise:

cannot live in p. system without profits, 158

industries left to hazards of p., 143

leave whole field [war] to p., 213

madness to let p. set habits of age of atomic energy, 89

no such thing as purely p. or public enterprise, 87

p. ceasing to be free enterprise, 89

run business as efficiently as p., 143

private initiative:

p. would give neither education nor employment to the poor, 86

private interests:

corporation . . . a body created for attaining public ends through appeal to p., 46

private property:

capitalism p. economy in which innovations are carried out by borrowed money, 27

God planted deep respect for p., 173

pure economics gives no criterion to choose between p. and socialist organization, 63

private sector:

anything p. can do, government can do it worse, 99

privilege:

people of p. risk destruction rather than surrender advantage, 106

privileged:

the P. and the People formed two nations, 35

privileged class:

no prettier sight than the p. enjoying their privileges, 37

prize:

best p. life offers is chance to work, 225

probabilities:

business proceeds on p. not certainties, 83

probability:

laws of p., true in general, fallacious in particular, 82

specifying conditions for prices to move only useful to estimate p. of event, 83

produce:

annual p. of land and labor divides itself . . . into three parts, 25

if men ceased to consume, they would cease to p., 40

in agriculture, doubling labor does not double p., 7

one must p. to have, 154

p. of labor not always to laborer, 115

riches of a community consume p. of my industry, afford me p. of theirs, 104

to work is not necessarily to p., 224

whole p. of labor to laborer, 115

production:

glut . . . implies p. without profit, 188

producer:

each successive addition to the population brings a consumer and a p., 41

producers:

p. to know public wants graph it as curves, 4

product:

p. will not sell without, will not sell with advertising, 4

production:

a country with great powers of p. should possess unproductive consumers, 40

household labor a necessary p., 222

improvements in p. and emigration of capital . . . do not diminish gross produce, 71

influence of cost of p. on value, 152

mass p. focusing principles of power, 155

method of p. determines social currents, 154

only p. in which no appropriated natural agent has concurred made under equal competition, 86

p. produces subject for object, 154

profit the proof that p. was for use, 157

saving to excess would destroy p., 175

taxes on p. fall on consumer, 192

war has given state important role in p., 213

whether state owns means of p., 178

inflation is r., 106

resources:
global corporation . . . diverts r. from where most needed . . . to where least needed, 47

respect:
unless prepared to accept "might makes right" philosophy, r. another's right, 33

respectability:
income the measure of r., 105

respectable:
business big enough, it's r., 17
virtues that make poor r., 218

responsibility:
corporation, . . . device for obtaining individual profit without individual r., 45
r. for lowliest assistant, 127

rest:
r. not quitting busy sphere, 122

restraint:
protective tariff a conspiracy in r. of trade, 205

retire:
to r. is death, 123

retirement:
good r. is two weeks, 123
looking at tax returns from first job to r., 196
r. ugliest word, 123

revenue:
devising schemes of r. should be left with representatives of the people, 95
government expands to absorb r., 98
no man divulges his r., 39
object of taxation to secure r., 194
three sources of all r., 151
workman's real r. not money but money's worth, 106

revolution:
inflation worst kind of r., 107
Marx's contribution to cause of r., 68
poverty the parent of r., 145
r. is transfer of property, 162

revolutionary:
a refrigerator can be a r. symbol, 5
I do not make the mistake of thinking every worker is a r., 38

revolutionists:
few r. if heirs to baronetcy, 219

revolutions:
commerce preserves men from r., 15

rewards:
business activity r. . . . . disciplined efficiency, 18
to escape from business despise the r., 14

Ricardo, David:
Marx . . . as a theorist was a pupil of R., 67

rich:

America . . . not a land of r. people, but successful workers, 9

barring luck few men get r. rapidly, 75

being r. is being able to give, 142

be neither r. nor a beggar, 36

eliminate advantages of being born r., 170

farmer r. next year, 6

for one r. man, five hundred poor, 159

honest r. can never forget [poverty], 148

ice: r. get it in Summer and poor in Winter, 33

if you aren't r., look useful, 148

in interest of r., get rid of [property], 161

in peace, r. make slaves of poor, 212

madness to live like wretch, die r., 174

man who dies r. dies disgraced, 141

most work night and day to become r., 85

nation wherein eight millions twice as r., 153

no longer a distinction to be r., 37

no sin but to be rich, 145

only the r. preach content to poor, 148

pleasures of r. bought with tears of poor, 146

poor do everything with their own hands, r. hire hands to do things, 38

poor don't know how r. live, and r. don't know how poor live, 38

poor have more fun than r., 149

potentiality of growing r., 129

r. before night, hanged before noon, 74

r. die but banks immortal, 11

r. different because they have more credit, 51

r. man is canonized as saint, 216

r. no right to property of p., 161

r. pay less taxes, 197

respectable means r., decent poor, 147

r. man may never get into heaven, 149

that some should be r., shows others may become r., 86

[the r.] advance the interest of the society, 85

what we give up makes us r., 141

when r. wage war, the poor die, 213

without frugality none can be r., 174

without the r. the poor would starve, 188

wonder is that poor consent to live out of America, or r. in it, 9

wretchedness of being r., 219

riches:
all r. have limits, 174
as r. increase so will pride, 171
be not penny-wise; r. have wings, 111
best r., ignorance of wealth, 216
chief employment of r. consists in the parade of r., 40
only the rich now have r., 34
r., a gift from Heaven, 172

small:
s. made large by advertising, 3
Smith, Adam:
always depressing to go back to S., 68
man who accepts S.'s statement that workman is kept honest by fear of losing employment is in damned state of soul, 71
smuggler:
s. a check on taxation, 167
smuggling:
high taxes encouraging s., 192
social contract:
foundation of s. is property, 159
social imbalance:
no scientific way of proving (or of disproving) that s. exists, 28
social reform:
taxation a dangerous instrument of s., 195
social relevance:
economics has ensured its technical virtuosity and internal consistency at the cost of its s., 66
social responsibility:
corporate officials s. to make as much money for their stockholders as possible, 29
social services:
unreasonable to expect business . . . have s. for principle, 16
values come with massive bills for s., 182
social system:
no s. will bring prosperity unless inspired, 181
social unrest:
advertising cause[d] s. of 20th century, 5
social values:
s. distributed equally unless unequal distribution is advantage, 106
Socialism:
capitalism hell compared to S., heaven compared to Feudalism, 26
confuse s. with unionism, 119
without socialization of agriculture, no complete s., 8
socialist:
s. a man with white-collar job, 179
economy one of basic principles of s., 176
s. idea that making profits is vice, 158
socialistic:
s. countries have lost technological leadership, 201
socialists:
s. today, directors tomorrow, 124
socialization:
without s. of agriculture, no complete socialism, 8
social work:
s. a band-aid on wounds, 142
societies:
advertising is in s. which have passed basic needs, 5

society:
American s. interlocking system, 10
as s. more complicated, functions of government increase, 97
composition of s. is arithmetical, 35
gold is the spirit of s., 93
history of all hitherto existing s. the history of class struggles, 35
if we seized property, s. would crumble, 159
in great s. men of business think greatly, 17
no s. can be happy of which greater part poor, 146
no s. operates entirely through cooperation, 170
no s. where wealth will not create an aristocracy, 35
not just here to manage capitalism but to change s., 99
nothing so cements all parts of s. as faith or credit, 48
ours a s., formally classless, nevertheless of differentiated social status, 37
poverty the hell beneath s., 147
profits mechanism by which s. decides, 158
s. divided into idlers and producers, 35
s. produces causes of unemployment, 181
s. rich when goods are cheap, 164
s. [that] cannot help poor cannot save rich, 149
thus does s. divide itself into four classes, 36
what s. isn't structured on greed?, 101
when labor of half the s. sufficient to provide food for the whole, 6
soldiers:
not hundredth part can be employed as s., 211
solution:
if economist certain of s. of problem, can be certain s. is wrong, 67
solvency:
s. a matter of temperament not income, 60
sophisters:
age . . . of s., economists and calculators has succeeded, 66
soul:
consider the s. reflected on advertising page, 3
gain the whole world, and lose his own s., 74
gold is the s. of all civil life, 91
promise the s. of advertisement, 3
s. abhors a vacuum, 15
sound money:
one of the uses of s. is to produce pain in the economic body, 55
sovereignty:
s. lost in various spheres, 56
unthinkable that countries would surrender s. . . . . to vagaries of gold production, 94
specialist:
mediocre man eager to cry wolf to the s., 32
specialists:
s. tend to think in grooves, 32

Swiss:
    S. a quite solvent business, 17

Taft-Hartley:
    nauseous effluvia of [T.], 119
    T. the first thrust of fascism, 119
take-home pay:
    they call it t., no other place you can go with it, 105
talent:
    t. without hard work a tragedy, 227
tariff:
    adoption of t. [led to] act for regulating labor, 167
    t. the mother of trusts, 168
    t. to protect producer against greed of consumer, 205
tariffs:
    government that raises t. kept in check, 167
    t. act similarly to cheap money, 168
    t. raise prices of things, 204
taught:
    my father t. me to work, 224
tax:
    support of family a hidden t. on wage earner, 222
    t. collector will continue with fury, 212
taxation:
    appropriation without t. as bad as t. without represen-
        tation, 79
    government cannot devise an efficient benefit scheme of
        t., 34
    inflation form of t. without legislation, 108
    monopoly the t. of industrious, 137
    power of t. by currency depreciation inherent in the State,
        55
    progressive t. obtained secure basis, 208
    purpose of t. to leave less in hands of taxpayer, 80
    t. must not lead men into temptation, 193
    [no] system of t. would operate with equality, 193
    owner of land has right of t., 162
    t. without representation is tyranny, 192
taxes:
    applying to people for t. to support war, 211
    never hesitate to open a business for fear of t., 111
    war . . . has one thing certain, to increase t., 211
"taxing machine":
    government to the discontented a t., 95
taxpayer:
    t. compelled to labor for other benefit, 193
teacher:
    prosperity a great t., 164
television:
    commercials on t. similar to sex and taxes, 5
temper:
    command t., 14
"testing hypotheses":
    t. euphemism for a priori theory, 84

theft:
    property is t., 160
theology:
    like t. . . . . economics deals with matters men consider
        close to their lives, 65
theories:
    economics has two sides: t. and facts, 66
theorist:
    the conviction, disturbing for a t., there is no such thing
        as economics, 66
thief:
    smuggler . . . the only honest t., 167
thinking:
    part of business is effect of not t., 14
    rich too indolent, poor too weak, to bear fatigue of t.,
        70
thirst:
    accursed t. for gold!, 91
thought:
    t. the real business capital, 24
thrift:
    majority prosper only through t., 175
    t. and adventure seldom go hand in hand, 42
    t. is care and scruple in the spending of one's means, 40
    t. is the great fortune-maker, 175
    t. should be guiding principle, 81
    to recommend t. to poor is insulting, 175
thrifty:
    it's well to be t., 173
    t. as if they would live forever, 173
time:
    work expands to fill t., 226
    free t. means t. to waste, 123
    t. is money, 133
toil:
    t. sweeter than idleness, 223
    tired millions toil inblest, 105
tools:
    without t. he [man] is nothing, 198
trade:
    advertising ministers to spiritual side of t., 3
    appetites of men main spur to t., 40
    banking watchful not laborious t., 12
    free t. . . . . never has existed, 204
    he that hath a t. hath an estate, 30
    if a man loves the labor of his t., . . . the gods have called
        him, 31
    it were better for t. . . . if rents were paid by shorter
        intervals, 51-52
    less inconvenience from banishment of philosophers than
        from extinction of any common t., 70
    men driving about from one t. to another sure to drive
        himself into ruin, 31
    man who on t. relies must advertise, 3

wage:
>you cannot help the w. earner by pulling down the w. payer, 105

wage rates:
>w. among least flexible prices, 72

wages:
>common w. of labor, 115
>high w. causes of high price, 151
>illogical for labor to resist reduction of money-w. but not of real w., 107
>man employed for w. a businessman, 117
>many a woman tempted by low w. to marry, 221
>profits tend more to raise price than w., 156
>that high w. retard progress refuted by number of establishments, 101

Wall Street:
>let W. have a nightmare, 185
>more crooks in W. than any other industry, 187
>to W. operator, everything seems possible, 186
>W. not to control International Bank, 186
>W. owns the country, 184

wants:
>all w. imaginary, 129
>utility represents common essence of all w., 208

war:
>business combination of w. and sport, 17
>commerce like w., 157
>declare w. in peaceful field of trade, 205
>every w. of trade becomes w. of blood, 205
>from w. sprang science, 198
>w. taught power of propaganda, 7
>what w. could ravish, commerce could bestow, 203
>taxes for w. support unproductive laborers, 192
>w. on poverty has been won, 149
>success of w. dependent on money, 211

wars:
>poverty never prevented w., 176

waste:
>greedy people w., 101
>organizations at least 50 percent w., 46

welfare:
>no boundary between economic and non-economic w., 152

welfare state:
>paradox of the w., 181
>w. compared to Santa Claus, 182
>w. softened harshness of capitalism, 181

wealth:
>abstention from labor, evidence of w., 122
>acquisition of w. the aim of life, 164
>adds to w. new utilities, 207
>America not land of money but of w., 9
>can w. give happiness?, 40
>capital that part of w. devoted to further w., 24

competitive commerce destroys mental w., 198
complain of influence of w., 167
consuming a maximum amount of w., 208
crises promote inequalities in distribution of w., 20
descent and deeds, unless united to w., are useless, 34
distribution of w. regulates industry, 104
economics is . . . a Science of W., 63
God shows contempt for w., 172
he lives poor and is jailor of his w., 175
health without w. is half a sickness, 180
increase [of w.] occasions rise in wages, 209
inflation arbitrarily redistributes w., 108
interest of commercial world that w. be found, 15
labor of women enables men to produce more w., 221
labor the father of w., 115
memorialize w. on tombstone, 164
misers amass w. for . . . death, 174
nobody who has w. to distribute omits himself, 97
no society where w. will not create an aristocracy, 35
only w. [kept] is w. given away, 140
power of producing w. destroyed by taxation, 193
power of producing w. more important then w., 154
predatory w. is found in stock markets, 184
that which has no value [not] w., 207
through industries we have built up w., 165
w. cannot satisfy desire of w., 100
w. conspicuous, poverty hides, 149
w. . . . . must be advertised, the normal medium is obtrusively expensive goods, 43
w. of nations arises from labor, 115
w. of nations is men, not silk, 117
w. or power must be put in evidence; esteem awarded only on evidence, 42
w. rarely begets sedition, 146
when rich are sick they feel impotence of w., 180
wherever excessive w., excessive poverty, 147
with progress w. will increase, 154

wealthy:
>taxation burden shifted onto shoulders of w., 195
>w. and poverty-stricken both too preoccupied with finance, 37
>w. urging privation for poor, 149

weapon:
>food is a w., 8

weapons:
>if sunbeams were w. of war, 214

weather:
>probable that crises connected with variation of w., 20

welfare:
>American farmers w. addicts, 8

well-being:
>taste for w. feature of democratic times, 41

Western Europe: